Portable Video

Fourth Edition

Portable Video:
ENG and EFP

Fourth Edition

Norman J. Medoff
Tom Tanquary

Focal Press

An Imprint of Elsevier
Amsterdam   Boston   Heidelberg   London   New York   Oxford
Paris   San Diego   San Francisco   Singapore   Sydney   Tokyo

∞ This book is printed on acid-free paper.

Library of Congress Cataloging-in-Publication Data
Medoff, Norman J.
    Portable video: ENG and EFP/Norman J. Medoff, Tom
    Tanquary. –4ᵗʰ ed.
        p. cm.
    Includes bibliographical references and index.
    ISBN 0-240-80438-4 (pbk.:alk. paper)
    1.   Television broadcasting of news. 2. Video recordings – Production
        and direction. I. Tanquary, Tom. II. Title.

TR895.M44 2001
778.59'80704-dc21
2001033905

British Library Cataloguing-in-Publication Data
A catalogue record for this book is available from the British Library

The publisher offers special discounts on bulk orders of this book.
For information, please contact:
Manager of Special Sales
Elsevier Science
200 Wheeler Road
Burlington, MA 01803
Tel: 781-313-4700
Fax: 781-313-4802

For information on all Focal Press publications available, contact our World
Wide Web homepage at http://www.focalpress.com

10 9 8 7 6 5 4 3
Printed in the United States of America

Table of Contents

Preface

The first edition of this book was written more than fifteen years ago. Since that time the number of people who shoot video professionally has grown considerably. There are more television stations, cable operations, and corporate video users. There are even new television networks that have come on the air in that time. Digital satellite services for the consumer and the large number of households having cable TV has allowed news operations to expand beyond the realm of broadcasting. Where CNN once stood alone, now a multitude of news operations can be found on cable and satellite. This growth is a response to needs of the organizations to disseminate information, find new audiences and, perhaps more importantly, it is a response to the growth of the needs of the audience. Viewers want choices.

Television viewers in the 1950s and 1960s often had three or four television viewing choices. In the 1970s, cable television raised the viewing channels to at least 12 and sometimes systems offered 30 channels or more. The number of viewing choices continued to grow, but the growth curve flattened out in the 1980s and 1990s somewhat as the cable industry went through consolidation and shakeout. But the growth curve in demand for video is about to once again become steep. The applications of video are going to dramatically increase once again because of the new technologies that utilize video.

Many computer users have endured the trials and tribulations of the changes that have occurred in the area of information transfer between computers. Eight years ago it was not uncommon to struggle with a 1200 or 2400 baud modem. Connections were often difficult to get and getting "bounced" off the connection occurred all too often. At those low transfer speeds, only text information was practical for transfer. Even the advances to 14.4 or 28.8 Kbps modems did not change things much. Although audio information transfer is possible at those speeds, it was not easy and the quality was often questionable. Even though most people who go online regularly now have 56.6 Kbps modems, full motion, full frame video still demands more speed than these modems can deliver. Cable modems, DSL, and other broadband connections however, do show the promise of data speeds sufficient to provide quality video in real time. Advances in codecs combined with faster Internet connections will eventually lead to the Internet as a source of video that can rival other delivery systems.

While images on the Web at this point in time are mostly graphic images that originated as still images digitized by a scanner or simply created electronically through software, this may change soon. As the technology to put full frame, full motion video on Web sites becomes more accessible, more sites with video will appear. As it occurred in the 1970s and the 1980s when portable video first became accessible to corporate, educational, and institutional entities, the demand will grow for people who can create professional quality video images and express ideas through those images. It doesn't seem likely that the same people who create the computer programming to create Web sites will automatically become the people who shoot the video for those sites. They don't have the appropriate education and the skills are different. In our optimistic view, this eventual reality will create many opportunities for college-educated people who can shoot professional quality video.

In the fourth edition we again find that although technology has changed (for the better), the basic ingredients for shooting professional quality video are not necessarily technology based. Although a better camera will help a skilled videographer or news photographer get better video across a wider variety of situations, the real keys to good video are variables like lighting, composition, framing, and exposure. We have noticed that lens technology hasn't changed that much. Also, lighting devices have gotten better and there are a few new designs, but they really aren't very different from what they were in the 1970s. What's more important is what has not changed at all. While cameras and tape machines are creating digital images and editing is being done on computers in a non-linear fashion, it's still the *content* of the pictures that creates the story or product.

Most of the advances in the technology deal with processing video, that is, manipulating the video images *after* the images are shot. The major technological growth area has been in the advent of non-linear, digital editors. There have been some advances in video signal storage, but generally videographers and news photographers are still shooting on some type of videotape. Once stored, the video images can be edited quickly and with tremendous creative flexibil-ity. The best part of this is that the digital technology is becoming accessible to lower end users.

As the processing of video becomes more and more involved with computers in the digital environment, we recall a saying that was rampant in the early days of computer programming: "Garbage in, garbage out." If your input to the computer was meaningless or low quality, the computer would give you meaningless or low quality output. The same is true in video. The best digital editor in the world can only do so much to improve bad video. The key to good video images lies in the basics that allow the video photographer to capture good images, on any camera, that, when edited together on any system, can tell a good story. Your computer can't do that for you. Your video camera will only be as good as you are. Hopefully, after reading the fourth edition of this book, you will have the skills needed to create video for traditional outlets, the new digital media, and whatever follows.

Norman J. Medoff
Flagstaff, AZ May 2001

Tom Tanquary
Costa Mesa, CA May 2001

Acknowledgments

It is hard to imagine creating a book like this without a tremendous amount of help from others. This help came not only in providing helpful information, but also reviewing, editing, proofreading, and moral support. No doubt we will accidentally leave off some names of those who have helped, but here are some of the people who have helped make this fourth edition a reality: the patient people at Focal Press; Marie Lee, Diane Wurzel, and Maura Kelly; Trena Payne, Rick Barron, Moira Tokatyan, Peter Stone, Kort Waddell, Jim White, and the many other working photographers whose collective experience is reflected in this book.

And speaking of moral support; Esther, Lynn, Natalie, and Sarah Medoff; and Nicole, Frank and Marie Tanquary.

1 Introduction

ENG AND EFP: THE WORLD OF PROFESSIONAL VIDEO

Portable video systems have been around for a long time. In the 1960s there was a video system called the Porta-pack that recorded fuzzy black-and-white pictures on a reel-to-reel style videotape recorder. The quality was outright bad and the product was almost impossible to edit. Some educational, government, medical, and experimental users found it helpful in conveying ideas where film would be too expensive. Mostly it was thought of as a toy with limited appeal. Even as color was introduced, the idea of using video in any big way in the field wasn't feasible. The equipment was just too big and too cumbersome.

The appearance of the U-Matic videocassette by Sony in 1971, coupled with the introduction of higher resolution color cameras, suddenly gave portable video a new appeal. This self-threading cassette system, in a machine small enough to be carried around and operated by battery, replaced the Porta-pack's reel-to-reel system and greatly improved the quality of the recording. The camera was still in two pieces—the camera head and the camera control unit, or CCU—but it too could be powered by a battery. Two people could easily walk around with the gear in backpack fashion to do taping. With the equipment mounted on a small cart, one person could operate it.

Knowing the power of video cameras in news and sports coverage—even though their use was limited by their size, miles of cables, and often days of setup time—the TV networks began to experiment with this new portable technology. Companies like Sony, Thomson, RCA, and Ikegami worked closely with the networks to deliver a smaller, higher quality camera that could meet their needs. Their primary focus of use was live TV and, in particular, sports. Having a smaller battery-powered camera could increase the coverage of a sporting event dramatically. One of the earliest uses of portable video in network news was President Nixon's historic visit to China in 1974. CBS decided to use video instead of 16mm film to cover the event. The ENG (electronic news gathering) revolution had begun. The 1976 CBS coverage of the presidential campaign put the video camera in the mainstream of news coverage. Reporters no longer had to wait for the shot film to be developed to air the story. They could now report live from the campaign stop with the use of these new camera units, or shoot tape and have it aired almost immediately. But an even more dramatic change was already under way.

By the second half of the 1970s, the video revolution began sweeping local television stations across the country. Starting with the early experiments at such stations as the CBS-owned and -operated (O&O) KNXT station in Los Angeles in 1974, video slowly began to create a foothold in daily news coverage. By 1976 it was widely recognized that KMOX in St. Louis had become the first all-video, or all ENG, newsroom in the country using the Ikegami two-piece camera, the HL-35. This novel approach to covering local events became an important factor in the competitiveness of the station's news ratings.

Fueled by the new realization that there was money in news—or more accurately, that there was a big and growing audience appetite for news—more and more stations started news shows or began aggressively expanding their current news operations. At the local level, it no longer mattered if a network's programming was the highest rated; what mattered was how big the audience—and therefore the advertising dollars—was for the local news show. The

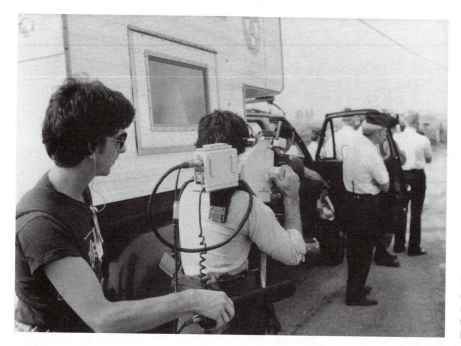

Figure 1.1 This early ENG camera, the Thompson MK-II MicroCAM, required two persons to operate it in the field. Courtesy of Larry Greene, KCBS-TV.

competition became fierce. Station and network management looked to any means to get a leg up on the other guy. The ability to get a breaking story on the air first epitomized the race in every way. Suddenly, that newly down-sized video camera and its videotape recorder were just what the doctor ordered.

The new-found portability of both the video camera and the videotape recorder that was being demonstrated at CBS and local stations like KNXT, KMOX, and WBBM in Chicago was now revolutionizing the film-dominated daily television newscasts in two very important ways. First, it was now possible for a videocassette of a breaking news story to be delivered to the station and, after just a few minutes of editing, be played on the air. Faster yet, the raw or unedited tape—which didn't have to be developed—could be put directly on the air allowing the viewer to see a live-to-tape presentation only minutes after it was shot. Second, because the camera was now electronic instead of mechanical, its video signal could be broadcast live from the field with little setup or fuss, aided by newly developed microwave technology. Live TV news on location was suddenly available to almost any station at a low price. That changed not only the look of the industry, but the various ways in which stories were covered, forever. This new form of acquiring pictures—and consequently the whole

business of television news—became known as electronic news gathering or ENG.

As the news ratings race continued at an ever-increasing pace, the demand for better, lighter, and more reliable camera gear also grew. Companies rushing to supply news departments with the latest advance in equipment began finding new outlets for their products. Mass production, better technology, and competition within their own industry had made video equipment cheaper and therefore more accessible to a wide range of users. Hospitals, government agencies, corporations, educational institutions, and independent production houses began to replace their film cameras with video cameras. The organizations that didn't have any production capabilities suddenly found producing their own projects on video to be cost effective because of the ever-decreasing price of video equipment and its ever-increasing quality. From hospital teaching tapes to TV commercials, any use of a single video camera with a portable videotape recorder that wasn't for a newscast became known as electronic field production or EFP. The similarities between ENG and EFP are many. Generally, the equipment and its operation are the same. Only the style of shooting often separates the two.

By the late 1990s, high-quality video camcorders (camera and videotape recorders in one unit) had not

Figure 1.2 News photographer in 1980. Each full set of gear weighed about 80 pounds. Photo by Joe Vitti.

only become affordable to the general public but had become commonplace. What this did was create a world where almost no event goes uncovered. Whenever something happens anywhere in the world, it is usually captured on video by someone. The most famous—or infamous—event was the police beating of Rodney King captured by an amateur photographer trying out his new camera from the balcony of his apartment. That home video began a chain of events that led to one of the worst civil disturbances in the history of the United States. It also secured the video camera's place as a powerful tool for a free society's ability to communicate. Some might say that that single moment was the culmination of the TV

revolution: the fullest realization of the power of television and its profound effect on society.

It is with this power in mind that the video professional sets about the job of creating both news and commercial product. Used properly and with ethical guidance, video can be the most persuasive means of communication regardless of the delivery system. Video is no longer just for broadcasting and industrial/educational uses but can be used by anyone in society. With broadening opportunities of streaming video on the Internet, anyone can have his or her own TV station. Learning and understanding the tools and techniques of the trade can make the video photographer an integral part of any modern com-

Figure 1.3 Shooting home videos.

munication medium whether that's the networks or the Internet or an as-yet unimagined delivery system.

ELECTRONIC NEWS GATHERING: CAPTURING THE EVENT

A Brief History

In its purest form, ENG is the art of shooting news—photojournalism for television. It is the descendent of a long tradition of documenting events with moving pictures. Just like the still camera, one of the first uses of the motion picture camera was recording historic events. Cameras rolled as trench warfare consumed the European continent in World War I. Later, a more organized effort by news services would show movie-going audiences World War II via the newsreel. With the advent of television and its growing acceptance in the 1950s, newsreels were replaced by newscasts. The style of shooting had changed little from the fields of

France to Edward R. Murrow's reports beaming into 1950s living rooms. The camera operators were a very select group of people that followed a tradition from generation to generation.

TV news grew as an industry in the 1960s, and the style of shooting began to change. Up until then, the film cameras used were rather large and heavy, so most shooting was done from a tripod in controlled situations. Small hand-held cameras had no audio-recording capabilities and were used mostly in hard-to-get-to places, such as in airplanes or on battle-fields. The lighter sound-on-film cameras of the 1960s, like the Cinema Products CP-16, allowed the camera operators greater freedom of movement without having to leave sound or quality behind. The handheld shot became more important. The cameraperson could now be part of the action like never before. The introduction of color-reversal film, which could be developed as fast as black-and-white film, added a new sense of reality to every newscast. But it was video that up-ended decades of tradition.

Figure 1.4 Home video capturing dramatic scenes can sometimes be sold to local TV stations, network news programs, or other TV production companies.

At the network level and at most of the large local stations, when video cameras came in and film cameras left, so did many of the operators. People who were trained in the art of cinema and experienced in the business of journalism were suddenly replaced by engineers from the studio who knew how the electronics worked in the camera but nothing about "shooting" or journalism. News events couldn't wait for these people to learn the craft, so stations and networks had to accept the new priority: just get any shot. The video revolution was not only painful to the displaced workers and confused managers but to the viewing public as well. Pictures on the evening news went from sharp clear images in realistic color to dull muddy visions with smears lagging behind moving objects and colors ranging from the garish to bright green. Sometimes it seemed that the operators were trying to master the technology first and find a good shot—or any shot—second. A lot of the respect for the pictures of TV news were lost when the film/video changeover occurred.

TV News Photography Today

By the late 1980s, after more than a decade of struggling for acceptance, the video photographer had come into his and her own. Most people still believe film looks better than video, but the people shooting the video are finally on the same creative level as their counterparts in film. Tune in any network news magazine show and you will see state-of-the-art creative photography that just happens to be shot on video. There are still plenty of examples of bad photography in daily TV news programs. Their unavoidable inclusion in the newscasts stems more from the changing nature of the news business than anything else. The proliferation of news outlets, the relentless competition, and the almost unrealistic deadline pressures of live TV have allowed quality standards to become a secondary concern at times.

If there is one driving maxim in the ENG world today it is "Any image that can be recorded is better than no image at all." To understand this statement,

Figure 1.5 An ENG crew shooting a stand-up on location during a breaking story.

you must understand the very nature of modern TV photojournalism. Yes, quality is important—very important—but nothing is as important as capturing the event. Bringing back the story is the ultimate goal. Because news cannot be planned or controlled—that is, staged—each situation a news cameraperson finds himself in is different. Decisions have to be made on a case-by-case basis and oftentimes on a second-by-second basis. This book will provide guidance for using a video camera in almost any application, but, specifically for the future news photographer, it will be a guide to making those quick decisions as well as making the creative choices that will set the photographer apart from the competition.

Many concepts differentiate ENG photography from any other form of shooting. The primary one we mentioned above: The event being covered is the most import thing. You can't go to the fire and not bring something back. A news shooter's mandate is to find any way to bring back the story. Beg, borrow, or buy whatever you need to get the shots necessary

to tell the story (within ethical considerations). There are five other areas in which a news shooter has a unique concern:

- Time
- Control
- Preparation
- Story line
- Responsibility.

Time

Anyone working in news has the sound of the clock pounding in their ears. On a normal day, the pressure builds as the time of the newscast comes closer. The show goes on at exactly 5 o'clock whether you're ready or not. And not being ready is a crime with a stiff penalty—one that can easily include termination of employment. A photographer's entire day revolves around when things take place, how long they last, and how long it takes to get to the next locale or back to the station. The press conference will take place at

10:00 A.M. sharp. The noon interview at the school lasted one hour. The 3 o'clock grape-pickers story is one hour from the station. How everything fits into the day and what can be done at each location is determined not so much by its importance as by the time involved.

The situation is doubly confounded when the story is breaking at the moment, such as a plane crash. A news shooter must be constantly aware of the time he or she is spending getting to the location, making the shots, and getting them on the air. It may involve driving them back to the station, driving to meet a microwave van to "feed" the pictures back to the station, or waiting in one spot for the van to arrive. Which method gets the pictures on the air the fastest? How far away is the station, the van, another photographer? On top of the pressure to take good pictures, the photographer must always be apprised of the time.

Control

The next factor that sets a news shooter apart from other photographers is the idea of control: Basically, there is none. News photography, with very few exceptions, must follow the mandates of good journalistic ethics. At the heart of those ethics is the rule against manufacturing an event or scene. In other words, you don't cause anything to happen that would not normally be happening. You can't go to a protest gathering and tell the participants that it would make better pictures if they marched around the building chanting. You can only show up and shoot what's there. If it's dull, then it's dull. Period.

Applying this rule, as well as working with an entire code of ethics (which are detailed later in this book), can make shooting even the most simple story difficult. What it all comes down to is this: You do not have, nor should you have, any control over your subjects. Even telling a housewife, whom you're shooting as part of a story on stay-at-home moms, to make a pot of coffee can be wrong. If you're asking her to do something she wouldn't normally be doing at that time of day just to give her something to do so you can have some action to shoot, then it's a violation. It may seem silly but if you make an exception here and there, you simply push the line further away from what is an accurate representation of the truth. If you get into the habit of arbitrarily drawing the line, then you tend to forget where the line was suppose to be in the first place.

Preparation

Anybody embarking on a video project of any kind needs to be prepared. The key difference for the news photographer is that he or she needs to be prepared for anything. You may haul a full set of lights up to the senator's office ready to do a three-light formal sit-down interview only to find out the senator is late for a vote and you must shoot the politician in the dark hallway and on the run. Having a battery-powered light—a sungun—mounted on top of the camera is what saves the day. You hadn't planned on using that unflattering light source, but having the correct exposure, as opposed to a dark low-contrast shot, is far better when seeing the senator answer important questions on camera. No matter how much planning goes into an upcoming news shoot, anything can change because of the concept mentioned above: You have no control.

To be prepared for anything, the photographer must have a full and complete understanding of the equipment and techniques available to him or her. Another thing this book will do is make sure the prospective shooter is up to speed on both of those points. The last thing necessary for good preparation is practice. Unfortunately, this book can't create that experience, but it will instruct the student about to how to get it.

Story Line

A typical assignment in TV news is to cover an event where little is known about the nature of the subject. A press conference has been called, but the information is vague as to what it's about—only that it's important. The photographer working in concert with the reporter, producer, or assignment editor must not only cover the event but also understand the event. The script for the story being covered won't be written until after all the shooting is complete—sometimes hours after the shoot. To obtain the necessary pictures and sound bites that, when combined, will provide viewers with a clear and concise presentation and fit with the script, the photographer needs to have as much knowledge and detail as possible about the story he or she is covering before and during the shooting. The photographer is the one primarily responsible for visualizing the story.

If that press conference was about a dangerous toxic chemical being found in the local landfill, then the first thing to be considered is getting pictures of that landfill. Paying close attention to all the details of the story can make a big difference in what gets shot and how. It may be that the source of the contamination is from liquid deposits to the dump. So, in shooting the landfill, most of the effort would be put into finding trucks dumping liquid waste, chemical drums, or any other evidence visible at the site. Even with that knowledge, the photographer needs more information. Which companies are doing it? If no one knows, then the shots of trucks dumping liquid waste must be made so that the identity of the company is hidden. You cannot imply wrongdoing by any one company unless they have been accused. One hopes that the writer of the on-air segment will convey the fact that the video seen is not the actual dumping but simply represents the kind of dumping responsible for the problem. You can easily see how shooting without the fullest understanding of the story can lead to more problems (like lawsuits) than just pictures that don't match the story.

The photographer never shoots in a vacuum. The pictures taken will have to be assembled into an edited story at some point. Having the correct mix and variety of shots that cover every aspect of the event or story can make the difference between a visual story line that is hard to follow, or one that speaks for itself. Each picture, every scene, must accurately depict what the photographer wants to convey. Before the photographer rolls tape, these questions must be asked:

- Why am I shooting this?
- What does it mean?
- What else do I need to go with to make it a complete story?

Responsibility

Despite the fact that a news photographer often works as part of a much larger team—the newsroom—she can, and often does, find herself as the only person responsible for getting the story. A shooter working alone in a smaller market may be the only one near a major story when it occurs. An event such as a plane crash can put that photographer on the front line of coverage with no reporter or other assistance for minutes or even hours—crucial time when the story must be fully covered. The photographer must not only gather the shots necessary but also gather information, find witnesses and/or survivors that can tell their story on camera, make contact with the authorities on the scene, and figure out a way to get all this back to the station to be the first on the air with it. That's why shooters are called photojournalists.

Even at the network level, a cameraperson must be able to do all the jobs needed in the field, including being on camera. If you are the witness to a major event as well as the documentor of it, then you may be called on to give your firsthand account to the audience, perhaps even live from the field. No job in the

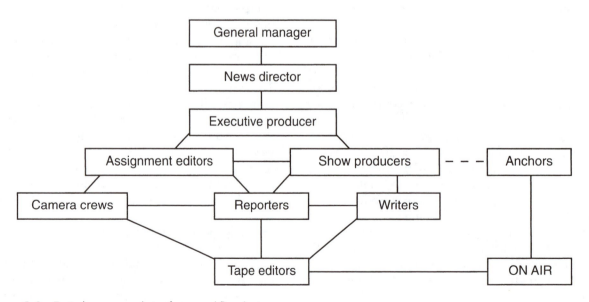

Figure 1.6 Typical newsroom chain-of-command flowchart.

news business should ever be considered strictly someone else's. But more than anyone else, the photographer is in the position to do it all. After all, television without the pictures is called radio.

This certainly doesn't preclude the photographer from being a team player. The overwhelming majority of time it really does take all those people to put a good show on the air. It makes for a better product when each member of the team concentrates on being the best at what he or she does and lets others be the best at doing their job. However, like so many other aspects of news, you must also plan for the worst case scenario. For the photographer, that means being prepared to go it alone.

Being a news photographer can be the greatest job in the world. It involves seeing history as it's made, experiencing the drama of life up close like very few in this society will ever do, going places that few will ever get to see—and being paid to do it.

ELECTRONIC FIELD PRODUCTION: STUDIO PRODUCTION ON LOCATION

Birth of an Industry

As news evolved from documentation to newsreels, only a few others outside the movie industry were making use of the moving picture. Making films of any kind was expensive, time consuming, and had relatively few practitioners. With the advent of television and smaller film formats like 16mm and 8mm, more organizations and even consumers began to use the medium. Health and science films produced by the government and shown on chattering 16mm projectors became common in the classroom. Home movies became a symbol of middle-class success. But it was the video revolution started by the news competition that sparked a whole new industry. Based entirely on the new portable video systems, electronic field production, or EFP, was born. Suddenly, for a slightly larger initial investment, the cost of shooting a minute's worth of moving pictures went from being measured in dollars to being measured in pennies. Without the punishing conditions of news coverage, the equipment could be easily maintained, and therefore last longer, so the reliability of it was no longer a question. Video productions that were once confined to and constricted in the studio suddenly broke free to take place in almost any location imaginable. This freedom from high cost and limited locations allowed anyone with the desire to communicate a message the method of doing it.

Video Production Today

As you go through this book you will notice the similarities between ENG and EFP. The equipment is basically the same. The shooting aesthetics are the same. The basic principles are very similar. Ideas and concepts in one discipline can easily be applied to the other in many cases. Learning news photography prepares you for doing production work and vice versa. But differences do exist that must be understood. The primary difference is the ultimate goal. By contrast with news, in which the event is of paramount importance, in EFP the overriding importance is on what the client—the person commissioning the video—wants. The sole purpose of the production is to serve the client's goals, whatever they are. It may be as simple as showing all the new Fords for sale, or as complex as teaching a group of teenagers that violence is not the answer to life's problems. Whatever the subject, the goal is to communicate the message of the client.

There are many other areas of difference with ENG. Most simply involve the reordering of priorities. Some involve approaching a situation from the exact opposite point of view. The following areas are of concern to a production photographer:

- Budget
- Planning
- Script
- Authority.

Budget

If time is the driving force behind the news photographer, money is what drives the production photographer. Before any work is done, a budget is set in place. Going over the budget can result in people and bills not being paid—not the kind of thing you want to happen in the business world. In EFP you can certainly say that time is money. This is especially true when it comes to the hours it takes to get something done. If a flat rate of $1000 is allotted to pay the members of the crew, then each member should have a reasonable expectation of how much work is involved for that amount of money. If the shoot starts to run longer than anticipated, then the hourly salary for those crew members begins to decline. That makes for unhappy workers and in some cases workers that walk away from the job in disgust. The producer, the person with the responsibility for getting the project done, has two choices: Go to the client and ask for more money, or find other items in the budget to cut and make up the difference.

Coming up with an accurate budget can be one of the hardest responsibilities in EFP. As the example above illustrates, a miscalculation can cause the entire project to fail. Unlike news, every aspect of the shooting must be accounted for in that project's budget. That means figuring in the cost of everything from duct tape to the wear and tear on the camera. Chapter 11, *Budgeting and Pricing,* will detail how to do an accurate budget that will keep you out of hot water—and possibly bankruptcy court.

Planning

The factor that allows budgets to be drawn up accurately is the extensive planning that goes into any EFP shoot. To control the budget, every aspect of the production must be planned well in advance. An accurate assessment of what's to be done, how many people will be needed for the crew, what equipment will be used, and any other items needed for the production must be compiled before the shooting begins. Most EFP projects also include editing as part of the overall job. How long will it take in the edit room? Are you going to need special effects?

In the real world, nothing ever goes quite as planned. A good production photographer should be intimately involved in the planning process. If the photographer makes up the entire crew, then he takes on the responsibility of being prepared for those unforeseen problems. On larger productions, the photographer may be working for a production manager but still should be included in any planning process. The best planning also includes what to do if things go wrong. What if it rains? Can the shoot be rescheduled? The EFP photographer must always be able to assess each situation and problem and offer constructive alternatives that meet not only the budget but the client's goals as well.

Figure 1.7 This EFP shoot involves a large crew, in which each member is responsible for only one aspect of the production.

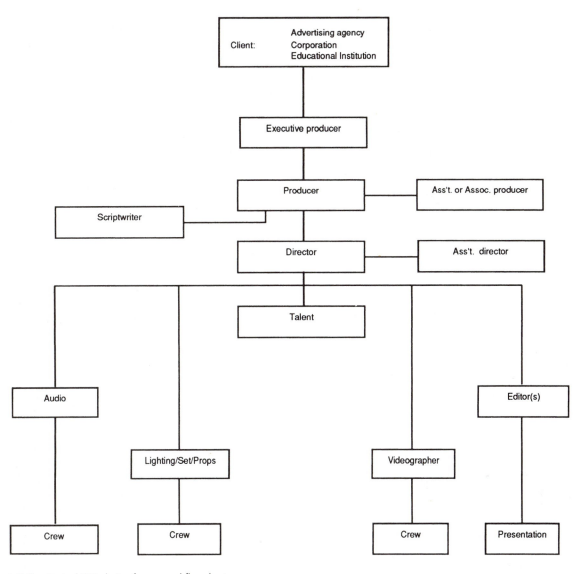

Figure 1.8 Typical EFP chain-of-command flowchart.

The Script

The blueprint for what will take place in the field and in the edit room is the script. Nothing gets done without one. The script, just like the blueprint for a new building, gives everyone the guidance they require to get the job done. In larger budgets and more sophisticated productions, the script is visualized in a series of drawings called the storyboard. Each shot is sketched out so every member of the production team knows what the finished product should look like. In smaller production crews where the photographer is also the director, she should have a well-defined image of what the look should be. How the shots are made, their framing, the camera movement, the action within the frame, and the lighting are all determined by the script, either directly or by interpretation.

A public service announcement (PSA) on boating safety may have a script calling for scenes of a boating accident. The producer and/or the director with the cameraperson will go over each sentence, indeed every word, of the script to find ways of illustrating the message being conveyed. Within the confines of the proposed budget, they will design shots and scenes that depict what the script is saying. They will come up with where the shooting will take place, how and where the camera is to be positioned, what kinds of actors are needed, all the props necessary, and how the action will be framed. If the script includes the emotions of the victim's families or another concept that for whatever reason can't be depicted directly by a specific shot, then visualizing it can be a creative challenge. That's when the production team and the talents of the photographer are stretched. The shots must now be symbolic of the message being delivered. They must convey the emotion of the script without showing exactly what the script is talking about. Seeing a hand toss a wreath onto the water may be all that's necessary to cover the narration describing a family's grief.

Authority

The final word on anything involved in a production shoot comes from the client. The client can reject the script, the actors, a particular shot, and even the photographer. The producer acts as the representative of the client in the client's absence. The producer makes all the decisions before, during, and after the shoot on authority of the client. The production photographer must understand her responsibility within that framework. It can be considerable or minimal. The EFP shooter needs to determine her level of authority as soon as possible when a production starts.

In a large organization, the photographer's duties are generally limited to work associated with the camera: designing and setting up shots, lighting, and executing the shot. The one thing the photographer won't have to do, unlike in news, is burden himself with the total responsibility of getting the project completed. In smaller productions, the photographer may be the producer, writer, sound tech, and even actor. Here the shooter-as-producer will have to get the entire job done on his own. What the EFP cameraperson must be able to do in any size organization is offer help and assistance whenever necessary. If the producer can't solve the problem of a shot that just doesn't fit the script, the photographer must be ready to step forward and offer a possible solution based on his knowledge of production skills and creative solutions.

Being a production shooter in today's ever-changing field of video can be both exciting and challenging. As multimedia becomes the way we communicate with each other, there will always be a growing demand for a video product. Unencumbered by the constraints of journalism, EFP photographers can explore the outermost limits of their creativity. They can reach into the highest realms of visual art.

Knowing the Basics

At this point, you should know the difference between ENG and EFP—and also know the similarities. In the real world, almost any job you get using portable video will include a combination of both disciplines. The news shooter will also work on commercials and PSAs done by the in-house production department at the station. The production shooter will be assigned a shoot that the client wants done ENG-style. In today's marketplace, most of the working photographers are freelancers—they work for themselves. The phone rings and they're off to a job that may last one day or one week. One day they work for ABC World News Tonight, the next day they're shooting a commercial for the local candidate for governor, and the day after that they're doing a training video on the new assembly line at the electronics plant. The type of shooting depends on who is paying them that day.

As the Internet and other forms of delivery continue to expand, the demand for video photographers will grow just as fast. As the world of digital video grows, the potential uses of that video also grow. Streaming video, webcasting, TV-on-demand, interactive TV, and broadcasting are all slowly becoming one and the same. But no matter what the format, no matter what the recording media, no matter what the delivery system, one thing will never change: It will always be photography.

From here on, this book will give the reader a complete course in the basics of video photography. All forms of shooting share a common goal: to tell a story. The methods and principles of storytelling are the same no matter what the story's end use. By learning the basics, a student or beginning-level video photographer can quickly learn to provide a certain level of quality to their work. Recipes for success come from the rules and formulas established over the years in news and production photography. They are a guide to get the novice cameraperson on the road to finding that elusive thing called style. That individual style is what creates those truly unique views that make video photography an art.

part one

The Tools

2 Basic Shots—The Language of Video

Before beginning any video shoot, you should have a goal in mind. In ENG work, the goal is to strive to represent the reality of an event or story in an appropriate context. It involves a lot more than simply pointing a camera at a scene or subject. To overcome the limitations of the medium, a news photographer must select what will be shown and what is to be left out. The goal is to accurately depict what he or she sees to be true at the location, both factually and emotionally.

In EFP work, the goal is usually dictated by the client or manager. The photographer is directed to tell a particular story in a way that will be perceived and understood by the intended audience. In a corporate video setting, the goal may be to effectively communicate the advantages and disadvantages of a new health plan to the employees. In a music video created for entertainment, the goal may be to visually capture a mood or statement intended by the musician's composition or song. No matter what type of presentation, you must assemble all the elements of the story.

Before deciding on what type of shot to make—how to frame it, how to move the camera, or what focal length to use—you also need to have a goal in mind. The camera simply can't think for itself. Every aspect of camera placement, focal length, camera height, and composition of the frame, plays a part in the audience's ability to understand what they are looking at. Filmmakers spend years in school and even more years on the job developing these skills. Entire books are written trying to explain the complex relationships of visual elements. But one thing is certain: Everything you place in your viewfinder must be there for a reason.

IDENTIFYING THE STORY LINE

Before you begin a shoot, ask yourself what you are trying to do. Reduce the task to its most basic description. If you can encapsulate the story in one sentence, you are well on the way to reaching your goal. A typical ENG example might be as follows: Students at a technical school are coming from other careers to study microelectronics and enhance their employment prospects. Every aspect of this story is contained in this one sentence. By giving yourself this starting point, you can expand the sentence outward until you have covered all points in as much detail as is practical. For an average TV news story, length is the factor that determines how much you can put into that story. Since TV news is more of a headline service than an in-depth documentary service, a story such as the technical school would probably last only 90 seconds on the air.

This example can easily be translated into EFP terms. If the owners of the technical school want to make a 1-minute commercial for the school, the basic ingredients of the story will be the same. In both cases, because of the limited on-air time, the photographer must make every shot count. Once you have a goal and a relative time constraint in mind, you need the means to reach that goal.

THE RANGE OF SHOTS

Just as a musician uses a finite number of notes to create a finished song, a photographer uses a finite set of shots to create a story. The musician can vary the way each note is played, and there are infinite ways to combine notes. Similar to the case of the musician, the uniqueness of the photographer's art comes from the execution of fairly routine camera shots and movements. There is a specific purpose and design behind each shot and movement. Before we talk about composition within any frame, it may be helpful to catalog shots as they might be called for by a script or a director. Each type of shot sets a tone for the type of information contained in the frame. After understanding the type of shots required and their position relative to other shots in a story, we will examine their composition.

A photographer has three basic types of shots available for use in any project. The first type is determined by the focal length of the lens. The second type is described by some type of physical move by the camera. The third type is a group of shots used to serve specific functions in the production process.

SHOTS BY FOCAL LENGTH

The early video cameras that were used in studios were equipped with a turret that had a selection of several lenses, each with only one focal length. The camera stayed at one position and simply rotated the turret to use a lens of a different focal length to get a closer or wider shot. Today's cameras have zoom lenses that effortlessly go to any focal length in the range of the lens. Nevertheless, the old terminology of early film and TV is still used to describe the content of the frame.

The Wide Shot

The **wide shot**, or **WS**, is sometimes called the **establishing shot**, the **master shot**, or the **long shot** and is generally the first shot a photographer should take when shooting begins. It is the most important shot.

The wide shot is made with a short focal length and, therefore, a wide angle of view. This shot should include all the visual elements of the story or scene, if possible. In the example of the technical school story, the wide shot would be used to cover or visually explain that original one-sentence description of the story. In this example, the wide shot would include the students, instructor, classroom, and electronic equipment. Every key element should be there. The shot should show relationships and activities that yield information: the older-than-expected students, the instructor in an active teaching role, and the equipment that is the subject of the lesson. These visual elements give the viewer the information that reinforces the comments of the announcer or newscaster. Usually each story contains more than one wide shot.

As the writer expands a single sentence into several paragraphs to make a complete story, so the photographer must expand the idea into visual sentences and paragraphs. A story can be broken up into its component parts. It has a beginning, a middle, and an end. These parts are a series of ideas or facts that combine to form the overall statement used to achieve your goal. Visually the story must be broken down into those same parts. Think of each part or sequence as a story unto itself. In this analogy, the wide shot would serve as the subject of the visual sentence, or as the beginning of the story. There are two characteristics common to any wide shot.

Establishing the Scene   The beginning of any sequence starts with a shot that establishes the idea of that sequence (or paragraph of the script). The wide shot begins a sequence by establishing what the viewer will be seeing and what the relationship is between all the elements to be used in that sequence. (See Figure 2.1.)

Within a typical sequence of shots, the wide shot should contain every object or subject that will be videotaped in the remainder of the sequence. If we are going to be seeing a man using a lathe while the reporter talks about him and his current job, then the first shot should show the man, the lathe, and his location. In the opening shot of the sequence, relate as much information as possible to the viewer. Questions that should be answered in this example's first shot would include:

- What is the setting of this scene?
- How large is the setting or location?
- What are the important objects?
- What is the main character doing in relation to the objects in the setting?
- What is the machinery or equipment doing?

The shots that will follow in the sequence further detail the answers to these questions. Without the wide shot, those details could be unrelated and therefore seemingly irrelevant or even confusing to the

Figure 2.1 This wide shot establishes the setting and what the sculptor is doing; it is clear that he is a sculptor in an older building.

viewer. Ideas that must be expressed in a story can often be said in a very short time, not leaving enough time for a visual sequence to develop. A wide shot most often takes care of this problem because it gives a maximum amount of information in a short period of time. Again, this is the idea of one shot expressing a complete thought or idea.

At other times a wide shot can simply be used to establish the location for the sequence that follows, such as showing the outside of the school building. In other storylines it may be showing the skyline of a city to let the viewer know what part of the country they are seeing. In these cases the WS stands alone and simply says, "here we are in/at. . . ."

Creating the Third Dimension The information included in a wide shot is only one of several components required for a good wide shot. If the framing is off, or the shot is too busy or otherwise aesthetically unpleasant, you have not maximized the impact it can have on the viewer. Since the TV is a two-dimensional surface similar to a piece of paper or a canvas, the third dimension must be created. The illusion of depth is what makes a two-dimensional picture come alive. The term **flat** is often used to describe a shot that has failed to show any three-dimensional characteristics. The wide shot is the best place to create the volume of the scene. More on how to do that a little later.

The Medium Shot

The **medium shot** or **MS** is the workhorse of most TV stories. It can be defined as the development shot. It concentrates on the subject with little attention given to anything else. In most cases, depth and relationships within the frame are brought out with subtleties of lighting or just a portion of other elements in the shot. If a wide shot shows someone from head to toe, then a medium shot shows a person from the waist up. Lighting can play a major role in bringing out the textures in a medium shot to enhance the feeling of three dimensionality. Medium shots are made with a narrowed field of view or a midrange focal length— not wide, but not telephoto either.

As with all shots, there is a need to maximize information when using the medium shot. In this type of shot, you do not need to show a subject's relationship to the surroundings, but you must show more detail of who or what the subject is or what the subject is doing. In the technical school story, one medium shot might be a student assembling a circuit board. The important elements of the shot are the subject's face, arms, hands, and the circuit board. An important difference between the execution of the wide shot and the medium shot is the number of angles available for the medium shot that are not always available for the wide shot. By keeping the same focal length and distance from the subject, the shot can be taken from the front, at a 45° angle from the front, at the side, over the shoulder, at low angles, or at high angles. (See Figure 2.2.)

Where one wide shot will suffice to start off the story or segment of a story, many medium shots are needed to supply the bulk of the storytelling material. The wide shot can contain many elements or subjects. Our tech school scene has the teacher and maybe a dozen students. Each of them can be used for the developing medium shots. Think of the wide shot as a completed jigsaw puzzle. We are now dividing the puzzle up into different sections for closer examination. These sections are the medium shots.

The key element in the medium shot is variety. If you can shoot—or look at—the subject from several different angles, you can quickly make quite a few medium shots. The more angles and the greater variety of shots you have available when the material gets to the editing stage, the more creative choices you have in assembling the finished story.

The Close-up Shot

The **close-up** or **CU** shot gives the intimate details of the subject. If the medium shot shows a person from the waist up, the close-up would be a shot of their head and shoulders. In our jigsaw puzzle analogy, the

Figure 2.2 These three angles are some of the possible medium shots of this sculptor at work.

section of the puzzle that made up the medium shot is now going to be taken apart to its individual pieces. The close-up is made with the lens at a telephoto

focal length. Now the individual subject is going to be examined part by part. A close-up shows the emotions in the face, the manipulation of the subject's hands, or the details of a craftsman's work. (See Figure 2.3.)

The close-up can be thought of as the final shot of a sequence or fully expressed idea initiated in the wide shot. In our technical school example, the close-up might be a shot of the student's hands positioning a chip or some other element onto the circuit board. The elements in the shot are the hands, the board, and the part being fitted to the board.

Depth in a close-up is completely reduced to the texture of the objects being photographed. The detail of the close-up subject will usually give the depth necessary for a good picture. The number of angles from which a close-up can be shot is often more limited than either the wide or the medium shot. The variety lies in shooting the many different elements of a subject in close-ups such as face, hands, or even feet (they may operate some tool with a foot pedal). Other possible close-ups in the technical school example might also be of a supply of parts or a book of instructions. In other words, you can shoot a detailed close-up of every element contained in the medium shot. It is always a good rule to include some form of relationship to the medium shot, however. The CU of the electrical parts would work better if a hand came into the frame and removed a part for use, or in the case of a CU of a textbook, if a hand reached across it to turn a page. Movement, especially by humans, is always interesting.

The Extreme Close-up

The **extreme close-up** or **XCU** adds drama or extra emphasis to a series of shots. In our example of a person, the XCU would be a shot of the subject's eyes. This shot is made at the very far end of the telephoto lens, zoomed all the way in. For many story lines, this shot could be out of place, but when used correctly it can greatly improve the quality of the piece. This type of shot brings the viewer into a world not normally seen in such detail. The extreme close-up presents a larger-than-life image that can be extremely interesting for a viewer. (See Figure 2.4.) The subject should be chosen carefully and the purpose of this shot should be clear.

The XCU in the technical school example could show the tip of the soldering iron as it melts some solder onto the part just put in place during the close-up

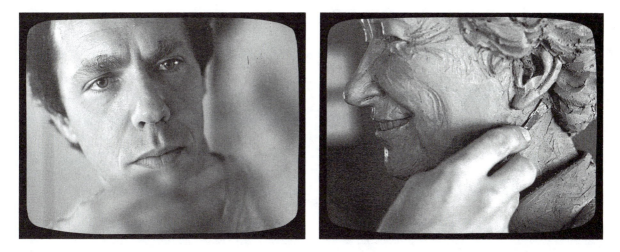

Figure 2.3 The left close-up shot shows the face of the artist clearly while maintaining his spatial relationship with the sculpture, and the right photo provides a detail of his work as he shapes the clay.

shot. Seeing the solder actually run and the smoke billow out from around it adds a sense of drama and visual excitement to a rather mundane classroom setting. An XCU of the student's eyes in a story like this may not be appropriate unless the student is wearing glasses and the reflection of the smoking solder can be seen in that reflection (thereby tying the shots together).

The XCU need not be action related but simply a detail shot: for example, a single stamp in a story about stamp collecting, or a hole in a leaf as part of a story on crop damage. If used properly, this shot

Figure 2.4 This XCU of the sculptor's tool shaping the clay demonstrates the texture and pliability of the clay, which is not normally seen.

can be the most memorable—and therefore most expressive—in any piece, but it must be used at the correct time, have a good relationship to the surrounding shots, and show an appropriate subject. By using the XCU, video pieces can demand a great deal of attention from the viewer.

CAMERA ACTION SHOTS

This category of shots is defined by moving the camera or changing focal lengths as the shot is recorded. In general, these shots add dynamics, drama, and interest to the story by having the shot's perspective change as the viewer watches.

The Zoom Shot

As probably the most overused and misused shot in the field of photography, the zoom is the ruin of TV news. The first thing any new photographer does is work the zoom control until it is worn out. The best way to teach a new photographer to shoot is to tape the zoom servo to *off*. A zoom should be considered a link between two static shots or a means of maintaining proper framing or perspective. Just as in any two individual shots, the ending shot of the zoom should contain different or, at least, more information than the beginning shot.

One common mistake many photographers make when starting out is zooming to or from the middle of the frame, keeping equal distance on all sides of the subject as they zoom. To add more visual interest to the movement, try keeping two sides of the frame static in reference to the subject as you make the zoom. (See Figure 2.5.) That means you will be zooming into or out of one of the four corners of the screen while adding a little pan to the movement. This makes the shot pivot on the subject, adding more emphasis to what the viewer should be noticing.

The two most commonly appropriate uses of a zoom are (1) to show relationships and (2) to emphasize a subject within a larger picture. The first is a zoom-out and the second a zoom-in. If the topic is a profile on an unemployed worker, you might photograph a scene at the unemployment office. By starting on a tight shot of the subject waiting in line and then zooming out to a wide shot that reveals the multitude of people waiting in line, you can show the subject's relationship to the surroundings by revealing them after establishing the subject. This also would give the viewer the perspective of this individual being buried in a mass of people. The relationship between the individual and the rest of the room is well established. Or, you might want to emphasize that individual after first establishing the situation. A zoom-in from a wide shot of that room to a tight shot of the very tired looking subject emphasizes this person. The shot draws the viewer's attention from the overall picture to the plight of one individual who is part of the situation.

The basic rules for the zoom shot are as follows:

1. Always zoom from something that's important to something else that's important.
2. Make sure the beginning and ending shots can stand alone as static shots.
3. Zoom out to show a spatial relationship.
4. Zoom in to emphasize a particular element contained in the wider picture.

Always keep in mind the time it takes to zoom. A zoom that is too slow may not be able to be used by an editor; a zoom that is too fast may not allow the viewer time to perceive and understand what is taking place. If you have the time and tape, shoot a zoom at two or three speeds and choose the best speed when the piece is being edited. A good rule of thumb is not to make any movement over 5 seconds in length, and generally try to limit them to about 3 seconds. This is enough time to execute most shots and still be short enough to fit with almost any editing pace.

When shooting for special effects or for an arty look, a slow zoom can give the feel of gentle movement and can add to the pace and flow of an edited piece. In a faster-moving piece, a snap zoom can be done by putting the auto-zoom servo on *off* and manually wrist-snapping the zoom ring from one extreme to the other. This produces a very dramatic result and should be used with that effect in mind. Too much of

Figure 2.5 A zoom from the subject in the field reveals the location. A good zoom always incorporates some panning and tilting of the camera.

any one technique may be bad for the piece. The more noticeable or dramatic the technique, the easier it is to overuse it.

The Pan Shot

In many ways the pan is like the zoom in how it is used, but it is harder to misuse. The two major uses of the pan are (1) to show relationships and (2) to show more information than is contained in just one static shot. A pan from a raging brush fire to a nearby house can show the danger the house is in by proximity. This type of shot does not work well if the pan lasts too long or if the angle of the pan is too great. If the pan lasts too long, it may not fit into the edited story; if the angle is too great, the relationship may be lost because too much ground was covered between subjects. Panning too fast can blur the picture to the point where nothing is recognizable during the pan. Generally, this is not acceptable. Try to pan slowly

enough so that you can obtain a good freeze frame from your video at any point in the pan. You may need to rehearse a pan several times—if you have the time—to find the right speed. Again, try to stick with the 3- to 5-second rule. There are, of course, many times when a long pan is desirable. (See Figure 2.6.)

For a shot of an extremely long line of people, a long pan in place of several static shots or a zoom can be more effective. The same is true for long angles of pans. While about 30 to 90° is as far as you should normally pan, 180 or even 360° can be made to work in the right situation. For instance, when showing how a small town has decorated the entire main street for Christmas, a 180° pan from one end of the street to the other may be very effective. In the middle of a neighborhood totally destroyed by a tornado, a 360° pan could give a viewer a very dramatic overview of the destruction. Again, as with the zoom, the purpose of the pan should be to impart as much information to the viewer in the least amount of time.

Figure 2.6   Within this scene, a good pan could be from the composition on the left to the one on the right. Together they form a complete picture of the area.

The Tilt Shot

The **tilt** is just like a pan only in the vertical direction. The same basic rules apply for its length, speed, and purpose. The shot must start on one properly framed picture and end on another, showing relationship to, or more information about, the overall subject.

The Dolly Shot

In all the shots previously discussed, the camera is in a fixed position while shooting. The **dolly** or **trucking** shot requires the camera to move while the shot is being made. For EFP work, this type of shot should be done on a dolly or a wheeled tripod. On uneven surfaces, tracks or a platform can be put down for the dolly to move on. This could make the shot very time consuming to execute, not to mention more expensive to the overall production. For ENG work, the use of such extra equipment is usually out of the question. Therefore, the dolly shot becomes a walking shot for most ENG work. Sometimes someone with a bit of ingenuity can improvise a dolly using a grocery cart, wheelchair, bicycle, golf cart, or car if there are crew members to help.

The point to keep in mind when using the dolly shot is that the *perspective* of the shot constantly changes as the camera position changes. This is the purpose of a dolly shot. It is similar to a zoom because it is a transition from one shot to another in real time. The difference, of course, is the type of perspective change. It can add a sense of drama by moving closer to the subject in a dolly-in shot, or moving away in a dolly-out shot. The advantage of the dolly shot is that the focal length can stay the same as the shot changes. If the focal length is short, the depth of field will be great; moving the camera in to a closer shot will not lessen that depth of field but would exaggerate the perspective. In a zoom, the depth of field would steadily decrease (as focal length increases) while you zoom in and the perspective would be compressed. The resulting size of the subject may be similar, but the effects are quite different.

The dolly shot can also be a point-of-view shot. In ENG, the walking shot gives the feel of a point of view, if not of a specific character, then certainly of the viewer as if actually present. This point-of-view idea can work in many stories. For example, in the earlier shot of the long line of people, a dolly shot along the line would give the viewer a firsthand look at what it would be like to be walking along that line.

Another use of the dolly shot is to replace a pan shot to maintain perspective. Instead of panning a long row of TV sets in a showroom, a dolly shot can keep each set in the same proportion (size and angle to the camera). The desired feeling of such a shot is not so much the relationship of the sets to each other and to the room, but the vast number of sets. A dolly shot has a beginning and an end, just like all camera movement shots, and each part must be a good shot. For any moving subject, such as a walking on-camera host, the dolly shot can keep the subject framed in the same way but let the background change to impart new information to the viewer.

To get a feel for the effect of a dolly shot, try doing a shot that you would use the zoom for as a dolly shot with a fixed focal length. Often you will notice that the dolly shot has a greater impact and is more pleasing than the zoom. The only drawback is that the shot requires more time and sometimes more skill than the zoom. A walking shot can be too shaky to look good in many segments because it looks out of place with all tripod shots in the rest of the story. While most ENG work should be done on a tripod, spot news is actually a good place to learn the effect and importance of a dolly shot because of its hurried, go-with-the-action nature. On the other hand, you can zoom a lot faster than you can dolly.

SPECIAL-USE SHOTS

This category of shots is defined by the function of the shot and not by the focal length or framing of the shot. These shots usually serve as some sort of transition from one part of the visual story to another or as an aid in the editing process to maintain continuity. The following shots allow the editor to take the viewer smoothly through the flow of the story while not affecting the visual style.

The Cutaway

As its name implies, the **cutaway shot** is used to cut away from the action. When an editor is putting together a series of shots and wants to avoid a **jump cut** (a break in continuity), a cutaway is used to take the viewer away from the subject so that time or subject position can change without disturbing the continuity within the overall flow of shots. (See Figure 2.7.)

The most basic example of this is during an interview in which two different sound bites will be

Figure 2.7 In the series of photos of the sculptor, this shot of his hands coming into the frame to exchange one tool for another is a cutaway from the main action of sculpting. It is still part of the story, but does not involve the main action of the subject.

butted (used back to back). The interviewee's head will not be in the same exact position from one shot to the next, and therefore the edit can result in a basic jump cut: The interviewee's head jumps instantly through space and time to another position. This is a break in continuity for the viewer who is used to having the illusion of real time within a story.

In TV news, the solution to the problem is a cutaway shot to the reporter listening to the interviewee. This shot (picture only) is often called a **reversal**; it is the reverse angle from where the camera was pointed in the preceding shot. It is inserted over the edit so that the audio is not disturbed and the bridge in time is not noticed by the viewer. This type of shot is often used in an action sequence in which time compression is necessary, that is, when the subject must get from one part of the scene to another in less time (or more) than it really took. In a sports story in which the beginning and end of one boxing round is to be shown, the editor must cut out the middle of that round. To avoid the appearance of the boxer instantly jumping from one part of the ring to another, the editor uses a shot of the crowd for a few seconds between the first and second shots of the fight. The audience's attention is momentarily diverted by the crowd cutaway. This type of cutaway is sometimes called a **reaction shot**; it shows the reaction of a person(s) to the action. Both reaction shots and reversals are specific forms of cutaways.

The generic cutaway is any shot away from the action or subject but related to it. It can be a wide shot, medium, or close-up. A good cutaway should fit with the other shots, just as all shots in a story should blend together. In the two examples above, the cutaways are shots of people involved in some way with the subject, either listening or watching. These usually make the best cutaways, but sometimes they are not available to shoot. Often you will have to find other related things to shoot. It may be the scoreboard at a sports event, or the clasped hands of a couple being interviewed, but it must always relate to the subject.

The cutaway is used within a sequence of shots involving the same subject in the same location; it is *not* a transition shot. (See Figure 2.8.) To go from a shot of the mayor in an office to a shot of the mayor at a fund-raiser is not necessarily a jump cut. The audience knows there is a jump in time with this edit and perceives it as natural. In the movies and higher quality video productions, very few, if any, cutaways are used and no one misses them. The reason is that the sequences are so well thought out that the action flows naturally from one shot to the next. Even in shooting news, with a little practice, you can learn which shots to get and how to piece them together so that no cutaways are needed. In general, cutaways slow down the pace of a story without adding any new information to the subject. In many instances, the reporter cutaway can be eliminated by editing in shots of what is being talked about. If the mayor is talking about cutting spending on street maintenance, then why not show shots of the major items that are being cut over the offending jump cut edit in the interview? If you find creative ways not to use cutaways, your video pieces will generally look much better and be more interesting.

The Transition Shot

The **transition shot** is an editing tool that allows visual continuity and flow while avoiding abrupt changes in the sequence of shots. Unlike a cutaway, which covers jump cuts in the middle of a single action such as an interview, a transition shot gets the subject or flow of action from one location or action to another. Any two shots edited together that are very similar in composition can create a jump cut. You can't go from the subject talking on the phone to the subject typing at the computer in the same location. A transition such as a tight shot (XCU) of the phone receiver being hung up or an XCU of fingers on the keyboard would bridge the two action shots. The former ends the phone action shot, leaving the subject free to start the next action, and the latter

Figure 2.8 Cutaways are typically framed like this shot. The subject is seen from behind with the camera as close to the line of interest as possible.

begins a new action. You would use one or the other because, by themselves, they are similar shots; they are both XCUs of the same hands.

A subject moved from one location to another in an edit sometimes results in a jump cut if the shots are too similar. The simplest example of a transition shot in this case is a scene where you allow the subject to move out of the frame. You are left with an empty picture and are now free to establish the character anywhere else you wish. The reverse of this is also true. Start with an empty frame for your next location and let your subject walk into the shot. In some cases it may be easier to pan to or away from the subject to get the subject in or out of the picture. One very common transition shot in broadcast TV is the building or room exterior shot. It is usually used to start the next sequence of shots. This is useful as a transition for a subject that is changing geographic locations, because it also establishes the location for the following series of shots.

As we said above, close-ups make excellent transition shots. Because viewers see so little of the scene or subject in a CU or XCU, it leaves viewers at the end of an expression or thought. Starting a sequence of shots with a CU begins the action or thought before revealing the subject, which also works. The close-up of a sculptor's hands shaping clay, or even the XCU of the tool working the clay, can be the end of one sequence or the beginning of another. If it ends a sequence, you could then cut to a wide shot of the artist placing the sculpture on a shelf at the end of the day. This jump in time is blended into the story by causing the viewer to concentrate on only one small aspect of what the sculptor is doing before coming back to another time in the same location. Use of this method makes it possible to maintain the level of action and information without wasting time on neutral transition shots, such as the subject leaving the frame. Each story has many ways of being told; the style and pacing often determine which type of transition shots work the best. It is a good idea to shoot for many different possibilities and make the final decision in the edit room.

COMPOSITION

Of course, standing back and pointing a camera with the lens at wide angle does not a wide shot make. The image created in the viewfinder must be recognizable by the viewer and contain some form of meaning. A jumble of elements all competing for attention with no unifying theme, direction, balance, or point of interest causes a viewer to look elsewhere.

Many aspects are involved in making a good picture. You can spend an entire college term just learning all the ways to create a well-balanced, pleasing picture. Elements such as size, color, relative position, brightness, darkness, and angle all contribute to the aesthetic forces within any frame. Some of these elements will be discussed in the lighting chapter. Several rules and guidelines exist, however, that will help you establish a good working knowledge of what good framing is and how to obtain it easily.

Creating the Third Dimension

One of the first things you try to accomplish in any picture is a sense of space. Lighting is a great way to create volume and it will be covered in the lighting chapter, but any shot you make needs to address this issue. The three ways to avoid a flat picture and create volume are (1) the use of the foreground, (2) the use of the vanishing point, and (3) the use of focus. Adding dimension or depth to any shot is the first tool to improve the viewer's perception of the shot.

Use of the Foreground   In the simplest form, the use of the foreground is establishing an area or object near the camera and placing the subject in the midground while lining up a good background. The picture will have a feeling of depth because the objects are at very different distances from the camera. (See Figures 2.9 and 2.10.)

Figure 2.9   The straight-on shot (left) is flat and uninteresting. All the architectural lines are horizontal and vertical with no foreground or background. Choosing a point of view with foreground (right) gives the picture depth, because objects are both near to and far from the camera.

Figure 2.10   While the left shot shows the building clearly, the total picture area is not used to frame the subject. By moving under a nearby tree (right), you can use a branch to frame the picture. The branch not only adds interest and balance to the scene, but also a foreground that increases the depth of the picture.

Many times it helps to exaggerate this effect (forced perspective) by placing the foreground object extremely close to the camera. Unlike backgrounds, if a foreground is out of focus, it should still be a recognizable form, such as a tree limb or a fence. If the foreground object is too out of focus, it may be a help in framing but not in adding editorial content or contextual information to the frame. As a general rule, the subject must not be minimized by foreground or overpowered by background. Lighting or, as we shall learn later, placement in the picture can make the subject stand out even with the other elements present. The subject need not be the brightest area of the picture or the largest if additional factors are present. Other elements can often serve to give the most emphasis to the subject, no matter how small it is.

Use of the Vanishing Point　In many shots in which a foreground is not practical or desirable, the use of angles can give the feeling of continuance in the picture. In a drawing or on the screen, diagonal lines seem to converge at some point, implying a third dimension or movement to a distant point. For example, when you look down a straight line of railroad tracks, you can see that, at a certain point, the two rails seem to come together. This is the **vanishing point**. (See Figure 2.11.)

Break the picture down into horizontal, vertical, and diagonal lines. The best examples of this occur when shooting buildings, because the lines are easy to see. As the camera's position and, therefore, perspective changes, so do the lines. When you walk around a structure, notice that from some angles there are almost all horizontal and vertical lines and no diagonals. At other angles, however, there are many diagonal lines and almost no horizontal lines. At the point in which horizontal lines appear diagonal in the field of view, you can easily create depth in a two-dimensional picture. Therefore, do not shoot objects straight-on unless you have a good foreground; try to shoot from an angle.

Besides creating volume, these converging lines can take the viewer's eye to a subject or important element of the picture. Our eyes naturally follow these lines, extending them even if they don't continue on their own. By creating a focal point, you can lead the viewer to the main element of the shot. (See Figure 2.12.)

Use of Selective Focus　Another way to create a sense of volume within the frame is to have well-defined areas of focus. This technique is particularly useful when working with longer focal lengths that tend to flatten a shot by the compression of perspective. A shot of a subject walking down a crowded street, as seen through a telephoto lens, would not highlight the subject if all the faces in the shot were equally in focus. By finding ways to decrease depth of field

Figure 2.11　Even though this sidewalk is the same width all the way down the block, it appears to narrow as it recedes into the background, thus creating a vanishing point.

(shooting with a lower f-stop, perhaps) you can bring the subject into sharp focus and have both the background and the foreground drop out of focus. This creates the look of depth and better expresses the distances between elements in the frame. Even without a foreground, this technique can greatly enhance the three-dimensional qualities of any picture. (See Figure 2.13.)

Effects of Focal Length

As focal length changes, many things change in the resulting picture. The most basic change is the size of the subject: It gets larger as the focal length increases (zooming in). This magnification of the subject also has other effects in the overall picture. As the field of view narrows (focal length increasing), the quantity

Figure 2.12 Here the angle of the rocks and sign create the movement to a vanishing point located behind the subject that, together with the horizon line, focuses the viewer's attention to the subject's face.

Figure 2.13 By framing a shot so both background and foreground are out of focus, the subject easily dominates the picture.

of background decreases as its size increases. Because the field of view is in the shape of a cone, as you zoom in the rate of size increase for the background is much faster than either the foreground or midground of the picture. This visual effect is known as **compression.** Objects at different distances from the camera and in line with each other appear to become closer to one another as the field of view narrows (the background seems to be moving forward), even though their sizes relative to each other never change.

This phenomenon can be used to great advantage by the photographer. For example, in a movie where the hero is running down the street toward the camera while being chased by a truck, a telephoto lens (long focal length) makes not only the hero appear large but the truck as well. The compression of perspective in the shot can make it look as though the truck is only inches from the hero when in reality the truck could be 100 feet away. The same shot done with a wide field of view would show the truck's position more clearly and not have the same dramatic effect. The drawback to this shot is the perceived speed at which the truck is closing in on our hero. Because of the compression, even if the truck is rapidly gaining on him, the truck's size would barely be changing. Image size doubles in reverse proportion to the distance change. For the truck to double in size, it would have to come half again as close to the camera as it is. For a telephoto shot that could be quite a distance.

On the other hand, at a very wide field of view, just the opposite effect of compression occurs. In wide-angle shots, things in line with the camera tend to appear much farther apart than they really are. If the object of our truck chase is to see the speed at which the truck is closing in on our hero, the wide shot would do it. With both elements close to the camera (our hero is still the same size in the frame, though), the oncoming truck could easily double in size within a second or two (halving the already short distance to double in size), thus exaggerating the speed. Even for static objects these effects can be used to bring objects closer together or farther apart in a picture.

Perspective

In place of focal length change, you can substitute camera distance to change the size of the subject. By simply moving the camera closer to the subject, you increase its magnification. In the early days of photojournalism when each lens had one fixed focal length, the photographer had to walk to or from the subject to change the size of the image. Many people still refer to a wide shot as a long shot because you had to walk a long way back to get a wide shot with a fixed focal length lens.

With today's zoom lenses and wider angles of view, you need not walk as far or as much. The thing to keep in mind is the **perspective** of each type of focal length, especially when shooting medium or close-up shots. (See Figures 2.14 and 2.15.)

Zooming in creates less depth of field and less of a three-dimensional view: The perspective is compressed or flattened. When the photographer walks

Figure 2.14 By changing the angle of view and distance to the subject, you can keep the plaza sign approximately the same size in the frame, but the background and perspective change dramatically.

closer to the subject, the perspective stays the same for the midground and background, but the foreground begins to distort in an effect called **exaggerated** or **forced perspective**. The depth of field does not change, but the three-dimensional effect is made more prominent by the rapidly increasing size of the foreground (the opposite effect of zooming in). Again, the objects double in size as the distance to them is cut in half. Unlike zooming, this effect is achieved by moving the camera closer to the subject while maintaining a constant focal length.

Balancing the Picture

Up to now we have just talked about composition as it relates to the camera, lens, and subject size and distance. The final aspect of composition is the arrangement of the elements within the frame. Before you push the record button you need to ask yourself, "How can I maximize the impact of this shot?" Too many photographers in television never ask that question. Flipping on almost any newscast, you can see the results of "point and shoot" photography. Shots are framed for a subject with no regard for the rest of the picture. A photographer's eye should be trained to look at the entire frame and all the visual elements within it, not just what initially attracts our attention while looking at a scene.

Too often balance is thought of in terms of being centered: having the same amount of space on all sides of the subject. Much of the time this is not the case. Balance is far more complex than that. As we

will learn in lighting, a little of something can go a long way. A very small but bright object can upset the balance of a picture quite easily, but can also be positioned to *add* balance to a picture. While there are some basic rules that can lead you to balance within a frame, there is no substitute for what your eye tells you as you look through the viewfinder. Some arrangements just feel better than others when you look at them.

Frame Dynamics   A well-designed garden maze ensures that anyone seeking the center has to make several circuits before they find that center, and they will still have to search for an exit once there. A well designed picture should do the same thing. It has one entrance for the eye, one main subject, and several points of departure away from it. There are three basic patterns to the movement of a viewer's eye.

1. **Pyramid**—the eye starts at the bottom left, traverses up to the pinnacle, down to the right corner, and finally back to the left to complete a strong and unified composition.
2. **Circle**—the classic symbol of unity forms the simplest compositions, allowing the eye to circle the image.
3. **Irregular shape**—allows the eye to move in a dynamic and asymmetrical flow adding energy and tension to the image.

Western culture has programmed our eyes to always start from the left side of any scene. In theater,

Figure 2.15   A wide-angle perspective (left) with a large angle of view can have an open feeling. A telephoto perspective (right) has a narrower angle of view, and objects appear closer because the perspective is compressed.

the left side of the stage is said to be the strong side for entrances. That doesn't mean that side of the frame is where the subject should go. The eye starts there, but your composition can take it to wherever the subject is in the frame. It is also possible to have the eye start in other places. A brilliant orange sun in the upper right corner of the frame can catch the eye first and send it down the right side to settle on a lone surfer in the lower left corner. (See Figure 2.16.)

Lines   As we have seen with the vanishing point, where our attention is directed to the point of convergence, lines can play a very large role in leading our eye. The diagonal lines create a vitality with their implied movement. Anywhere in the frame where two lines cross or one line suddenly changes direction (a corner) will draw the eye. An isolated vertical line, such as a tree, pole, or even a standing person, is noticed first in the picture and takes precedence over any horizontal or diagonal lines in the scene. (See Figure 2.17.) To achieve a pleasing composition, a horizontal line must cross this vertical element at some point. When a vertical line is not interrupted, it simply splits the screen, creating two disconnected sections of the frame.

Color   A very important tool in the design of a frame is the color of elements within it. This can be a difficult task for the video photographer because of the black-and-white viewfinder. A red rose may stand out as the dominant element in the frame when viewed in color, but in the viewfinder it may be next to impossible to pick it out in the field of grays. A TV photographer needs to use one eye to see color and one to look through the viewfinder, combining the two versions to realize the actual outcome of the video. Composition includes giving weight to brighter colors.

The Rule of Thirds   One very easy way to frame objects is by using a nine-square grid as an overlay to the picture. This concept, called the **rule of thirds**, divides the screen up by thirds vertically and horizontally. (See Figure 2.18.) It is based on the ancient Greek discovery called the **golden rectangle,** or as Da Vinci called it, the **divine proportion**. An accurate golden rectangle has an aspect ratio of 1.618:1. That ratio is found by dividing the longest side of the rectangle by the shortest side. A true golden rectangle is more like the aspect ratio of a movie screen. The TV aspect ratio of 4:3 does not contain the same geometric properties as a golden rectangle, but the one-third and two-thirds divisions are a close approximation. As high-definition television with its movie-like as-

pect ratio makes its way into homes, the TV screen will take on more of the artistic look seen in other forms of Western design.

As you look at any composition, try to fit the elements of the scene into the grid, centering them on the four intersections of the lines. Try this idea with a sunset and a very flat horizon such as the ocean or a large field. You'll find that long or tall objects, such as the horizon line and maybe a telephone pole, will look better lined up along the lines of the grid and not centered in the spaces of the squares. You'll also find that smaller objects like the sun look better placed at the intersection of the lines.

Figure and Ground   One way to organize the elements of the frame is to use the concept of figure and ground, figure being the main visual element or subject of the picture—the shape that you notice first—while ground gives it the context in which to exist. Figure can only exist with a ground to place it on. You cannot see figure and ground at the same time. Photographers who point and shoot run afoul of this concept all the time. A figure is any element in the frame that achieves prominence over the rest. By concentrating on just the element you *want* to be the subject of the shot, you cannot see the entire frame—a version of not seeing the forest for the trees. The best example of this is the infamous tree positioned so it comes perfectly out of the top of someone's head. The photographer is so focused on the subject that the other aspects of the frame are literally not seen. But the viewer is not concentrating in the same way, they are just discovering the shot and see it first as simply figure and ground. In this case the figure is a person visually attached to a tree. The tree and the head are one continuous form. Signs can work the same way. If they are too large or too overpowering in the shot, they become the figure and the person standing in front of them becomes the ground. (See Figure 2.19.) This is not effective communication.

It is easy to control figure within ground just as you would any object you wish to highlight. Through lighting, color, focus, position, and so on, you determine which object will be figure and which will be ground despite the complexity of the shot.

Balance   A balanced shot is one in which the elements within the frame are at equilibrium with all the forces of the frame. And there are many. The frame is like a scale; elements and groups of elements have visual weight determined by size, shape, contrast, direction, or just plain interest. Large dominates small; a black bean will dominate when seen in a

Figure 2.16   The bright sunset catches the viewer's eye first then moves it to the surfers in the foreground.

Figure 2.17   A lone vertical element will dominate the picture.

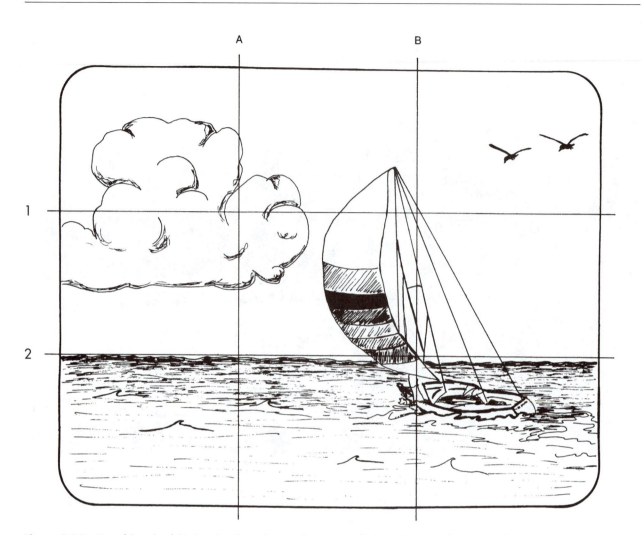

Figure 2.18 Use of the rule of thirds makes the sailboat and seascape a balanced picture. The sea is in the lower third of the picture, the boat is at B2, and the cloud is at A1.

group of all white beans; a regular shape such as a circle will dominate within a group of irregular shapes, and certainly a snake sliding across the floor will dominate any picture regardless of composition.

Balance is determined by two factors: visual weight and the visual pattern's direction of movement. Position in the frame has a lot to do with the relative weight an element has. A large object near the center of the screen can be balanced by a small object close to the edges of the frame. Objects at the center of the frame or on the vertical centerline of the frame have less weight than the same object at the sides of the picture. An element at the top of the frame is heavier than when it is at the bottom. Because of our left–right conditioning, an object on the right side of the frame has less visual weight than one

on the left side. A picture can be balanced by total symmetry, but these compositions rarely hold visual interest; they are boring. By using a more dynamic framing scheme, such as the rule of thirds combined with the concepts of eye movement, you can design an image that holds the viewer's interest and therefore imparts more information.

The movement, or implied movement, within the frame is the other part of the balancing act. Converging lines create movement to the point of convergence. Your eye will follow a curved line in a field of all straight lines. But one of the most important movements that you will deal with in TV is the movement created by the human face. The direction in which a person looks creates a very strong movement in that direction; it is a force that needs to be neutral-

Figure 2.19 Here the reporter is overwhelmed by the sign. The subject becomes ground while the sign becomes the figure. This diminishes the importance of the subject.

ized in some form within the frame. Later, in the Interview Shot section of this chapter, we will deal with this specific problem.

COMPOSING SPECIFIC SHOTS

Just as shots can be described by their focal length to quickly communicate the size of the subject within the frame, there are specific shots that can be called for by using common names. Their execution is done by convention. The most common specialty shot is the interview. When a producer or reporter says, "Let's set up for an interview," they have a specific style of framing in mind. The conditions of the location or situation or artistic inspiration can change this, but for the most part, an interview shot looks the same from Maine to California, from small town local news to the networks.

The Interview Shot

The basic framing of the interview shot is the head and shoulders of the subject, hence the name "talking heads." The standard reference point for where the bottom frame line would cut the subject is the "necktie knot." If the subject, man or woman, were wearing a tie, the bottom of the frame would be just below the knot. A looser version of this shot cuts them off at the top of the breast pocket. A shot tighter than the

necktie is sometimes called a "choker." To simplify all the compositional information we learned above, there are two basic rules for framing the talking head and have it look good virtually every time.

1. *Never let the subject's eyes go below the horizontal centerline of the screen.* If the focal length changes from the waist up to a close-up of the face, the eyes of the subject should always be in the upper half of the screen. (See Figure 2.20.)

2. *Keep the tip of the subject's nose on the vertical centerline of the screen.* If the subject is talking to a reporter off camera, you will notice that this rule puts the subject's head slightly off center. Because the subject is not talking to the viewer directly, this type of framing leaves a space in front of the subject that helps counter the movement created by the direction of the subject's eye line, and it also implies that someone is there just out of the frame. That implication becomes yet another force in the dynamics of the picture. You can start to see how these simple rules support the concepts of composition.

You may at times want to include the interviewer in the shot. If this is the case, you must pay close attention to the balance of the picture; you don't want the reporter to be the figure and the subject to become the ground. If only a portion of the reporter's head is in the frame, make sure the subject is not centered but off to the other side. As more of the reporter

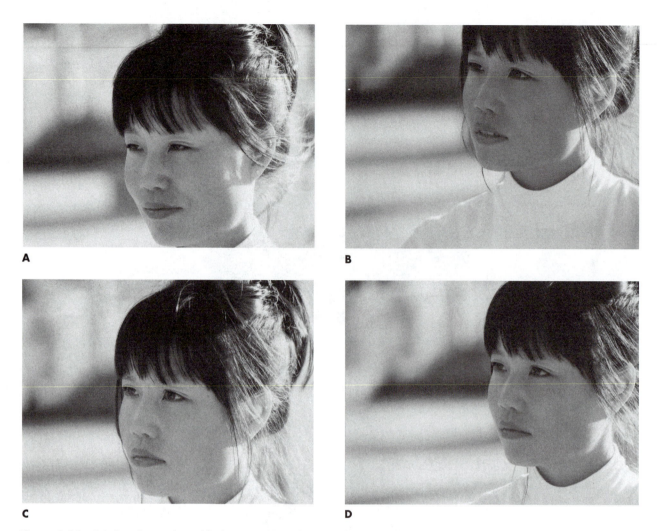

Figure 2.20 (A) The subject is framed for her entire head placing her face too low. (B) The subject's face is framed too high, as if she's pushing out the top of the frame. (C) The subject's head is framed dead center, leaving too little room in the direction she is looking. (D) A properly framed head for this focal length.

is seen, make sure you are using the tools of composition to keep the subject the main point of interest.

As mentioned above, the standard framing for the talking head should be tight enough to show the subject's face clearly on the average TV screen. In the case of chokers, as on a probing interview on *60 Minutes*, the framing may be extremely tight. You will notice that as the top frame line closes in on the face using the rules stated above, it begins to cut off the top of the head. One of the biggest fights you will ever have over composition with coworkers will be over this effect. Untrained producers will call for head room or scream that the top of the head is cut off; they can't see all of the subject's hair. Take refuge in the concepts of good composition. By allowing the face to slip to the bottom half of the frame (eyes below the mid-

point) you have given added weight to the hair of the subject (top of the screen is heavier). You are throwing the picture out of balance. The edges of the frame have a force all their own. As an object begins to near or partially exit any side of the frame, the frame acts as a pull on that object. For a talking head, the face is the center of interest and therefore the main element. For it to sink in the bottom of the frame it gives the appearance of falling out of the frame. The hair being cut off by the top of the frame produces a feeling of the subject rising, but because the hair is not a major element or focus of the picture, its force carries little weight and is easily countered by the grouping of eyes, nose, and mouth—the figure of the scene.

Be careful when framing subjects too tightly, though. An interview with a welfare mother who has had her food stamps stolen could be a close-up of her face to show the viewer her emotion. However, the same type of shot in an interview with a city official regarding an upcoming change in street signs would not have the same meaning. Reserve the close-up of faces only for emotional or dramatic subjects. Children are the biggest exception to this rule—they almost always look good in close-ups.

It is possible to overdo the facial close-up. It is basic conditioning to zoom in for a tight face shot when the grieving mother of a dead child starts to cry. While some may argue that the emphasis is needed to convey the full impact of emotion to the viewer, there is also the argument that this type of shot is an uncaring, vulgar invasion of the woman's privacy. It may indeed be more dramatic to actually zoom out from such a scene to give the subject some "space," if only symbolically.

TV is the best medium for conveying emotions, especially in news photography. While the emotions portrayed should be true to your subject, they should not be offensive to your viewing audience. Some subjects deserve more respect than to have their worst moments seen larger than life in everyone's living room. The moral values or degree of good taste you express in your shooting should be the same as you would express any time in your life. The tight head shot can be a powerful tool both artistically and emotionally, but you must be careful how and when you use it.

Effects of Background and Focal Length   In some cases, the background can be of such importance that the framing or placement of the subject in the frame is dictated by that background. The best setup for an interview with a farmer about a flooded field may be a wide shot of the field that includes the standing farmer (remember how a single vertical figure can dominate). The farmer may be framed head to toe, and if you place the farmer on the edge of the flooded field (rule of thirds), the impact is enhanced from both a visual and informational point of view. An interview background should add to—*not distract from*—the interviewee (figure/ground concept). If an appropriate background cannot be found, then choose a neutral one, or use a focal length that produces a depth of field shallow enough to take the background out of focus.

When setting up an interview shot with a specific background, first choose the background. Add the subject to the shot. If the subject does not conform to the framing rules mentioned at the beginning of this section, do not bend the rules but "tweak" the cam-

era location and/or focal length to satisfy the framing concepts. A very common misuse of background and subject occurs when the photographer tries to put a sign over the shoulder of the subject. If the sign is too high, many new photographers shoot the interview from a low angle or frame the shot so that the subject's eyes are below the middle of the screen. Both generally produce a very uncomfortable shot and overemphasize the sign (again, object/ground). Never let the eyes of the interviewee or the interviewer go below the horizontal midpoints of the screen. Simply move the camera and subject farther from the sign, so that the sign can be placed in the deep background to maintain good framing. Do not force bad framing on your subject just to get a "good" background. A little experimentation usually shows a way to make both satisfactory.

The Reporter Stand-up Shot

This shot is a specialized version of the interview shot used especially in TV news. For EFP this concept can be used as any on-camera appearance by a narrator who is talking *directly* to the audience. Because of this direct link to the audience, the framing of the stand-up is very important. A general rule for this shot is to never frame the subject looser than the waist up or tighter than the breast pocket top. This allows the viewer to have good eye contact with the talent and feel a personal link, which helps establish credibility.

If the shot is framed too loosely, the importance of the subject can be reduced or even lost in the background and the impact is greatly reduced. (See Figure 2.21.)

Again, there are ways around this if careful attention to the rules of composition are applied. The talent must be the focus of the shot or why else have him or her in it? Background is important but very much a secondary part of the picture. The subject's monologue should help design the shot and determine the type of background used. If the script is general, then the background should be as well. If the script deals with a power plant, however, perhaps the power plant should be in the background.

Many of the same rules that apply to the interview shot apply also to the stand-up shot, such as placing the subject correctly in relation to the background and keeping the subject's eyes above the middle of the screen. As in the interview, the best camera elevation is eye level. One thing this does is place any visible portion of the horizon at the eye level of the subject. The horizon line running through the picture directly behind the eyes of the on-camera subject draws added interest to their face. This is good. Any other angle tends to be either unflattering or can either add or subtract too much importance to other elements in the picture. Sometimes, however, a different angle does work; for example, if you are shooting a reporter in front of a field of flowers. When the camera is at eye level, the background covers about half of the frame, but the sky may be overcast and "blowing out" (overexposing) the upper portion of the frame behind the top of the head. (See Figure 2.22.) If you raise the camera above eye level, however, the viewer has a different perspective on the background. The horizon line can be taken to the very top of the shot, leaving the reporter framed against nothing but flowers. This composition can be more dramatic.

Figure 2.21 The reporter in this picture blends into the objects in the scene, becoming part of the background. There is no separation.

Figure 2.22 Any time the camera is at eye level with the subject, their eyes will be at the horizon line. This draws attention to the subject's eyes, which is desirable.

The difference between the stand-up and the interview shot is that the subject is talking directly to the camera. The need for the implied second person, the listener, is gone. This allows you more latitude to frame the subject in different areas of the frame and to fit the background in around the subject. For any off-center positions, the talent's inside shoulder (closest to the middle of the picture) should be angled slightly away from the camera to help add a three-dimensional quality to the shot and visually direct the viewer's eye to the return journey to the background as part of the overall eye movement. Again, the subject is always the dominant element in the frame, even if they are part of the background. A good rule of thumb to simplify stand-up framing is to never let the talent be more than 6 feet from the camera if you are using wide or medium focal lengths. (See Figure 2.23.)

A

B

Figure 2.23 (A) The reporter is too low in the frame and the sign overpowers the shot. (B) The reporter is dominant in the foreground, but the sign is still visible.

The stand-up shot has many variations. The most common is the walking stand-up. As with any shot, it should have a purpose. The reason for a walking stand-up shot can be as simple as adding a little movement to an otherwise static composition. The movement should be slow and comfortable. A relaxed walk not only provides the necessary movement but also visually adds to the conversational tone appropriate for a stand-up. The subject should already be walking when the shot starts and can either stop partway through it or continue to walk throughout the shot. The correct framing needs to be maintained on the walking subject. Depending on other compositional tools, it may be necessary to zoom out as the subject approaches to maintain her in the waist-up framing. Other frame dynamics may work, such as having the reporter grow in size as she approaches the camera, thus drawing the viewer's eye. This works as long as the reporter is the center of attention right from the start of the shot.

As a general rule, the zoom-in is used much more frequently than the zoom-out in the stand-up shot. The zoom-in, or **push**, adds emphasis to a stationary subject, whereas the zoom-out, or **pull**, usually de-emphasizes the subject by bringing attention to the ground of the shot. A zoom-out can also be effective when there is some additional information to be imparted by expanding the shot. But keep in mind that doing this generally renders the reporter as insignificant and leaves only his words to convey continuity in meaning. His physical presence has been diminished by the new subject of the shot. An example of this is a reporter doing a stand-up in an area that is very dry due to a recent drought. The shot starts as a waist-up shot; as the talent talks, the camera zooms out to show the reporter at the end of a lake's dock with no water in sight. The dry lake bed becomes the new subject of the picture and the reporter fades to ground.

Another factor in stand-ups is direction. The audience is being spoken to, and therefore the direction of the stand-up should always be toward the camera or audience. If the talent is entering the frame from off camera, the direction should still be toward the camera and not at a right angle to it. This usually requires some camera movement to get the talent into the frame in the least amount of time, but the feeling of positive motion (motion toward the camera) is worth the movement. Walking into a static shot is time consuming and usually awkward because of the transition period of being half in the frame and half out of the frame. If the transition can't be made

quickly, find another way of doing it. The only time a talent should have negative motion (motion away from the camera) is when taking the viewer to another location or showing the viewer something behind the place where the stand-up starts. This can be very effective if the shot is well thought out in advance. The audience does not like to have subjects turn their backs to them without good reason. The main goal is always to communicate—every shot, every subject.

Following the Action

Following the action combines all shots and camera moves. Spot news is the best example of this concept because of the severe time constraints on getting the visual story and the level of action during the shooting. As a story unfolds under the fast-paced conditions of spot news, the photographer tries to stay with the subject or the important aspects of the story. To do this, the photographer's position and camera zoom must be used to maintain good framing and get all the different shot types necessary to tell the story. Because of the fast pace, the camera should never stop rolling. Often a zoom is necessary or a camera position must change, but the important idea is that the action must always be followed. The action can be allowed to leave the frame (a transition shot), but it must be picked up again with a minimum of lost time.

Sports coverage is the easiest example of following the action (or "staying with the ball"). The action should determine how the shot is framed and what the camera must do. If the action involves more than one subject, such as in basketball, then frame for them all. If it only involves one subject, such as a football running back, then stay with that subject in the best framing to visually describe the action. In some cases it may be best to hold the same focal length and let the action take place while panning to keep it in the frame. Too much camera movement or zooming can ruin the visual presentation of an event.

All the rules in the previous sections apply to following the action, especially the rule that too much of anything is bad. A photographer needs to do what is necessary to get the shot, but if the piece overuses pans and zooms it may be too annoying to watch while yielding little information to the viewer.

The one rule for composition is to always lead the action in the frame. A runner on a track, or an ice skater on an ice rink, or a paramedic rushing a gurney to an ambulance, should not be framed in the center but slightly off center with the empty side of the picture in front of them. (See Figure 2.24.)

Through the use of the empty space in framing an action, you give the impression that the subject has someplace to go, and the dynamics of the frame make the figure's movement in that direction seem natural. The subject should not be running into the side of the frame (creating a look of falling out of the picture). There should always be space left for the subject to run into, even before they start any movement (a runner in the starting blocks should have the space ready to fill before the gun sounds).

Breaking the Rules

Rules are simply guidelines to help understand the basics of portable video. Once you become proficient

with the basics, you will begin to see the ways you can break the rules and still achieve truly great results. The talking head is a perfect example of this. By ignoring the basic rules of framing, it is possible to put the interviewee anywhere in the frame if you know what you are doing. Producer Ray Farkas has built a reputation in the TV news business by using unusual framing for interviews. At first glance, you would think they violate everything known about framing. On closer examination, you discover that the frame is not only emphasizing the subject strongly but adding editorial content to the environment. His frames pack quite a punch. (See Figure 2.25.) The framing as well as the content sticks in the viewers' minds. They not only remember the subject's words but other things about the subject as well. The Farkas style is not easy to copy. Without the fundamentals of

Figure 2.24 As the camera follows the skater, the framing leads the subject to give her room to skate into.

Figure 2.25   This style of framing, made famous by Ray Farkas, uses the subject's environment to add editorial content to the composition.

SUMMARY

Stories can be told with nothing more than tight shots or wide shots if a photographer truly understands how to use them. A popular term in today's television business is **cinéma vérité**. A character on a TV sitcom once described it as meaning "something in French, but in America it just means shaky camera." Even though the description comes from a comedian, that is exactly what it has become. The true art of cinéma vérité is rarely seen on today's TV. Simply having the camera on your shoulder does not mean that you are being artistic in a French way. Unless you are chasing a subject, it mostly means you are lazy or simply do not care to provide the audience with pictures that let the subject be the center of attention instead of drawing that attention to yourself. The camera has become the subject. Form has overcome substance.

Style is what separates the truly artistic from the basic, but style can only come from the basic. If you are just learning to shoot video and tell stories with a camera, you need to concentrate on the fundamentals first and then learn to apply style. There is no substitute for good composition.

good photography, a novice attempt would simply look as though someone made a mistake or was trying to be arty and failed.

3

Video: The Process of Image Acquisition

LIGHT, LENSES, CAMERAS, AND RECORDERS

Like any craftsperson or artist, a successful photographer wants the most information possible about the tools of the trade. Knowing how a piece of equipment works reveals its limitations and its possibilities. To become truly proficient at creating video, a TV photographer sooner or later has to learn the technical things too often left just to the engineers and maintenance staff. As camcorders move toward simpler and simpler operation, it actually becomes more important for the user to know how each part of the system works. The reliance on the camera to do all of the thinking reduces the level of creativity by reducing the attention to detail. To master the craft—or indeed the art—of video, the photographer must master, and understand, the tools in every respect. This book will give the photographer a good start on the road to that understanding.

The medium of TV involves three basic forms of communication: sight, sound, and motion. The basic tools for creating these for TV are a camera, a recording device, a microphone, and a source of illumination. In Chapters 3 and 4, the basic elements of each piece of video equipment are introduced. This chapter discusses the camera with its lens and the recorder—the two most important elements in capturing sight and motion. Chapter 4 deals with microphones and recording technique—the sound element. Chapter 5 presents light sources and their control—the one component necessary to accomplish any type of photography.

There is no end to the machines, gadgets, and accessories that any photographer can consider prized possessions on a shoot. There is a big difference, however, between a basic set of gear and the ideal set of gear. Although budgets will determine the type and quantity of equipment, there will always be several items that simply cannot be left out. These may be of the lowest or highest quality, but they constitute the minimum needed to do the job.

Today's TV photographers have a wide range of equipment available; therefore, it is hard to provide a definitive list. The list in Table 3.1 will satisfy job requirements at the minimum standards of quality almost anywhere.

This chapter will introduce the reader to most of the basic forms of equipment used in portable video today. As more and more manufacturers and newly

Table 3.1. A photographer's basic set of gear.

Camera with lens	Omnidirectional hand mic
Videocassette recorder, or VCR, either mounted on/in the camera or separate (stand-alone)	
Tripod with fluid head	Two-lavalier mic
Set of three AC-powered (120V) location lights and AC extension cords	4–6 hours of battery power
Camera-mounted light, 30V or 12V, with batteries and cables	Several audio and video cables of varying lengths

Figure 3.1 The interior of a production van viewed through the side door. Custom shelves are made to organize and store equipment.

developed technology enter the market, no one book can describe them all in detail. The following text will go through the basics of how any typical device works. It is always a good idea to get the service and operating manuals for the equipment you will be using and read them thoroughly to truly understand that particular piece of gear. Today's marketplace underscores that thought. With a growing number of tape formats, recording formats, and delivery systems, a photographer can easily find herself in a situation where nothing seems compatible, where analog and digital are used side by side. Just keeping up with the changing technologies is a full-time job. Understanding them is a career. But the basics of what they do will always be the same.

PRINCIPLES OF LENS OPERATION

The lens of the human eye is a truly amazing mechanism for directing and focusing light on the light-sensitive rods and cones in the back of our eyes. In video cameras, the zoom lens tries to perform the same tasks. While our eyes have a single lens, video lenses are complicated devices with many individual pieces of glass that can be physically moved to direct, focus, and magnify the light from images in front of it. If the lens cannot focus properly, the picture is fuzzy; if it cannot transmit light efficiently, then the picture is dark or distorted.

Lens Components

No less valuable than the eye's lens is the lens on a camera. While most discussions of video equipment center on the camera and tape machines, the lens is a crucial part of the image-gathering process. A high-quality lens can make the best camera the best performer, and a poor-quality lens can leave the camera's picture out of focus and distorted. The eye has one simple lens that does amazing things. The camera needs several lenses called **elements** to duplicate the complex workings of the eye. Nonzoom lenses used in photography are made up of as many as five elements in two groups that properly place an image on the recording surface or **focal plane**. A zoom lens, which is used on most TV cameras, has 13 or more elements.

A lens is basically two prisms joined together. If joined at their apexes, they form a **concave lens** that refracts light out from the center. If joined at the base, they form a **convex lens** that converges the light to a single point.

Light refracted through a prism can be broken down into areas of different wavelengths. Even after prisms are joined to make lenses, small defects can cause aberrations in the sharpness and color of the image by not transmitting all frequencies evenly. By combining groups of concave and convex lenses and using special coatings, almost all of the defects of any single lens can be overcome. Such defects as **chromatic** and **spherical aberrations**, curvature of the field, distortion, flare, and astigmatism are all corrected by the many elements contained in the average TV lens. Each of the elements in the lens serves a specific purpose in controlling the quality and quantity of the visual information.

Focal Length

The distance from the optical center of the primary lens to the point where the light converges on the focal plane (the principal focus) is the focal length of a lens. On TV lenses the focal length setting can be read off the zoom portion of the lens. The focal length determines the **field of view** of the lens. A lens with a very short focal length has a very wide field of view and is called a **wide-angle lens**. A lens with a long focal length has a narrow field of view and is called a **telephoto** lens. Focal lengths are measured in millimeters (mm). The average TV zoom lens starts at about 8mm and goes to 100mm or more. Focal lengths between 4.8mm and 25mm are considered to be wide-angle fields of view. From 25mm to 75mm a lens is said to have a normal field of view, meaning that the lens sees things in a way similar to how your eye does. From 75mm to the longest focal lengths available, the lens has a narrow field of view and is referred to as telephoto.

The field of view of a lens is often expressed as the horizontal angle of view and is measured in de-grees. The widest setting on the most common professional lens is about 8mm. This focal length represents an angle of view of about 50 degrees, which would have a view about 6 feet wide of a wall 6 feet from the camera. A wide-angle lens, about 5.5mm, has an angle of view of about 75 degrees, which sees an area 10 feet wide of a wall 6 feet from the camera. Similarly a lens of 300mm would have an angle of view of less than 2 degrees and would cover only a span of about 1 foot of a wall 50 feet from the camera.

The advantage of a zoom lens over lenses of fixed focal lengths is that the focal length can be set at any point from 8mm all the way to 100mm or whatever the parameters happen to be on that lens. More on the zoom lens a little later. While fixed focal length lenses, sometimes called **prime** lenses, are generally of a higher quality than zoom lenses, they are simply not practical for most TV shooting styles.

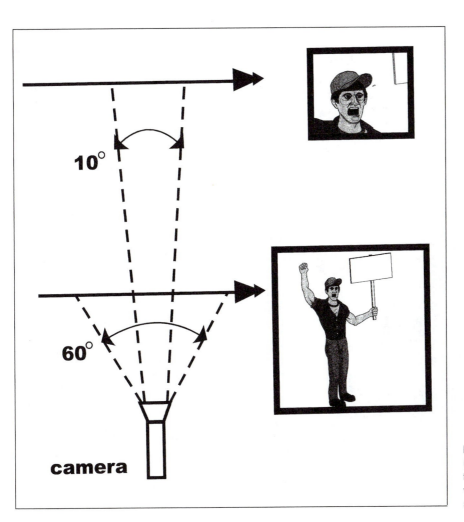

Figure 3.2 A wide field of view (60°) would see the subject head to toe. A narrow field of view (10°) would see only the head and shoulders of that same subject.

Focus

Another set of elements in the lens determines the sharpness of the image sent to the **principle focus** or **focal plane**. These elements are usually at the front of the lens. By moving these elements further away or closer to the remaining elements, objects at different distances to the focal plane can be brought into sharp focus. The point of focus in front of the camera determines an area called the **plane of focus.** Almost all lenses have focusing marks on the barrel that read in feet and meters. If the focus barrel is turned in order to line up the number 10 on the focus mark, then the plane of focus is at 10 feet from the camera (more precisely, from the focal plane of the camera). Often objects at other distances are also in focus with the barrel set at 10 feet. The range of acceptable focus in front of and behind the plane of focus is called the **depth of field**; on older 35mm still cameras, this information can be read right off the lens for any focal plane setting. Video lenses do not have this convenience; the eye must judge what the range is. (See Figure 3.3.)

Three factors have an effect on the depth of field for any chosen plane of focus: the focal length, the iris opening, and the distance from the camera. As the focal length increases, the depth of field decreases; as the iris is opened up, the depth of field decreases. As the lens is focused on objects closer and closer to the camera, the depth of field also decreases. The greatest depth of field occurs with wide-angle focal lengths with the iris opening very small and the lens focused

at infinity. The shortest depth of field comes at telephoto settings with the iris wide open and the lens focused at its minimum focus point.

Take a video camera outside and play with the zoom and focus, first in full sun and then in deep shade. Notice how much more depth of field you have in the sunny areas even as you zoom in. Also notice how much easier it is to stay in focus when the lens is at it widest setting. As you begin to use a video camera more, you will get used to combining the effects of focal length, focus, and iris to achieve the results you want.

Although it is still rare to see an auto-focus function on a professional style camera, it is a standard on consumer and prosumer cameras. The auto-focus function can make shooting moving objects easier to keep in focus but as we have mentioned earlier, a true professional likes to maintain as much control as possible over the tools. As anyone who has used an auto-focus camera can attest, the system doesn't always do what you want it to—a situation unacceptable to a professional.

The **hyperfocal distance** of a lens is the distance from the lens to the first point where an object is in focus when the lens is focused at infinity. In shooting news or any uncontrolled action where there is little time or ability to focus properly, this number comes in handy. The number will vary depending on the iris setting and focal length, but at full wide angle the iris settings will have little effect on the hyperfocal distance. This translates into the ability to focus the lens at infinity and know that everything at the hyperfocal distance or beyond is in focus.

Macrofocus

Although every lens can focus on infinity, each lens has a limit on how close it can focus. This varies from one type of lens to another and is called the **minimum object distance**. For the Canon J14X8B lens that distance is 27.5 inches. Most typical TV lenses have a minimum distance similar to this. Therefore, a very valuable feature to have on any lens is a **macro-focusing ring**. The macrofocus is usually a pull-out knob on the rear area of the lens barrel that allows a rotation of the rear elements inside the lens to change the focus distance. (See Figure 3.5.) It is possible to macrofocus as close as the very surface of the front element of the lens itself when it's at the wide-angle focal length. The macrofocus can be used with the lens focused at any point and set at any focal length.

Figure 3.3 The still camera lens has its focus set at 10 feet and its f-stop at f5.6. The middle scale on the lens lets us read off the depth of field for those settings. At f5.6, everything from 30 feet to approximately 7 feet will be in focus.

However, with the macrofocus engaged, the focal length cannot be adjusted without disturbing the focus of the picture. In macro, a zoom lens in effect becomes a fixed focal length lens because of this limitation.

Creative photographers have found unlimited uses for the macrofocus. The macro's effect on the front focus and zoom can be used to a creative advantage. With a lens set in macro, any change of the focal length changes the point of focus, which gives

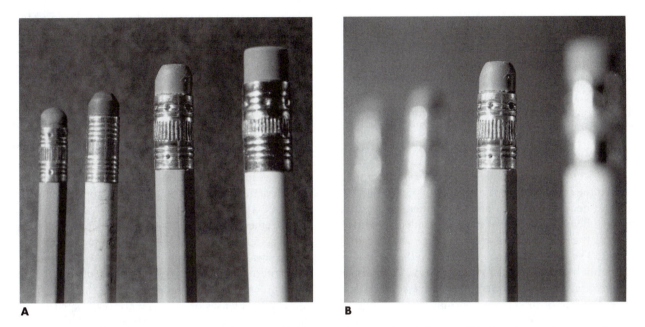

A **B**

Figure 3.4 (A) Deep depth of field. (B) Shallow depth of field. Frame A was made with the iris at f22. Everything is the same in frame B except that the iris is at f2.8. The same exposure was maintained by adding neutral density filters to the camera lens.

Figure 3.5 The small macro knob at the base of the lens must be pulled out slightly to allow its rotation.

you the ability to use the zoom to change focus. This abnormal behavior can lead to some very unusual shots. An understanding of the relationships among the various elements that make up a TV lens can lead to interesting shots that enhance the visual quality of the product.

Aspect Ratio

Even though lenses are round, the pictures they make are rectangular. The ratio between the width and the height of the TV picture is always the same. All standard TV cameras have an **aspect ratio** of 4:3 (or 1.33:1 in cinema terms): For every 4 units of width in the picture, its height will be 3 units. This limitation becomes most noticeable when, for instance, a TV photographer tries to shoot a still picture of a military officer printed in a book. The still photographer turned the camera on its side to get the portrait of the general head to toe. For the video camera to see this picture head to toe, extra space is needed on either side of the photo because the aspect ratios do not match. The full shot of the general from the book will probably be just head and shoulders or a tilt up from boots to face to avoid the empty or undesirable space on either side of the photo. Learning to see things as the video camera sees them means getting used to seeing everything in this 4:3 aspect. Video shot for high-definition TV (HDTV) will almost always be in the 16:9 ratio.

Iris

Every lens has an aperture for controlling the amount of light passed on to the focal plane. Just like the mechanism in the eye that controls the amount of light, this aperture is referred to as an **iris**. This control over light quantity is done by a series of overlapping metal leaves or fins that can be rotated one way to make the hole very small or rotated the other way to make the hole very large. The efficiency of a lens to pass light is referred to as its **speed**. A fast lens can transmit a large amount of light, whereas a slow lens transmits a much smaller amount of light. The speed is measured in **f-stops**. An f-stop is the ratio between the size of the aperture and the focal length of the lens. f-stops are a standardized way of measuring the passage of light on every lens; the numbers refer to a specific amount of light. Any lens set at f8 gives the same amount of light no matter which camera or format of recording. The differences in lens speeds come

from how wide the iris can be opened. The smaller the f-stop number, the more light the lens transmits. A lens that can go to f2 is not as fast as a lens that can go to f1.4.

Most lenses range from f16 to f1.8. Each f-stop shown on the lens represents twice as much light as the one before it, or half as much as the one after it. The f-stops would normally be f16, f11, f8, f5.6, f4, f2.8, f2, and f1.4. An iris at f8 lets in twice the amount of light as a setting of f11 but only half as much light as f5.6. If the exposure is increased by one stop, you are allowing in twice as much light. The smallest f-stop number tells you how fast a lens is. The typical lens mentioned above can only go to f1.8, which is only one-quarter of a stop faster than f2 and three-quarters of a stop, or 75%, darker than the next full stop of f1.4. A small increase in the fastest f-stop does not greatly affect the lens's ability to gather light, particularly in low-light situations. For most cameras, a lens faster than f1.4 would not show any improvement in gathering light. Each camera has an internal optical system; most of them are rated at f1.4. New ENG cameras coming onto the market have internal speeds of around f1.2. Lens makers are making lenses with speeds to match this, but both cameras and lenses of this type are very expensive. It does no good to place an expensive fast lens like an f1.2 on a camera that can only receive an f1.4 amount of light.

Video lenses allow the increase or decrease of exposures by fractions of stops because the iris is free moving (unlike a still camera) and can be set at any point within the range of the lens. At the stopped-down end of the iris (the smallest aperture), there is always a position labeled "C" for **cap**. When the iris is in this position, no light at all is being sent to the camera. This feature protects certain workings of the camera when not in use and also shows the camera true black. (See discussion on black balance later in this chapter.)

Most lenses operate best at the middle range of their f-stops. The optimum is usually f5.6 and one stop up or down from there. Only in very controlled situations is it possible to always operate at optimum. At f5.6 the flaws that may be inherent in the lens will be at their minimum and all the lens elements will be performing at the best degree possible. The iris has an effect not only on the exposure but on the look of the shot as well. The f-stop setting is only one factor in setting up a shot and does not have to be dictated by lighting conditions.

Auto-Iris

All video lenses have servos that control the iris setting. A **servo** is an electronically powered gear that adjusts the setting. A switch can easily change the iris from manual to auto to allow the camera to set the proper exposure for you. This can be as big a minus as it is a plus to the photographer. Another small button on the lens allows the operator to briefly put the lens into auto-iris only for the time the button is depressed. This method is generally the choice of most photographers, because it can set an exposure quickly but not stay in auto all the time where it is likely to **roam**. Roaming is where the iris reacts to everything that comes into the frame. In a scene with much action or many camera moves, an auto-iris can fluctuate wildly as dark-clothed subjects and bright light sources pass through the frame. The result is an amateurish scene with an exposure that fluctuates from dark to light with every movement in the frame. Most scenes require only one constant exposure setting. Auto-iris also does not guarantee the proper exposure. It merely "averages" the scene exposure between the brightest and darkest elements. Auto-iris would leave the face of an interview subject wearing dark clothes shot against a dark background overexposed because of this. The photographer determines which element is most important and exposes for that element. Once again, allowing a machine to make critical decisions can leave the photographer at a creative disadvantage.

Zoom Lenses

Most lenses used by still photographers and a great many cinematographers generally have a fixed focal length. Video cameras almost without exception have a **zoom lens**, a lens that can change focal lengths through a series of sliding elements within the lens. Zoom lenses permit changing the field of view without changing the point of focus or the aperture. Unlike the two optical groups that make up a fixed focal length lens, four different optical groups make up a zoom lens.

1. The **focusing group** gathers the light into a sharp, clear image.
2. The **variator group** moves inside the lens to change the image size from wide angle to telephoto.
3. The **compensator group** moves with the variator group to keep the image in focus and reduce aberrations caused by the first two groups.

4. The **prime lens group** focuses the image on the recording surface, such as film or a TV camera chip.

When setting up a shot for proper focus, it is customary to zoom all the way into the object you determine to be the focus plane, focus the lens, and then zoom out to the desired focal length for shooting. (See Figure 3.6.)

TV zoom lenses also come with a box of electronic servos formed into a hand grip and attached to the side of the lens. (See Figure 3.7.)

The servos drive a series of gears that turn the zoom barrel as well as the iris ring (mentioned earlier). A rocker-style switch on top of the hand grip controls the zoom servo, which allows you to move the elements continuously at speeds from a mere crawl to a fast snap zoom. The zoom and the iris can be operated electrically from a remote location with the proper cable and control unit. The most popular remote zoom is the pistol grip handle. (See Figure 3.8.)

With an extension cable, the zoom control can be operated from anywhere the operator wants within the length of the cable. On all lenses the power zoom can be turned off, leaving the lens to manual control. By simply twisting the zoom portion of the lens tube, you can adjust the focal length or do zooms. This method of zooming generally cannot be done as smoothly as the power zoom but can be done faster than most servos can operate. Zooms that are this fast are generally not used except as special effects or in certain types of sports coverage. An adjustment within the zoom-control housing can change the speed range of the power zoom.

The range of the zoom can vary greatly from one lens type to another. Older consumer camcorders have a 6:1 or 8:1 zoom ratio. If the widest focal length is 9mm, then the longest is either 54mm or 72mm, respectively. The zoom ratios for professional lenses are more often 14:1 or as high as 22:1. Lenses are often listed as simply a 14× or a 20× or whatever the multiplier is for the maximum focal length. Sometimes the multiplier is followed by the minimum focal length, such as the standard TV zoom lens, or the 14×8.5 lens, which has a minimum focal length of 8.5mm and a maximum of 119mm (14 times 8.5). Lenses with focal length ratios as high as 30:1 or more are made but require extra support brackets to attach to the camera. At such extreme focal lengths, it becomes very hard to maintain a steady picture on a

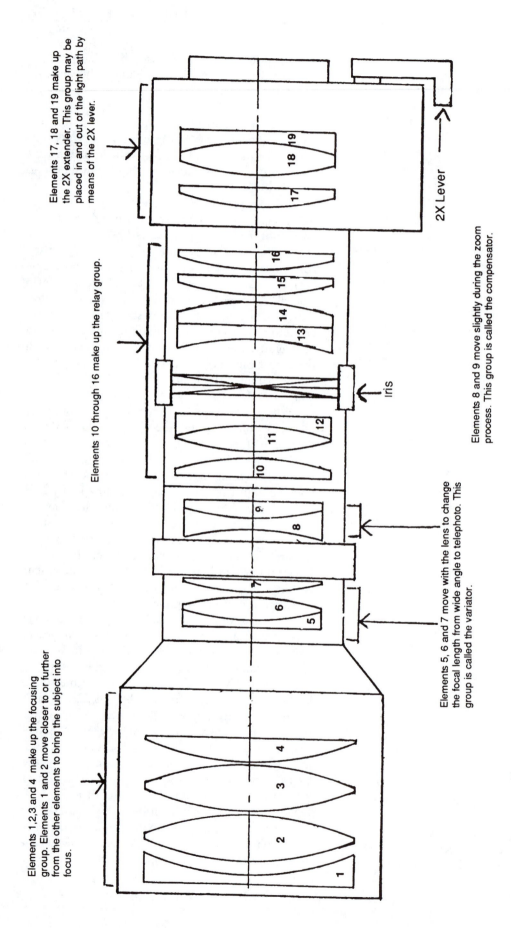

Elements 1,2,3 and 4 make up the focusing group. Elements 1 and 2 move closer to or further from the other elements to bring the subject into focus.

Elements 5, 6 and 7 move with the lens to change the focal length from wide angle to telephoto. This group is called the variator.

Elements 8 and 9 move slightly during the zoom process. This group is called the compensator.

Elements 10 through 16 make up the relay group.

Elements 17, 18 and 19 make up the 2X extender. This group may be placed in and out of the light path by means of the 2X lever.

Iris

2X Lever →

Figure 3.6 Optical groups for a typical TV zoom lens.

Figure 3.7 The typical TV zoom lens has a hand grip like this one with a rocker-style zoom control, a button labeled "RET" to see return video from the deck (either from confidence heads or on playback), a switch to select auto/manual/remote control for the iris and a button to set camera exposure if the iris is in manual control.

lightweight camera even on a typical tripod, but especially when handheld or on the shoulder.

The widest focal length available on a zoom lens as of the early 2000s is about 4.8mm, which is considered an ultra-wide-angle lens, but this lens does not have a large zoom ratio. Most professional wide-angle lens zoom ratios are about 10:1. Consumer and prosumer camcorders have lenses with greatly enhanced zoom ratios compared to older such cameras from just a few years ago. A ratio of 40:1 is not uncommon. Most of this high ratio is not made by the lens itself but done electronically by magnifying the picture in the camera. Most of these camcorders have built-in image stabilizing devices to remove the annoying shake from the shots but they generally only help a little.

A common feature on TV zoom lenses is the **2×range extender.** This small device, which is part of the last elements at the rear of the lens, has a lever that can be moved to a 2× position; this drops an optical system into the light path, effectively doubling whatever focal length at which the lens is set. (See Figure 3.9.)

The zoom can continue to be used with the extender in place, but all focal lengths will be doubled. In effect, a lens that ranges from 10mm to 100mm would become a 20mm to 200mm lens with the extender in place. In the highly competitive news business, this addition to the lens is an absolute must. It is less important for field production, because the 2× range extender slightly degrades the quality of light passing through it. Whenever the 2× range extender is engaged, the amount of light passing though it is reduced by about one-half (the equivalent of losing one f-stop) and the sharpness of the image is reduced by a sometimes noticeable amount. This makes the extender of limited use in low-light situations. If the highest technical quality is required, use of the 2× range extender is not recommended and should be considered only if it would enhance the value of the shot.

Figure 3.8 Many photographers prefer to use a pistol grip attachment on their zoom lens. This handle offers more control, even when the camera is on a tripod and contains a rocker-style zoom control, a VCR record switch, and a return video button.

Figure 3.9 The lever on the back of this lens can be moved from the "X1" or normal position to the "X2" or double position.

A minor drawback of zoom lenses is that they lose some light at the very end of their focal length range. For example, the Canon JI3X9B zoom lens has a maximum relative aperture of f1.6 from 9mm to 99mm, but at 117mm the maximum aperture is only f1.9. In low-light situations this sudden darkening of the picture at the very end of the zoom can be noticeable. Therefore, for high-quality work, it is best not to use a zoom at the end of its range. Using the auto-iris can make up for this effect as long as there is enough light to set the exposure in the middle range of the f-stop range.

When the lens is zoomed all the way in, it is nearly impossible to get a steady picture. Any small movement of the camera will be greatly exaggerated by the long focal length; this makes steady telephoto shooting off the shoulder next to impossible. Today, many **image stabilizers** are available to take the shake out. Some are part of the lens itself, and others fit onto the front of many normal zoom lenses. Most modern home camcorders have similar devices built into them. One drawback to their use is the difficulty in **panning** (moving the camera left or right) or **tilting** (moving the camera up or down). These types of actions must be done slowly or the motion control device overcompensates for the movement. Nevertheless the image stabilizers can produce spectacular results when compared to ordinary zoom lenses.

Light Quality Control

The elements of the lens combine to make the sharpest image possible with the smallest loss of brightness at the focal plane where the image will be recorded onto a light-sensitive medium. Because lenses are sealed units, the operator has no control over how well the lens works inside. The last layer of quality that the manufacturer puts on the lens is a special coating on the glass. This coating helps with color reproduction and aids in correcting many minor flaws in the ability of the glass to transmit a sharp image. Special care must be taken when cleaning a lens so as not to harm this coating.

The best way to insure against damage to the front element of your lens is to always keep a clear filter or a **UV (ultraviolet) haze filter** on the lens. Most TV stations prescribe that a camera never leaves the lot without one of these filters on the lens. Neither filter has any noticeable effect on the picture quality or the amount of light transmission; they merely serve to protect the front element from scratches, dirt, and

other problems that could cause costly repairs or lower the quality of the lens.

One of the most common problems in maintaining picture quality is glare on the lens from light sources. At certain angles to a light source, light rays reflect off the front element, causing a glare across the lens surface. This glare reduces the contrast of the picture as well as its sharpness. Just as our hands often function as a sunshade for our eyes when we look in the general direction of the sun or any bright light, the camera lens needs the same protection to work at its optimum. The sunshade or **hood** that comes with the lens is an absolute must to prevent direct light from striking the front element. As the light source comes closer and closer to the camera's field of view, it becomes increasingly difficult to protect the lens. Glare is actually the worst when the light is just outside the shot. You may find yourself using your hand to shade the light from the lens. Once the light source is in the shot itself, there is little that can be done. When a light is in the shot the glare is reduced, but other effects called **flares** (circular patterns of reflections in the lens) can be just as objectionable if not used in an artistic fashion.

Accessories

Many attachments are available for lenses that will enhance their performance. Many photographers like to take shots at more than the 8mm focal length allowed by their standard lens. Although changing to a wide-angle zoom lens is probably the best way to get a wider angle shot, it is also time consuming to change the lens, not to mention the inconvenience and expense of having a second lens available. A wide-angle **retrozoom** is another set of optical elements that can be mounted on the front of most normal zoom lenses. This attachment works like the $2\times$ extender only it decreases the focal length by multiplying them by around $0.8\times$. This would make a normal lens 6.4mm instead of 8mm and allows zooming and focusing as normal. The other way to get a quick wide-angle shot is to attach a single-element wide-angle adapter. This curved lens either clamps or screws onto the front element of your normal zoom lens much like a filter. The drawback here is that the picture can be focused only with the macrofocusing device, thus preventing the use of the zoom: The lens becomes a fixed focal length instrument.

There are teleconverters that look and work like retrozooms to make objects even larger. Teleconverters multiply the image size by about 2.8×. One drawback of both the retrozoom and the teleconverter is the added weight on the camera and lens itself. This can put added stress on the camera body at the point where the lens is attached.

Close-up lenses or **diopters** are single-element attachments that reduce the minimum focus distance of the lens. They also reduce the maximum focus distance so the lens can only be focused on objects close to the camera. Diopters come in different strengths, such as +2, +3, and so on. A strong diopter on a good lens will allow a camera to zoom in to the mint date on a dime so that it fills the entire picture. One drawback to diopters is they require a fair amount of light to be useful. A diopter will somewhat degrade the sharpness of a lens in high light levels but *greatly* reduce the sharpness in low light with the lens' iris wide open.

Filters

The clear glass and UV filters mentioned above are just two of the many types of filters available for a video camera's lens. Most lenses have a threaded lip on the front element onto which a round filter or filter adapter can be screwed. The most common size diameter is the 77mm filter, although filter size may vary from one type of lens to another. Some lenses have no threads on the front element and require an adapting ring that clamps to the outside of the lens

barrel. Most filters are threaded on both sides so that they can be stacked or combined with other attachments. Generally, no more than two filters can be used at one time without the filter edges showing in the corners of the picture. This is called **vignetting** and may also be caused by other factors, such as a poorly aligned lens. Many photographers always leave the clear filter and add any other filters on top of it to make sure that the front element stays protected at all times.

Two other types of filter mounts are available for professional use: the round nonthreaded filters, such as the popular Series 9 from Tiffen, and the film-style square filters, such as the 4-by-4 inch and the 6-by-6 inch. These filters require special adapters, which are made for every lens. With the larger unthreaded filters it may be necessary to obtain a larger sunshade for the lens to avoid glare problems. The square filters are generally used with a **matte box**. A matte box is a rectangular, tapered box that looks like a bellows and attaches to the front of the lens in a way that allows the lens to be focused without rotating the matte box. (See Figure 3.10.)

A series of slots at the back of the box permits the use of up to three square filters. These filter slots may be rotated independently of the lens to orient the filter as desired. (See the discussion of star and graduated filters below.) The rest of the box acts as a sunshade for the filters. The matte box is the most versatile and effective system of using filters with the

Figure 3.10 This simple matte box attaches directly to the front of the lens. It has two slots for 4-by-4 filters and has a "French flag" fixed to the front for added light flare protection.

lens, although it may be too cumbersome for most ENG work and some EFP shooting where weight and maneuverability are important considerations.

Filters fall into three broad categories:

- Color enhancement
- Diffusion
- Special effects.

Color enhancement filters can be used to change the perceived color of light used in a particular shot. This type of use is generally unnecessary because of the white balance circuit in the video camera, but they can be used to achieve very controlled, known artistic results. **Diffusion filters** reduce the sharpness and/or contrast of the picture. They are often used to give a film-look to the video or soften skin-tone detail. **Special effects filters** do everything from creating multiple images to split-screen fields of focus. Many of the effects of filters can also be done electronically in postproduction. Some of the new digital cameras can create these effects internally. It is a good idea to shoot a scene calling for filters at least once without filters so that the producer or editor has the choice of using or not using the effect. Today, as more and more editing is done digitally in nonlinear systems, the need to use a filter in the field has been greatly reduced. So many of the same effects can be done easier in the computer without permanently changing the original image.

The following is a partial list of the more popular filters used in TV work. Most are used for EFP shooting or feature stories in ENG. They are not recommended for general news use. Most of these filters come in different degrees of effect rated from 1 to 5. A number 1 filter has only a slight effect and a number 5 has the maximum effect.

Sepia Effect Filter. This filter gives the scene a warm brown tone similar to that of old photos from the turn of the century. It can be used to imply a look back in time.

Enhancing or Warming Filter. This filter creates a warm look by selectively improving the saturation of reds and oranges with little effect on other colors. It is used to bring out better skin tones on light-complexion subjects and give dark-skinned subjects a deeper, richer color. It is also good for the fall color shots of autumn.

Polarizing Filter. This filter reduces glare and reflections on surfaces, such as glass or water, in the picture, while saturating colors and darkening in the blue of the sky. The polarized filter is made to turn in its housing to achieve the correct angle to the reflections. As you turn the polarizer, watch the effect in the viewfinder to find the optimum orientation. It can make white clouds really stand out from the blue sky or take away annoying reflections from car windows.

Fog Effect Filter. This filter creates the look of real fog in the scene. The effect is most noticeable in overexposed areas of the picture or around light sources in the shot. It can add a dream-like quality to scenes or give atmosphere to interior scenes. (See Figure 3.11.)

Low-Contrast Filter. This filter lowers the contrast in the picture and mutes the colors. It allows

Figure 3.11 This with/without fog filter scene shows the effect of a number 4 fog filter, which adds the look of atmospheric fog and lowers the contrast in the scene.

black areas to become lighter and reduces the density of shadows, allowing more detail to be seen while not affecting the white areas of the picture. It is a good filter for scenes where shadows are particularly dark and can help give video a film look.

Double-Fog Effect Filter. This filter combines a soft fog with a heavy low-contrast effect that allows a sharper image than fog alone. It is particularly good to reduce the effects of overexposed windows in interior shots without adding a dense fog look to the picture.

Diffusion Effect Filter. This filter uses a slight ripple effect in the filter glass to reduce the sharpness of the picture without creating a fog-like effect. It is often used to hide skin blemishes or wrinkles from the camera and looks good in backlit situations. It also causes a halo effect around light sources in the shot.

Softnet Filter. This filter uses a net material between laminated glass that creates a soft diffusion without the halation, or blurring, of highlights in the shot. The net comes in several colors allowing multiple effects from one filter: black net leaves the dark areas dark; white net lowers the contrast as it diffuses; red net warms the colors of the scene; skin-tone net enhances skin color.

Dot Filter. Instead of a net to cause the diffusion in the picture, this filter glass is covered by thousands of dots in varying sizes (similar to a paint sprayer mist). It comes in white, black, and skin tone. The filter is similar in effect to the net filters but without the slight star effect on highlights.

Star Filter. This filter has engraved lines forming a grid on the glass surface that causes highlights, such as the sun, candles, and headlights, to appear star-like. The grid comes in different sizes from 1mm to 4mm spacing; a 1mm grid has the longest rays and a 4mm grid the shortest. Star filters also come in varying numbers of points; stars with 4, 6, 8, or 12 points can be created. The filters can give a glamorous quality to pictures with highlights in them, making them sparkle or helping reduce the sharpness of light sources (by using a 12-point 4mm star) without affecting anything else in the picture. They are also free-spinning within their housings to allow the points of the star to be rotated to any angle.

Split-Field-Effect Filter. This filter is basically a close-up lens cut in two. It allows you to have a close object in the bottom half of the picture and a faraway object in the top half of the picture all in sharp focus. The one-half close-up lens is a fixed-focus element; this means that the lens must be focused first on the background and then the foreground object or the camera must be moved in or out until that object is also in focus. This filter creates the ultimate depth-of-field lens where everything from just in front of the lens to infinity is in focus.

Graduated Filter. This filter contains the effect only in one-half of the filter, while creating a smooth transition from that effect to clear near the middle of the filter. Graduated filters come as sepias, corals, oranges, and neutral densities. They are generally used over the sky portion of the picture to change the color of the sky without changing the color of subjects on the ground. They can create the look of a sunset sky without turning the ground pink too. The neutral density filter can be used to gain an even exposure on the sky as well as the ground on overcast days. The filters work best in a matte box setup where they can be positioned at just the right place in the frame without adjusting the shot.

A problem of some filters with nets and dots is that the diffusion material can sometimes be visible in the picture. This can easily happen when the lens is wide and at maximum aperture. The net or screen can be faintly visible across the entire picture. A good way to avoid this is to get filters that fit behind the lens. For video cameras, this would mean having them in the filter wheel of the camera. If this is not possible, it may limit the use of some filters to smaller apertures or longer focal lengths so that they will not be seen.

A homemade way of getting around this is making your own diffusion filters. By taking a small piece of lady's hosiery (like panty hose) and stretching it across the back of the lens, holding it there with a rubber band, cutting off the excess and reseating the lens into the camera mount, you can create a very good behind-the-lens net filter. Try different colors and textures of hosiery to see what effects are possible. (See Figure 3.12.)

Interchangeable Lenses

Most cameras on the market cannot use just any lens. A lens for a Sony camera cannot be put on an Ikegami camera without being modified at the factory. Some models of cameras may share the same

Figure 3.12 A small piece of hosiery attached to the back of a lens and held with a rubber band can create a net filter look. Be sure to stretch the material as tight as possible.

lens specifications but they are the exceptions. Each camera manufacturer has a different design for the way a lens works with its internal focus plane. And every camera must be shaded to any lens (that is, adjusted to the light characteristics of the lens) that is being used on it to achieve the optimum quality.

Care and Cleaning of Lenses

The greatest enemy a lens has is dirt, and it does not take much to get a lens dirty. Besides the huge amount of dust in the air, there is always the chance that something will come in contact with the lens and smudge it, such as your hand or fingers. For the lens to work at its optimum, it must be free of all dirt and smudges. Loose dirt or dust can be blown or brushed away with the proper tools but not wiped away. Touching the lens with dry cloth or tissue may actually grind the dirt into the glass. For loose dirt a soft photo brush and an air blower can be used. Simple squeeze-style blowers or air-in-a-can can be purchased at any photo store.

Do not, however, blow air from your mouth. If the squeeze-style or other type of blower does not clean the lens, switch to a liquid cleaner. Always try to use a cleaner made to be used on high-quality glass. Lenses, and even some filters, can be very expensive. A deep scratch or other blemish can require an equally expensive trip to the factory for regrinding

or replacement. Most photo stores sell lens-cleaning solutions along with tissues to wipe the lens clean. A homemade solution of a few drops of dishwashing soap and distilled water works well as do some commercial products. A very clean, soft, lint-free cloth can also be used instead of the photo tissues. There are also products on the market that have premoistened towelettes in individual packets for cleaning lenses on location.

No matter what you use, the method should be the same. Never use more fluid than you need and never grind the pickup material (such as a tissue) into the lens. Always use a circular motion and try not to go over the same place more than once if you can help it. A good cleaner used sparingly will do the job and any excess will evaporate quickly. Never use plain water; it has too many mineral deposits in it and does not evaporate quickly enough.

Keep a cap on the lens at all times when the camera is not in use, such as when it is in transit, storage, or in any hazardous environment (a desert or beach, or in windy conditions). Often the dirt on your lens will not be visible in the viewfinder. Visually inspect the cleanliness of the lens often. The time when dirt really stands out is when there is any glare on the lens or a highlight, such as the sun, in the shot. While a little glare and the sun may be part of the shot, any dirt on the lens will stand out like a huge sore thumb. The time not to find out that you have a dirty lens is in the middle of a shot where you pan past the sun. It may have been the only chance to get that shot.

Modern TV lenses are made to work in the harshest environments. This does not mean that the nonglass parts never need cleaning. The rotating barrels of the focus, zoom, and iris all must be kept clean. Wipe the lens free of any dust and dirt as often as possible. Use a compressed air blower to get in the small places, possibly with the help of a soft brush such as a toothbrush. Never use water to clean the lens. Never use any cleaner that has an oil in it. All the moving parts of the lens and servos are on sealed bearings and need no further lubrication. If they are stiff to use, they are dirty, not in need of an oiling. Make sure the gears and teeth of the lens barrel are always clean and free of dirt and dust. Most lens units are considered waterproof but are really just water resistant. If exposed to excessive dampness, they may short out or dirt may collect in the condensation and foul the servos at a later time. If the lens does get a bad drenching, allow it to dry out completely by putting it in a sealed plastic bag with silica gel or another desiccant (a substance that absorbs moisture).

Check the tightness of all the accessible screws on the lens (including the back of the lens) as well as the lens control unit on a weekly basis. Like most TV equipment, any repair work or extensive servicing should be done by experienced people. If you wish to do more than the very basic care, have someone with more experience show you the right way to do it. The final word on lens care is to know the lens's factory service center near you. Most offer overnight service or even loaner lenses; they can certainly help you over the phone with small problems. Keep a heavily used lens in topnotch shape by having a factory overhaul every 2 years.

VIDEO CAMERAS

A current-model portable video camera barely resembles the huge, heavy studio camera of TV's early years because of the numerous design changes made over the years. But the color video camera of the earlier days of TV had to perform the same basic functions as today's cameras: light filtering; the separation of white light into red, blue, and green; image sensing; and signal processing. Today's cameras are simply smaller, lighter, and more accurate.

Camera Basics

We have now taken the light that makes up a real image, traced its progression though the lens, and seen how the lens may manipulate it. It is now time to transform that image into a form we can record.

In a film camera, this would be as simple as having a light-sensitive material on a celluloid backing exposed to the image. The camera would simply be a means to move and position the film. For a video camera, recording the image is a more involved and complicated process. The inside of a TV camera is filled with circuit boards and other wiring with at least a dozen places to make adjustments. Since making a change in any one of the adjustments causes a change in the remaining unadjusted areas of the camera, the proper equipment as well as the proper training is required to touch anything on the inside. Unless you have been shown by a qualified maintenance person how to make adjustments inside your camera, do not try it.

In the new world of digital cameras, making adjustments is considerably easier. A digital camera is software driven. In older cameras, adjustments were made by turning tiny screws. In today's digital cameras, they are made by calling up menus in the viewfinder screen and using buttons to raise or lower selected values. If you don't like the way your changes look, hit erase and start again. Anyone can play around with the camera perimeters and always be able to reset the camera to its normal setup. (See Figure 3.13.)

Filter Wheel

The first thing an image passes through in any broadcast-quality camera as it comes from the lens is a filter wheel. This wheel (sometimes two wheels) contains typical photographic filters just like those on the front of a film camera lens. It is much more convenient for the video camera, as well as the operator, to have them behind the lens. Normally, there are three types of filters in the wheel: clear, color correction, and light reduction. The electronics of any camera is just like a roll of film: It has a specific speed or **ASA** (level of sensitivity to light) and is designed for a specific color of light. All TV cameras are made to work their best with light at 3200 degrees Kelvin, the color temperature of typical TV lights. (See Figure 3.14.)

Shooting a scene lit by TV lights is done with the filter wheel dialed to the clear (3200-degree or in-

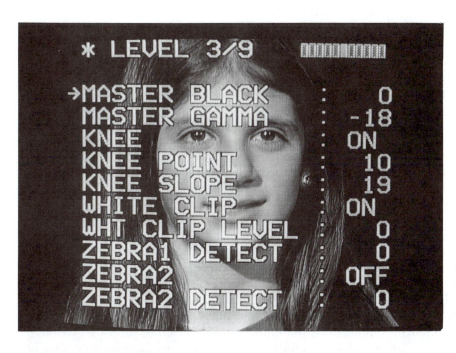

Figure 3.13 One page of a Sony D600 setup menu as it appears in the viewfinder. Buttons on the camera allow you to scroll the pages and items to change their values.

Figure 3.14 The front of this Sony D600 camera has two filter wheels. Here they are set in the "1" "B" combination.

doors) position. If the shoot is outdoors in sunlight, then the filter wheel is turned to a daylight or 5600-degree position. This filter is nothing more than an orange-colored filter designed to convert daylight color temperatures to that of tungsten (TV lights). A similar filter in film is the 85B. The camera can be balanced to any light temperature, but for now we

will assume it is operating at its factory-designed optimum (or preset) of 3200 degrees. As the amount of sunlight increases, a video camera can increase shutter speeds to regulate the amount of light it receives if the range of the iris has been exhausted. This usually has an adverse affect on any movement in the picture, however. The most effective way for a video camera to handle high brightness levels is to simply dial in a **neutral density filter (ND)** on the filter wheel. In single filter wheel cameras NDs are usually combined with a daylight color correction filter.

The standard one-wheel camera has four positions on its wheel:

1. Clear—(3200 K) used for interior shoots, or exterior at night.
2. Daylight—(5600 K) used outdoors in moderate amounts of sunlight intensity or in shaded areas.
3. Daylight + 1/4 ND—used for open sunlit areas on clear days.
4. Daylight + 1/8 ND—used for very bright daylight scenes, such as a sunny day at the beach or the ski slopes.

A 1/4 ND allows 25% of the light to pass through it without affecting it in any other way. A 1/8 ND allows 12.5% of the light to pass through. Although each camera model has different nomenclature or different combinations in its filter wheel, they all operate on the basic principles stated above. These filters allow a camera to shoot in any typical lighting condition.

Prism

The light forming the image passes through a prism after going through the filter wheel. Unlike most consumer and low-end industrial cameras that have only one pickup device, a professional camera will split the beam of light into its three primary TV colors: red, blue, and green. These are not the primary colors of art classes, and should not be equated to them in any way. The way a TV camera arrives at all the colors of the rainbow is considerably different from the way an artist would on a canvas or even as a filmmaker would in making a color print. The camera prism delivers a very pure blue, green, and red picture to three targets or light-sensitive surfaces. These three colors can be recombined later to represent the true colors of the object being photographed. It is the intensity of each TV primary color that determines the true color when the information is recombined into a video picture.

Charge-Coupled Devices

In the 1980s cameras were switched to using charged-coupled devices, or CCDs, from the older methods of using light-sensitive tubes. The CCDs be-

came known simply as chips. After about 1990 camera manufacturers stopped making cameras with tubes because the chip technology far surpassed tubes. Many problems that were inherent in tubes, such as **smear, lag,** and **burn-in,** were eliminated by the use of chips.

Most chips are rated by the number of **pixels** that each chip has. Each pixel is like a grain of emulsion on a film; the greater the number of them present, the sharper the image. The more pixels present on a chip, the more sensitive the chip is to light. The latest cameras can almost see in the dark. They are capable of making good pictures in no more light than that of a single candle. This is something a tube camera could never do.

Video Signal

Electronic impulses from the chips are sent on to the rest of the camera called the processor. Much of the camera's insides makes up the video processing unit of the camera. This complex series of boards and circuits shapes the video image into its many parts, mainly **chroma** and **luminance**. Before that information leaves the camera, it can be recombined into one **composite** signal or left separate in its **component** state to be recombined later.

Fields and Frames

The images of the video signal are relayed in a similar manner to that of film. Each video image is just like a frame from motion picture film. Video is recorded at a rate of 30 frames per second, however, instead of 24 frames like the movies. Each video frame is made up of two fields, sometimes called odd and even. (More about this in Chapter 9.)

NTSC, PAL, and SECAM

Whether a video signal is component or composite, it is based on a reference system. In the United States the reference system is called the **National Television Standards Committee** or **NTSC**, which was set up by the federal government. Only a few other countries use the NTSC system, most notably, Canada, Mexico, and Japan. NTSC has 525 lines of resolution and scans at 59.85 fields (29.97 frames) per second. Common practice for discussing frame speed is to round off to 30 frames per second. One drawback to the NTSC system is that it allows the viewer at home to adjust the color on their TV set. This led NTSC to be jokingly referred to as "Never Twice the Same Color." Having no guarantee that the viewer's set is properly adjusted can mean a great deal of loss for the artistry of video.

The other two reference systems in the world are the PAL and SECAM standards. **Phase Alteration by Line (PAL)** was developed by Germany, England, and Holland in 1966. PAL has 625 lines of resolution and scans at 50 fields (25 frames) per second but does not have color controls on the TV receivers like NTSC. Consequently, PAL has less color distortion than NTSC, but because of the slower scan rate, many NTSC viewers see PAL pictures as flickering too much. In 1962, France introduced the **Sequential Couleur a Memoire (SECAM)** system, which was later adopted by the Soviet Union and several other European countries. SECAM has 625 scanning lines at 50 fields (25 frames) per second like PAL.

These three systems are not compatible with each other. A special device is necessary to translate one system to another when making dubs.

CAMERA FUNCTIONS

On the outside of every professional quality camera are the operational controls. These switches and but-

tons are the primary means of controlling the electronics inside the camera. Each model and each camera manufacturer can have widely varying controls and placement of controls on the camera body. Although cameras generally don't have many switches, just one those switches in the wrong position can affect the quality of the video or even prevent the camera from operating. (See Figure 3.15.)

Power Switch. There is always a main power switch on the camera that sends energy to all parts of the camera or camcorder. Another switch on the camera may control the power to the record device and also acts as a power saver to the camera itself. This switch can be a three-position switch: Standby, Save On, and On. **Standby** is used when you do not need to operate the camera but want to start up the camera suddenly. A trickle current from the power source keeps the circuits warm and allows the camera to be ready to shoot in just a couple of seconds when it is turned on from the standby position. **Save On** gives you a picture in the viewfinder, but if the camera is hooked up to a VCR in any way, it prevents the VCR's tape servo from coming up to speed, thus saving power. If you try to record when the camera is in this mode, it will take a couple of seconds for the VCR servo to come up to speed before the recording can begin. In a news situation, this is clearly a disadvantage, but if you are spending quite a lot of time

Figure 3.15 All of the camera function switches are located on the lower front and side of this Sony D600. On this camera, "Save" keeps the tape servo off, whereas "Standby" puts the camera and VCR in instant record mode.

lining up or waiting for a shot, this function lets you work with the camera picture without running the deck battery (or camcorder battery) down until you need to roll. But more importantly, if the servo is left running without recording, you are needlessly wearing down the video record heads and the drums of the tape machine and running an increased risk of damaging the tape itself. The **On** position is when everything is up and ready for instantaneous recording as soon as the button is pushed.

Camera/Bars Switch. This switch makes the output of the camera either the picture or the color bar generator contained within the camera.

Gain Switch. Most cameras offer the user three choices of gain in the sensitivity of the chips. Gain, which is measured in decibels (dBs), is usually left at zero or normal for most shooting but can be raised as high as +24. To raise the level of exposure if the lens is wide open, you can shift the gain switch by one position. Under extreme low light, you can go to the last position of the gain switch. Each position increases the sensitivity of the chips by the amount labeled on the switches or on some cameras by the amount you have predetermined. Gain increases also increase the **picture noise** (graininess). A +18-dB picture gain is not considered to be of broadcast quality unless it is a news tape shot under terrible conditions. Even +9-dB gain can be objectionable in some news and almost all EFP situations. Use gain only when you cannot get a picture without it.

White Balance Button. To allow the camera to work under any type of light, each professional camera has a white balance circuit. By showing the camera something white (zooming in on a white card, wall, or paper) and pressing a button or flipping a switch, the camera sets the reference volts on each chip to make a white picture with that color of light. An indicator in the viewfinder tells the operator when the white balance is done (usually in 2 or 3 seconds or less). Some new cameras also show you what the color temperature is on completed white balance.

Some cameras also have a **black balance** switch to set the black reference in the camera. This is done automatically in most cameras, but heat can affect the black balance. If your camera has a black balance, you should use it every time you white balance or any time the atmospheric (hot/cold) temperature changes even if the light does not. A good camera should white balance under most colors of light when the proper filter wheel is dialed in. Again, in con-

sumer and prosumer cameras, the white balance function can be automatic. That is great for saving time and avoiding mistakes but it once again relinquishes creative control to the machine and can lead to subjects being shot in the wrong color.

White Balance Channels. Many modern cameras have three channels of white balance circuits from which to choose. The first two are normally called "**A**" and "**B**." They both work the same way and allow you to balance for two scenes. If a shot requires you to follow a subject from a sunlit area to a room lit with only incandescent light, you can set the white balance on A for daylight and the B balance for incandescent. As you follow the subject from one room to the other, only a quick flip of the switch is needed to maintain the proper colors. The third position is **Preset**. This setting puts the camera in its factory-preset white balance of 3200 degrees Kelvin, the normal TV lights' color temperature. The camera now acts like a film camera with a constant color reference (that is, it is the same as using a selected film stock); any correction for color temperature has to be done by means of filters in or on the camera or on the lights themselves.

Shutter Selection. Many cameras now have variable shutter speeds much like film cameras. The normal shutter speed of a video camera (usually an electronic shutter) is $1/60$ of a second. Speeds of $1/125$, $1/500$, and $1/1000$ of a second are usually available. These additional shutter speeds allow the camera to do certain special effects or let the operator shoot at low f-stops in bright light, but they are not useful in most situations. The most common use is in an isolated sports camera. The faster shutter speeds allow for brilliantly clear and sharp slow-motion pictures and freeze frames of fast-moving objects. The trouble is that when these pictures are played at normal speed, they appear to stutter or strobe on the screen. You should only use the faster shutter speeds for shots to be played in slow motion or frozen, or for shots with little movement.

Clear Scan

You may have noticed that when computer screens are shown on video they often have an annoying flicker or rolling as though the horizontal hold is broken. Computer monitors, unlike NTSC TV sets and monitors, do not scan their CRTs at the same rate as normal television (59.85 Hz). They can scan at rates both higher and lower than that of video. Many modern cameras can change their own scan rates to match any computer monitor by use of a selection switch, usually as part of the shutter switch, called **clear scan**. This option allows the camera to show very clear, flicker-free computer screens. Matching rates to some monitors with really low scan rates can leave the camera's ability to shoot moving subjects greatly reduced, and any movement by the camera such as a pan will result in blurred pictures.

Monitoring the Picture

Up to this point we have only discussed the inner workings of the camera and the means of controlling those functions. Now it is time to see the results of what the camera is doing, starting with what the camera sees and on up through analyzing the quality of the video output.

Viewfinder. In some early video cameras, the viewfinder was simply a glass window with some crosshairs in it. The operator never even looked through the lens. Today's cameras have high-resolution video mini-monitors as viewfinders and some are in color. Because the picture appears after it has been processed, the operator sees just what the recorder or any output destination of the camera sees. The only difference is that the picture is usually in black and white. The viewfinder has brightness and contrast controls that need to be set at proper levels. The contrast control should be turned up all the way and the picture quality adjusted by the brightness knob only. A good picture should show whites as white and any deep shadows as a rich black.

Most cameras have a considerable amount of information available to the operator in the viewfinder. Some information is contained in the picture itself, such as the zebra striping. The **zebra bars** that appear over parts of the picture are a graphic display of the exposure level. Most cameras come from the factory with the zebra bars set at 70% video or 70 **IREs** (Institute of Radio Engineers) of video; this means that any portion of the picture with an exposure of 70 units, as measured on a waveform monitor, will have these stripes. This measure, 70 units, corresponds to the proper exposure of skin-tone highlights on a subject with a light complexion or the proper exposure of a white piece of paper. If a person's face is the part of the picture that needs proper exposure, then the zebra bars should appear over the brightest highlights on the face, usually the cheeks and center of the forehead. (See Figure 3.16.) Many photographers prefer that skin tones be more in the 55- to 65-unit range to avoid that *video* look and back the iris off (reduce the exposure) to just remove the zebra bars from a face. Some photographers prefer to set the zebra pattern at 100 units to better see overexposed portions of the

Figure 3.16 Zebra bars appear on the cheeks of the subject as seen through the viewfinder of a Sony D600. These bars are set at 70 IREs and their appearance on the highlight areas indicates proper exposure.

picture, especially when people are not in the shot. In analog recording any portion of the video picture at 100 units will have greatly reduced definition and appear **washed out**. Video above 110 IRE will be seen as simply a white glow. For digital recording, anything above 100 IRE will lose all detail and turn to that white glow. Zebra bars can be set at any level by a service person and many cameras can show two different sets of zebras at the same time: one a standard crosshatch at 70 units and the other a square mosaic set at 100 units.

Other warning lights or indicators show low battery power, end of tape, low-light levels, which filter is in use, and if the shutter speed is other than normal. By holding down the **RET** button on the lens control unit you can show return video in the viewfinder. This return video may be the confidence playback function of the deck while the actual recording is being made (on some camcorders), or the scene played back from its tape machine or other source if the camera is connected to it by a multi-pin cable.

Color Bars. The color bars are the most common reference point in any TV work. Any professional camera has a switch that turns on a color bar generator within itself and feeds it to the camera output. This internal color bar system is essential to track down any problems in the video system because it is such a known reference. If the color bars do not look right, nothing else will.

Associated Test Equipment

Waveform Monitor. The waveform monitor is needed to make adjustments on the electronics of a camera. Generally, only camera maintenance people use this device, but the data it provides are needed for any high-quality work with cameras, tape recorders, digital devices, microwave or satellite transmitters, or time-base correctors. This monitor, sometimes just called a scope, is the window to the inner parts of the video signal. Any problem with the video signal can be found by analyzing the different information available from it. A photographer wishing to truly master a video camera should learn to read and use the waveform monitor. (See Figure 3.17.) Hooking a camera up to a monitor and experimenting with exposure should give some information on how a video signal works and how to recognize problems in the camera.

Vectorscope. The vectorscope also checks the color or chroma of the TV signal. If reds in the pic-

ture do not look right, this scope can identify whether it is the operator's eye, the TV set, or the camera that is wrong. (See Figure 3.18.) The waveform monitor and vectorscope are the two most important means of analyzing the quality of your video signal.

Color TV Monitor. The most common but technically weakest form of monitoring the video picture is the color TV monitor, which can be a plain TV set. (See Figure 3.19.) It is good for showing composition to others such as the director, producer, or reporter. Unless the monitor has been carefully set up and adjusted and viewing conditions are optimal (no glares or high room light, for example), any other information such as true color reproduction or even exposure cannot be judged from the picture on the screen. The viewfinder and the waveform and vector monitors are the most accurate indicators.

A color monitor is also good for the cameraperson to use as a viewfinder on lengthy shoots where the camera is in a fixed place on a tripod. The strain on the eyes, neck, and back can be greatly reduced by having a conveniently placed monitor (to line up and maintain the framing).

Maintenance. To maintain your camera, protect it from shock and keep it clean. There is virtually nothing inside a camera that the typical operator can repair or adjust. Take good care of the camera, and notify qualified maintenance personnel if there is a problem. It is the operator's job to keep the outside of the camera in the best possible shape. Screws holding the side panels in place or any other screws must be checked for tightness on a regular basis. Protect the camera from the elements as well as from bumps, jolts, and drops. Although most cameras are water resistant, none of them are waterproof. A rain jacket, a plastic protector shaped to fit the camera and keep moisture out, is an absolute must.

Troubleshooting. You must be able to tell when something is not right with your camera. More important, you should also be able to accurately diagnose the area of the camera problem. Many times the correct diagnosis can lead to a very simple operator-capable fix. A switch in the wrong position is the most common error. Know where all switches should be set and check them first in case of trouble. Check your power source. Put up color bars and see how they look. If the bars look good, then you know the problem is not in the output of the camera but in the input before the image gets to the video processor section of the camera. Unfortunately, most internal

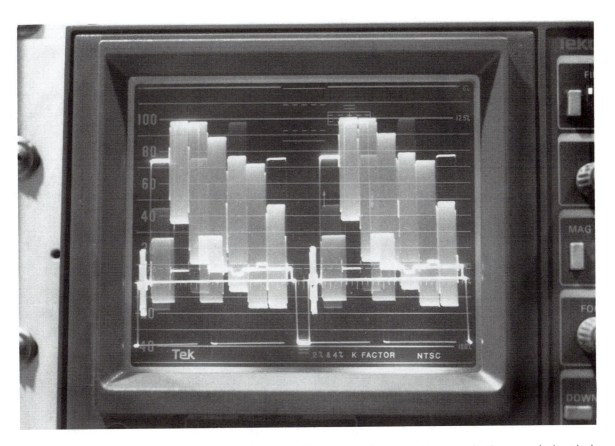

Figure 3.17 The waveform monitor shows what color bars look like when everything is working properly. This picture looks at both fields of one frame of video and shows both chroma and luminance.

problems cannot be fixed in the field. Identify a good maintenance person or factory service center if you do not have an in-house repair facility or when you are out of town.

VIDEOTAPE RECORDERS

It is almost unheard of to see a camera that doesn't have the video recorder built into it: the camcorder. While it is easy to see the unit as one piece of equipment it is necessary to think of each component as separate.

Videotape recorders are used in a wide variety of applications. New VHS consumer videotape recorders can be purchased for less than $100. A professional-quality digital format deck can be up to well over $75,000. The major differences among the various decks stem from the format of the videotape and the application for the deck. Portable decks must be con-

structed to be lightweight, to run on batteries, and to have the ability to withstand temperature variations and be somewhat protected from dirt, dust, and water. Professional-quality decks feature high resolution, good picture stability and color, the ability to encode or record a number of different types of information like time code onto the tape, and have a multitude of inputs and outputs to accommodate any situation.

THE FORMAT WARS

In what has become a dizzying array of formats, the selection of a tape machine has moved from what just a few years ago was two or three choices to now over a dozen. A survey by Intertec Publishing's Corporate Planning & Research Department in February 2000 found that 50% of people shooting and/or editing video—across all fields of use—were using

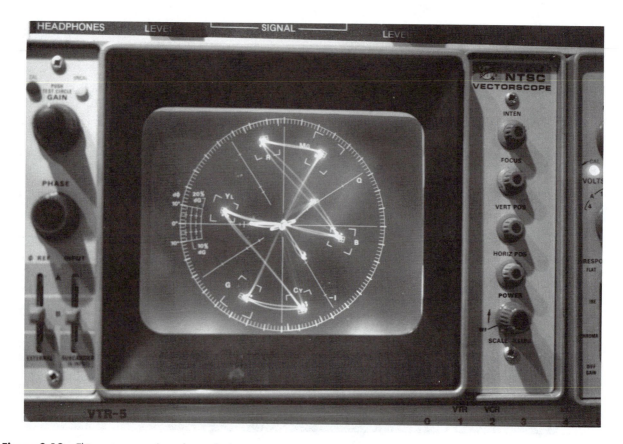

Figure 3.18 This vectorscope shows how color bars are represented when the video signal is at optimum.

Figure 3.19 This Sony PVM 8044Q 8-inch color monitor can run on both AC or batteries and be fitted with a protective soft case for easy carrying.

the Betacam SP format. S-VHS was the next most popular. Only about 28% were using digital formats in some capacity. Since its introduction in 1982 until the time of this writing, Sony Betacam has dominated the professional world of videotape for portable recording. But as video slowly converts to digital, a host of new formats have arrived on the scene. It is unlikely all of these formats will survive over a great length of time. Conversely, it is likely that more formats (and recording media) will be introduced in the near future. If this process of advancing technology follows the computer world, then any prediction today as to what the future will bring will be wrong. No one knows the future. The only thing you can say for certain is that the future is digital. The following is a brief rundown of the formats in use, past and present.

Older Formats: Hi8, S-VHS, and 3/4-Inch SP

The biggest revolution in the video world came when broadcast-quality equipment became available to the average consumer. The 35mm film format allowed anyone to take a still picture of the technical quality needed for print publishing. By the mid-1980s the average citizen could make TV of technical broadcast quality. The Hi8 and Super-VHS (S-VHS) formats had the minimum 425 lines of resolution necessary to be considered broadcast quality. In the early 1990s network news turned to these formats during the Persian Gulf War because of their small size, lightweight, and relative high quality. Parts of one episode of a popular TV sitcom, *Growing Pains,* were shot on Hi8 without any consciously noticeable dip in quality. Both the Hi8 and S-VHS formats came in models that featured all the options of a professional format in a slightly larger package than the regular consumer models, and both made dockable decks that could go on camera heads designed to be used with higher quality formats.

The **3/4-inch U-Matic** format was the standard of the portable video world for more than a decade but was quickly replaced and is no longer being manufactured. For users who still have considerable 3/4-inch libraries, and for those who wanted an inexpensive broadcast format just a notch below new broadcast forms, Sony offered the **3/4-inch SP** format. This format made use of the great number of 3/4-inch tapes already out there but allows users to upgrade to metal tape and much higher quality without making

the older machines obsolete. Camcorders were not made with this tape format. Because of the vast libraries of 3/4-inch tapes in the world, this format will be around for a long time as a playback system, but has already disappeared as a portable record format.

Standard Analog Formats: Beta SP, 1-Inch, and MII

In 1982, Sony developed a 1/2-inch format for broadcast use out of their Betamax consumer format. The new format was introduced as part of a one-piece camera recorder unit they called a **Betacam**. The term went on to mean the Beta format for professional use as opposed to home-use Beta tapes. Many people still mistakenly refer to any professional camcorder as a "Betacam" whether it is made by Sony or not. The original Betacam format is no longer made and has been replaced by Beta SP. Like 3/4-inch SP, this format allows for the use of the older format tapes but greatly improves the quality of the video when metal particle tape is used.

The old standard for studio tape, the 1-inch C format, has had very limited use in the field. Although portable 1-inch decks are made, they are just barely portable and certainly not dockable with a camera. They are usually mounted on a cart and cannot be subjected to any movement, such as being carried, while recording.

Another 1/2-inch tape, the M format, was introduced by Panasonic in the mid-1980s, about the same time as Beta. It was an offshoot of VHS but never developed a professional following. In 1987 the **MII** format was introduced to compete with Beta SP. MII also makes use of 1/2-inch metal particle tape but uses a cassette shell unique to its format unlike the Beta tapes, which still use the original Beta cassette shell. Blank Betamax tapes (if they can still be found) purchased at the local discount store could work in any professional Beta machine. The M formats, which never found a wide following, are no longer manufactured. Panasonic has replaced them with digital formats.

Digital Formats: D Series, Digital Betacam, Betacam SX, DV, DVCAM, DVCPRO, and Digital S

While digital tape is definitely the tape of the future, no one standard has come to the forefront to dominate the industry. As you'll see in the descriptions of the different formats that follow, confusion is the best way to describe the situation. As we will keep mentioning in this book, it is unlikely that all—or even many—of these formats will survive. Just like the MII format, rising technologies will overtake the weaker, less popular forms. But for now, here's a thumbnail sketch of what's out there today.

Many postproduction (editing) facilities have been using digital recorders for some time to create the edit master. Earlier 3/4-inch cassettes and the later models with 1/2-inch cassette tape systems were made by both Sony and Panasonic and designated by a "D-x" such as D-1, D-2, and so on, have generally replaced the 1-inch type recorders. These machines are still primarily used in studios and not taken into the field.

Standard 1/2-Inch Formats

In 1993 Sony introduced the **Digital Betacam** format using a discrete cosine transform (DCT) recording technique referred to as the ITU-R 601 with a 2.34:1 compression ratio and a recording data rate of 127.76 Mb/s (megabytes per second). The resulting files are similar to JPEG files in the computer world. This format is often referred to as Digi-Beta, and as of 2000, it was still recognized as the gold standard of standard definition digital recording. One version of this format comes as part of a one-piece all-digital camcorder, the BVW-D700. Sony also introduced in late 1996 another digital format, **Betacam SX,** which uses 10-bit MPEG-2 digital encoding with a 4:2:2 sampling rate, 10:1 compression format, and an 18 Mb/s data record rate. MPEG-2 is the digital method used in most digital editing and all digital transmission. The 4:2:2 sampling means that for every four luminance samples taken, two red samples and two blue samples are also taken. This format is particularly interesting to news departments because the signal can be transmitted via microwave at two times normal speed, thus redefining transmission time. Sony has also recently introduced yet another format called MPEG IMX as an edit format but not for field use. Also, JVC introduced **Digital S,** also known as D-9, which is based on their S-VHS system, with an 8-bit 4:2:2 sampling rate in a dual-DV recording format (two DV chipset processors used in tandem) and a 50 Mb/s data rate.

The 6.35mm Tape Formats

During the same time period, the consumer and lower end professional or industrial market transformed virtually overnight to a digital format called **DV** using a smaller tape width of 6.35mm. DV refers to a specific method of recording a digital signal on the tape similar to JPEG files but differs from other means like MPEG-2 and DCT. All DV formats use an 8-bit 4:1:1 sampling rate where only one red and one blue sample are taken for every four units of luminance, a compression of 5:1, and a data recording rate of 25 Mb/s. While DV with its 4:1:1 sampling rate is often comparable in quality to that of Beta-SP, the lower chroma sampling compared to 4:2:2 can mean greatly reduced picture quality when the video is going down in generation (copying) such as in editing, being translated to other formats, or going through multi-layered special effects. Despite DV being digital, Beta-SP can actually hold up better when making multiple-generation copies. Also remember that when comparing DV to Beta SP, the performance of the tape machine is only one component of the many factors involved. A $4000 DV camcorder will never look as good as a $40,000 Beta-SP camcorder. The better camera and lens will always outperform the lesser regardless of the tape format. There is no question that the DV formatted camcorders look better than their Hi8 and S-VHS cousins. Nevertheless, DV, made by both Sony and Panasonic, has become the format of choice for consumers, prosumers, and budget-minded professionals. The development of this format—especially the new mini-DV cassettes—has led to the design of camcorders so small they fit into a shirt pocket and has brought professional quality to almost any user for a reasonable price. DV has become as generic as the old VHS format, and each company has its own upgraded version of it.

Sony introduced its DVCAM version of DV to appeal to the industrial or prosumer market. The major difference between DVCAM and Standard DV is a larger spacing of the recording tracks (called track pitch), which requires the tape to run at a faster speed. This becomes a benefit in editing because it allows more accurate edits and fewer audio problems.

Panasonic's upgraded version of DV is the DVCPRO. Again, the only real difference is the track pitch for better editing capabilities. Unlike the larger professional formats, DV tapes can be recorded and played in different manufacturers' machines. Sony's DV and DVCAM can be played in Panasonic's DV and DVCPRO decks and vice versa. For all practical purposes, there is no quality difference among any of these four formats. DVCAM and DVCPRO are better formats for professionals because of the increased editing capabilities and other added features of their respective machines but the actual quality of the recording is the same.

Panasonic has also taken the DVCPRO to an additional height with their DVCPRO50 version of the format designed to compete against the Digi-Beta and Beta SX. DVCPRO50 has increased quality due to its 8-bit 4:2:2 sampling at a data recording rate of 50 Mb/s and a lesser compression ratio of 3.3:1 in a dual-DV processor format.

Confused? That certainly describes the marketplace for tape format choices. And we haven't even talked about high-definition formats yet (we'll cover those in the new technologies chapter). The one thing to carry away from this discussion of tape formats is their compatibility. Close attention has to be paid as to where and how the material on a recorded tape is to be used. How many points of transfer or translation is that tape going to have to go through? In the transfer/editing/transmission/storage process the different machines or systems handling the signal can go from 8 bit to 10 bit, DV to MPEG-2, 25 Mb/s to 50 Mb/s, and so on and vice versa, with the resulting picture ending up worse than an old analog picture.

It would be a disservice to the reader to try to predict which if any of the current formats will survive or dominate in their current form. The acceptance of digital format acquisition methods at the professional level has been slow because of the above-stated confusion and the mismatching formats. DVCPRO has made great inroads by replacing the aging MII and 3/4-inch U-Matic SP systems in broadcasting, and DV has done the same by replacing Hi8 and S-VHS formats in the general marketplace. Because of so many competing formats, the professional market is still dominated by Beta SP. Sony is likely to dominate in the overall format wars within the professional arena because of the vast libraries of Beta tapes in the world. Sony's new generation of studio tape machines plays all formats of the basic Beta cassette from the original Betacam to the newest MPEG IMX. No other company or format can cover such an array of material. It is likely, however, that we will see videotape replaced with some sort of random access medium some time during the 2000s. Only then will video be truly digital. The only thing that is certain is that many of the functions of the recording device will remain the same.

Time Code

One of the most important pieces of information to be recorded on a tape is the time code or **TC**. Similar to edge numbers in film, the time code allows each frame of the video to be numbered. In whatever ma-

chine a tape is played back, scenes or shots can be referred to and found by their time code number. Most time code in professional analog machines is recorded like an additional channel of audio on the videotape. It has a separate track and its own space on the tape. This type of encoding is called **linear time code**. On newer tape formats there is also a form of time code recorded in the picture portion of the video signal. The numerical information is added to the vertical interval space left as the tracing beam shuts off to return to the top of the picture. This channel of time code is simply called **vertical interval time code** (**VITC**).

Time code in a professional machine can be recorded as either drop frame or nondrop frame. Because video in NTSC is recorded at 29.97 fps, numbering each frame will not be an accurate counting of the time of the recording. A 1-hour recording will have 1 hour and 3.6 seconds of time code. Drop frame TC skips two frames every minute except every tenth minute. This allows the counting of frames to meet the real time of the recording. Almost every user of video prefers to use drop frame TC.

User bits are stored in yet another portion of the video signal. They can store characters of the alphabet as well as numbers. Whatever is entered into the user-bit channel will be recorded within every frame of video just like time code. Once set, user bits do not advance or change as the recording takes place. Each frame has the same information. That makes user bits a good way to label tapes. The operator's name, initials, date, or unit number can be placed in this channel to aid in cataloging later. The limit, however, is eight characters.

On machines that allow it, one of the more popular uses for vertical interval time code is as that of a clock. While linear time code is usually set on **Record Run** so the numbers only advance when the tape does, VITC can be set on **Free Run** so the numbers continue to advance no matter what the VCR is doing. The VITC can be set in sync with any clock such as a wristwatch. Many news photographers set the VITC in sync with their reporter's watch. In this way, reporters can take time code notes using the time of day while the photographer is shooting. During a long interview, sound bites can be noted easily without looking at the tape machine. Later in editing, the reporters can simply have the editor switch the playback machine to VITC and search quickly for the sound or shots referred to in their notes. This can save valuable minutes when editing under deadline pressure. Linear time code can also be set to free run, but this can make editing more difficult (see Chapter 8 on postproduction).

Professional camcorders and decks always have TC in and out ports. On multi-camera shoots, one camera or deck can be designated as the master TC source and feed the other units—a process called slaving—so all the tapes will have the same TC while recording. This makes the editing process much easier by allowing the editor to sync up the same scene shot from different cameras and intercut them as if the scene were being edited live at the location.

One of the great disadvantages of the newer DV formats at the prosumer level is access to time code. Although most recorders have TC, it cannot be set by the user and has no separate in and out ports. Each tape put into the machine starts at 00:00:00 and they don't allow multiple recorders to be synchronized to the same time code during recording.

Typical Control Functions

The standard video recorder operates in the same manner as any audiotape recorder. There are positions for play, record, stop, fast forward, rewind, and pause. More up-to-date models have a search function that allows the operator to scan the pictures on the tape at a fast rate with the machine in the pause or play mode. Some older models of video recorders have an audio dub function that allows the recording of audio on only one of the audio channels (usually channel 2) as long as there is video already recorded on the tape. The small video recorders or decks that fit on the back of, or are included in, a professional camera have fewer functions than the stand-alone models. Although many of these onboard decks have a complete function panel, it is usually covered by a door and rarely used by the operator. These types of decks are generally thought of as record-only decks because of their limited functions for other uses. The play function on the typical nondigital onboard broadcast-quality deck only plays the tape back in the viewfinder and must use a playback adapter unit to be seen outside the camera. Professional nondigital onboard decks and one-piece camcorders cannot record a video signal from any source other than the camera. That limitation usually means that a second deck may be needed in certain situations. On-board digital decks allow the recording of other signals in addition to the camera and play back recorded video in full color without an adapter.

Typical Inputs

The functions of nondigital dockable decks or built-in recorders are very limited and, thus, they have fewer input points. They accept video only from the camera to which they are attached, but they do permit audio to be recorded either through the connectors in the back or from the camera's own mic. Professional onboard decks have input/output points for time code to allow one deck to be "slaved" to another deck or source to share a common time code.

A typical stand-alone nondigital videocassette recorder (VCR) can receive a video signal in one of two ways: via the **BNC** connector, which carries a standard composite video signal, or via the multi-pin cable connector, which carries a component signal. The origin of the acronym BNC is often debated, but one popular thesis is that it stands for **"Baby N Connector."** This name comes from a similar connector used during World War II by the Navy.

Most one-piece camcorders also have an input point for **Gen-lock**. This BNC connector is used to link the unit to other machines or cameras to synchronize the timing of the video signals. This is necessary whenever more than one camera or recorder is used together or used as part of a live transmission.

The multi-pin connector on most professional decks is the 27-pin Beta connector. This supplies component video to another machine, either another deck or an edit machine. On prosumer models this connection is usually an S-VHS or just an S-video connector which again supplies a component signal.

Digital decks have an additional input/output (I/O) port for delivering an all-digital signal of not only the video but the audio as well. It's called **FIREWIRE** or **i-Link** and often referred to by its more technical name IEEE-1394. The information can flow in either direction so the port can be used for playback, recording, or editing.

Typical Outputs

The video output of a stand-alone VCR such as the BVW-35 usually comes from three types of connections and forms. Component format decks have a multi-pin connector that allows the video signal to stay in its separated state as it leaves the deck for another source that can handle component video. The next output is the NTSC composite signal that comes out of a BNC connector. On lower quality machines,

Figure 3.20 BNC connecting ports for the Sony D600 camera. TEST OUT can be used as a simple video output port. An additional video output is in the rear of the camera.

this signal may come out of an RCA-style plug. All professional decks have two of these composite video outputs. The other possible output path is through an F connector that carries a standard TV signal on either channel 3 or 4. This may be hooked to any TV set just like an antenna so it can function as a monitor. (See Figure 3.20.)

The standard male XLR connector provides the audio outputs of any professional deck. Switches on some decks allow the mixing of the output of both audio channels into just one connector for more flexible uses. The audio output levels can be controlled on each channel separately, and the signal usually comes out at line-level impedance (see Chapter 4). Less expensive decks may have RCA or miniplug connectors to get audio from the deck. There is always a socket for a headphone or ear piece to monitor the sound recording and playback. This connector is usually a female 1/4-inch phone plug but can also be a 1/8-inch miniplug. Some decks have sockets for both.

Camcorders also have an output for the time code, which works both as the video is being recorded and on playback, and a BNC (video connector) output for a TBC (time-base connector used to correct minor playback problems) if one is used. A switch called **confidence playback** on some professional decks permits the audio and video to be moni-

tored while it is being recorded. The audio confidence, delayed by about 1 second, can be heard on the headphone output only. The video confidence can be seen on any of the video outputs of the deck or in the return position through the camera's viewfinder. Meant only to serve as a quick check on whether something is indeed being recorded on the tape, the video confidence picture is black and white and of poor quality in appearance. The same is true of the audio confidence: The quality is poor, but it shows that something is being recorded. Confidence playback is often used to spot-check the recording in progress and ensure there is no head clog or other failure of the system. It makes no sense to waste time shooting if the machine is not working properly.

Onboard Decks

Many professional camera systems come as true one-piece camcorders. These machines make it easy for one person to shoot from the shoulder and eliminate one cable and battery. These nondigital decks are not made to play back video without the use of a playback adapter. They can play back the recording "in the camera" to check to see if something was recorded or to review what was recorded but it will only be in black and white and the signal doesn't

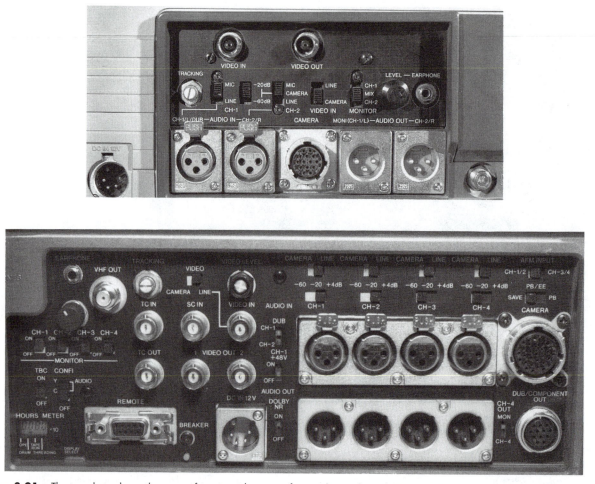

Figure 3.21 The top photo shows the array of inputs and outputs of a standard industrial U-Matic VCR. The bottom photo shows the much larger array on a professional Beta SP VCR.

leave the camcorder without the playback adapter. Because of this, there are no output connectors on these decks except for a headphone, a time code BNC (for jamming or inserting time code to another deck), and a video BNC out for use with a monitor that only shows the camera output, not the recording. A multi-pin plug on the deck allows it to be attached to the playback adapter. Dockable decks do not have as many functions as the stand-alone VCRs, but they record with the same level of quality. With an added adapter, any record-only dockable deck can be converted into a stand-alone deck and used with a multi-pin cable or BNC coax cable to record from the camera or any other video source.

Meters

The audio record levels are always visible on analog VU (**volume units**) meters or the newer style LED

peak meters on the deck. The meters, calibrated from −20 decibels to 0 decibels in the green, and 0 to +3 decibels in the red (for analog meters), indicate the strength of the audio signal. A good recording should have the loudest passages or sounds peaking at 0 dB with most of the signal around −10 dB. If the meter needle goes above 0 dB into the red, it may mean that the audio is being recorded with distortion. The ability of a deck to record audio over the +3-dB level is called **head room**. Some machines have little or no head room and distort any sound hotter or stronger than +5 dB. Others can handle signals up to nearly +10 dB without distortion, although the sound may be somewhat compressed. (See Figure 3.22.) For digital recording, the audio has no head room. Anything over 0 dB is distorted.

One of the meters usually has a scale to read off video signal strength as well. This is usually a short green line. When the meter select switch is in the

Figure 3.22 The display panel of a Sony D600 camcorder shows audio level at –4 dB. These peak-style meters react differently than VU-style meters.

video position, the needle should be somewhere on that green line. A dark picture can give the needle a low reading, and a very bright picture a high reading. If no video is present, the needle does not register. A third scale is there to measure VCR battery strength. A **Batt Check** button shows the relative strength of the battery. Most battery scales are not calibrated; the needle position means something only if you know what a fresh battery reading looks like on that particular machine.

Warning Lights

Every deck has warning lights that tell the operator that something has gone wrong or needs checking. The most common of these is the **tape-end warning.** When the tape is in the last two minutes of record time, this light flashes and an audio warning can be heard over the headsets but nowhere else. This method of alert is the same for all the warning functions. Other warnings usually include **RF** or **Clog** (no video being recorded), **Servo** (VCR receiving poor video signal), **Dew** (excess moisture inside the machine), and **Battery** (battery's power nearing end).

Time-Base Correctors

The complicated electronics of TV operate on very precise timing for the various functions involved in

creating the TV signal. Any time two or more signals are mixed, such as videotape mixed with live pictures from the studio during a live newscast, the timing of their electronic functions must be in sync. The **time-base corrector (TBC)** is one way to bring the video in sync with the broadcast signal of the TV station. It also improves the stability of the picture by replacing the control track of the video with a newly generated one, thus eliminating any errors or defects in the original information. The functions of the TBC are becoming almost invisible to the user and are simply part of the machine.

Maintenance

As with a camera, there is very little you can do to fix a VCR unless you have been trained in a factory-sponsored school or by experienced technicians. Like any other piece of equipment, the VCR must be treated with respect. Do not let it get dirty; if it does, clean it as soon as possible. Do not let it get wet, and keep it away from harmful environments, such as cigarette smoke. For news use, the deck will go into some of the worst imaginable conditions. If the deck is not at its top performance level, it is not likely to bring home good-quality video. The best professional decks are made to take abuse but up to a limit. The best protection for stand-alone decks is a cloth carry bag custom made to fit the deck. This offers not only protection from dust, dirt, water, and shock but also a good shoulder strap and plenty of pockets for carrying extra equipment, such as a spare battery, tapes, or audio gear.

Most VCR manufacturers recommend using a cleaning tape on a regular basis. This tape cleans the machine's video and audio heads of any dirt particles that may interfere with the recording process.

Troubleshooting

There is always a time when things simply do not work. One of the most likely things to fail for the portable video photographer is the tape machine. Because of the highly accurate moving parts and their exposure to the environment when tapes are changed, the tape deck is subject to more wear and tear than the other equipment. A mental checklist should be second nature to anyone using a portable VCR in the field. On such a complex machine, the solution to a problem can be easy if you know where to look for the cause of the trouble.

The most common reason a deck will not work is also the simplest: no power. It is often easy to tell when there is no power present, but a drained battery can sometimes work some functions but not others. Check the battery first. The next most common is the tape itself: Is the record tab in place? (If not, the machine will not record.) Is the tape being threaded? (If not, it may not be seated properly in the tape carriage.) Is the tape rewound? Once these things are checked out, the problem may be in the circuits that control the mechanics, sometimes called the machine's logic. Shutting the power off to the deck for a minute or two may clear the logic circuits and allow them to reset. The last area of possible trouble is the mechanics of the deck. A dirty pinch roller can cause the tape not to thread properly. Most problems such as this, however, require a trip to the maintenance department.

You should know the position of every switch on the deck for every function you wish to use. You may never use some of the switches because of the type of work you do, but if they are in the wrong position for some reason, they may prevent the correct operation of the machine. Study the manuals for your equipment carefully. It is not uncommon to have just the playback function of a deck fail, so in certain circumstances you may want to play the tape back on another machine just to be sure. Very little field repair

work can be done on a VCR, although one easy fix is that of cleaning clogged video heads. They can be easily unclogged without a trip to the shop even if a head-cleaning tape is not available on location. A new unused tape can be played or fast-forwarded in the clogged deck. The rougher surface on the new tape can often break the clog loose.

BATTERIES

More power-efficient cameras and decks with higher capacity battery technology have considerably reduced power worries in recent years. Most people are familiar with lead-based batteries like those in our cars (wet cells) or flashlights (dry cells). The standard alkaline dry cell type of battery is rarely used to power a large piece of equipment, because it does not pack enough punch per ounce of battery weight; also it generally cannot be recharged. The most popular source of battery power today comes from the **nickel-cadmium (Ni-Cad)** cell. This battery gives quite a bit of power for its size and weight and can be recharged many times before wearing out. Today new technologies are changing the once heavy batteries into fairly light, compact units. Like the technology used in cell phone batteries, many battery styles are going to nickel metal halide (NiMH) versions. Their power-to-battery-weight ratio makes them a good choice for field use. Additionally, lithium ion technology is also being used in battery production, replacing a Ni-Cad type battery weighing several pounds with one that weighs several ounces yet gives the same or even more power.

The battery's power output must match the power requirements of the equipment to which it is hooked. A 30-volt power belt made for portable lights would fry a 12-volt system camera. In today's world of camcorders, one battery generally powers both units. The most popular is the clip-on **brick** battery, a generic name for any cube-style battery. The 13.2- or 14.4-volt capacity of these batteries gives them the reserve power to operate the equipment at its rated volts (12 volts) for the maximum amount of time without harming them.

Battery capacity is rated by **ampere hours (Ah)**. The typical brick battery has a rating of 4 Ah, that is, it can deliver 1 amp of power for 4 hours. The manual with your camcorder will tell its power consumption and how many watts the camcorder uses, say, 18W. Amps are watts divided by volts. In this case 18 watts /12 volts = 1.5 amps; this means that a 4-Ah battery should run the camcorder for a little more than 2.5 hours (1.5 amps = 2.7 hours). Of course, the exact time will always vary depending on the age of the battery and the operating conditions.

Three types of packaging are generally used for the batteries used in today's video productions. (See Figure 3.23.) The small, thin NP-1 battery and the larger flat BP-90 style battery, both originally developed for Sony, were primarily designed to be used as deck batteries, although both can power cameras and camcorders. The larger square brick batteries are designed primarily for use as onboard sources of long-lasting power. The brick concept was developed by Anton Bauer using a patented three-point attaching plate. These plates can be easily mounted on cameras, camcorders, decks, monitors, and belts to provide power in any configuration. (See Figure 3.24.)

Recharging

The first step in proper battery care starts with proper recharging. A Ni-Cad battery should always be fully drained before it is recharged. Many new charging systems on the market finish draining half-used batteries and condition them before recharging. If the charger does not do this, try to discharge the battery fully without overdraining the battery to avoid what is called a **memory**. A battery will memorize the amount of power it is accustomed to giving. If the battery is always only half drained when recharged, the battery will learn to have only that amount of power. Both NiMH and lithium batteries do not have memory problems.

The two types of battery charging are fast and slow (trickle). A fast charger works only on batteries designed to be fast charged and takes about 1 hour.

Figure 3.23 The three most common batteries in video production. Starting clockwise from upper left: (1) a BP-90-type battery used primarily in VCRs; (2) a snap-on-type "brick" commonly used on cameras and camcorders; (3) an NP-1-type used in both VCRs and cameras as well as monitors.

Figure 3.24 The standardized Anton Bauer Snap-On® system is patented and has become the most common way of providing power to professional video cameras.

The slow charger usually takes about 12 to 14 hours to fully charge a battery. Most chargers will prevent overcharging and automatically switch to a maintenance cycle once the battery is charged. At 14 hours per charge, one charger is needed for every battery in everyday use. The charger must also match the battery. While many types of batteries are made to fit the same brackets, they do not necessarily work on the same chargers. Make sure your batteries and chargers are compatible. The newer types of batteries are charged on smart systems that allow for fast charging times and a self-diagnosis of battery condition.

Life Span

The order of battery use needs to be rotated so that no battery gets more use than the others. This makes the batteries reliable to the same degree; one should not wear out while others go without any usage, which can also be harmful. A professional battery should be able to undergo hundreds of recharges be-fore the drop in capacity makes the use of that battery too impractical. The life of the battery may be extended by regular checks on the condition of the individual cells within the battery. A bad or weak cell can hasten the demise of the other good cells by shifting too much of the load over to them. Unfortunately, this check can only be done by trained maintenance personnel.

Proper Care

Batteries are very susceptible to temperature, both hot and cold. The ideal temperature for a battery is about 75 degrees Fahrenheit, but as temperatures drop below freezing or go above 100 degrees Fahrenheit, the ability of the battery to deliver power starts to fall off rather quickly. In very hot climates or when batteries are left in the car for long periods of time, a cooler with a no-leak ice pack is a good way to ensure fresh batteries. The reverse is true for very cold weather: Keep the batteries as warm as possible.

Temperature also comes into play when recharging the battery. Never try to recharge a frozen or a blazing hot battery. Always allow the battery to reach a normal temperature before putting it through the rigors of charging. Once charged, the typical battery has a shelf life of about 2 days at full capacity. After that it will start to lose about 5% of its power every week; the decay accelerates as time goes by. If the batteries cannot be left on a trickle charger, their shelf life should be kept in mind.

TRIPODS AND CAMERA-MOUNTING DEVICES

Portable cameras are made so they can be used on the operator's shoulder for handheld photography. Although this is essential, it is not the optimum way to use the equipment. Most professional uses of portable cameras and camcorders involve a tripod mount. The tripod raises the production values of photography more than any other element except lighting. (See Figure 3.25.)

Fluid Heads

Most professional tripod heads involve a combination spring/fluid mechanism for giving pans and tilts a smooth motion. The fluid acts as a dampening agent to resist movement so that the camera does not simply jerk up and down or to the side. There are two adjustments for the fluid (one for tilt and one for pan) that can make the resistance as heavy or as light as the operator likes. There are also locks for the pan and tilt to keep the camera in one place without drifting. A third function on the head is the **counterbalance**. This adjusts the internal springs to the exact weight of the camera.

To make a fluid head work, the camera's center of gravity must be perfectly balanced on the head. To do this, the head itself must be leveled (using the plumb-bubble bull's-eye found on the head), the pan and tilt locks must be off, and the pan and tilt friction must be set at the lightest setting. There should be an adjustment on the quick-release plate to slide the camera back and forth to get its center of gravity over the center of the head so the camera stays level without touching it. Lock the sliding plate in this position. A good fluid head should permit you to tilt the camera forward and back with minimal friction dialed

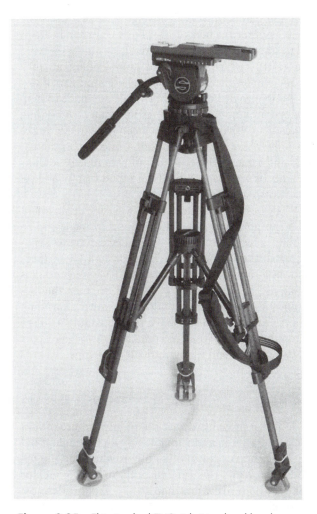

Figure 3.25 This standard ENG-style tripod and head, a Sachtler Video 18p, has two-stage legs, a midlevel spreader, and a shoulder strap for easy carrying.

into the tilt function, and take your hand off the camera at any angle and have the camera stay in that position without drifting. If it does drift, it means the spring portion—the counterbalance—of the head is not adjusted properly. The head must be rated for the weight of the camera. If the camera is too heavy or too light for the head, all the functions of the head will be of little value. Trying different levels of friction can help you find the point where the camera can make very smooth movements with little effort.

Tripod Legs

The days of the wooden tripod or sticks are long gone. Most tripods today are made of alloys, graphite, or aluminum and are very lightweight. The lightness is a great asset for the news crews, but weight can be helpful to stabilize the camera, particularly on windy days. Never trust a tripod to hold your camera up in a strong wind or in any situation where things are likely to bump into it. Lightweight tripods are made to help the operator, not to take the responsibility for holding the camera. If you walk away from the camera, make sure that the camera cannot fall, or take it off the tripod and set it on the ground until you return. Anchor weights or sandbags to hold the tripod firmly in place are always worth using.

The best tripods have a two-stage leg deployment that can go from a height of about 26 inches up to around 6 feet. The length of each leg can be set separately so the tripod can be used on uneven surfaces with minimum leveling at the head. Most leg designs make use of the spreader, or spider, to keep the legs from sliding out from under the camera on slick floors. These spreaders have an adjustable span to bring the legs in closer or spread them further apart or be removed entirely in difficult situations.

Dollies

A dolly is a movable device that allows you to mount the camera on it and shoot steady video while moving. The simplest form of a dolly is wheels on the tripod legs. While this type of dolly may be good for some basic moves, it is hard to control and almost impossible to steer once movement starts. Many dolly platforms are made to use a standard tripod attached to them. The most common dolly, a **doorway dolly,** accommodates any tripod but is small enough to fit through most doors. This dolly has large inflated tires that give a smooth ride over fairly flat surfaces. For uneven or rough surfaces, the tires can be replaced with special wheels that run along rails laid on the ground called **track.** (See Figure 3.26.) This type of dolly obviously takes time to set up, and any dolly usually requires a second person to push it. On larger dollies, like the **crab dolly,** the operator sits on the dolly itself while the built-in tripod raises or lowers the camera hydraulically.

Homemade or common items can be used to make a dolly without much cost or hassle. The most popular is the wheelchair. While the operator sits in the chair with a shoulder-mounted camera, another person can easily roll the chair. Another possibility is the grocery cart. Just about anything with wheels can be made to work in certain situations.

Figure 3.26 Dollies can be used with rubber wheels on a smooth surface or with hard wheels on specially laid tracks like this one. This type of dolly provides a very solid base for the camera and incredibly steady pictures while the dolly is moving. Because the operator rides on the dolly, one or two extra persons are required to execute the move. The camera in this photo is also equipped with a video-prompting device. A remote sending unit relays the text to the TV monitor and is reflected in the two-way mirror in front of the lens. Photo by Tony Burke.

Cranes and Booms

The crane shot is a favorite of the movie industry. The shot starts out high and wide as the camera slowly descends to eye level in the middle of the action. On a **crane,** the operator sits on a platform that is raised or lowered at the end of a long arm. A **boom** has the camera remotely mounted on an arm. All camera functions such as pan, tilt, zoom, and focus are done at the base of the boom arm. The smaller versions of these booms are very popular in video field production and can be operated by one person. (See Figure 3.27.) They can also add an incredible amount of production value to the shoot by moving the camera through a space where no person could go, such as sweeping over the heads of the crowd.

Figure 3.27 This portable boom or jib can be operated by one person. A monitor located at the base shows the operator what the camera sees. Courtesy of Stanton Video Services, Inc.

Steadi-Cam

The **Steadi-Cam®** revolutionized the handheld camera. This complex system of counterbalanced arms is worn by the photographer with the camera mounted at the end of the armature. Although it is rather strenuous to operate, the Steadi-Cam combines many of the effects of the dolly and crane to achieve an incredibly stable picture even with the operator running over obstacles or down stairs. A video screen mounted in the arm near the hand grip allows the operator to see the picture from the camera no matter which way the camera is pointed. A new, smaller version is made specifically for EFP. It is lighter and easier to use but still takes a considerable amount of practice to learn.

Car Mounts

Shooting in or into moving cars can be very troublesome. For the time when the camera must be mounted outside the car, a suction device with a cam-

era attached grips the hood or door. This mount can provide some dramatic angles, but safety lines should always be used in case the suction doesn't hold. Sets of bars and clamps that fit almost every car are also available that allow a camera to be placed almost anywhere.

Aerial Mounts

Shooting from aircraft can be very limiting because of the air turbulence and the vibration of the engines. Even in a helicopter, the picture really only looks steady on the wide shots. As soon as the photographer zooms in, the viewer can see the chop of the ride. The old standard in aerial photography used to be the **Tyler Mount,** which functions as a Steadi-Cam in the air. Attached to the frame of the aircraft, this mount removes the vibrations and minor bumps of the ride and lets the camera produce a steady picture even at long focal lengths. The aircraft must be approved for using it, but the Tyler Mount offers excellent aerial photography.

Several devices are available today that mount externally onto aircraft that contain the camera in a large spherical housing. The direction and zoom of the camera are controlled remotely by an operator from inside the craft. The most famous result of this type of mounting can be seen in the pictures of O. J. Simpson's freeway chase. The rock-steady shots were made by several helicopters all using some form of external mounted camera stabilization system. (See Figure 3.28.)

Special Mounts

Many types of mounts can be made with a little ingenuity. The key is making them strong enough to hold the camera and withstand other forces. If you can think of a place to put the camera, then someone can surely devise a way to get the camera there. Anything attached to the outside of an aircraft would have to have FAA approval. With the advent of new color cameras called lipstick- or cigar-cams that are the size of their namesakes, it is possible to put a camera just about anywhere. A lipstick-cam can be placed at the end of an audio boom to get shots from odd places, such as holding the pole with the camera out of one moving car to shoot another car. You can move the camera from the wheels, up the side, over the hood, and then raise the camera to let the car speed on past under the camera. (See Figure 3.29)

The key to mounting any camera is always safety—for the camera and the operator and any

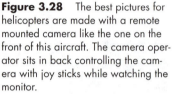

Figure 3.28 The best pictures for helicopters are made with a remote mounted camera like the one on the front of this aircraft. The camera operator sits in back controlling the camera with joy sticks while watching the monitor.

members of the crew or public. Mounting a camera on a roller coaster might seem like a good idea, but only if you have taken into account the G forces of the ride. Is the mount strong enough to withstand being whipped around at several times the force of gravity? It could be a life-threatening disaster to have the mount break and the camera sent flying in the middle of the ride. Safety first.

Miniature Cameras

One of the great benefits of the new DV format cameras is their small size relative to their quality. Where at one time mounting a Betacam in a difficult situation would be time consuming and possibly dangerous, a small DV camera can be placed with ease and secured safely. By the use of fiber optics and these small cameras, cameras can now be hidden on a person. No longer is a bag or briefcase necessary; the camera lens can be hidden in a pair of sunglasses and the recorder hidden in a jacket pocket.

Figure 3.29 This tiny camera, sometimes referred to as a lipstick-cam because of its small size, is actually only the bottom third of what is shown here. This camera is connected to a small camera control unit (CCU) by means of a thin cable. The CCU in turn sends video to any recorder hooked up to it. The camera has several interchangeable lenses including a fiber optic lens that can be run up the operator's back under clothes and placed through the front of a baseball cap to appear as a decorative button, creating a totally hidden body camera.

4

Microphones and Audio-Recording Techniques

Microphones are the first link in the technical chain that forms an audio production. The choice and placement of the mic along with its quality help determine how strong this link will be.

Microphones (mics) have existed for more than 100 years. The first was used in Alexander Graham Bell's telephone to change audible voice signals into electrical energy. It was a simple and inexpensive carbon microphone sensitive to the frequencies of sound typically generated by the human voice. Carbon microphones are still used in many telephones today.

MICROPHONE STRUCTURE

A **microphone** is a transducer, a device that changes energy from one form to another. Microphones change sound or acoustical energy into electrical energy, or more specifically, sound waves into electrical signals. The microphone **diaphragm** catches the sound waves while the microphone **element** translates that mechanical energy into electrical energy.

Four basic designs have been used for microphone elements over the years: **carbon, ceramic, dynamic,** and **condenser.** The first two, carbon and ceramic, were the elements used in early mics but they are rarely used now in professional audio work. The latter two, dynamic and condenser, are the mics of choice for almost all professionals. Because each element has a unique electrical and sonic property,

knowing the differences among them will help you choose the right mic for the right job.

Dynamic Elements

Dynamic elements have parts inside them that physically move when struck by sound waves. This movement creates an electrical current, which becomes the audio signal. Although many different variations of dynamic elements have been manufactured by various companies, there are two general classifications: the moving-coil type and the ribbon, or velocity, type.

Moving-Coil Microphones

Most moving-coil microphones are made up of a Mylar diaphragm attached to a coil of wire called a voice coil, which is suspended within a magnetic field. As the term *dynamic* implies, dynamic elements are designed to allow movement. In a moving-coil element a finely wrapped coil of wire moves when the diaphragm is struck by sound waves. This movement within the magnetic field induces a very small voltage in the coil, which becomes the output signal.

A moving-coil microphone is the most widely used in professional audio applications for several reasons:

1. They have a very good frequency response, close to what our ears hear, and can gather audio from many different kinds of sources.

A common frequency range for a professional dynamic mic is 40 to 15,000 Hz.
2. Generally the most ruggedly designed mics available, they are shock resistant, unimpaired by most temperature extremes, and insensitive to extremes in humidity.
3. They are generally inexpensive.

Ribbon, or Velocity, Microphones

Another dynamic microphone similar to the moving-coil mic is the ribbon, or velocity, mic, in which a thin ribbon-like piece of corrugated metal is positioned between the poles of a magnet. When struck by sound waves, the ribbon vibrates between the magnetic poles, causing a small voltage in the ribbon that becomes the audio signal. Because the ribbon is flat, it is sensitive to sound pressure striking it directly from either the front or the back. Ribbon mics were used extensively in the 1930s and 1940s in studio-produced radio. Although they are very sensitive and have a very good high-frequency response, their drawbacks include shock sensitivity, fragility, and noncompact size.

Condenser Elements

Condenser microphones have a light diaphragm that serves as one plate of a two-plate capacitor. Capable of storing electrical charges, a capacitor is an electrical component with two electrodes (+ and −) separated by a small distance. Unlike the dynamic element that makes use of electromagnetism to generate elec-

trical impulses, it operates on a principle known as variable capacitance. The diaphragm and the backplate act as the electrodes of a capacitor. (See Figure 4.1.) When sound waves strike the diaphragm, the distance between the two electrodes changes, producing a change in its capacitance, or its ability to store an electrical charge. This results in a very small signal voltage that becomes the start of the audio signal.

The quality of a condenser mic depends on the design of its capsule, which is the condenser element and its acoustic system or housing. The capsule plays a major role in how the mic responds, not only to different frequencies but to different directions of sounds.

A condenser mic requires two additional features to produce its audio signal. One is an impedance-converting preamplifier that converts the signal immediately to low impedance to enhance signal quality. The other feature is a power supply of DC voltage to the capacitor element to polarize the two plates and provide power for the preamplifier. In electret condenser microphones, the voltage needs of the mic are smaller because the diaphragm is capable of holding a permanent charge; the power supply is needed only for the preamplifier. A good electret mic should hold its internal charge for 10 years or more but will eventually wear out. A disadvantage is its inability to respond to the higher frequencies as well as the externally polarized condenser mic.

In condenser microphones, the power supply can be located in the microphone itself or at the end of a short cable to the capsule. In a configuration referred to as phantom power, the power may also come from the console, mixer, or VCR to which the mic is connected. (See Figure 4.2.)

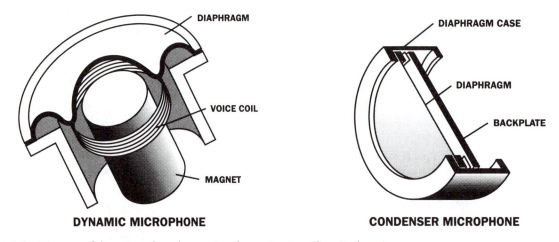

Figure 4.1 Diagrams of dynamic and condenser microphones. Courtesy Shure Brothers, Inc.

Considered the mic of choice for accurate sound recording in professional work, condenser microphones are sensitive and have excellent frequency response. One drawback is that it is more expensive than its dynamic counterpart; a second is that it requires a battery or power supply. Although a single small battery does not at first seem like a serious drawback, a condenser microphone battery is quite small and sometimes difficult to install properly because of polarity; beginners often install the battery upside down. This type of battery may be hard to find at local stores, thereby making replacement more difficult. Finally, condenser microphones are sometimes too sensitive for extremely noisy situations or sudden loud noises and are sometimes inappropriate for outdoor use.

SENSITIVITY

Microphones can also be categorized by their sensitivity—their ability to reproduce sound in sev-

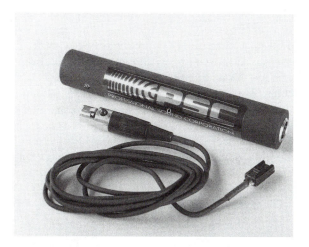

Figure 4.2 This lavaliere mic has a detachable power supply allowing it to be used with a wireless transmitter.

eral different ways. Directional sensitivity is the mic's ability to pick up sound from various directions. Frequency response is the mic's ability to pick up sounds of differing pitch or wavelength. Sound sensitivity refers to a mic's ability to generate a signal from a sound source. The more sensitive a mic is, the more signal it will produce.

Directional Sensitivity

Microphones have different abilities to pick up sound from varying directions. A **polar response** chart shows the pickup or polar pattern where sounds can originate and still be transduced into an electric signal. Manufacturers usually provide polar response charts to provide technically accurate information about the pickup characteristics of individual microphones. These standardized charts depict the angle of sound sensitivity relative to the element of the microphone and sound pressure levels. In effect, they show how a mic will respond to sounds that come from various angles and at various levels of sound pressure. The head of the mic is at the center of the chart and its base is at the bottom. Sounds coming from the top, or 0 degrees, are called **on axis** and those from the side, or 90 degrees, **off axis**.

A microphone's ability to gather sounds at various degrees off axis is what determines how directional the mic is. The further the distance from the tip of a mic, the less the sound level is transduced. On the chart this is shown by the concentric circles around the tip of a microphone, which represent sound levels that decrease in intensity as you go away from the mic. These charts are especially helpful because there are many variations of the general pickup patterns. Also, many mics have slightly different patterns at different frequencies. In addition, there are some hybrid and altered versions of the standard patterns. (See Figure 4.3.) Two major polar patterns describe professional mics: omnidirectional and directional.

Figure 4.3 Pickup patterns of microphones.

Omnidirectional

Omnidirectional mics have patterns that pick up sounds equally from all directions. The pickup pattern is three dimensional and almost spherical. If you place an omnidirectional mic in the center of a circle of people, the sound level coming from any of those people should be almost identical to the others, assuming that they are all equidistant from the mic and all persons are speaking at about the same level. The design of this type of mic is based on the mic's response to acoustic sound pressure, which is nondirectional. The mic's diaphragm can react to sound pressure changes equally from any direction. However, a pressure-type mic does tend to be more directional at higher sound frequencies; it is best to point the mic in the direction of the primary sound source to be recorded. In other words, even for an omnidirectional mic, sound on axis will tend to sound better in quality than sounds off axis.

Directional

A **directional mic** uses a pressure-gradient device to achieve its polar pattern and achieve directionality in one of two ways. It can respond to differences in audio pressure between the two faces of its diaphragm (the pressure-gradient device) or achieve directionality by the use of reflectors. Directional mics are good at reducing background noise from two sources: (1) off-axis sounds and (2) excessive reverberation (usually found inside small rooms). They can also be placed at a greater distance from the sound source while maintaining their frequency response and sensitivity. These are the mics of choice in stereo recording because of their ability to give a sense of sound location.

Bidirectional   A bidirectional microphone picks up sound equally from only two directions. Resembling a figure eight, its pickup pattern is achieved in mics that are purely pressure-gradient devices (no reflectors used). The most common of these mics is the ribbon mic. One of the oldest mic designs around, the ribbon mic is still widely used today in radio and studio work. Larry King has made the ribbon mic familiar to a new generation of TV viewers by using it as his desk mic and logo on *The Larry King Live* show on CNN. If you interview someone who is at the same but opposite distance as you are from the mic and who speaks at about the same volume, a bidirectional mic will be equally sensitive to both voices and

eliminate any side audio. This assumes that your locations are at the correct angles relative to the mic.

Unidirectional/Cardioid   By combining pressure and pressure-gradient designs into one mic, the resulting pattern variation is called a cardioid. **Cardioid microphones** are unidirectional and pick up sound primarily from one direction. The word *cardioid* comes from the shape of its response chart, an inverted heart-shaped pattern. Cardioid microphones pick up sounds almost entirely from the area directly in front of the mic and almost nothing from the far sides or rear, which makes them very desirable in noisy situations. By varying the ratio of pressure versus pressure-gradient in the mic design, several types of cardioid patterns can be found. The three basic patterns are cardioid, supercardioid, and hypercardioid. (See Figure 4.4.)

Ultradirectional   More directional than the hypercardioid, the **ultradirectional** or **shotgun microphone** uses an entirely different capsule design to achieve its special purpose. The shotgun mic allows even greater distance between mic and source and greater rejection of off-axis sounds. Shotguns are usually more sensitive over the entire frequency range than other directional mics. The design is simply a tube with the diaphragm at one end. The tube has slits in it covered by an audio-dampening material to assure the full frequency response of the on-axis sounds. This allows sound to enter the tube from straight on (parallel to the tube or on axis) while reflecting off-axis sound through the slits. In general, the longer the tube, the more directional the shotgun mic is. Because its polar

Figure 4.4   An Electro-Voice® RE-10 dynamic supercardioid microphone. The ribbed shaft aids in the directionality of the microphone.

pattern is more sensitive to a wide range of frequencies, it is more directional for higher frequencies than for lower ones. Many shotgun systems have audio filters that cut out lower sound frequencies to make the mic more directional, which makes the sound received more tinny in quality with a lack of bass.

The shotgun is the workhorse microphone of ENG and EFP work. For the stand-alone newsperson, a shotgun mounted on the camera is the primary source of natural sound and sometimes even interview sound. A two-person news crew uses the shotgun for almost all sound gathering. In production, the shotgun is often boom mounted for precise sound gathering in the studio and on location where hidden mics are not possible.

Frequency Response

The goal of a sound technician is to accurately capture the sound source for reproduction. This requires a microphone capable of picking up the entire frequency spectrum of the sound waves that strike the mic's transducing element. A mic used for picking up conversation needs to be sensitive to the frequencies of the human voice, a range of about 100 to 10,000 Hz. A mic used in a sound studio for picking up the sounds of a piccolo must accurately transduce frequencies as low as 500 Hz and as high as 15,000 Hz. Although the construction and pickup pattern of a mic may qualify it for a particular application, it should not be used unless it has the appropriate frequency response capabilities.

Most professional-quality microphones can reproduce sounds within the frequency range of about 500 to 15,000 Hz. A chart can show a mic's frequency response or sensitivity to various frequencies of sound. (See Figure 4.5.) Ideally, the microphone will have a flat response curve, which implies that the mic is equally sensitive to all frequencies in its range. The most common fault of microphone frequency response appears at the upper end of its frequency range where the response curve drops off considerably, demonstrating an inability to reproduce sound waves at high frequencies. This drop off is present at low frequencies but is not quite as common and often less important. Many mics are designed with special characteristics to slightly alter their frequency response.

It is common to have a mic with a **bass rolloff switch** of some sort, allowing the user to purposefully de-emphasize frequencies at the low end of the audio spectrum. This helps correct the proximity effect, or

Type
Dynamic
Frequency Response
50 to 12,000 Hz (see Figure 1)

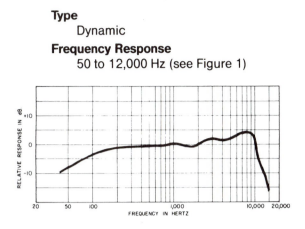

Figure 4.5 Frequency response chart for a dynamic microphone. Courtesy Shure Brothers, Inc.

the tendency of unidirectional and bidirectional mics to emphasize the bass or low-frequency response when the sound source is close to the mic. Other mics used in vocal work sometimes have a **presence boost** in the upper midrange to enhance the voice. These features also help add brilliance, clarity, and general intelligibility to the sounds recorded.

Sound Sensitivity

Microphone sensitivity refers to the amount of signal a given microphone produces from a given input sound source. Different mics have various sensitivities; some mics simply put out a stronger signal than others. Sensitivity is determined by measuring the mic's output power when the microphone is placed by a sound source of a known intensity or pressure. At first it may seem that the more sensitive a mic is the better, but experienced audio production practitioners realize that good audio production consists of an absence of the sounds you do not want to hear as well as the presence of the sounds that you do want to hear. Overly sensitive mics can be just as much a problem as those that are insensitive.

Overload

Dynamic mics are very hard to overload. They have very low distortion across their entire 140-dB dynamic range. The same cannot be said for condenser mics. At high acoustic levels the output signal of the capsule can overload the impedance converter circuit in the microphone. Some mics have built-in pads that can reduce that signal but at the cost of adding noise to the sound quality.

IMPEDANCE AND OTHER FACTORS

Microphones can also be differentiated by several technical factors. One factor, **impedance**, is very important because selecting the wrong impedance mic can cause immediate and sometimes serious problems. Other factors, like output noise and maximum sound pressure, are important only in very specific situations where the production requires specific sound pickup other than typical voice or music, or in situations that have a lot of interfering signals or sounds.

Impedance

Microphone impedance refers to the amount of resistance a signal encounters in a microphone circuit. The more impedance in a circuit, the less signal will flow out of it. Therefore, all other things being equal, low-impedance microphones produce more signal than high-impedance microphones.

Most professional mics have low impedance, which allows long audio cable runs without significant loss of signal. Their higher level of signal relative to high-impedance mics gives better rejection of hum and other types of interference. Also, low-impedance mics are compatible with almost all professional audio and video equipment.

Although impedance levels are rated as either high or low (corresponding to the designations high Z or low Z), mics can be found that are somewhere in between. Table 4.1 lists typical microphone impedance levels and their corresponding measurement in ohms, the unit of electrical resistance.

The impedance of a professional mic is usually 150 ohms; it is measured as −60 dB, which is referred to as **mic level**. After an audio signal has been passed

Table 4.1. Microphone impedance levels.

Rating in Ohms	Impedance Level
38 to 150	Low
600 to 2400	Medium
9600 and above	High

through a mixer, VCR, microwave transmitter, or any other processing device, the signal coming from that device is usually sent at a medium impedance of 600 ohms and is measured as +4 dB, which is referred to as **line level**. When audio signals are called high or low in professional situations, that usually means the line level is high and the mic level is low.

Other Factors

Besides the major considerations of element construction, pickup pattern, frequency range, sensitivity, and impedance, several other factors should be considered when selecting a microphone. Hum and radio frequency interference, signal-to-noise ratio, output noise, clipping level, and maximum sound pressure are often specified by the manufacturer. Some of these factors are critical for broadcasting applications but are not as important for less exacting applications.

STYLE

Of all the equipment manufactured for the reproduction of sound, microphones display the widest range of appearance and design. Although there are many different brands of compact disc players or reel-to-reel audiotape recorders, they vary only slightly in appearance. Microphones can range in size from a lavaliere smaller than a dime, to a shotgun mic more than 2 feet long, to a studio overhead mic the size of a large grapefruit. Because microphones vary extensively in size, weight, appearance, and application, knowledge of these factors provides a better understanding of how to use microphones and select the one appropriate to the task.

There is a direct relationship between microphone size and weight; obviously, the larger the microphone, the heavier it is. Size is a concern only some of the time. When a microphone is seen by an audience, such as in TV work, the mic must be unobtrusive. Because a variety of mic styles can achieve the same sound, other factors determine which mic is used when and where it will be placed. After considering polar patterns, frequency response, and sensitivity, you can choose a style.

Hand Microphones

The hand mic category is the broadest of the style categories. It is not a question of which mics are in it but which are not. A typical hand mic found throughout the world today is the Electro-Voice 635A. (See Figure 4.6.) This omnidirectional dynamic mic is so rugged, it could be used as a hammer. Built to last a lifetime, it is virtually the generic mic. The mic is small enough to fit in a hand and light enough not to be a strain. It is the general-purpose hand mic. Almost all hand mics are similar to the 635A in appearance. They have a relatively small head or capsule for the diaphragm at the end of a 4- or 5-inch staff. Today, many hand mics, including the 635, come in an extended handle model. The shaft of the mic is now closer to 12 inches to give it added reach and to better accommodate being attached to wireless transmitters. Hand mics can have any polar pattern, be it dynamic or condenser, and have various quality levels.

A hand mic is generally held by a person, such as a singer or someone addressing the camera or interviewing a subject. Because it is easily manipulated, it is good for gathering sound quickly from multiple sources, such as when a reporter doing an interview points the mic at the person talking with little effort or even walks the mic closer to the source. Almost all hand mics are made with a pleasing appearance so that they will not be distracting on camera. Hand mics can be mounted on a desk or a floor mic stand. In ENG work, where speed can be the overriding factor in getting the job done, the hand mic is indispensable because of its versatility despite any limitations. However, the disadvantages are (1) limited pick-up range and (2) sound quality that is not the best.

Mounted Microphones

Designed to be supported by a mechanical system such as a desk stand or overhead boom, a mounted mic can be one of two types: studio or shotgun.

Studio mics are designed purely for the highest quality sound reproduction. Because appearance is not important, these mics may be larger than those that appear on camera or on a speaker's podium. The on-camera or podium mics are sometimes referred to as desk mics but are still designed for studio use only. Studio mics are not moved often, especially not when sound is being recorded. Many have solid or integral mic-attachment devices for use on mic booms and floor stands. The ribbon mic is a classic example of a studio mic.

Shotgun mics are also not meant to be handheld. You can mount a shotgun mic in any of three primary ways: (1) on a camera, (2) on a studio boom or stand,

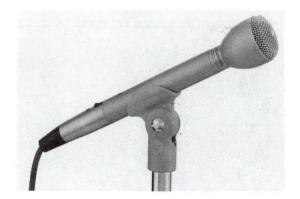

Figure 4.6 EV-635A, a rugged dynamic omnidirectional mic. Photo courtesy of Electro-Voice, Inc.

or (3) on a portable boom called a **fishpole.** Both studio and shotgun mics require a fair degree of isolation from mechanical noise, that is, noise caused by handling or brushing up against something. A good camera mount for a shotgun has a rubber pad in the holder surrounding the mic to cushion it from shock. A boom usually has a suspension system of heavy-duty rubber bands so that the shotgun literally floats within the holding bracket. Generally. shotguns are not meant to be seen by the camera so their appearance does not matter. They can gather quality audio at a good distance from the sound source. Because they are so directional, a boom allows the operator to position them at the best possible angle to get only the desired sound while keeping them out of the shot.

The disadvantage of mounted mics is their need to be fixed to a certain location. The most widely used mic system in professional production, the fishpole shotgun, is fixed to the fishpole and also requires a full-time operator. (See Figure 4.7.) If the shotgun is fixed to a camera, it cannot always be at the right angle to cut out unwanted background noise; it will gather any and all sounds in front of it.

Lavaliere Microphones

Lavaliere or mini-microphones became quite popular when TV presented new problems for audio production professionals. The mics used on TV had to sound good and they also had to have an acceptable appearance on camera. The lavaliere mic was one answer to this appearance problem. Designed to be worn by the person whose voice is to be recorded, lavaliere mics, or lavs, are quite small and unobtrusive. Often used as tie-clip mics, lavs usually have a

Figure 4.7 Soundman with mixer and mic boom or "fishpole." Audio from mixer is transmitted to receivers mounted on the camcorder.

condenser element. (See Figure 4.8.) This means that all lavs need a power source to work.

The microphone head or capsule is at the end of a long, thin cable run from the power unit. Like all powered mics, they generally work on a small watch-type battery that lasts quite some time. Some use a more common AA battery. The end of the power unit acts as the connector end of the mic with the standard male XLR receptacle. Lavaliere mics are almost always constructed with an omnidirectional pickup pattern because the sound of the human voice em-

anates from the mouth in an omnidirectional pattern as the head turns during speaking. Designed to be worn either against the clothing of the person or beneath an article of clothing, such as a tie, scarf, or shirt, lavaliere mics are designed with a built-in boost in the high-frequency range because the sound reaching the mic may be filtered by the cloth and cause higher frequencies to be missed. For live TV, two of these mics are often placed on the same tie clip in a technique known as **dual redundancy** to provide a backup if one fails.

Figure 4.8 A Sonotrim lav with windscreen and attaching devices surrounding it.

SPECIAL APPLICATIONS

In addition to the considerations of structure, sensitivity, impedance, and style, the type of application for the mic may influence which mic is best for your audio needs. Special application microphones have been developed to meet the needs of some atypical applications.

Performance Microphones

Microphones designed for performances will usually have special characteristics or devices built into them to suit the needs of audio performers. Consider the needs of a performer like Mick Jagger. Because of his bouncing, swinging, and jolting style of singing, he needs a mic that will take some abuse. First, his mic should have a shock mounting that dampens the noise created from rough handling. He would also need a mic that would withstand the explosive wind and breath sounds generated from his movement and style of singing. Mics designed for this purpose have a special filter called a **pop** or **blast** filter that will stabilize the diaphragm and thereby minimize the distortion and allow truer sound reproduction. Performance mics are often used at very close range. Any viewer of rock stars on TV will see that they practically swallow the mic as they sing. Mics used for this purpose must have the characteristics that enhance the singer's vocal qualities, including a bass rolloff feature to minimize a booming low-frequency sound or a boost of the upper midrange frequencies. Another common design feature of performance mics is the ability to reject background noise to permit a higher amplification level for the desired sound before getting audio feedback in the system. For artists who prefer holding their microphones, lightweight mics are a necessity.

Multiple-Application Microphones

Some microphones are now designed and marketed to be used in a wide variety of applications. These mics are designed so that they are able to provide different pickup patterns in different situations. The mics designed in this way are also known as convertible or system mics. These mics often come with a standard power module and several attachments that allow different configurations for various applications. Some mics change configuration by the flip of a switch. Essentially, this type of mic can function as a handheld, omnidirectional, unidirectional mic, or even one or more variations of the special cardioid patterns to provide the pickup abilities of various types of shotgun mics. As with any multi-purpose tool, this type of mic may not be as good in any one configuration as the best mic of that type. However, this slight trade-off of some excellence for versatility is a worthwhile one for many users with limited budgets but a wide range of audio pickup needs.

Headset Microphones

Headset microphones are mounted on a bracket with one or two earphones attached. This headset is worn on the head of announcers in both radio and TV. Their use in TV can be seen most often in sporting event announcing and network reporters on the floor of the political conventions. (See Figure 4.9.)

The headset mic has a mini-boom that holds the mic in place very close to the announcer's mouth. This is especially important in situations where the announcer may have to turn his head to follow action or receive information from another person. This mic can have either a dynamic or condenser element. Its pickup pattern is cardioid, because the important sounds are coming from one source, the announcer's mouth, which is located an inch or less in front of the mic.

Surface-Mount and Pressure-Zone Microphones

Surface-mount and pressure-zone microphones, also called boundary mics, are usually used in situations where two or more people are the sources for audio to be recorded or broadcast, and these people are positioned in front of a flat surface such as the floor or a table. (See Figure 4.10.)

The polar pickup patterns of these mics are somewhat different than conventional mics. The mics come with both omni- and unidirectional patterns, but only one hemisphere of the omnidirectional sphere or unidirectional heart shape is available.

When this type of mic is unidirectional, it can be used to isolate a particular vocalist or part of a musical group. It can also function as a single instrument mic, for example, for a bass drum, by placing the mic on the floor directly in front of the instrument.

You can create your own boundary mic with mics you already have. By taking a hand mic or lav and laying it parallel to the floor or any boundary surface, pointing it to the center of the sound source, and raising it just slightly (1 or 2 mm) off that surface with a bit of tape or something else small, you can achieve a close approximation of an actual boundary mic.

Wireless Microphones

In numerous situations a standard microphone is appropriate for the audio needs of a production situation, but the use of audio cable is not. The wireless microphone, often referred to as a radio-frequency (RF) mic, frees the person being mic'd from the tether of an audio cable, which is often aesthetically undesirable or downright impractical in film or TV shots. (See Figure 4.11.)

A wireless microphone system can consist of any standard mic connected to a small portable radio transmitter. (See Figure 4.12.)

The belt pack radio transmitter is attached to the person being mic'd, or a plug-on is attached directly

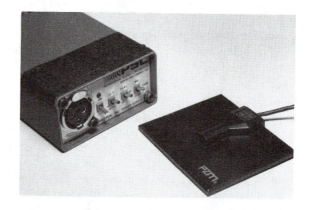

Figure 4.10 This boundary mic by Crown called a PZM® can be mounted on any surface such as a tabletop or a floor. The power supply with this mic has controls to change the sensitivity and filters to shape the frequency response to get the best sound from varying conditions.

Figure 4.9 Headset mics like those used by sportscasters. Courtesy of Shure Brothers, Inc.

Figure 4.11 Wireless hand mic. Courtesy of Shure Brothers, Inc.

mon in the 1970s and 1980s are no longer available today. Many older RF mics are now actually illegal per the FCCs rules. For that reason most wirelesses sold today are UHF (450 MHz and above). They provide much better range and reliability although they do cost more. When you buy a professional wireless mic, you will be asked where the mic will be used before being assigned a VHF or UHF frequency depending on which you buy. Many of the UHF frequencies are the same as those used for digital TV transmitters. So you now must avoid not only the analog transmitters but the digital ones as well. The spectrum is truly getting squeezed throughout the country. Therefore, a mic bought for use in Boston may not work well in Chicago, and so on. Production crews traveling

to the mic or any other audio source, and sends the radio signal encoded with the audio information to a receiver. With a very good system the receiver may be at a location up to one-quarter mile away, although the standard receiving distance is usually no more than 100 feet. Some hand microphones have the transmitter built into the mic shaft itself.

Although wireless mics are essential in location TV work, they should be treated as temperamental. A great many factors can arise to interfere with the signal. This is particularly true in urban environments where various electrical sources and other RF signals from standard broadcasting and point-to-point communications generate radio-frequency interference.

RF mics come in two frequency ranges: VHF (very high frequency) and UHF (ultra high frequency). Years ago VHF frequencies (174 to 216 MHz) were very popular because they worked fairly well and were cheap to buy. But they were also very susceptible to interference of all kinds. Toward the end of the 1990s the entire radio-frequency spectrum was reshuffled by the FCC to accommodate digital TV and a host of new users. Most frequencies com-

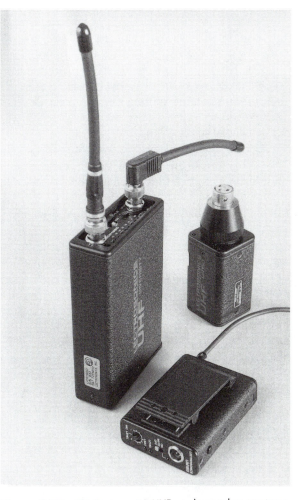

Figure 4.12 This Lectrosonics UHF wireless set has two transmitters, a plug-on and a belt pack (only one can be used at a time). The receiver is a diversity type with two antenna systems.

around the country try to carry wireless systems that can change frequencies to adapt to the local airwaves. These wireless mics are called **frequency agile**. Even with these, if more than one set of wirelesses is being used, the soundperson must take care to make sure the frequencies are spread out from one another to avoid interference. A large production or a network news crew may use up to eight wireless mics at one time. Keeping them all clear can be a headache, especially when traveling.

One of the biggest causes of interference is reflected radio waves from the transmitter striking the receiver at different times, just like reflected audio waves cause echo. The path between transmitter and receiver must be as clear of obstructions as possible, especially anything made of metal. To further improve your chances of getting a good signal, make sure the receiving and transmitting antennas are parallel; in other words, one cannot be horizontal while the other is vertical. Also be sure that they are not curled or bunched up if they are the soft type.

One type of wireless that cures some of the interference problems is the **diversity** system. In effect, in this system each transmitter has two receivers. The system switches seamlessly to whichever receiver has the best signal so there is no interruption of the sound.

Getting the signal into the typical wireless **belt-pack** transmitter (the type most commonly used) is not as easy as it might look. Each brand of transmitter has its own special cable connector, and it is not usually compatible with anything else. You will need an adapter cable that goes from a female XLR to the particular transmitter's connector type in order to attach a microphone to it. Because most wireless situations call for the use of a lav mic, it is beneficial to have one wired to plug directly into the transmitter. The transmitter will supply the lav with the necessary power to operate so the lav power supply is not needed. Some transmitters, called **plug-ons**, can be plugged directly into an audio line or the bottom of a mic. They are more bulky and cannot be hidden on a person as easily as the belt-pack can.

ACCESSORIES

Differing applications and locations demand that microphones be flexible enough to be positioned in various places under numerous conditions. To get acceptable sound, many accessories are available to the audio technician for mounting the mic and ensuring that quality sound can be gathered under adverse conditions.

Mounts

Microphones are not freestanding instruments and require a device or mounting system to keep them secured in place. For interviewing or sound collection on location, this is most often accomplished by simply holding the mic by hand. Mics without a built-in feature for mounting require a bracket or most commonly a mic clasp. (See Figure 4.13.) After a clasp is put on the hand mic, the mic is adaptable to the vast majority of mic-mounting devices, including studio booms, floor stands, desk stands, gooseneck stands, and a variety of stands for special applications.

Acoustic Filters and Windscreens

Some microphones are designed to cope with problems inherent in close mic'ing. Inexperienced announcers and people who are being interviewed may pop their *P*s, speak too loudly or forcefully, or blast the microphone with too much sound. Many mics now have pop-and-blast filters built into them to correct these problems. These filters are contained inside the mic housing; the sound must pass through them before striking the diaphragm. Some pop filters are designed for use in front of the mic rather than inside it. These filters, made of a mesh material, can be positioned between the speaker/singer and the mic.

Windscreens are foam-rubber-like casings designed to fit over the top of a microphone. Almost all hand mics, lavalieres, and headset microphones can be used with windscreens to reduce the sound made by air currents or wind. The effectiveness of this type of

Figure 4.13 Mic clasp for attaching a mic to a stand. Courtesy of Shure Brothers, Inc.

windscreen can vary greatly depending on the nature of the mic. In general, the more directional a mic is, the more susceptible it is to wind noise and the harder it is to protect. Because shotgun mics are the most affected by wind, a simple foam windscreen is not enough to achieve quality audio under windy conditions. For optimum sound, a shotgun is used in a basket-type windscreen called a **zeppelin**. This device surrounds the mic with a space of dead air while allowing most audible frequencies to pass through. (See Figure 4.14.)

AUDIO CABLES AND CONNECTORS

To complete the technical chain of an audio system, the signal must get to a recording device through an electrical interface: a cable and its connectors.

Balanced and Unbalanced Lines

An unbalanced line is the type of audio line found in most consumer-level audio products, such as home camcorders and cassette recorders. The cable consists of a single conductor carrying the positive signal and a shield carrying the negative signal of a circuit. While this type of line is fine for most consumer needs, it is limited to cable lengths of less than 10 feet to maintain quality and can be susceptible to outside electrical interference, especially in cable lengths of more than 10 feet. This type of line is not recommended for any professional use.

In a balanced audio line, the mic signal is carried by two leads instead of one. The shield is the ground

so that the conductor leads are completely isolated from other electrical components. A balanced line is far less susceptible to RF interference and ground loop hum found in unbalanced lines. If you must connect a balanced line to an unbalanced line, it is best to have a one-to-one isolation transformer between the two. This device keeps the ground loop of the unbalanced line from inducing hum or noise in the balanced line.

Connectors and Adapters

The standard connector for balanced audio lines is the three-contact **XLR**-type, sometimes referred to as a **canon connector**. The input end of an XLR cable is always a female connector (receptacles for the connector pins), and the output end is always a male connector (the connector pins). A microphone always has a male connector. The XLR connectors are the only type used in professional audio recording but may not be the only types encountered in field production or news gathering. (See Figure 4.15.)

It is typical in ENG work to be asked to record audio sources from a wide variety of systems in the field. A good audio kit should include adapters to tap into any of these systems. (See Figure 4.16.) The most common is the 1/4-inch phone plug. This plug comes in balanced (stereo) and unbalanced (mono) versions. In most cases you will not need a stereo signal. This 1/4-inch connector is the most common way to tap into a house PA system or audio mixing board not designed for video production. The output of such systems is usually labeled "monitor out" and is typically mono at mic level but can be line level or even a nonstandard level. Many video supply companies sell

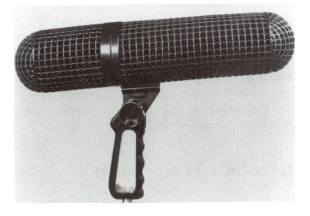

Figure 4.14 A zeppelin system is used for cutting down wind noise. Courtesy Light Wave Systems, Van Nuys, CA.

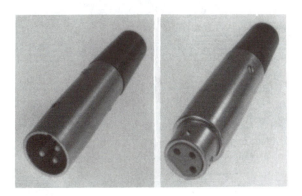

Figure 4.15 Audio-balanced line (XLR) connectors. Courtesy Comprehensive Video Supply Corp., Northvale, NJ.

adapters that are 1/4-inch phone (stereo or mono) at one end and XLR at the other.

Other connectors that you are likely to encounter in the field are the 1/8-inch or mini-plug, the RCA-type connector that your stereo uses, the micro-plug, such as those found in those miniature tape recorders, and a modular telephone line plug. While adapters are available to convert these plugs to XLR, it is quite easy to make up short cables with the different types of connectors at each input end and an XLR at the other.

Signal Loss in Audio Cable

A mic level signal is able to travel up to 200 feet or more with insignificant loss of signal strength. On very long runs, a loss of some audio frequencies may occur as well as an increased susceptibility to hum or electrical interference. For long distances, it may be necessary to amplify the audio with a mixer near the source end to deliver enough signal strength to the cable destination. By amplifying the signal to line level from mic level, a higher quality signal with less hum can be transferred over a greater distance.

Phase

If the polarity of the audio cables or mics used in a single system does not match, the signal may be out of phase and cause the cancellation of some frequencies or the entire signal itself. This can be a very tricky problem to track down without the use of a volt-ohm meter or a cable tester. While this problem is not common, it is possible. If you find a cable or source that is out of phase, a small in-line adapter can reverse the phase (polarity) of the audio line, or you can rewire the cable or connector.

Filters and Pads

A variety of in-line filters and pads in barrel style are available that aid the audio-gathering process. These items can be invaluable in getting the most out of your mics and overcoming weak points in your audio system. The barrel style allows you to put the filter or pad in the audio line at any point where there is a connection.

Switchable Attenuator Pad. A switchable attenuator pad reduces impedance by 15, 20, or 25 dB to avoid overload distortion at the recorder from too strong a signal. It also comes in handy for matching audio signals of nonstandard strengths.

Line Adapter. A line adapter is a 50-dB attenuator that reduces line level to mic level. Whereas the output level of many mixers, VCRs, and amplifiers is at line level, many recorders and most wireless transmitters only accept mic-level input.

High-Pass Filter. A high-pass filter reduces bass and rumble by rolling off the low frequencies. This filter is good for reducing air-conditioner noise and wind rumble.

Low-Pass Filter. A low-pass filter reduces hiss by rolling off the high frequencies.

Presence Adapter. A presence adapter gives a slight boost in the upper midrange of frequencies to enhance the quality of the human voice.

Response Shaper. A response shaper puts a slight dip in the upper midrange of frequencies to reduce the sibilance that can sometimes be present in certain mics or mic'ing situations.

SELECTION AND PLACEMENT

Now that the numerous characteristics of microphones have been explained, it is appropriate to discuss how to use this information to complete the processes of mic selection and mic placement.

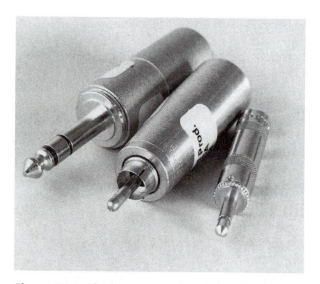

Figure 4.16 The three most popular unbalanced audio connectors; from left to right, 1/4-inch phono plug, RCA type, and 1/8-inch mini-plug.

Choosing a Mic

Mics have varying elements, pickup patterns, frequency responses, impedances, appearances, applications, and special accessories, such as built-in filters. In addition, some mics even have a type of personality, a sound different from other similarly constructed or designed microphones. Because of the variety of choices, it seems that the selection process could be lengthy and complicated. Fortunately, this is not usually the case. Most audio production facilities have a finite selection of mics available for production work. This selection consists of representatives of the different types of mics available: omnidirectional, unidirectional, dynamic, condenser, and so on. Not many production houses would stay in business if they decided to buy an additional microphone whenever the producer or production manager decided that a different mic might be somewhat better than those already owned. High-quality microphones are expensive. Good-quality microphones can often yield high-quality sound in a variety of situations, and many good mics often overlap each other in what they can do well. For example, a cardioid mic is best for many interview situations, but an omnidirectional mic might work just as well if you can keep the extraneous noise in the room low and keep the omnidirectional mic close to the source.

Four factors should be considered when selecting the best mic for any production:

1. What are the general production goals, such as what is the end product supposed to be, how will it be distributed, who will the audience be, and what quality level should be obtained?
2. How much control will there be over the sound environment?
3. How many sound sources are involved in the production?
4. What are the technical aspects of the sound sources, such as frequency and volume?

Placing a Mic

Not only must you choose a mic based on its design characteristics but also based on where the mic must or can be placed. Limitations such as personnel, budget, time, boom shadows, and environmental concerns can dictate which mics you can use. Knowing how to place a particular mic lets you know if that mic is right for the job you have to do. (See Figure 4.17.)

Hand Microphones

A hand mic is often the easiest to use. You simply pick it up and point it at the source of the sound. Singers, TV evangelists, used car salespersons, and TV reporters often use hand mics, which are made for gathering audio close to the source. Meant to be seen on camera most of the time, hand mics do not require a boom person or as much time and hassle to put in place as a hidden lavaliere would require. There is just one hard and fast rule: They must be within about 1 to 2 feet of the source of audio. Some hand mics are shock-mounted within their outer shell to withstand rough handling without creating excessive mechanical noise. The Electro-Voice RE-50 is a shock-mounted mic well suited for ENG work. (See Figure 4.18.)

A news photographer working without a soundperson may have no choice but to give the reporter a hand mic to gather almost all the audio, especially for interviews and stand-ups. The hand mic allows the reporter to place the mic where it can get the best sound. If the news crew is talking to a gathering of steel workers outside a closed factory, the reporter can maneuver the mic to whichever person is talking while being able to bring the mic back to record the questions as well. The biggest problem is, if you are not using a shock-mounted mic, the sound of fidgeting fingers on the mic can be very distracting.

In EFP work the hand mic is used more often as a prop and not out of necessity as in ENG. Because the quality of the audio is more important in EFP, it is not a good idea to leave the handling and placement of the mic in the hands of the talent. That is why most EFP crews have a soundperson. Some talent, such as a used car salesperson, likes to have a mic to hold onto like a security blanket. It may in fact be just a prop with the actual sound being recorded by an unseen mic. If you have time, budget, or personnel, there are usually better ways to get that audio in many situations. The best exception to this rule is in the case of singers, but even they are now going to the new micro-headset mics (such as those Madonna and Garth Brooks have used) to free their hands for instrument playing or dancing.

Even when a hand mic is used on a floor or desk stand, it still must be within the 2-foot range to obtain good-quality sound. As the mic is placed further from the sound source, the risk of the audio sounding hollow or having an echo is increased. For a news conference at which several people seated at a long table are to speak, using more than one mic is a good alternative. It is best to follow the rule of three to one

Figure 4.17 Sometimes good sound pickup requires unusual microphone placement.

Figure 4.18 An RE-50 omnidirectional dynamic mic with a shock-mount housing. Courtesy of Electro-Voice, Inc.

in the placement of the mics, however many people are present. This principle says that for every unit of distance between the mic and the audio source, the distance between mics should be at least three times greater. The greater the directionality of the mic, the less chance there is of phase problems from reflected sounds or multiple mics.

Camera-Mounted Microphones

The best mic to mount on a camera is the ultradirectional type, although any type of mic can be used. A shotgun microphone will pick up audio mostly from the camera's field of vision. Distant sounds that come from the sides (outside of the picture) are not picked up nearly as well. Even in highly directional mics, there are still flanges (off-axis lobes) of sound pickup to the side and rear areas of the mic. Although those flanges are not as sensitive as the on-axis lobes of the polar response chart, they may still pick up some unwanted sounds, such as the reporter whispering in your ear next to the side of the mic while you are shooting.

Sound gathered at the camera is usually referred to as **background (BG) audio.** Most producers refer to it as **natural sound,** or the sound the camera naturally hears. It is the most valuable sound an ENG person can get. Natural sound is what makes many pictures come alive. Having it can mean the difference in keeping your job or losing it. Some news photographers try to use their camera mic to do reporterless interviews. Under certain time pressures or acoustic conditions this may be acceptable, but most of the time it is not. The photographer places the camera (and therefore the mic) as close to the subject as possible to reduce the amount of background noise (unwanted audio) from this interview so the person sounds more on-mic. The net effect here is okay sound but a picture that has its perspective (and therefore its subject) distorted. It can make people's heads and their features seem enlarged or out of proportion. Of course any mic can be used to gather natural sound or BG, but for one-person crews, the camera mic is the standard tool for achieving that end.

Boom Microphones

Although any microphone can be placed on a boom, the most common one used on booms is the shotgun. The portable boom or fishpole allows its operator to place the mic in the optimum position to gather the best audio. This is a common way for production crews and larger news organizations to gather audio in the field. Good teamwork between the photographer and the soundperson can keep the mic out of the picture but in the right place to get the best audio. The task of the boom operator is to keep the desired sound source on axis while aiming the mic away from other distracting sounds. In the case of the reporter interviewing people on the street, a fishpole can be used by an audio person to do what a hand mic does, only without the mic being seen. This gives a more natural, realistic look. The audio person lines the mic up with the person's mouth at an angle to avoid having it also pointed at, say, the street or an idling car at the curb. Most of the time the mic is at waist level, as close to the person as possible and pointed up. The fishpole can also be held above and pointed down to the audio source, but this increases the possibility of

reflected sound being gathered if the ground is a hard surface, such as concrete. (See Figure 4.19.)

Mini-Microphones

Lavs or mini-mics can be the best sounding but most frustrating mics to use in field productions. They are by far the most susceptible to mechanical noise caused by material rubbing against not only the capsule but the cable as well. Extra care is needed when using this type of mic. The most common use of a lav is on someone's tie, jacket, or shirt. The most common lav clasp is the alligator clip. You simply clip on to any edge or fold of material. The two most common mistakes in using lavs are not hiding the mic cable and not properly securing it. (See Figure 4.20.)

Seeing people being interviewed on TV using a lav simply hanging from the front of their clothes is a major distraction. It just looks sloppy. This leads us to another problem. It is natural for everyone to move somewhat during a conversation. If the mic is placed incorrectly or the cable is not secured, a little movement translates into a horrendous scratching sound called mic rustle.

You must use considerable care when choosing where to attach a mic to a person. Look for a spot that is nondistracting to the camera and will not be brushed against by any part of the person's clothing or jewelry. Next, make sure the cable is fastened down so that it cannot pull on the mic. The easiest way is to loop the cord to the back of the alligator clip and pinch it with the material used to hold the mic. The other way is to use a fabric tape or a similar product such as surgical tape (from any drug store) to tape the cable to the inside of the clothing. For an active subject wearing a lav, both procedures are highly recommended.

Many other devices are available for attaching lav mics. The second most popular is the pin or "vampire" clip. This holder attaches to the cable and has two fine stick pins that catch the subject's clothing. It is used extensively when hiding the mic under clothing. Care must be taken not to damage the material or prick the subject.

Because lavs are so small, most EFP users prefer hiding them in the person's clothing. This is not an easy job, but the results are well worth the effort. This mic placement can make everyone wearing one sound good in any kind of production without any hint of a mic being present. There are many ways to

Figure 4.19 A soundman using a shotgun mic on a boom pole can get good audio from the subject without having the mic in the shot.

hide a lav that is often no bigger than a small pea. The dangers are clothing rustle and muffling. The mic capsule must be as unobstructed as possible even if it is already under the clothing. The mic must be taped down with several inches of tape between clothing layers with the capsule taped on both sides and only the grill area of the capsule left exposed. If the mic goes between clothing and skin, the mic can be taped directly to the skin using surgical tape or the equivalent. Sometimes a little funnel made of tape or even very soft leather can be fashioned to shield a hidden mic from rustle. This process is tricky and may take some trial and error to perfect.

Wireless Microphones

The distinguishing factor about a wireless mic is not the mic, but the means of transmitting the audio from a mic to a receiver at the recorder. Of all the types of mics, using a wireless is the most dramatic in its results. There is nothing like hearing someone perfectly and seemingly "up-close" who is obviously some distance from the camera or who is moving about the set or location, yet without seeing a microphone or cable in the shot.

Combining the use of the wireless with the hidden mic can truly free up your subjects to be as natu-

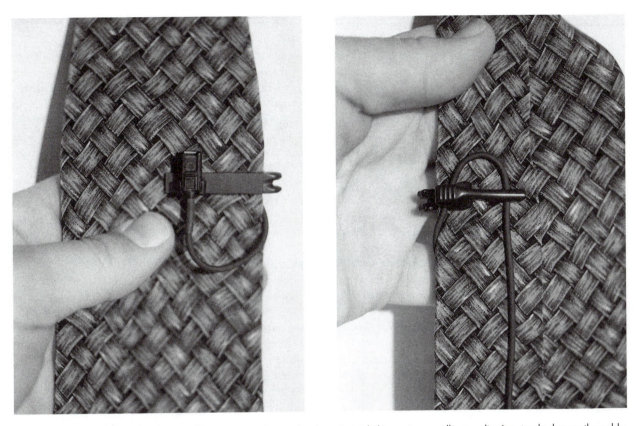

Figure 4.20 A front and back view of how to properly attach a lav mic to clothing using an alligator clip. It not only dresses the cable but helps dampen cable noise.

ral as they can be. Wireless mics have become so popular in all forms of EFP that most producers simply will not work without them. They have become as important as, if not more important than, boom mics to get high-quality audio without a mic being on camera. A wireless allows the talent to roam the location cable free, to turn backwards to the camera while still being on-mic, and to have close-in mic sound. With extensive use of wirelesses, any production can take on a more natural sound, as if the viewer were actually there.

The use of wireless mics has also made quite a difference in news gathering. Veteran news producer Ray Farkas has made extensive use of wireless mics on stories for the networks and other news outlets. Farkas has been the pioneer in using wireless sound and leading photojournalism into a new sound era. By eliminating the boom mic and placing the camera and crew a great distance from the subject, Farkas is able to relax the video subjects so completely that they forget they are wearing a mic and being video-

taped. The results have commonly become known as the "Farkas interview," an interview that is not only more conversational in tone but actually looks like the viewer is eavesdropping on a private conversation. This technique can make a simple news story more compelling to watch and more convincing. Although no staging is allowed in journalism, the obvious presence of camera, lights, and mics can make an interview look more like a TV show than a slice of real life. Farkas's highly stylized technique may not suit all or even many of the traditional looks of TV news, but it does represent what attention to the audio-gathering process can do for editorial content.

Even without the more complex uses that Farkas has developed, the wireless is an invaluable tool for any everyday news crew. Besides wiring a subject for better natural sound or walking interviews, the wireless can be plugged into PA systems or placed on podiums at meetings and gatherings so that the camera can go anywhere within the location and still have a house audio feed. The wireless can be quickly and easily placed anywhere within a scene to get a close-in presence to the sound.

Even if you cannot plug in directly or put the mic at the source of the audio at an event that has a PA system (**house sound**), you may be able to place the wireless directly in front of the PA speaker. The audio is not as good as a direct feed, but if the sound system does not have excessive buzz or hum, you can still get house sound. The small size of wireless transmitters allows you to place the mics just about anywhere. If you are shooting a long line of Super Bowl ticket buyers, you might simply set the wireless on the counter at one of the ticket windows. You could then make a shot from anywhere around the window and still have great audio from the activity there. One shot may be from the end of the line with the window in the background as the viewer hears the conversation at the window. This helps focus the viewer on what is taking place. The technique may also be as simple as putting the mic at the stream's edge for a wide shot of a beautiful valley as canoeists pass through it. The camera is up on the side of a small hill, but the audio is of the water flowing in the stream below and the sounds of the canoeists as they pass through the shot. Synchronous sound that you could not get with the mic at the camera position can now be gathered with creative use of the wireless. It is this simple and subtle use of close-in sound that can make a good video story into a great one.

MONITORING, MIXING, AND STEREO

After you have selected the appropriate mic, mount, filter, and screen, and achieved proper placement, you need to consider other aspects of the sound-recording process. Multiple microphones for any given sound situation require combining signals, called **mixing**. To ensure that your sound is appropriate for your situation, you must also learn to monitor the sound. A brief mention is also made here about stereo-sound recording.

Monitoring

While the performance of your equipment may be well known, you cannot really know if everything is working fine unless you actually hear what you are getting. (See Figure 4.21.)

A good pair of headphones is absolutely mandatory for any audio person, and at least a good ear piece is essential for a one-person operation. Without hearing what you are getting, an unheard problem can make all your efforts worthless. Most professional VCRs offer a confidence playback head in the audio-recording circuit. This system allows you to actually hear the sound on the tape after it has been recorded while you are still recording. The playback head passes over the tape about 1 second after the record head lays down the audio. Because of this delay, confidence audio sounds weird because it is out of sync with what you are seeing. Most photographers and audio persons only spot-check the confidence circuit occasionally during the recording process because of the distraction.

It takes some practice to "hear" audio. Even with a good set of isolation headphones it is hard to separate the audio you are monitoring and the sounds that are bleeding through the headset. If the headset is turned up too loud, you may think the background noise is excessive when in reality it is not. It takes the experience of doing field recordings and playing them back in the studio to become comfortable with knowing what you're getting on location.

Mixing

The last stage that audio is likely to go through is some form of mixing before it is recorded at the VCR. To mix audio it first needs to be monitored. Whenever more than one mic is being recorded on a single audio channel, it is best to use a mixer to make sure each mic can be separately controlled to ensure the best performance.

Popular professional, portable mixers have three or four input channels, frequency cut filters on each, a tone generator, two bridged output lines, and a master output volume control. They can take line or mic-level impedance inputs and send mic or line level out. They can also feed phantom power to condenser-type mics on any channel. Most importantly, they are usually stereo with each channel capable of being panned right or left. This ability lets the operator place only the audio of channel 1's input on the channel 1 output by panning channel 1 to the left. Panning channel 2's control to the right would place its audio on the channel 2 output only. Additional channels can also be panned to either output channel. The audio person then has the flexibility of isolating or combining signals to the recording tracks in the camera.

Figure 4.21 Even where there is a one-person crew, it is necessary to use headphones to constantly monitor the audio and its quality. Photo by John Lebya.

Figure 4.22 An M4A+ stereo mixer from PSC designed to be used in the field for ENG and EFP.

These portable mixers are very popular for use with camcorders. Two record channels on the VCR can be set up with a tone signal from the mixer; the input volume adjustments can be made at the mixer and no further attention is required at the camera. In some cases, the sound person will use a wireless mic to send the output of the mixer to the camcorder, thus allowing the photographer to roam freely while the audio person can go wherever the best sound-gathering location is.

Stereo

At the time of this writing and for the foreseeable future, stereo audio in most field productions and news gathering is not practical. Such factors as the mics used and critical mixing techniques make stereo recording a very demanding job in the field. More effort is required at the time of recording than most productions can afford—and typical news gathering will never allow the time needed for stereo recording.

5 Light: Understanding and Controlling It

Lighting is probably the most overlooked, misunderstood, and feared aspect of ENG and EFP. Very often, light kits are low-priority items in budgets for field gear and subsequently, especially in days of lean budgets, well-appointed light kits are never purchased. Existing kits often go for months without replacement bulbs, again a result of the low priority assigned to remote lighting beyond the camera light and one basic light for live shots. Today's cameras boast of their low-light capabilities, creating the impression that lights simply aren't needed anymore. That impression, coupled with the limitations of trunk space, crew members, and setup time, means the portable light kits are often left at the station, in the studio, or in the vehicle. And that is a huge mistake.

It seems odd that lighting equipment gets such casual treatment; after all, without light there would be no photography—video or otherwise. Especially when using relatively inexact video cameras, you must pay constant attention to the lighting factor to produce a realistic image.

Portable video practitioners may treat lighting casually because much of their work is done outdoors. Available sunlight provides enough light to allow the video cameras to see the desired scene and record the action. But seeing is not always good enough. With some additional lighting effort and consideration, the camera will not only see the scene and the action, but it will also detect additional mood, dimension, interest, focus, and indeed understanding in a good video segment.

This chapter looks at the very nature of light. Its qualities, its quantities, and the instruments that create and shape it. We will also discuss the basics of lighting theory and technique and how they relate to the content of any video production—both ENG and EFP—to go beyond simply making the subject visible to the camera.

PART ONE: THE PHYSICAL PROPERTIES OF LIGHT

WHAT IS LIGHT?

Without light there would be no picture. A good knowledge of the physical and artistic characteristics of light is a prerequisite of understanding TV photography in any form.

Photons and Light Waves

Light is just one part of the total electromagnetic radiation spectrum, but, unlike other forms of this type of energy, light is visible radiant energy. Actually made up of very small energy particles called **photons,** light follows the common rules associated with all wave physics. The big difference between light and x-rays or radio waves is its inability to penetrate solid objects. Light is easily deflected. In fact, except for the light source itself, reflection is the only way light can be seen. Shining a bright light into a dark night sky produces no evidence of that light from the side or below unless some dust, fog, or other material crosses the path of the light and reflects it. Light is visible only when we see its effect as it strikes an object.

The photons released by the light source travel in a straight line away from the source at the same speed. The sun is the best example of a light source. Points at the same distance away from any side of the sun receive the same amount of light.

Photons travel in that straight line until they encounter something. In space, that may be quite a long time, but once they reach Earth, it doesn't take much to start blocking them. Our atmosphere, which is actually very thin by the standards of physics, blocks a great deal of sunlight striking Earth. Some of the light is absorbed by the air and converted into heat; some is reflected by the air, which is the source of our beautiful blue skies. The same is true as light strikes the surface of the planet. Everyone notices that a black car sitting in the sun gets a lot hotter than a white car. The black car is absorbing the light and its energy, while the white car is reflecting most of it. Photography concerns itself with both the reflected light and the absorbed light. Knowing that light always travels in straight lines and how light is absorbed or reflected is the key to understanding so much of what is modern photography and how today's video equipment works.

Spectrum

Like all electromagnetic radiation, light can be classified by its wavelength or frequency. In addition to its speed (186,282 miles per second), light waves can be measured in units called **nanometers** (**nm**). Visible light, or white light, contains all the wavelengths between 400 and 700 nm. Wavelengths shorter than 400 nm go from ultraviolet and x-ray to gamma and cosmic (the shortest). Wavelengths longer than 700 nm go from infrared and radar to broadcast signals such as TV and radio transmissions (the longest).

Shining any light through a prism reveals the various frequencies that make up that light; these frequencies will be bent at different rates according to their wavelengths. The resulting light on the other side of the prism appears as a rainbow. This represents the spectrum of frequencies contained in that light. In nanometers, the colors in the rainbow range from violet (400 to 430 nm) to green (492 to 550 nm) to red (647 to 700 nm). Lights that have a continuous spectrum have all of the wavelengths between 400 and 700 nm present. Not all light sources have continuous spectrums and not all wavelengths within any spectrum are present in equal amounts. Sunlight has much more energy in the shorter wavelengths (blue, indigos, and violets), whereas filament light (such as the common household lamp) has more energy in the longer wavelengths (oranges and reds). (See Figure 5.1.)

THE COLOR OF LIGHT

The brain is color-adaptive to what the eyes see. We tend not to notice the difference in the relative colors of light sources. The light in our homes at night seems to be the same color as light in our yards at noon. To the optical prism or the objective camera, the color of light in those two situations is very different. Taking

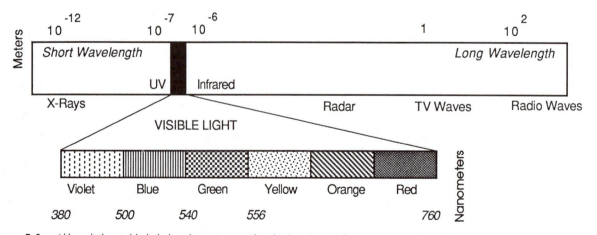

Figure 5.1 Although the visible light band is narrow, within this band are differences in wavelength that determine the color of light. Graphic courtesy Manny Romero.

still photos with standard film stock indoors at night using just the lamps in the room for light results in pictures tinged with orange. The film, rated for daylight use, is designed to recreate realistic colors only in daylight. A video camera operates in much the same way as the film. Thus, the understanding of light is crucial for us to create the end product we desire.

Primary Additive Colors

The color emitted by any wavelength of light is referred to as its hue or tint. When all the wavelengths are combined we get white light. But when just specific individual colors (frequencies) are combined, the result is yet another color. For example, combining a pure green and a pure red light produces yellow light. Within the visible spectrum, red, blue, and green are known as the **primary additive colors.** Combinations of these three colors in various ratios can be made to create all other visible colors. This gives a very basic explanation of why three-chip cameras divide the light coming through the lens into red, green, and blue. Mixtures of the information from these chips can be regenerated into the full-color image the camera is shooting. If these primary colors of light are combined in equal amounts, the result is white light.

Subtractive Primary Colors

The primary colors that an artist uses for painting or that a lab uses to make a color photograph are magenta (reddish blue), cyan (blue green), and yellow. These three primary colors are called the **subtractive primary colors.** Mixing materials such as dyes or pigments of these colors will yield different results than mixing the colors of light. Mixing magenta, cyan, and yellow paint together yields black, not white.

Color Temperature

Although our eyes generally perceive most light as being white, it generally is not, technically speaking. Although the additive properties of any light's spectrum allow objects of any color to be perceived correctly once our eyes and brain have made the necessary adjustments, the amounts of each frequency in the spectrum may vary by quite a bit. Light sources with a predominance of higher frequencies (more energy) tend to be bluish, and those with lower frequencies (lower energy) tend to be red. Thanks to Lord Kelvin, we have a very convenient way of quan-

tifying the color of a light source. The thermometric scale he invented is used to measure the temperature of a light source in degrees of Kelvin (K). This measurement is known as the **color temperature** of the light. Low temperatures (around 2000° K) are very red, and high temperatures (around 9000° K) are very blue. (See Figure 5.2.)

Because all artificial light is created by heating or applying energy to a known material, such as a tungsten filament inside a light bulb, it is possible to predetermine the color temperature of that source.

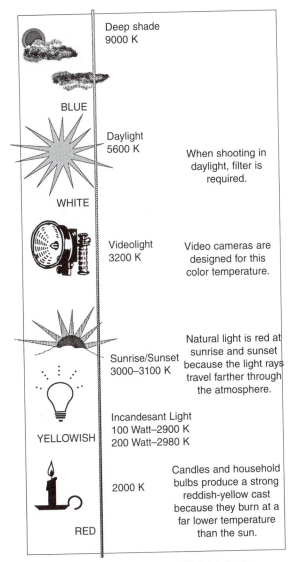

Deep shade
9000 K

BLUE

Daylight
5600 K

When shooting in daylight, filter is required.

WHITE

Videolight
3200 K

Video cameras are designed for this color temperature.

Sunrise/Sunset
3000–3100 K

Natural light is red at sunrise and sunset because the light rays travel farther through the atmosphere.

Incandesant Light
100 Watt–2900 K
200 Watt–2980 K

YELLOWISH

2000 K

Candles and household bulbs produce a strong reddish-yellow cast because they burn at a far lower temperature than the sun.

RED

The Color Temperature (Kelvin) Scale

Figure 5.2 This chart represents how video cameras respond to different kinds of light. Graphic by Manny Romero.

Indeed, even the sun acts as a huge filament burning at a constant temperature. This consistency allows a photographer to judge with some certainty what color of light exists within any scene.

THE DIRECTION AND SIZE OF A LIGHT SOURCE

Two additional factors that determine the quality of light are its direction or angle to the subject and scene and the spectral quality or harshness of the light source. Again, our eyes tend to make up for a lot of the things the camera simply cannot do. We see in stereo, or three dimensions, so depth perception is generally not a problem. The camera does not. And, for the most part, we see details equally well in the shadows of a scene or face as we do in the areas that are lit. Again, the camera does not.

The Angle of Light

In the two-dimensional world of the TV screen, the only way we can perceive depth—the third dimension—is by the shadows present. The shadows or dark areas of the picture convey a multitude of information about the subject or scene. Shadows can let us see the texture of a surface. They can give us the time of day or even the season of the year. They can relate the mood of the situation. They can define the area of main interest within the frame. But above all, they define the space we are seeing.

With the source of light behind the camera and very close to the lens, a scene is almost without shadow. This look is referred to as **flat lighting**. It is hard to perceive depth, texture, or spatial relationships in the picture. As the light source moves away from the lens, we start to see how the shadows fall both on the objects creating them (attached shadows) and on their surroundings (unattached shadows). These shadows are the chief determinate of the quality of light. When any great photographer refers to the quality of light he or she is talking about the direction of the light or, more simply, the shadows created by it. Flat lighting of an area of a scene or a face within a scene may be desirable at times, but flat lighting an entire scene should be avoided. Later, we will discuss the manipulation and meaning of shadows in more depth, in the section on lighting styles and technique (Part Three of this chapter).

Hard and Soft Light

It is impossible to describe the quality of light without talking about both the shadow and its edge: the area of transition between what is lit and what is not. One simple factor determines the difference between hard and soft light: the size of the source in relationship to its distance from the subject. This factor is often referred to as a light's ability to **wrap**. Hard light is created by very small sources of light as seen from the area being lit.

The sun is an excellent example of a hard source. It may be many times the size of the Earth, but because of its distance, it appears to us as a very small object. The shadows created by it on a cloudless day are razor sharp. As you look at your own shadow on the pavement, you see a perfect outline. Now, let a small cloud move in front of the sun. The sun is no longer—technically speaking—the light source: It is now the cloud. To us, the cloud is much larger than the sun. Now look at your shadow on the ground. It's fuzzy and the shape is ill defined. We now have an example of a soft light source. That fuzzy nature of the shadow is the result of the light wrapping around the object (you). The source is larger than the subject; either wider or taller or both. That defines soft light.

Keep this distance relationship in mind as you go through the rest of the chapter, and certainly when you are on location setting up lights. Lighting instruments that are called soft lights are only soft at certain distances from the subject. A soft light set up at 30 feet from the subject is not going to be nearly as soft (have as much wrap) as when that light is 10 feet from the subject.

THE QUANTITY OF LIGHT

Intensity

The intensity of light has traditionally been measured in units of **foot-candles (fc)**. One foot-candle is the amount of light given off by one candle 1 foot away. Today, more and more, you will see the units of light quantity being expressed in **lux**. One lux is the amount of light at 1 meter from a candle. One foot-candle equals about 11 lux. Because foot-candles are still the more popular way of measuring light, because of all the light meters already in existence, we will continue to use the term here. When you see a camera's low-light performance ratings listed by its manufacturer, it will be in lux.

Light Meters

Light meters are indispensable in film work but are rarely seen on a video shoot because of such factors as auto-iris and seeing what the picture looks like with respect to exposure in the viewfinder and monitor. However, one way to judge your camera's performance and your light's settings is to measure it with an incidence light meter (one that measures the light falling on an object and not reflected from an object). Try all the different lights in your kit one by one and measure the foot-candles at various distances and angles to the light. You will quickly see how much light is given off and how the lights may be aimed or manipulated to put the desired amount in the desired place. You will also see how much light your camera needs to make a good picture. This experiment is particularly good for adjustable lights.

The meter can check the ASA rating (the speed) of your camera or show how many foot-candles it takes to get a good exposure at different f-stops. To do this, set up a gray scale in the light you wish to use. If you don't have a gray scale, use a plain gray card of any form, or even a dull white one in its place. Zoom the camera in so the card fills the frame. Put the camera in auto-iris mode and read the f-stop off the lens. Now measure the amount of light falling on the card with the meter. Adjust the meter's ASA setting until the amount of light measured gives the same f-stop that the camera shows. That will be the ASA rating for that camera when it's on the filter you currently have dialed in. An advanced professional can use a light meter to light a scene without the camera present, to light by a certain formula without a lot of trial and error, or to achieve a certain amount of light to work the lens at a specific f-stop. The light meter can be invaluable in doing site surveys when looking at the quantities of available light. (See Figure 5.3.)

The Inverse Square Law

A lamp placed near us gives off a certain amount of light. If the lamp is moved closer, there is more light; if the lamp is moved away, there is less light. The actual relationship between distance and illumination is often critical in location video work in order to achieve the desired quantity of light on a subject. This relationship is described by a law of physics known as the **inverse square law**, which states that the amount of light diminishes by a factor equal to the

Figure 5.3 A Sekonic light meter that measures the amount of light reaching the subject.

inverse square of the distance change. When the distance between a light and the subject is doubled, the amount of light falling on the subject is reduced to one-quarter of the original amount. As an example, if a light placed 10 feet from the subject produces 100 fc, moving it back to 20 feet away would result in the subject's foot-candles being reduced to 25 (a distance change by a factor of 2; square that to get 4, and then invert it to get 1/4, thus one-fourth the amount of

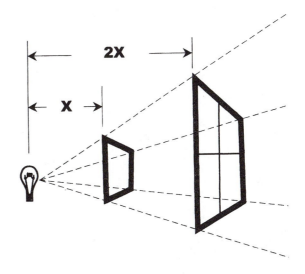

Figure 5.4 Both squares in this drawing receive the same amount of light. Because the second square is twice the distance from the source, that light is spread across four times the area as the first square, or is 1/4 as intense: the inverse square of the distance change.

light). If you move the light to only 5 feet from the subject, you would get 400 fc (a distance change factor of $1/2$; square that to get $1/4$, and then invert it to get 4 or four times the amount of light).

This relationship is of particular importance when lighting subjects that move around within a scene, such as a walking stand-up by a reporter or other on-camera talent. As the subject moves closer to the camera, he or she is also moving closer to the light. If the light is already close to the subject, that distance can easily be cut in half during the walk. As we have just seen, that would increase the amount of light on the subject by 4 times from the start of the walk to the end of it. Not a pretty picture. One way to minimize this effect is to have the lights set as far as possible from the area of the walk. If the subject started at 50 feet from the light and moved to 40 feet from it, the multiplying ratio would only be 1.6 times the amount of light at 40 feet—a much better, and more acceptable, rate of change than 4 times the brightness. We'll discuss other solutions to this problem later in this chapter.

Absorption and Reflection

Earlier, we talked about light's ability to be absorbed and reflected by different colors. These characteristics now come into play when dealing with quantities of light. It is virtually impossible to light a black object. The more light you put on it, the more light is absorbed. What you will quickly notice in doing such an exercise is that it's the reflected light that we really see. If the black object has a shiny surface, we'll see the light's glare. The object never gets any brighter as we add light, but the glare gets worse. The reverse is true for white objects. Just a little addition of light shows up right away: It's almost all being reflected by not only the surface but the color.

These properties of light have to be considered when lighting any scene or subject. A dark wood-paneled room is going to take more light to show up than a room with white plaster walls. But there is more to absorption and reflection than just the color of the surface. Factors such as texture and the angle of the incoming light can change things dramatically.

Texture

A very smooth surface of any color is going to reflect more of the light than a rough surface. The light striking a very smooth surface is efficiently absorbed

by the color and reflected back. As the surface of the object becomes rougher, more and more of the reflected light is restriking raised areas of that surface as it's bouncing up from the recessed areas. The overall amount of light reflected is greatly reduced. If you have a scene with red velour curtains and vinyl seats of the same tone of red, the seats are going to appear much brighter than the curtains. The added texture of the velour is absorbing more of the light.

Angle of Incidence

Another law of physics that applies to lighting is the one governing reflection. As we learned earlier, light travels in straight lines much like a bullet. As a beam of light strikes any surface, some of it is absorbed and turned into heat, some is radiated back from the pigment of the surface revealing its color, and some of it is just plain reflected in the form of what could be called glare. The smoother the surface the more the glare. Unlike the portion of the light coming back as the color of the object, glare is somewhat subjective in where it comes from. A smooth surface acts like a mirror. The light striking it is reflected at a predictable angle. If the beam of light strikes the surface at an angle of 45° measured from the surface in the direction of the light source, the beam will be reflected at a 45° angle to the surface measured from the opposite direction on the surface. The angle of incidence (incoming light) is equal to the angle of reflection (outgoing light). (See Figure 5.5.)

This law of physics will come into play in almost every lighting setup you do. You may have placed the light in the perfect place to create the perfect shadows

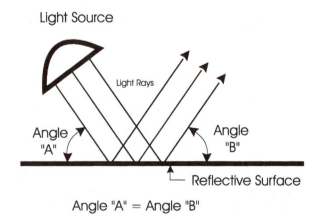

Figure 5.5 Light is reflected at a predictable angle.

but discover that the surface of the object being lit is producing nothing but glare in the direction of the camera. What to do? By remembering the relationship of the light source and where the reflection will be visible, you can readjust whichever element is easiest to eliminate from the picture. In other words, move the light to send the reflection to a point other than at the lens, slightly change the position of the object, or move the camera location or height.

Glare can also work in your favor. Let's go back to that black object we were trying to light earlier; let's say it's a statue of a black cat. By placing one light behind the statue we can create a glare around the edges of it, giving it form and separating it from the rest of the picture. Now by placing a white surface such as an art card at the side of the statue, the card's reflection on the surface of the cat will be seen by the camera. That reflection will show the contours of the statue. The cat will appear to be lit, but in reality it was all done with simple reflections.

To summarize, the quality of light is dependent on two things: color and shadow. Just as the video signal is divided into chrominance and luminance, light is also divided into its color and black-and-white elements. Color depends on which sources you use and what, if any, filter you place in front of them. Shadow depends on the size of those light sources and where you place them. As you go about the job of dealing with light, you should always keep these two factors separated. Each must be dealt with in its own way.

PART TWO: CREATING LIGHT

LIGHT EMITTERS

Even though today's cameras can shoot in nearly any type of light, not all light sources will produce the quality of light you desire. With an understanding of each type of light source, you will be better able to judge the performance of your camera, particularly when it comes to reproducing realistic colors.

The Sun

The single best source of light for portable video, the sun, is also the cheapest and, in many locations, the most readily available as well. The sun can be the hardest light source to manipulate but usually helps make the subject's skin tone appear natural. This is not surprising, because the sun is our natural supplier of light—the light by which we judge reality. Almost everyone has bought clothing in an artificially lit store only to perceive its color quite differently in the sunlight. Mismatched sock wearers often realize the color disparity only after the sun reflects off the socks. Since the sun follows its own schedule, it is necessary to go to great lengths to control it.

As Edison and other early filmmakers quickly discovered, the sun is a great source of illumination for making movies. Unfortunately, this cheap and easy source of natural light has some annoying qualities in addition to the beneficial ones. First, it is not always visible in the daytime. Clouds, smog, mist, trees, buildings, mountains, billboards, and even large people can prevent sunlight from reaching the subject of the video camera. Second, the sun changes position in the sky continuously throughout the day. At early morning, the sun rising in the East strikes the subject in a scene at a low angle. Despite having a constant color temperature before it reaches the earth, sunlight displays varying color temperatures at different times of the day. In the morning, when the sun is low in the sky, its light must travel through a great deal of atmosphere to reach your position. The sun's shorter wavelengths are absorbed faster than the long ones, thus leaving only the redder frequencies. If there are few pollutants or dust particles in the air, the sunrise will be a beautiful yellow or gold color. With dirty air, the rising sun first shows up as a red disc on the horizon giving the scene a pink glow. By noon, the sun is shining almost straight down. The amount of atmosphere it is going through is considerably less. Midday light has regained those bluer frequencies to the point where they dominate. In early morning, sunlight measures about 3500° to 4500° K. Noontime sunlight is 5600° K or higher, and in the late afternoon, the color temperature is similar to early morning, about 2500° to 3000° K. Sunsets are often more red than sunrises because of atmospheric changes created by the midday sunshine adding more moisture and dust to the air. This low-angle sunlight yields less light than the higher angle sunlight characteristic of midday.

Color temperature changes occur throughout the day: You need to white balance every time anything changes, not only for time of day and such things as clear or cloudy skies. The same idea holds true for white balances in sun and shade. This is where many new photographers make mistakes. The temperature on the sunlit street may be 5600° K, but in the deeply shaded courtyard of the apartment complex, the indirect daylight can be 6500° to 7500° K—very blue. Without correction, your video will be very blue, too. Many photographers prefer to balance their camera for 6500° K and not change it as they go from full sun to full shade. Color reproduction in the shade will read true and the colors in full sun will appear slightly warm, which can be good for skin tones and take some of the coldness out of direct sunlight on the subject.

Because of these differences in the angle of the sun and the quality of light at different times of the day, when more than one shot is required to complete a particular scene, it is best to shoot the scene at the same time of day with similar amounts of cloudiness. Many directors of TV commercials favor the early morning light because of its golden glow and will shoot an entire commercial with that type of light. This may require several shoots at that location on successive days. Some photographers attempt to manipulate the overall light appearance by performing the white balance procedure while the camera is aimed at a light blue card. This procedure tends to give the video that golden hue. The color of the scene can also be manipulated by filters on the lens just as in film photography. Despite the fact that early morning and late afternoon color temperatures are lower in degrees Kelvin, it is incorrect to call the reddish-orange color at 3000° K cooler than the noontime blue of 5600° K. Although photographers refer to blue and green as cooler colors, and gold, red, yellow, and pink as warmer, the technical concept of color temperature needs to be separated from the emotional response to colors. The term **warm light** refers to a cool-color temperature or a slight pink or golden look.

Traditional standards of photography contend that sunlight reflected off objects yields the most natural (and hence most eye-pleasing) light. Therefore, objects or subjects need to be placed in such a way that sunlight is reflected from them into the lens. This can be accomplished most easily by positioning the camera between the sun and what is to be shot. If the subject is between the camera and the sun, there are two possible results: a strongly backlit shot or direct sunlight shining into the lens. Both effects can be undesirable if handled incorrectly by a novice camera operator; however, as we'll see later, they can be used to great advantage by a skilled operator.

Artificial Light

The two broad categories of manmade light sources are incandescent and fluorescent. While most modern video cameras can white balance for these types of sources, they are inconsistent and therefore unreliable to a professional video maker. The light from typical office ceiling fluorescents is highly diffused but top heavy. They eliminate the shadows necessary to give subjects the appearance of depth, leaving only the shadows of the eye socket on a subject—not a flattering appearance. Light from typical house lamps is usually too dim and, like the fluorescents, not the optimum color. For these reasons, common incandescents and fluorescents are usually avoided in portable video, if at all possible.

Today's low-light cameras allow the photographer to shoot anywhere without the need for additional lighting, but they still do not satisfy some of the basic needs of photography. For a news photographer, shooting available light is a major blessing, but just helps somewhat for a discriminating photographer in EFP and stylized ENG work. We come back to the definition of photography: manipulating light, shadow, and color to achieve a specific artistic or editorial result. Professional video practitioners use specially designed lights that give a better color temperature for more natural skin tones (either 3200° or 5600° K) and enable them to have control over light quality and intensity.

Incandescents

Incandescent lights make use of a filament, usually made of tungsten, to create the light. Whereas it is easy to measure the temperature of the light coming off a known material, other factors can greatly change the ultimate color of the light. For example, ordinary household bulbs should be around 2800° K. Because of their design, these bulbs vary greatly as to their exact temperature. As the atoms of tungsten are given off when the filament is heated, they stick to the inside of the glass bulb. Over time the glass darkens and the color temperature drops. Other factors, such as whether they're clear, frosted, or tinted, can change their color.

Tungsten/Quartz

Professional tungsten halogen or quartz lights are the most common light sources used in video production.

While using a tungsten filament within a halogen-filled sealed quartz globe to produce light, these professional lights are quite different from common household light bulbs. They are often simply called tungstens. In video production, tungsten, quartz, or halogen all refer to the same type of light. Tungsten filaments give off a very constant 3200° K over their life span, which may only be around 75 hours of use. Most tungsten bulbs are used in some sort of housing that enables the user to control the light. (See Figure 5.6.)

One form of the tungsten bulb comes with its own reflector and focusing lens. This type is called a **parabolic aluminized reflector (PAR).** It is similar to the headlights in a car and is often referred to as a **sealed beam** light. Unlike the bare bulb tungsten lights, PAR lights can come in different color temperatures, such as daylight (called a PAR 64) for use outdoors.

Lamps

The bulbs used for professional lighting are often referred to as lamps or globes. They come in a variety of shapes and sizes; they can be 110, 220, 30, or even 12 volts, and the globe can be clear or frosted. They are usually described by a three-letter code such as DYS, which refers to a 600-watt, 120-volt bulb with a particular connecting pin configuration.

Lamp handling requires a note of caution. Lamps can become extremely hot during use and remain hot for some time after operation. They should not be handled when hot; not only can they cause severe burns, but the lamps are also extremely fragile when hot and that causes the filaments to break easily. Lamp handling, even after a cooldown period, must be done with care. Handling a lamp with bare hands can leave a slight oil deposit on the quartz glass that will hasten the lamp's burnout. The area of glass that was touched can be weakened, leading to a possible bulb explosion when the lamp is turned on. If lamps must be handled, do so with cloth or plastic gloves, but only when the lamp is cool. It is wise to carry some heat-proof gloves in your lighting kit to avoid any possibility of burns or lamp-glass contamination from the oil on your skin. Some companies will supply you with small plier-type tongs designed for lamp removal and installation.

Spare lamps are always necessary. Every light kit should have them. Even though most lamps are rated for about 75 hours of use, a burned-out lamp after fewer hours is not uncommon—often occurring in the middle of a story or production shoot. Make sure the replacement lamp is designed and rated for the housing into which you are putting it. If you replace a burned-out lamp with one that has a higher wattage rating, you may damage the housing or even start a fire. Using a replacement lamp with a lower voltage

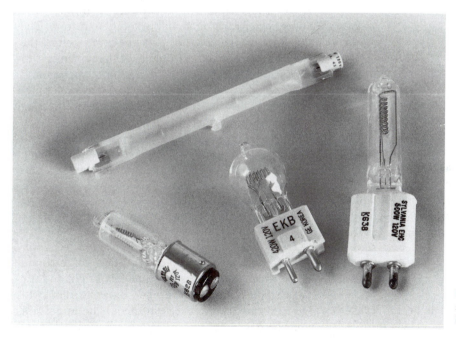

Figure 5.6 Four of the most popular styles of tungsten bulbs used for TV lights.

rating than is required can cause a nearly instantaneous burnout of the new lamp.

Fluorescents

Fluorescent bulbs, part of a larger group of lighting devices called discharge lamps, give off light by electrifying a metal vapor inside a glass tube. Contacts at each end of the tube allow electricity to flow through the gas causing it to glow. Much like filament lights, many differences exist between consumer tubes and those used in film and TV production. A consumer grade tube's color temperature may vary from brand to brand, but most are around 4200° K. The real problem with fluorescent lights is their spectrum. Unlike the smooth mix of frequencies from a filament bulb, fluorescent tubes often have a higher degree (a spike) of green in their output and can actually be missing some frequencies altogether. While our eyes compensate for this, the camera does not. Pictures can have a very ghastly green pallor to the skin tones. White balancing may not fully compensate for this effect because of the missing hues and all that green in the light. Professional tubes compensate for this and can come in either 3200° or 5600° K, which will match the professional tungsten lights or daylight, respectively. The consumer versions of these lamps are called warm white (3200° K) and cool white (5600° K). If you're doing quite a bit of shooting in a space that has many fluorescent fixtures, you may want to change the bulbs to one of the color correct ones.

Color-Correcting Fluorescents

Because the typical fluorescents found in the home and office can vary greatly in color temperature, great lengths are taken to avoid them or correct them in color-critical productions. Professional lighting handbooks have long charts and tables to deal with the wide variety of these lamps in correcting them to different film stocks. There are specially designed filters that can be put over fluorescent bulbs (minus green gel) to reduce the green spike in their spectrum, and other filters to be placed over tungsten lights (plus green) that, when used with a matching lens filter, allow the camera to compensate for the added green of the fluorescent light.

Mixed Light

Situations with mixed sources of light can cause problems. Imagine the face of a subject whose right side is lit by a tungsten-halogen lamp and whose left side is lit by a fluorescent bulb. If the camera is set for 3200° K, the right side would look normal and the other side could be that sickly greenish blue. Because the video camera compensates for only one color temperature at a time, it is best to avoid mixed lighting situations. In the above example, it would be best to turn off the fluorescent and add tungsten-halogen light to the left side of the face. This may not always be possible, however, because some lights must stay on to prevent disruption of others (such as shooting at just one desk in a large office workspace).

The biggest advantage of modern video cameras regarding color temperature is that they white balance under any light if the lights are evenly blended. As long as the scene has a consistently even mix of any number of light sources that are within a limited range, the picture should be close to the true colors. When the mix changes because the distance from any of the light sources varies, the ratio of relative intensities changes; that is, the subject moves closer to the windows in a fluorescent lit room. Mixed-light white balancing works best when each light source is about the same intensity and close in relative color temperature. It is hard to mix tungsten and daylight (3200° and 5600° K), but tungsten and household incandescent or fluorescent are much closer in temperature (3200° and 2800° K or 4400° K). In our example of the face above, a possible solution would be to get the tungsten light on the face from directly in front of it. Although fluorescent light would still be mixed in, the resulting white balance would reveal fairly true colors. The background will be a different story. The face would look good, but someone sitting behind the subject at another desk would have that green cast to their skin tone and possibly to the entire background of the scene as well. One trick is to use as little tungsten light as possible on the subject, thereby reflecting more of the fluorescent light in the white balance. The tungsten is just enough to give some red hues to the skin and minimize the greens without throwing the background so far out of color balance.

Carbon Arcs

The most famous light in Hollywood is the big carbon arc light that has been used on movie sets ever since filmmaking was invented. These large round lights, called studio arcs, are intensely bright and use two carbon electrodes and high, direct current voltage to create an arc between them. The important word here is large. The arc lights still used today are very big in size and weight and not only produce large amounts of light but large amounts of heat as well. They are mostly used outdoors in movie productions and seldom used in video production.

Hydrargyum Medium Arc-Length Iodide Lamp

Another type of arc lamp uses alternating current instead of direct current. The most common arc of this type is the **hydrargyum medium arc-length iodide (HMI)** light. The light is created by a mercury arc between two tungsten electrodes sealed in a glass bulb or globe. HMIs are a daylight temperature light. As they age, the temperature tends to decrease, however. A new light may be as high as 6000° K, but a very old bulb may be as low as 4800° K. HMI lights have been very popular in filmmaking and are becoming very popular in video as well. Unlike tungsten lights, there is much more involved in HMI operation. (See Figure 5.7.)

HMI lights take a very large amount of power to start the arc in the bulb, up to 60,000 volts for the 1-second starting surge. After the surge, it takes about 1 minute for the light to come up to operating strength and color temperature. HMIs operate using a 220-volt AC circuit and require a ballast not only for the starting surge but to regulate the voltage to the lamp. Each light runs at a specific voltage and no two bulbs operate at the exact some voltage. The ballast for most small HMIs, such as the kind you would use for a video production, runs on a normal 110- to 120-volt power supply and increases the voltage up to 220. Even though HMI lights can be small enough to use on top of the camera, the ballast must be attached to the light, usually by a cable. Two mini-HMIs are available that have built-in ballasts and can be powered by the camera's battery just like a normal tungsten camera light.

Ballast comes in two forms, magnetic and electronic. The older magnetic styles are very heavy and bulky, even for a small 200-watt HMI. The more modern electronic solid-state ballasts are very lightweight and compact but still make the smallest HMIs more space consuming than tungsten lights.

HMI lights have many advantages. Because the light is at sunlight temperatures, color perception is at its best. They come in sizes ranging from 28 to 12,000 watts. You get much more light from an HMI lamp than from a tungsten lamp of the same wattage, roughly five times as much, in fact. A 1200-watt HMI puts out the equivalent of 6000 watts of incan-

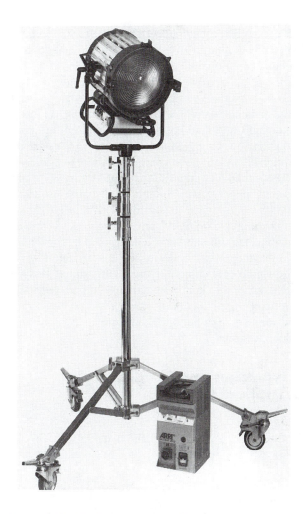

Figure 5.7 HMI light. Courtesy Arriflex Corp.

descent light in a similar fixture. The lights may cost more to buy, but they are cheaper to run per foot-candle of light output, a major consideration if only a limited amount of power is available. HMIs also come in a DC-battery version for portable use. A simple 30-volt battery belt operates a light of about 200 watts for around 20 to 30 minutes. That's like having a portable 1 K (battery-powered 1000-watt light) with you, if you were using tungsten. HMIs come in almost any type of housing, so there are few situations where they cannot be used.

Industrial High-Intensity Discharge Lamp

High-intensity discharge (HID) refers to another type of arc-discharge that produces light through vapor or gas pressure in a glass globe. The three most common types of HIDs are mercury vapor, metal halide, and sodium vapor. For video use, the metal halide is the only one of interest. Metal halide lights are used in sports stadiums, parks, airports, and malls to light large areas at night. The color temperature is closest to daylight and similar to HMIs. Metal halides tend to be yellow-green, but the camera can be easily white balanced in their light. The other two types of HIDs are also used primarily for industrial night lighting or city street lighting. Because of their strange line spectra, it is difficult to white balance under these two lights. Mercury vapor has no blue or red wavelengths, and sodium vapor has almost no blue or green, which means those colors cannot be reproduced by the camera (a red object cannot be seen as red when the light illuminating it has no red in its spectrum). They have no value for video production and make it very hard for the camera to reproduce colors accurately.

Advantages and Disadvantages of Artificial Light

Artificial light is, for the most part, a necessary evil in portable video. There are many disadvantages to using artificial lights:

1. Expense
2. Weight and size
3. AC power requirements necessitating extension cords
4. Excess heat
5. Artificiality or sickliness of subject's appearance if not properly placed and the camera is not white balanced.

This might seem like enough reasons to justify leaving the light kits in the studio, but there is one compelling reason to bring them: If you do not, you will miss quite a few important shots. Even today's video cameras are not sensitive or accurate enough to allow us to always use available light.

There are also more subtle reasons for using artificial light:

1. You must often add light to maintain a realistic appearance; existing light may create an unrealistic appearance to the camera, and you must compensate with added light to make the subject appear more normal on tape.

2. The existing light may be undesirable: too harsh in some areas, too dim in others. Added light can give the proper balance.
3. Added light can enhance the shot aesthetically. You can highlight important visual elements and de-emphasize the less important ones.
4. You may sometimes want to create an artificial environment to achieve the mood of the story. This is particularly true in EFP work, especially when making commercials or dramatic presentations. Though less common in ENG, creating the environment with the addition of artificial light is as old as filmmaking itself.

To put it bluntly, the light kit helps the portable video cameraperson achieve proper exposure and maintain the necessary control over the environment. Artificial lights are tools that a good ENG or EFP practitioner uses to help get the shot that will make the video piece a professional product both for exposure and for creative reasons.

LIGHTING EQUIPMENT

Lighting equipment comes in three categories: housings, mounts, and modulators.

Light Housings

To gain control over artificial light sources, the bulb must be housed in something more than a simple socket. The light housing or fixture provides the primary control over how the light reaches the subject or scene. The housing can direct, focus, or limit the illumination coming from the bulb. The housing can also dissipate the heat a bulb produces. Almost every year new and improved housings are developed. The lights available in 1980 seem old and outdated when compared with the lights available in 2001. Like cameras and VCRs, lighting is a fast-changing part of video production. On the other hand, the basics have not changed in decades. A light made in 1950 still has plenty of uses in today's digital video world. This is another reason that lighting equipment is the best investment you can make: It simply never loses its usefulness despite all the new designs entering the marketplace.

Light housings fall into two broad categories: floods and spots. Although dozens of variations exist within these two groups, a few simple types usually account for most lights available in a typical video production.

Floodlights

Floodlights are the simplest of all lights. They provide even illumination of wide areas. The flood's primary use is to provide overall illumination for a scene or to fill shadows created by other lights. The housings are simple with little means of controlling the light.

Scoops The most basic floodlight is the **scoop**. (See Figure 5.8.) As its name implies, the scoop is simply a large metal bowl, 8 to 18 inches in diameter, with a bulb in the bottom of it. Because of its size, although it weighs practically nothing, a scoop is mostly used in studios. The lights just take up too much space in a vehicle and on location. However, they are cheap. You can get the type that has a traditional screw-in socket, the same as a household socket, and use *photoflood* bulbs purchased at a camera store. These bulbs come in 3200° and 5600° K colors and up to 500 watts in power.

Broads **Broad** lights have a small reflector behind a linear-filament (or tubular) bulb. (See Figure 5.9.) They are usually between 250 and 1000 watts. Broads are easier to control than scoops. Most have small **barndoors** to regulate the light spread. The

light from a broad is fairly hard, producing well-defined but low-density shadows. Because of their small size, broads can be easily placed anywhere in a room as long as there is no danger of heat damage to the surroundings. Small broads are often called **nook lights** and are often used to light backgrounds.

Floodlight Bank This light is made up of several sealed-beam-type lights in a rectangular housing. The overlapping of the lights creates the soft effect of a floodlight. Sometimes called **modules**, they can contain from 4 to 12 lamps, usually laid out in banks that can be switched on individually. They are also referred to by the number of lights in the module, such as a **ninelight**. Only one version of this type of light is used in most video productions, because the size and power requirements are too great for small-scale location shooting.

Internal Reflector Soft Lights Usually referred to as just **soft lights** or sometimes **zip lights**, these instruments shield the bulb(s) from lighting the scene directly but reflect their light into a curved plate at the back of the housing. This white or silver plate reflects the light onto the scene. While reflected light cannot be focused, the light from a soft light is the easiest floodlight to control. Remember, the degree of softness in a light source is determined by the size of that source, that is, the size of the bulb and/or any reflector

Figure 5.8 Scoop light. Photo courtesy Colortran, Inc.

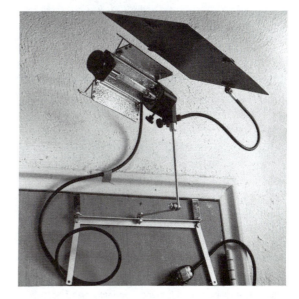

Figure 5.9 This Lowel Tota broad light is attached to a door bracket and has a flag to prevent light from striking the ceiling.

used. For scoops and broads, the bulb shines directly onto the scene softened only by the small reflector areas behind the bulbs. A soft light uses only the reflected light from the large backplate of the housing making that plate the source of light. (See Figure 5.10.) The shadows created are very soft and fall off quickly. Soft lights come in strengths from 200 to 2000 watts. Reflecting the light in this way reduces the efficiency of the bulbs. The output of a 1000-watt bulb is 40 to 60% less in a soft light than in a broad light.

Spotlights

Spotlights are used to light specific areas of a scene. These lights can be easily controlled and focused. Traditionally, the main source of illumination in most scenes is provided by a spotlight of some sort. The sun is the best example of a spotlight. The opposite of floodlights, spots use a very compact source of illumination to produce well-defined, dense shadows. A spot is made up of a small bulb and some form of parabolic-shaped reflector to concentrate the radiant light into a direct beam.

Open-Face Spot The **open-face** spot is the most commonly used light in all of video production because it is the most economical and efficient light to use. (See Figure 5.11.) Almost all open-face spots have the ability to focus from a spot position (called "pinned") to a flood position. The focus ability is accomplished by moving the bulb closer to the internal reflector (flood) or away from the reflector (spot). This takes the bulb into and out of the reflector's parabolic focal point. While the flood position is not as even and uniform as that of a broad or other floodlight, this housing allows most users to get double duty out of one light housing. The disadvantage of this type of light is the quality of its light pattern. The light beam is uneven in intensity, and the lack of a focusing lens can prevent getting distinct, hard-edge shadows. For most work in EFP and almost all work in ENG, these drawbacks are minimal.

Fresnel Spot The **Fresnel** spot (pronounced fre-*nel*) can also be adjusted from spot to flood like the open-face lights. But it differs from the open-face light in two ways: A Fresnel has a glass lens at the front through which the light passes and a different

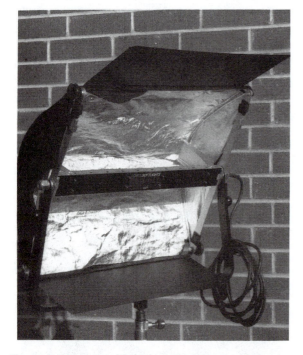

Figure 5.10 A Lowel Softlight 2. This light uses a heat-resistant cloth reflector and two independently switched 1000-watt bulbs. The light folds down for easy carrying and storage.

Figure 5.11 A Lowel Omni open-face light. Focus is achieved by moving a lever in back of the light.

method of focusing the light. Unlike the open-face light where changing from spot to flood is achieved by moving the bulb closer or further from the reflector, the Fresnel light moves the bulb and reflector closer or further from the lens as a single unit. A Fresnel also allows a much narrower spot (around 10 degrees). The focus of the lens gives shadows created in the light beam a hard, well-defined edge but leaves a

softness to the outer edge of the overall beam so that the blending of several lights to cover a large area is possible without unevenly lit spaces. Fresnels come in tungsten and HMI sources and range from 100 to 10,000 watts. The one disadvantage is the loss of light because of the lens. A 1000-watt Fresnel only puts out the light equivalent of a 650-watt open-face light. (See Figure 5.12.) However, this system is designed for maximum light control.

Ellipsoidal Spot The **ellipsoidal** spot (sometimes called a **focal spot**) is the most specialized in its application. Here, the lens moves back and forth in front of a fixed bulb and its ellipsoid-shaded reflector to focus the edges of the light pattern on a particular surface. Often stencils (called **gobo patterns**) are inserted in the light housing to throw a well-defined shadow (such as those created by venetian blinds, prison bars, or tree limbs) on the surface of a wall. (See Figure 5.13.) Generally, this type of light is too expensive, big, and limiting to use for portable video. It is usually used in theater productions and dramatic applications in the studio, *but*, if you have the time and budget, it can add greatly to the look of your field productions.

Several companies make projection lenses that attach to Fresnel-type lights making them an ellipsoidal spot. This relatively inexpensive solution can add greatly to the production values of any shoot by allowing the photographer to project symbolic patterns on surfaces.

Figure 5.12　An LTM Pepper light with a Fresnel lens and barndoors.

Figure 5.13　A Dedo light with projection lens. The window-blind pattern or gobo gives the effect of sunlight coming through a window.

Mounts

Most TV studios have a system of crosshatched pipes called a **lighting grid** on which lights are hung. Lights designed for studio use ordinarily have a C-clamp for this application. In the field, lights are most often attached to tripod stands, some of which have small wheels to allow for easy repositioning. Lights made for stands have receptacles that fit over the standard 5/8-inch stud on the top of tripod stands called **kit stands** (compact) or **baby stands** (heavy duty). Larger lights, like many HMIs, have a 1 1/8-inch stud on the light and slip into a receptacle at the top of large stands called **rollers, juniors,** or **combos.**

Gaffer Grip   Small lights are more flexible than large lights to mount, since their weight does not require a sturdy tripod. Small lights, such as open-face spotlights, are often attached to poles, cameras, or kit stands, or on items like shelves and bookcases by means of a large clamp called a **gaffer grip.** (See Figure 5.14.) Some companies offer wide varieties of clamps, mounts, and special poles for securing lights in the field.

Grip Arm   There are many variations of this device in lighting. A standard **grip arm** is a metal rod that attaches to a stand by means of a **grip head** and is used to hold other light modifiers. These arms can be of various lengths and flexible instead of rigid. (See Figure 5.15.)

If you have ever seen a production lighting crew at work, or even a network news crew, you would have seen a box containing a multitude of clamps and other devices made to mount lights and accessories in just about any fashion anywhere. It's called a **grip kit.** Such things as C-clamps, pipe clamps, door brackets, furniture clamps, vice grips, putty knives, and more, all with the standard 5/8-inch stud attached, can be found in the box. A good location crew—even if that's just you—should be able to set up lights using something other than the standard kit stands. In a room where the camera may be panning 360 degrees, or there are too many toddlers running about, you may need to mount the lights out of the camera's view and harm's way using the furniture or other stationary objects as stands. (See Figure 5.16.)

In a situation in which there are excess crew members, it may be possible to have a crew member, or **grip,** hold a light for you while you are shooting. It

Figure 5.15   A grip head and arm attached to a light stand and holding a flag or solid gobo in place.

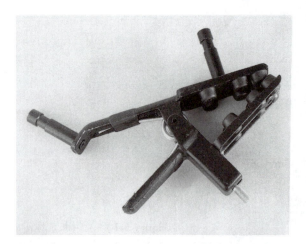

Figure 5.14   An alligator or gaffer clamp with two light studs attached.

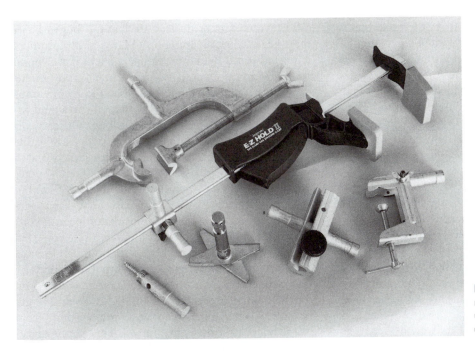

Figure 5.16 Just some of the many clamping devices or "grips" used to attach lights to almost anything.

is not recommended, however, because the lights get hot and the holder often cannot hold the light steady, but if all else fails, have a crew member don the heat-proof gloves, avoid puddles of water, and stand as still as possible.

Gaffer Tape   The most popular item to have in a grip kit is **gaffer tape**. Lights, if you're careful, and grip equipment can sometimes be taped to poles, trees, or equipment cases with gaffer tape. Gaffer tape is usually silver or black (preferred) and, although it is sometimes referred to as duct tape, it is not the same thing. Gaffer tape is expensive and has a cloth backing, and while it has good bonding strength, it is much easier to remove than duct tape. It is strong, but not nearly as reliable as the gaffer grip. Exercise a considerable amount of caution when using tape to mount lights. Do not forget that lights generate heat on all sides. They can scorch paint and material and cause a fire. Falling lights break and often explode. If you stick tape to anything, you better be able to remove it without removing part of what it's stuck to. Good tape may stick too well to most surfaces. Removing it may also remove paint, wallpaper, floor tiles, or even wood veneer. Removal may leave tape gum deposits on the surface. The owners of the property may not take kindly to your ruining their decor.

Modulators

Although some lights have built-in adjustments to allow for focusing the light beam, many that are used for field production do not. When using remote lighting, you must have control over both the amount and size of the light beam. You must also control where the light does and does not fall on the scene you are lighting. In addition to selecting the appropriate fixture for size and function, you must often use additional equipment to maximize light control.

Shaping the Beam

Barndoors   **Barndoors** are rectangular pieces of metal (both two- and four-door) with hinges and are attached to the front of lights to direct the light beam more selectively. Barndoors give you the control to prevent light from falling on areas that do not require it or areas that simply should remain in shadow.

Snoots   Shaped like a tube or coffee can, a **snoot** contains the light beam in a narrow, circular pattern. Barndoors can be added to the front of the snoot to further control or shape the light. They are useful for lighting very selected areas far from the light itself.

Gobos   **Gobos** are similar to barndoors in that they shade or deflect light away from areas that should not be lit. The most popular form of the **gobos** is called a **solid** or **flag**. They are commonly rectangular pieces of metal or black cloth in a frame that may be attached to a light mount such as a stand with the use of a grip arm. They are not attached to the light itself. Gobos come in a wide variety of shapes and sizes. Small round ones are called **dots** and **targets** and are used to shade areas within the light-beam's pattern instead of at the edges. Narrow ones are called **cutters, fingers,** and **sticks;** they are used when a long, thin shadow is needed in the scene. As they increase to a size big enough to control large light sources such as windows, they are referred to as **teasers.** They are also referred to by where they are placed, such as **toppers, bottomers,** and **siders.** Gobos or flags are the most effective way of controlling light in the cramped spaces of location-shooting but usually require more time to set up than the photographer has to spend in ENG situations.

Shaping the Quantity

Dimmers   In the TV studio, lights can be dimmed by use of **faders** (lighting controls that electronically reduce light output), but those are rare in most ENG and EFP situations. Some manufactures make field faders or **dimmers** that work with lights up to about 1000 watts. Larger devices are just too big to be of practical value on location. Many photographers have fashioned their own dimmers out of items found at the local hardware store. Consumer-grade extension cord dimmers made for table and floor lamps can handle lights up to 300 watts, which would include many used in location lighting. Other wall-mounted household dimmers can be wired with cable and made to work as a dimmable extension cord with careful attention to safety standards. These home-made dimmers can handle lights up to 500 watts. Carrying consumer dimmers is also good for reducing the output of any table lamps that appear in your shots, which are often too bright.

A word of caution about using dimmers to cut down the amount of light. If the output is reduced by more than 20%, you will notice an appreciable drop in the color temperature of the light: They will get very red. You might also notice a buzzing sound from some lights after they are dimmed. This can be objectionable if the mic picks up the sound. Also, dimmers do not work on HMI lights, although many of them have built-in dimmers.

Scrims   A wire mesh screen called a **scrim** can be used on the front of a light to effectively reduce the amount of light from that instrument. (See Figure 5.17.)

Figure 5.17   A Pepper light with scrims and a gel holder. A half double scrim is on the light.

Scrims come in predictable strengths labeled single (cuts the light by one-half stop) and double (cuts one stop). They also come as full and half. The full covers the entire light and the half just half the light. The half is used to even out the amount of light falling on surfaces that are at an angle to the light. Say you wish to throw a slash of light across the wall in the background of a shot, and the only place for the light to be placed is off to the side of the room. You line up the light to form the slash, but the part of the slash closest to the light is a lot brighter. To even it out you need to position a half scrim over the light with the wire mesh on the side of the light closest to the wall. You have reduced the closest half of the beam now leaving the entire slash of an even intensity across the wall.

Screens and Nets   Similar to scrims, **screens** and **nets** (both refer to the same item) are used out in front of the lights as opposed to attaching onto them. Made of either metal or fabric mesh, they also come in full and double strengths (again, one-half and one stop, respectively). They are either square or rectangular and usually held in frames with the smaller ones being open ended, or held in a three-sided frame. This reduces the chance of seeing the shadow of the frame when it only partially covers a light. Like gobos, nets are held in place by grip arms or similar means.

Neutral Density   One way to reduce the amount of light coming from a fixture is to place a **neutral density (ND)** gel in front of the light. This grayish gel is calibrated to know exactly how much light each one is cutting. The three most popular grades are referred to as N3, N6, and N9. N3 (1/2 ND) allows a 50% transmission of light, which is a one-stop reduction. N6 (1/4 ND) has only a 25% transmission, or two stops less light. And N9 (1/8 ND) has a 12.5% transmission, or three stops less light.

These gels do not diffuse or color the light in any way. ND gel also comes in large sheets and rolls for covering windows in rooms or cars to reduce the light coming through those windows and to match interior light levels. ND gel can also come combined with color correcting gel to match interior light temperatures as well.

Shaping the Quality

One of the quickest and easiest ways to increase the quality of light is, as we learned earlier, by increasing the size of the source. There are many ways of doing that.

Umbrella Lighting   The most common way to produce a very soft quality light is to attach an umbrella to it. Umbrellas are a must in any portable lighting kit. They are attached to the light housing so that the light is aimed directly into the umbrella. (See Figure 5.18.)

Broad lights make the best umbrella sources, but spotlights in a flooded position can be used. The reflective surface then returns the light past the housing and onto the subject. Umbrellas are made with silver reflective surfaces to bounce the light, but some are made of silk so the user may face the umbrella in either direction to get reflected light or diffused direct light. Others have a blue reflective surface to turn tungsten light into a daylight color.

Soft Boxes   Several companies now make cone-like boxes that cover almost any light fixture. They have a diffusion material over the front of them to soften and increase the size of the source. Generally referred to as **soft boxes**, these tools are increasingly becoming the standard lighting instruments of both the film and video industries. Their design allows them to be more easily controlled than other forms of soft light by attaching **baffles** (rigid material attached to the front sides of the box that help shape the light beam) and **egg crates** or **louvers** (a grid of material placed over the front of the diffusion surface that contains the spread of the light by forming the beam into a shaft of light). (See Figure 5.19.)

Figure 5.18   A Lowel Tota light with an umbrella.

Figure 5.19 A Lowel Rifa Soft Box light. The front panel diffuses the light from the bulb inside.

with anything in contact with a light, it must be fire-proof material. The next position for diffusion is *just* in front of the light. By stretching diffusion over the front of the open barndoors, or on a small frame made to fit close to the light, the effective source can be made larger still. But with this arrangement, it is now harder to contain the light's beam.

The actual diffusion material is usually some type of flameproof gel, spun glass, or frosted glass. Frosted glass is usually placed over the opening of the light housing. Its use is limited in field production because of its breakable nature. Several companies make a multitude of diffusion materials. Don't be fooled by some of the names, such as **tracing paper, soft frost,** and **shower curtain.** These products are designed to be used with hot lights. Do not use home-made or nonprofessional materials anywhere near a light. Some of the most popular materials are **opal, tough frost, tough spun** (spun glass), **216,** and **brushed silk.** Competing companies can have different names for the same material. (See Figure 5.20.)

Silks and Butterflies   Just like the cloud over the sun, the further out front the diffusion material is from the source, the more diffused the light. (See Figure 5.21.) **Silks** have the same type of frames used by nets and gobos, either three- or four-sided. Silks are a very white silk material that passes light at a known rate. A full silk transmits 50% of the light. They also come in half, quarter, and eighth strengths. When the size

Figure 5.20 Spun glass can be stretched across the front of a light and held in place by clothspins to create a diffused light source.

of a silk becomes larger than a 4-foot square, the silk is usually called a **butterfly** (6-foot square) or **overhead** (12-foot square or more). These larger sizes need to be attached to more than one stand and, if used outdoors, carefully weighted to avoid wind gusts blowing them over.

Reflectors Unlike flags, **reflectors** have a light-colored surface that reflects light into desired areas rather than blocking it from certain areas. Reflectors can be stiff boards, metal, or even light-colored cloth, and can come in sizes ranging from a 6-inch square to panels 6 feet square. Far and away the most popular form of the reflector is the circular flex-type cloth using a highly reflective silver material on one side and a bright white material on the other. These reflectors can be mounted but are generally handheld by the cameraperson or other crew members and are usually used to reflect light onto nonmoving subjects, such as a reporter appearing on camera. No lighting kit should be without this inexpensive but invaluable tool. (See Figure 5.22.)

White Cards One of the simplest forms of bounced light comes from the common picture-mounting material called **foamcore**. This is a thin layer of Styrofoam sandwiched between two layers of very white, heavy paper to form rigid cards in sizes ranging from a couple of feet square to 6-foot by 8-foot sheets. These inexpensive cards can be cut to size, mounted by almost any means because they weigh nothing, and used to reflect any light source from tungsten to the sun.

Figure 5.21 A full, open-ended silk used to soften and reduce the direct sunlight falling on the subject.

Figure 5.22 Here the white side of a collapsible reflector is all that is needed to fill in the subject's shadow.

Walls and Ceilings   Sometimes the solution of a bounce material is as easy to find as the room you are in. Because white is the most popular color for most walls and ceilings in both homes and offices, they make good bounce surfaces. Of course, any surface can be used to reflect light to some degree. The one word of caution is to be conscious of the color of the surface. A light blue wall will reflect that blue onto the subject. Try to always use just white surfaces and always remember to white balance for that bounced light: It will not be the same temperature as the direct light.

Shaping the Color Quality

In addition to changing the *amount* of light that comes from an instrument, we can also manipulate the *color* of light by placing a colored, heat-proof, cellophane-like material over the front of the lighting instrument. This modulator is called a **gel** and is common in EFP work. Many lights have **gel frames** that attach to the housing. Color gels can be divided into two categories: *color correction* and *color elimination*. The most common correction gel used in video production is the **daylight-blue** that converts tungsten light to a daylight temperature. (See Figure 5.23.)

Daylight blue gel is often called a **CTB (color temperature blue)** and comes in several strengths: full, half, quarter, and eighth. Another use for this gel is matching the color temperature of a TV screen. Most color TVs have a temperature of nearly 9000° K. For the camera to see true colors on any TV

set picture in the shot, you will need to correct any lights you're using to a high-color temperature (or make the TV's picture very red to compensate for the lights). A full CTB on a tungsten light will raise the temperature of the light to match daylight.

Another popular and useful gel is the **CTO (color temperature orange)**. It also comes in various strengths. This gel shifts the light from high temperatures to low. A full CTO takes daylight to a tungsten temperature. This gel can be used on HMI lights to match tungsten ones or used in large sheets to cover windows converting the daylight streaming in to the same color as your video lights. Most often this gel is used in lower strengths to simply warm the light after you have white balanced for the uncorrected sources. By white balancing for the main light in the scene, you can add a quarter or eighth CTO to give skin tones a slightly redder (warmer) tone.

Color elimination gels remove all or most of the color from a light source except the color of that gel. A green gel casts only green light (unlike CTOs and CTBs, which only shift the temperature of the light). For instance, a primary-green gel covering a light allows the transmission of virtually no red wavelengths. A white sign with red lettering will appear as a green sign with black lettering under this light. The red pigment contains no green and therefore can't reflect that color, and the green light is simply absorbed and leaves the lettering to appear as black. This type of gel can come in any color or shade of color. Except for the primary-color gels, most color-elimination gels do transmit a little of all wavelengths so objects will retain some of their natural color. Using a light-green gel (nonprimary) on lights used to illuminate foliage in the shot can make the leaves stand out without discoloring areas around them too much.

Some Technical Considerations

Nothing is worse than setting lights for a shoot only to have them suddenly go out due to a blown fuse. If you're in a commercial building, that event cannot only be bad for you but for other tenants, workers, and customers. To add to the misery, you may not know where the circuit board is located, and it may take a maintenance person to open it. Valuable time can be lost and bad feelings can start to grow. Before you attempt any location lighting, you must have a thorough understanding of the amount of power required and whether or not you have that amount available for use.

Figure 5.23   Light with daylight blue gel in a gel frame.

Volts and Amps

All the lights you will be using out in the field run on 110 to 120 volts AC—normal household current. Only battery-powered lights use direct current (DC), which is why the two types of bulbs are not interchangeable. The amount of current available is measured in amperes (amps) and multiplied by volts, giving you the power expressed in watts. The equation would therefore be *watts = volts × amps*. It can be remembered as: <u>W</u>est <u>V</u>irgini<u>A</u>. Because each of your lights has a watt rating, you can figure the amps needed for each light. This equation would be *amps = watts /volts*. To build in a safety factor, it is a good practice to use 100 as the voltage even though it may really be 120. Any long extension cable runs can increase the amount of amps and, unless you figure that in, put you in danger of an overload. If you wish to put up two 600-watt lights in a room, you would divide 1200 watts by 100 volts to find that 12 amps of power are needed to safely run the two lights.

Most homes and offices have electrical outlets divided into many separate circuits. In an older house each circuit may be only 15 amps yet have several outlets (in different rooms) on that circuit. Most modern homes and offices have more circuits with fewer outlets per circuit, and each circuit has 20 amps. This means you should never have more than 2000 watts on any one circuit. Finding more than one circuit may be difficult. The first place to start is by finding the circuit breaker box for the area you are working in—a good idea if you plan on using more than one light. The circuits may be labeled in the box. If they are not, and you need more than 20 amps, try to find outlets as far from each other as possible to increase your chances of getting two separate circuits. The other obvious thing is to see if anything else is being used on the circuit you are using. A coffee maker can limit the amps available to you. If you know you will be working in an older home where fuses may still be in use, have spare fuses available.

Avoiding Overloads

For on-location shoots that require a lot of power, either a professional gaffer is used to tap into the electrical system or a generator is rented. Many types of generators are made for TV and movie work that can supply power with little or no noise. Electricity is dangerous and should be dealt with accordingly. Make sure all fixtures are grounded, do not stand in water while touching anything connected to the power, and do not overload any system you are using. Some lights are only meant to be used with bulbs under a certain wattage. Many extension cords are made to carry only a certain number of amps. The length of the cable also determines how much of a load can be carried. A 2000-watt light with 200 feet of cable would need an 8-gauge wire (sometimes just called #8). The lower the number, the more amps it can carry. A 500-watt light could use a 16-gauge cable to go 100 feet. The more wattage you use, the smaller the gauge number should be; the longer the cable run, the smaller the gauge number. All the cables should be three-wire cables. An overheated cable or light housing can easily start a fire. An underground cable could lead to an electrocution.

PART THREE: BASIC LIGHTING TECHNIQUE

THE STARTING POINT: EXPOSURE

In every shooting situation, indoors or outdoors, the first thing a good photographer looks at is the amount of light available. There may be enough to shoot in or you may need to add some of your own. How much is enough? Relying on auto-iris to set your exposure can lead to some undesirable shots. Knowing how to set the proper exposure on any scene without the help of the automatic functions is a requirement in the professional world.

Base Lighting

One of the drawbacks to early video photography was that the video camera required a large amount of light to record a good image. Unlike film cameras that can use extremely light-sensitive film stock or developing procedures that maximize a small amount of light, the light sensitivity of video cameras was limited by the quality and sensitivity of the pickup tube, a component not subject to easy replacement or change. Therefore, the first requirement in video lighting was to provide the camera's pickup tube with a quantity of light large enough to enable the camera to function properly. This minimum level is the **base light**.

Today's chip cameras require very little base light to make a good picture. Very little does not mean no light, however. Base light should be thought of as the minimum light required for shooting. The scene always looks better, especially in EFP work, if the light levels are somewhat above the base. The first requirement in lighting a scene is to make sure you have enough base light on every area of the scene for which you wish to see detail. Areas with less than base light (like shadows) appear gray or go black in the picture, which you may want to happen. By knowing your camera's ASA or lux rating, you can determine the base-light level in foot-candles or lux for any f-stop you use. A typical professional camera available for ENG or EFP applications, the Sony BVW-400A, requires 2000 lux at f5.6 for an acceptable image, or 200 lux at f1.7 (the typical widest opening for a broadcast quality lens), which is about 19 foot-candles of light. Therefore, you would want the main area of the scene you are about to shoot to have the base light of 19 fc. Lux is a measure of light quantity used in countries that use the metric system and has become the standard measurement for judging video camera sensitivity; 10.74 lux is equal to 1 foot-candle.

Finding the Correct Exposure

Exposure is both a scientific and subjective point. A light meter can give you what the manufacturer says is the proper exposure similar to how filmmakers do it. You can put the camera on automatic iris and let it tell you what the exposure should be. But just as filmmakers decide *what* subject and *where* to measure the light to achieve the end result they want for the film's look, a video maker must also choose to go beyond the auto-iris to get aesthetically pleasing results. The proper exposure for a piece of white paper shot full frame may be without argument, but the correct exposure of someone sitting in front of a window may be quite subjective.

The problems of not enough light are easy enough for most beginners to notice. The picture is muddy, dull, and looks to be of all the same shade of gray in the viewfinder. Most of the newer portable cameras have a signal of some kind that alerts the camera operator to a potential low-light problem. This indicator is sometimes a **light-emitting diode (LED)** that glows when there is insufficient signal level output from the camera. A slightly different version of this type of indicator is a white line across the picture that indicates either too much signal (requiring a reduction in iris opening), a proper operating range (requiring no iris setting change), or too little signal (necessitating an increase in iris opening or a general increase of light on the scene). Many other aids are visible in the viewfinder of different cameras that help find the right exposure, such as the zebra stripes in all professional cameras.

The problems of too much light being let into the camera can be difficult for many first-time video shooters. They may think the picture is better when everything is bright and you can see details in all the shadow areas of the picture. It usually is not. Overexposure usually shows up as the loss of detail in the brighter areas. Areas of the picture or subjects within the picture that become overexposed start to lose texture and definition. The writing on a white piece of paper starts to disappear as the paper is overexposed. If that paper is on the desktop in your shot, you may indeed have to overexpose it to get the proper exposure for the entire picture. As we shall see a little later, it's the contrast ratio that helps determine what the proper exposure should be.

Use of High Gain

Use of the high-gain circuit increases the sensitivity of the pickup device, thus increasing the range of light in which the video camera can supply an image. However, use of this additional amplification enhances the noise, or graininess, in the video as well. The resulting picture often appears somewhat grainy, and darker areas of the frame are muddy and have confetti-like specks of color. Scenes or stories shot in high gain that require editing or duplication will suffer noticeably.

Obviously, some stories must be shown despite minor video flaws. Unfortunately, too many important news stories occur at night. Shooting these stories requires as much boost to the lighting situation as possible. The 12- or 30-volt battery-powered portable light that is often used gives acceptable illumination only on subjects 6 to 20 feet from the camera. When shooting outdoors at night, these battery-powered lights offer only a little help on large scenes, but they are still necessary. The +6- or +9-dB gain is quite often used when more light is needed but cannot be added. Because of the graininess of the resulting video image, the +12- or +18-dB gain should be used only on very important shots that cannot be done any other way.

These large gain enhancements may be used at night to record objects at a distance or in special situations; for example, when the lights would interfere with the actions of a SWAT team's operation. The resulting video will be noisy and the video level (the amount of video signal) will probably be low, but there is a common procedure to improve the look of the picture. When the tape is played or edited, the chroma level can be lowered on the shots done at low light and high gain. Lowering this level causes the colored, confetti-like speckles in the darker areas of the picture to lose their color. This technique produces a nearly black-and-white picture, but since our eyes see very little color at night, the loss of some chroma is not objectionable. However, the brighter areas of the picture retain some chroma, and the perception of overall noise in the picture is greatly reduced.

Contrast Ratio

Unlike the human eye, video cameras are severely restricted in their ability to perceive large variations of brightness within a given scene. When extremely bright objects are framed with very dark objects, many video cameras do not reproduce details well in either the light or dark areas. Excessively bright areas, such as a pure white shirt, may tend to glow and appear otherworldly. Very dark portions of the screen may be muddy and lack detail, resulting in an unappealing, two-dimensional image.

In an overall scene, most video cameras can properly show bright areas that are no more than 20 times brighter than the darkest areas of that scene. The newest chip cameras for general use have contrast ratios of as high as 100:1. The typical film used in motion pictures has a contrast range of about 200:1 and our eye sees at about 1000:1. This is primarily why film looks better than tape and why our eyes see the best of all. As technology improves the contrast range of video, the quality of the look will increase dramatically. But for the present, it is still a good rule of thumb to stick with the 20:1 rule. For example, if when using a reflective or **spotlight meter** you measure the reflected light from the brightest area of the picture and it is equal to 400 foot-candles, then any area of the picture reflecting less than 20 fc of light is beyond your camera's contrast range.

A piece of typical white paper reflects 60% of the light that strikes it, whereas black paint reflects only 3%. White plaster, however, reflects 90%. If you have 200 fc of light falling on a white plaster wall in a scene, it will reflect 180 fc. A dark brown chair in that scene reflects only 6 fc, which is beyond your 20:1 contrast range. If you expose for the wall, the chair becomes underexposed, even though the same amount of light is striking it. Therefore, you must keep in mind not only the amount of light striking the objects, but also their ability to reflect that light. Going back to our earlier example of the white paper on the desktop, if the shot is of a person sitting at a dark wood desk in a dark suit, then the proper exposure for the overall shot would have the paper overexposed, because it falls outside the contrast ratio of the main subject. The darker areas would need to be seen more than the paper.

These considerations demonstrate why it can be very difficult to expose for two subjects in the same scene when one is in the shade and one is in the sun. When using a TV camera, you try to expose for the brightest area, but the difference in brightness between objects in both sun and shade can be well over 200:1. Exposing for the brightly lit person sends the other into darkness and exposing for the darker one causes a total loss of detail in the bright one.

In a practical sense, photographers must watch out for bright/dark combinations in every shot. The contrast ratio problem becomes more apparent when the brightest and darkest areas of the scene are right next to each other or where one is much larger than the other. If your subject is wearing a bright white shirt and dark trousers, suggest lighter trousers or a pastel shirt. White blouses can be less harmful to the overall look if partially covered by a scarf or jacket. A small area of overexposure is much less noticeable.

A dark-skinned subject can present problems to a video camera operator. A light-colored shirt and light background can make a proper exposure difficult. In daytime shooting, extra light is often necessary to brighten the subject's facial features. You must pay close attention to lighting and background to avoid having a dark-skinned face blend in with the background.

Do not forget that an extremely dark or extremely light portion of the screen can often be compensated for by an iris adjustment. The problem arises when two extremes appear in the same shot. If you cannot get detail in both areas of the picture at the same time, find a way to adjust the shot to reduce the amount of too light or too dark areas, or adjust the lighting to reduce the contrast ratio. (See Figure 5.24.)

In ENG work, you are often forced to work with shots that have more than a 20:1 contrast ratio. An example might be an interview with a tall plane-crash

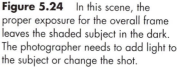
Figure 5.24 In this scene, the proper exposure for the overall frame leaves the shaded subject in the dark. The photographer needs to add light to the subject or change the shot.

eyewitness wearing a hat on a heavily overcast day. The white sky reflects large quantities of light, but the shaded face of the subject reflects very little light. The contrast ratio between sky and face will be far in excess of 20:1. The iris must be pushed, or opened, beyond what the overall picture requires, to get the face to show on tape with some detail. In this case, the background will be overexposed. If the background is overexposed, the edges of the subject's face may be undefined, making the subject look abnormal.

There are some possible solutions in this case, however:

1. Try to find a dark background, for example, against a wall, fire truck, or tree.
2. Frame the subject's face as tightly as possible to reduce the amount of background in the shot, thereby reducing the overall contrast in the shot.
3. Anticipate these conditions and use a camera-mounted battery light with a dichroic filter to brighten the face. Even without the filter, the extra light on the subject's face will help the contrast despite being too red; a reddish face is certainly better than no face at all.

In ENG, if you do not get the shot, a competitor probably will. It is your job to find a way to make the shot work with few technical distractions. In some ENG situations, you may have to shoot despite adverse lighting conditions because the story is too important to miss. The audio may be usable, even if the video is not. As chip cameras get better, it is possible to drive the contrast to greater extremes and not have the picture look bad. In fact, in many EFP projects overexposure of certain areas of the frame is a specific style. Overexposure can be used as a creative force if done with purpose. A shaft of sunlight coming through a window can blow out (overexpose) part of the picture or even part of the subject to show the intensity of that light or draw the viewer's attention to the light and thus to the subject.

Increasing the Quality through Contrast

The flat lighting created by the light very near or on the camera puts no shadows on a subject's face, nor does it show tone differences on a subject's face. After a tape with this type of lighting is dubbed (copied) in an analog system (nondigital), the resolution begins to decrease and, because there is no contrast to the subject's features, the face begins to disappear completely. The face washes out and has no texture or features. A news station often airs third- or fourth-generation dubs. The quality of these is already lower than the original tape and if the lighting is very flat the picture will have almost no detail.

Good cameras can see a 100:1 contrast ratio or more, but nondigital videotape can record only about a 20:1 contrast ratio. Most home TV sets have only a

10:1 ratio because of high levels of room light. This is one more reason for keeping the lighting ratios within about 20:1 for the overall scene, and even less for the subject itself—but *a contrast is always necessary*. There should be light and dark areas in the picture and the topography of the subject's face must be clearly distinguishable. Having shadows—the modeling effect—adds texture and more of a three-dimensional feeling to a picture, which makes it is easier to see on the home screen and therefore easier to watch.

There are some things you can control so that the picture showing at home is as close as possible to the way things are. For example, you may think you are changing the picture too much by setting up several lights. You probably are not, however, if the end result is a picture with light levels high enough to properly expose the picture, a contrast ratio in the proper range, and a picture that looks natural and pleasing to the viewer. Because the camera does not see things in the same way you do, you must help it to see that way.

THE ART OF CASTING SHADOWS

You should now know what light is, how it travels, what creates it, and the tools for controlling it. Now you need to know how to use light to your advantage beyond simple exposure for the camera. Too often ENG and even some EFP shooters rely on just a camera light to give them exposure. This is certainly necessary in adverse conditions, but it lacks character and artistic purpose. The purpose of good lighting is to cast shadows. The absence of shadows—flat lighting—adds nothing to a viewer's visual understanding of the shot or scene. The world around us is literally defined by shadows. Without them we could no longer see depth or texture. We couldn't even tell the time of day without a watch. During a shoot, you will need to light many different scenes indoors and outdoors, both to control contrast for the camera and to help the viewer better see what the pictures are saying. Although each lighting situation is unique, there are some fundamental guidelines you can follow that will help you light any scene.

BASIC THEORY

The History of Lighting

Most of what we know about lighting comes from a single period of art history. A painter named Caravag-

gio in the early 1600s developed a style of painting that used shadows to express depth on the two-dimensional canvas. An admirer of his went on to perfect this style and become one of the most famous painters in history: Rembrandt van Rijn (1606–1669). This painter from the seventeenth century created a way of working with light and shadow that transcended its own time and medium and survived well into modern times. The technique is called **chiaroscuro**, an Italian word meaning "light–dark." Rembrandt's paintings have very clear—but not necessarily visible—sources of light that only illuminate selected parts of the frame. Even his outdoor scenes make use of clouds and their shadows to provide areas of light and dark within the picture. The number one rule was that every light source be natural. Light in his paintings—as in life—could only come from a naturally occurring source. No one has ever found a better way of lighting since. There are three main characteristics of chiaroscuro lighting, as discussed next.

The Source and Intensity of Light   There is only one apparent light source that selectively lights only parts of the scene. The overall illumination is low—called low-key lighting—and the overall background is darker than the subject of the shot.

Shadow Direction and Fall-off   Dense, attached shadows make the direction of the light readily apparent. The quick fall-off or diminishing of the light's intensity before reaching the background allows darker areas of the frame to dominate, thus directing the viewer's eye to the lighter areas, that is, the subject.

Object Texture   This highly directional light source accentuates the texture and form of objects in the frame. Faces, clothing, furniture, walls, and even dust in the air take on a three-dimensional quality.

Chiaroscuro lighting can convey both high and low emotional intensity. The quantity of dark and light areas helps determine what the perception will be. This type of lighting uses a low key, usually a Fresnel with barndoors, and very little fill. The background is usually lit with other very directional, narrow beam lights to control the amount of the scene receiving light. Chiaroscuro lighting intensifies the three-dimensional properties of the subject, clarifies the space around them, and gives an emotional quality to the scene. The particular emotional quality should be selected on the basis of the subject you are photographing in ENG work and by what the script calls for in EFP. Each lighting setup should have a predetermined goal beyond making a good exposure for the camera. Chiaroscuro lighting is the basis for almost all the motivational lighting you will do. (See Figure 5.25.)

The Rembrandt Way

Chiaroscuro lighting is now more popularly known as **Rembrandt lighting**. There are a few simple tricks to getting the flavor of the master in anything you light. By sticking with these principles you can't go wrong. As we said, after nearly 400 years, nobody has come up with a better way. These five points can be used as a guideline to Rembrandt lighting:

1. Place the key light, or angle the subject, so the shadowed side of the subject is closest to the camera (so it appears the subject is looking into the direction of the light but not at it).
2. Move the subject away from the background.
3. Look for a dark background.
4. Make the subject the brightest and/or biggest area of the shot.
5. Have the darkest area of the background directly behind the subject.

This theory can work for everything—not just for setting up lights but in simply positioning subjects

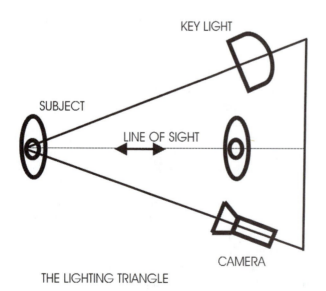

KEY LIGHT

SUBJECT

LINE OF SIGHT

CAMERA

THE LIGHTING TRIANGLE

Figure 5.25 This is the basic lighting triangle formula that will give a Chiaroscuro look. The idea can be applied to almost any situation.

in any shot. Our plane-crash witness earlier can have a chiaroscuro feel by positioning his head in the shot against the dark foliage of a tree and having him face in the direction of the flashing fire truck lights. The red lights become the subliminal key light source giving texture to his face, even though they do not overpower the diffused daylight. The dark tree makes his face the brightest area of the picture. Simple, quick, yet meeting the artistic standards of Rembrandt on a very basic level. (See Figure 5.26.)

Zone Lighting

Along the same lines as chiaroscuro lighting, **zone lighting** selectively lights only certain areas of the picture, which are divided into zones by distance from the camera. This is usually foreground, midground, and background. The subject is usually in the midground. Each of these areas is lit separately with dark or shadow areas separating them. This technique helps to create a three-dimensional look and draw the eye to whatever you wish to emphasize in the frame.

FORMAL LIGHTING

Three-Point Lighting

The technique of three-point lighting has been used for years in both professional TV and photography studios. It is based on the principles of chiaroscuro but doesn't try to disguise the artificiality of the light. This method of lighting is simple but effective for many situations that call for lighting a particular subject or object. Three carefully placed directional lights—the key light, the fill light, and the backlight—can light a subject in a way that provides an appropriate level of base light for the video camera; gives sufficient shadow for definition of shape, size, and texture; and separates the subject from surrounding objects and the background. The three-point technique is appropriate in most ENG or EFP situations to satisfy basic lighting needs. Figure 5.27 displays the same shot under four different lighting conditions. Figure 5.28 gives guidelines for light placement in a situation in which the subject is facing the camera.

Key Light   As the name implies, the **key light** is the most important light and is, therefore, placed first. The key light should be the brightest and most direc-

A

B

Figure 5.26 (A) A simple example of Rembrandt lighting: dark shadows and background with a single motivating light source opposing the direction of the subject. (B) The lighting setup used to create the Rembrandt scene.

tional. A key light placed on the camera–subject axis (right over the top of the camera) produces a very flat, shadowless picture. In most cases, this is not flattering to the subject.

Start with these guidelines for placing the key light:

1. Place it off the camera–subject axis, anywhere from 10° to 90°, depending on the effect or look you are creating.
2. For a subject not facing directly toward the camera, focus the key light on the opposite side of the subject's face from the camera position.

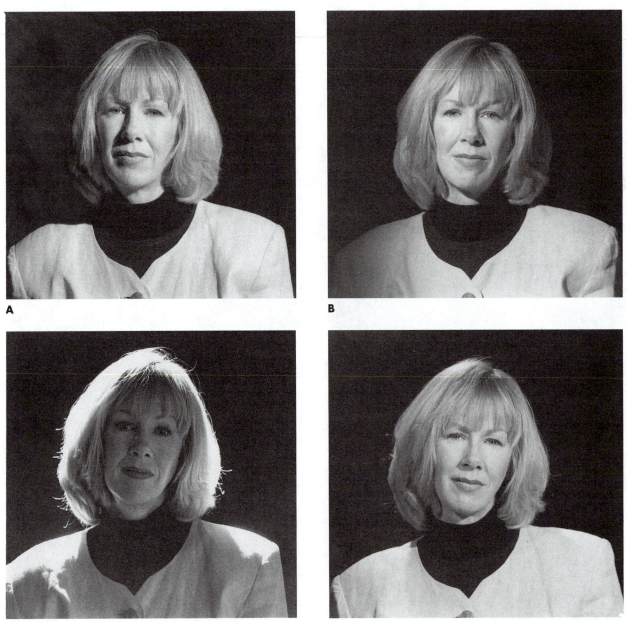

Figure 5.27 (A) Key light only; it creates the shadow. (B) Fill light only; it lightens the shadow of the key. (C) Back light only; it separates the subject from the background. (D) The three lights together.

3. Elevate the light above the subject at about a 45° angle from the camera–subject plane.

The key light creates a strong shadow, sometimes called the **draw**, on the subject's face. This is called the **modeling effect.** The photographer is responsible for bringing the viewer's attention to the most important aspect(s) of the screen. Since the audience is naturally drawn to the brightest part of the screen, and since the key light illuminates an area so brightly, the key light is used to focus the viewer's attention. For subjects not looking directly into the camera, the key light should be the light that the subject faces towards but not at—thus, the short side of the face (the side away from the camera) is lit by the key. Focusing the key light on the long side of your subject (the side nearest the camera) makes it seem like the subject is looking away from the light. This gives the appear-

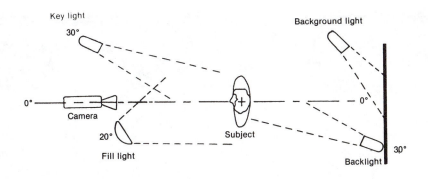

The standard three-point lighting setup with an added background light.

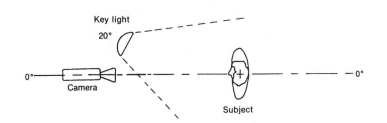

A single light source should be near the camera and flooded as much as possible.

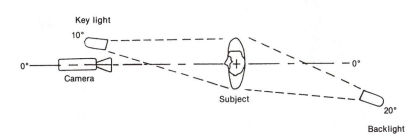

When only two lights are used, the combination of the key and back is effective.

Figure 5.28 Light placement when the subject faces the camera.

ance of subject discomfort or avoidance, which can be misleading, distracting, or unpleasant for the viewer. It also casts the draw, or shadow, out of view for the camera, thus losing the three-dimensional effect.

Fill Light The next light to set when using the three-point lighting technique is the **fill light**, located at an angle about 10° to 45° from the camera on the opposite side of the camera from the key. Again, the light should be placed above the subject to give a more

normal appearance. In studio TV the fill light is often a scoop or a Fresnel spot adjusted to give a wide or flooded-out beam. These types of lights are preferable because they are less harsh and soften shadows created by the key light without eliminating them. Unfortunately, portable kits rarely contain scoops or other diffused lights. Typically, portable kits have small spotlights without lenses. Since the key and fill lights are usually of equal strength in portable kits, the fill is often placed at a slightly greater distance

A

B

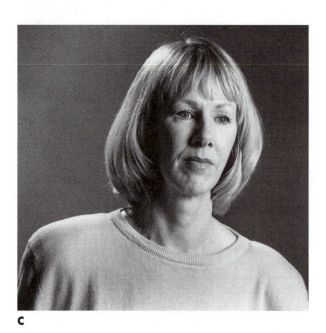

C

Figure 5.29 Here are three examples of interview lighting based on a three-point concept. (A) A single hard source creates a serious tone. (B) A single soft source creates a more open feel with less dense shadows. (C) A soft source and a backlight create an easy, formal look.

from the subject, resulting in a less intense light for fill (remember the inverse square rule!).

Many portable kits have adjustable lights that allow the light to be pinned to a narrow beam that gives sharp, bright light, or flooded to give a softer, less bright light. For example, the fill light could be set at a distance from the subject equal to the key light and set in the flooded or wide position, and the key could be pinned. *As a general rule, your key light should be twice as bright as your fill (a 2:1 ratio), but a key that is four times as bright as the fill (a 4:1 ratio) is not uncommon.* The combination of properly set key and fill lights should give enough base light for the video camera to operate at an acceptable level and create a perception of depth, giving your subject a three-dimensional quality.

Backlight   The third light in the three-point lighting technique is the **backlight**. The primary purpose of this light is to separate the subject from the background by highlighting or framing the subject with a rim of light. The backlight is most often a spot, both in the studio and in the field. It is focused on the back of the subject and aimed so it's not shining into the camera lens. Barndoors are a must on backlights. The light is placed directly opposite the key light, behind and above the subject at an angle of about 45°. It is not unusual for a backlight to be as strong as the key light for a key–fill–back ratio of 2:1:2. A more subtle 2:1:1 is the most common choice. Because the effect of a backlight as seen from the camera position is more reflection than illumination, the strength of the backlight must be considered in relationship to the subject or object being lit. A person with golden blond hair will reflect a great deal of the backlight toward the camera, so only a little is needed. A person with a lot of very black hair can absorb a great deal of light and may need a very strong beam from the backlight. There's a saying among cinematographers that a backlight should be felt and not seen. It is best to judge the strength of the backlight with your eyes and get the brightness just to the point where it is noticeable. (See Figure 5.29.)

Adding to Three-Point Lighting

Other light placements are common in the photographic world and a good TV photographer should take advantage of their availability. With a minimum of setup time, you can properly light most ENG and EFP assignments using the basic light kit. Three lights are more than adequate to light any medium-sized meeting room or interview. With the addition of a couple of extra lights and some accessories, creativity need not take a back seat to expediency.

Background Light The **background light**, or fourth light, is often used to locate the subject in the set, that is, to show the relationship of the subject to the background. The placement of this light can vary, but the idea is to illuminate part of the background to show its texture, shape, and depth relative to the subject. It may be extra trouble to purchase, carry, and set a fourth light, but it becomes very important when you must videotape a subject with dark hair or a dark shirt against a dark background. The fourth light can give the viewer a better understanding of volume within the shot. (See Figure 5.30.)

One way to use a background light is to light the area directly behind the subject if the subject is centered, or on the empty side of the frame if the subject is not centered. But it should not light the entire background, only a portion of it. Many times a well-placed background light can be substituted for a backlight to achieve subject/background separation. This is also the light that can add special effects to the scene. For example, you can make the background interesting by using a cookie or another shadow-forming device placed in front of a narrow-beam background light. A very common technique in movies is to use a venetian blinds effect. A slotted pattern on the background light gives the effect of window light coming through blinds. The light serves its purpose by giving highlight and detail to the background while also making it seem natural. Experiment with background lights using different patterns and also different directions.

Kicker Light An additional light often used in EFP is the **kicker light**. It is a light set from a low angle to the side of the subject and slightly behind. Its purpose is to highlight the subject's hair or face. The kicker is often used in hair product commercials to add a glamorous look. In drama scenes the kicker is used to denote time of day. A very soft, flat kicker on an actor's

Figure 5.30 Putting light on the background opposite the subject adds interest, separation, and motivation for the key light and the mood.

face represents early morning or late evening while a hard, spotted kicker says midday. (See Figure 5.31.)

Eye Light   In some dramatic EFP presentations you can use a small, highly directional light to illuminate a subject's eyes. The **eye light** is usually a lower wattage lamp aimed at the eyes from the camera position. The next time you watch an old *Star Trek* rerun, watch for the eye light used in close-ups when Commander Kirk plays a dramatic or love scene. This light in a more subtle form is sometimes called an **obie light**. The name comes from the silent movie star Merle Oberon who had her cameraman use a light mounted on top of the camera to shine directly on her face and nowhere else. This flattened her lighting but also took away any and all wrinkles. Today the eye light or obie is used to fill shadows in facial creases and give a reflective sparkle in the subject's eyes.

Lighting with Color

For most work in EFP and ENG, keeping the color of light the same from all sources in a scene is the standard. However, for creative work you will find yourself mixing colors of light more and more. By knowing what color any particular light source is, you can predict how it will look on the screen when added to your shot. If you are doing an interview inside a room during the day, but for some reason you wish it to look as though it were night, you may light the sub-

ject with tungsten, balance for that, and let some daylight spill into the background. The area lit by sunlight will appear blue, similar to that of moonlight (as used in TV and movies), especially if the daylight is of a much lower intensity than your key light. You may use daylight from a large window as your key on a subject, but tungsten as the backlight to give the hair a warm glow. Once you have mastered the idea of color temperature, you can balance the camera for any key light and paint the rest of the picture with color created by temperature or gels or both. You will quickly find that the use of CTO and CTB on backlights, background lights, and even kickers gives your pictures a creative edge.

NATURAL LIGHTING

As cameras have gotten better and better over the years, popular lighting styles have changed. No longer is it necessary to literally pound a subject with light to get proper exposure. Artificial light has become something that is simply added and manipulated primarily to suit the needs of the photographer, not the camera. Three-point lighting looks like something from the studio. Since location shooting is all about being on location and having it look that way, finding alternatives to this formal approach to lighting would only make sense. Using some of the tech-

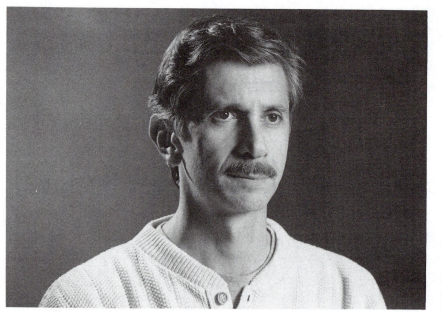

Figure 5.31   The kicker gives a stronger jaw line and a more natural look.

niques mentioned below, you can create a pleasing natural light with soft shadows that meets your lighting requirements without disturbing the natural look of your location shoot. It also takes you a step closer to the master's style of Rembrandt.

Adding to Existing Light

Too often hundreds of pounds of delicate equipment are bounced around in a truck only to result in a scene that looks as if it could have been shot in the studio. The addition of artificial lighting often gives an artificial look to a remote scene and destroys the natural appearance of a location setting. If the subjects can easily perform or be interviewed in the studio, why bother hauling out the remote equipment? One reason for a remote shoot is to preserve the natural environment of the subject. Sometimes there is the need for minimum base-level lighting. Some situations simply demand additional light. The best way to fulfill the technical requirements of the video camera is to *add* to the existing light without overpowering it. Unlike studio scenes in which three-point lighting is the standard, many locations need only the existing light levels raised to produce a pleasing, well-lit scene.

Preserving Color Temperature By taking what you learned about color temperature, you can size up the color of any scene. Whether it's daylight streaming through the windows (5600° K), or ambient reflected daylight coming in (6500° K), or just household lamps (2800° K), you should now know how to adjust your lights to match the natural light in the scene. You may wish to use the natural light as the key and use your lights as the fill, back, or background sources.

Preserving a Natural Look To preserve the natural look of the location, keep the direction of the natural key light the same as it was without enhancement. If there isn't enough natural light to satisfy base requirements, add your light source near to or in line with the existing light source. If your additional lighting produces shadows that are too dark, fill light may be necessary. The fill light should be as subtle as possible, such as using bounced light, but bright enough to fill the shadows. Many times natural light is nondirectional or flat, such as in an office building, so the additional lighting you provide should also lack directionality for the most part; that is, it should have no shadows. In these situations it is necessary to find

natural elements of light and dark to gain a three-dimensional look.

Creating a Natural Look

Soft Lighting Except for standing outside in the sun, humans are almost never seen in any kind of direct light. We don't put spotlights in our homes or offices that shine in our faces. So any time we light someone like that the visual message is artificial and conspicuous. The goal of a natural look is a type of lighting referred to as simply **soft lighting**. Shadows are undefined or have very hazy, soft edges. It is hard to recreate this type of light with standard lighting equipment alone. You can create soft light effects using hard lights by adding umbrellas, boxes, or a diffusing material, such as spun glass, in front of them, or by bouncing the light off another surface such as we discussed earlier in this chapter. Larger diffusing material can even be hung from the ceiling in front of the lights to produce a wall of light. Any of these methods will yield a natural soft light on the subject or scene, but you must remember that the amount of light reaching the subject will be greatly reduced and the color temperature lowered by the diffusing material. Light from an umbrella source is only one-half to one-third of what it would be if the light came directly from the fixture. (See Figure 5.32.)

Bouncing light is the best method of adding soft light in situations where the room is small. If a room's ceiling is light colored, relatively smooth, and no higher than 8 or 10 feet from the floor, you can aim a light at the ceiling and the reflected light will enhance the base illumination level. Almost any type of light can be used for this purpose, but very weak lights will lose much of their lighting power before reaching the subject. How much of the ceiling you light can make a big difference in the resulting look. Lighting only a small portion can produce a very "top-heavy" light with dark eye sockets on any subject too close to that part of the room. Lighting the entire ceiling is better most of the time, but you have to make sure the direct light doesn't hit the walls or it will show up in the shots.

Direct Light You can also achieve a natural look with direct lights. By aiming them not into faces but from other directions or onto other parts of the scene, the direct light will create its own ambient or reflected light. As an example, a person sitting at a desk can be lit from behind by a strong direct light in the kicker or backlight position. The light can look like daylight from an off-camera window (very strong), or light from an unseen lamp (diffused) hitting the subject. As that light also hits the desk top, some of it will be reflected back onto the subject, or you can add more fill of your own. In this example the key light—the direct light—is actually behind the subject, which is not an abnormal scene in real life. (See Figure 5.33.)

Backlight There is an entire theory of natural lighting that uses a key behind the subject; it's called **backlighting**. This type of shot creates difficult problems for cameras and photographers, but the results are well worth the trouble. This style is used most often outdoors using the sun as the backlight key. To make the shot work, most of the objects in the shot need to be backlit as well. A subject with too much of the background directly lit may not show up well on camera. This type of backlit scene may need to be done with a manual iris to achieve the proper exposure on the subject. Most backlit scenes will have an area of overexposure. When using this style, try to overexpose as little of the picture as possible. Even in ENG and EFP applications, a backlit shot can produce warm or pastel colors and good textures as long as the background is also shaded and as little as possible of the sky is in the shot. This effect may be desirable for many reasons; for example, to soften the features of a subject's face. (See Figure 5.34.)

A backlit scene is lit with ambient or reflected light—nature's soft light. This reflected sunlight tends to be more blue than direct sunlight, but white balancing in this reflected light offsets the problem. In effect, by using this reflected light you are getting the best qualities of sunlight without the drawbacks. You can get great skin tones without the horrible dark shadows caused by harsh, direct sunshine.

At certain angles, sunlight can reflect off an object's surface creating glare. This is when backlighting can be troublesome. Paved surfaces such as concrete can be very hard to include in backlit shots. That is why in backlit TV commercials they wet the streets down with water to darken the surface. Wet concrete actually reflects less light as long as there are no puddles.

Lens flares, caused by backlights striking the lens, could be desirable. The rows of flares created by the light can be used to add dynamics to the shot and help emphasize the sun or light source. A story on solar power practically requires a shot of the sun and such effects can add interest.

Source Lighting

Source lighting is the best possible natural lighting; you see it most often in the movies. All the artificial light sources are cleverly placed so the viewer is unaware that any are used. The scene looks as though it is lit only by the natural light sources in the picture or perceived to be just outside the camera's view; this is why it is called source lighting. This is modern-day chiaroscuro lighting.

It may actually take many lights to make a scene appear as though it has no added light. A room with windows should look as though the only light comes from those windows. To make a scene look like this,

Figure 5.32 To create a natural look, this interview setup was done with two lights. The key light was a 3- by 3-foot foam core with a 1000-watt broad light bounced off of it and the backlight was a 100-watt Fresnel. The window light was blocked by a Duvetyne curtain to allow the use of uncorrected tungsten lights and to allow the camera to use a larger f-stop. The slower lens setting allowed better use of the practical, or incandescent, light on the table and a more out-of-focus background.

you can use artificial lights to fill in the shadows or accent certain highlights (thereby controlling the contrast ratio). (See Figure 5.35.) You can also use artificial lights to make the lighting appear as though it is coming from table lamps in a room, the light from a fireplace or candles, or any natural light source that happens to be there. These natural sources of artificial light are called **practicals**. They generally do not provide the amount or quality of light necessary for

shooting but simply provide the motivation for how a scene is lit. It is helpful to the viewer if the light source is incorporated into the shot or shown in a setup shot so that there is at least a subliminal awareness of where the light is coming from—but it's not necessary.

Balancing the lighting contrast ratio of the subject in the room to the daylight in the windows can be very difficult in source lighting. In EFP work as in the movies, large sheets of neutral density gels can be

Figure 5.33 The only light source for this scene is from behind the subject. Reflected light from the book and table fill the subject.

Figure 5.34 With the subjects backlit and against a dark background, you can expose for the softer reflected light.

Figure 5.35 It is the natural light, like the illumination provided by this window, that photographers seek to recreate.

taped to the window to cut down on the amount of light coming in. These can also be combined with color correction gels to bring the color temperature down to the temperature of tungsten if it is easier than changing all of your artificial sources to daylight temperatures. It will take some practice to become proficient at balancing contrast ratios, but you can follow these rules to start:

1. Choose a natural light source and make it your key light.
2. Color correct so all light sources match (if desired).
3. If the key is too weak, add light from the same direction as the key and light only the areas originally lit by the natural key.
4. Add fill light to bring the contrast ratios down.
5. Make sure the shadows caused by the fill lights are not evident in the shot; only the key light and effects lights should produce any noticeable shadows.

Lighting on the Run

News photographers will often use a small spotlight mounted on the video camera to provide enough light to properly expose the subject or scene being shot. (See Figure 5.36.) This method is usually used outdoors at night when no other light source is available.

However, it can also be used when the subject is moving in low-light situations and the photographer must keep the subject lit. This technique is also used in crowded situations when stationary light placement is impossible and in rushed situations in which the photographer has only enough time to shoot the scene and move on to the next location or get back to the station.

Speed is very important in many ENG situations. The run-and-gun method of news coverage requires a news photographer to have that camera light in place at all times so that subjects can be grabbed at a moment's notice for a quick shot off-the-shoulder interview or "bite." If there is no light, or if existing light is poor, the camera light or **sungun** is the best chance for a proper amount of illumination.

Using a Camera-Mounted Light

It has many names: sungun, peewee, beanie, headlight, Frezzi, or news light. But those terms all refer to the same thing: the camera light. Although the camera-mounted light is expedient, it has both practical and aesthetic drawbacks and is therefore not recommended for general field production. There is, however, an art to using one, but be forewarned:

1. Any light mounted close to the lens of the camera will shine almost directly into the eyes of the

Figure 5.36 Any camera used for news gathering must have a camera-mounted light available. This Anton Bauer Ultralite operates at 12 volts and uses the on-board camera battery for power.

person being interviewed, causing that person to squint or be uncomfortable. Often, the subject will turn away from the camera because of this.

2. The light may be reflected off the subject's skin or glasses, causing a hot spot in the picture.
3. A camera-mounted light aimed directly at a subject will yield a flat, washed-out image that prevents the desirable depth effect that can be obtained from three-point or natural lighting. (See Figure 5.37.)
4. The light used on a subject close to a background (such as a person against a wall) may cast an undesirable shadow on the background surface.
5. The camera light can create overexposed foregrounds and underexposed backgrounds.

The older style 30-volt power belt for a 250-watt portable light lasts only about 15 to 20 minutes. Today, many camera lights run off the same battery that the camera is using. They are also 12-volt lights and generally no more powerful than 20 or 25 watts. Some are as high as 75 watts. Since the average camera uses about 20 watts of power, using a 20-watt sungun attached to it will drain your battery twice as fast. A 75-watt light will drain it three times as fast. If you do much shooting early in your workday using that light, you may not have batteries available for later shots. A photographer working a night shift may have only two or three batteries to use, so it is important to conserve them and use AC lights when-

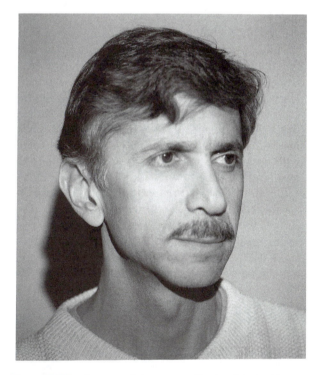

Figure 5.37 A camera light creates a flat, harsh look without beneficial shadows.

ever possible. It is advisable to use a separate battery belt for the sungun if possible. A 12-volt belt can run a 20- or even a 75-watt light for a long time.

If a dichroic filter is available for your battery light, daytime shadows on subjects can be filled with that light if the subject is close enough. A reporter standing in the shade, or backlit, can be helped out with a battery light and a dichroic filter. The effective distance for this application is only about 4 feet in open shade, so its use in this way is limited. And since most 12-volt lamps are 25 watts, they are ineffectual compared with direct sunlight.

Many photographers add a bit of diffusion to their sunguns to help minimize their harshness. The diffusion gives a more even spread to the light beam. This also allows the camera light to be used as a colorizing fill light. In fluorescent situations, for example, a little boost from a diffused sungun can give the subject a better skin tone and fill the eye socket shadows without washing out the entire shot or drawing attention to the fact that light was added.

One-Light Setups

Speed can be absolutely crucial in the news business. A good photographer is always looking for shortcuts to quicken the pace of production but at the same time keep that competitive edge. The biggest drawback to the camera light is the look: It just screams "down and dirty." To avoid this look, many photographers have set up a one-light package they can easily carry with them and set up quickly. The most basic one is a single-light head, such as the Lowel Omni, with an umbrella (to diffuse it), a stand, and an extension cord. The umbrella light gives a pleasingly soft high-quality light that is directable. You can create soft-edged shadows or place it over the top of the camera to simply raise the base light of a scene. Even in the most rushed setups, the light works well because it can be placed almost anywhere. The lighting may be flat in some situations, but if all you need is base illumination, you've got it and it's still a step above the sungun look.

LIGHT AS AN EDITORIAL TOOL

Just as the painters of the Renaissance found, light can be used for so much more than mere illumination. Light, or more accurately the shadows it creates, can tell us so much about a scene. Even in news situations, the photographer still needs to interpret and communicate what he or she sees using the camera and all the tools at hand. At every lighting seminar ever held, it seems, there is someone who asks the

A

B

Figure 5.38 (A) Here, the interview is lit in a high-key fashion and conveys a somewhat neutral tone. (B) In this photo, the interview is lit in a low-key style. The dark areas dominate and create a serious mood.

speaker how they would light a particular location. The answer is always the same: "Show me the script first." Lighting must match what's going on in the scene whether it's news, commercial, or fiction.

High Key/Low Key

Lighting communication styles fall into two broad areas: **high key** and **low key**. High-key scenes are bright with a low contrast ratio. They have few shadows and any modeling is very subtle. This type of lighting is usually thought of as upbeat, happy, positive, successful, and energetic. It's the lighting of comedies. Low-key scenes are mostly dark, with many dense shadows and little fill light. The key light seems to be the only light being used. This lighting is thought of as serious, sad, concerned, negative, failing, and low energy. It's the lighting of dramas.

The best place to see examples of the these two types of lighting are on the network news magazines like *Dateline*, *20/20*, and *60 Minutes*. A story about a swindler and his victims will have most of the interviews done with dark backgrounds and subjects with well-defined attached shadows modeling their faces: the serious, somber tones of low-key lighting. A story profiling a popular singer will have interviews with bright lighting, very thin shadows, and bright backgrounds (usually looking out windows): the cheery, glowing tones of high-key lighting. (See Figure 5.38.)

Time of Day

One of the oldest tricks of lighting is to show time of day. The long shadows of early morning and late afternoon are unmistakable. Add color to them—gold for morning and orange for evening—and no one will miss the meaning. This not only applies to outdoor shots but more importantly to indoor setups. By placing a light outside a window, shining it into the room at a low angle, and adding color you can get the time of day effect quite easily. You can also keep the light

in the room and, by adding gobos in the shape of windows, create both the look of window light and the time of day. (See Figure 5.39.)

Mood Lighting

Once your basic lighting setup is completed, use the remaining time before the actual shooting to experiment with mood lighting. By simply modifying the setup, you can easily manipulate the mood of the shot. When lighting in the field do not forget that adding light to a scene starts to change the mood of the scene. The more subtle and indirect the lighting, the more natural people tend to appear and behave.

The mood you are trying to convey will dictate the type of lighting for a particular shot. Imagine that you must shoot an interview with a welfare mother in a darkly lit apartment. The easiest way to bring up the base light level would be to use the camera-mounted light. But a sungun interview with bright light shining in the woman's eyes would look like a harsh, uncaring invasion by the media into the woman's life. If that's the look you want, okay. But you can do better for her and yourself while more accurately portraying her situation. You can shoot this interview using just one light, but its placement is crucial.

One possible solution might be a diffused light placed at a 90° side angle to the camera. Attach barndoors to the light or flag it to keep the light off the

Figure 5.39 By adding a light outside the window at eye level, this scene appears to take place in either early morning or late afternoon light. Coloring the light can determine which it is: gold for morning, orange for evening.

background behind the woman so it remains dark. The dreary apartment retains its character and the woman is lit, but she is less likely to be distracted by the light. Your audience will focus on the woman and her story, rather than the bright lights in her eyes or a distracting background flatly illuminated by the camera-mounted light. The subtle lighting allows the woman to be the most important element in the story, not the expensive equipment that has intruded into her life. The strong shadows on her face convey the serious tone of the subject matter. Good lighting is lighting that is not noticed. Good lighting techniques enhance the mood and bring out the subject for the audience. Good lighting does not challenge or distort the existing mood of the scene or direct attention from the subject.

There are many styles to creative lighting. Most are derived from master painters—like Rembrandt—whose work can be seen in art history books or art museums anywhere. If you want to be more than just a basic photographer, you need to study the styles that make up the creative world of lighting.

Directing the Viewer

Across the broad range of lighting styles, there is one element that should always be present: showing the viewer what's important. Most of the time that will be the subject. It can also be any aspect of the frame you wish to draw attention to. By only lighting selected areas of the frame you show the viewer which elements you want them to notice. The subject, such as the interviewee, is the obvious choice, but additional aspects such as background items can add both to the editorial meaning and the aesthetic value of the shot.

An interview with the CEO of a large corporation can be enhanced by not shooting him or her seated behind the desk but out in front of the desk. At the desk would leave little background to be used in the frame and thereby eliminate added visual editorial content. By placing him or her in a chair far from the desk—but with the desk in the background—you can shoot the CEO with a close-up and have a pertinent element still visible. Selectively lighting the desk and its large chair to make it stand out while leaving the remainder of the background dark, will emphasize the CEO's powerful position. We see, literally, the position of power (the large desk and chair isolated by the light), while at the same time we see the CEO in a close shot. You have maximized the information given to the viewer visually while the viewer listens to the dialog.

As you set up for any shot, look around for elements that can add to the understanding of the picture. Even in noninterview shots, look for items that are important to the story. Selectively, even if subtly, make them brighter than the rest of the shot. A story about a teenager's success on the baseball field might contain a shot of his room with a wall of trophies. You should find a way of lighting the trophies (light from a window?) while letting the rest of the room remain at least slightly darker. Even a wide shot of the room will immediately show off the trophies to the viewer. With today's fast-paced editing and limited screen time for any one shot, no matter which form of media, this added visual emphasis helps the viewer understand the scene quickly and easily. (See Figure 5.40.)

To Light or Not to Light?

In ENG work, because of time constraints, you will repeatedly face the dilemma of mood preservation versus mood contamination. You don't have the time to recreate the mood with better lighting, but the existing light levels or color are just not quite right. When do you forgo the existing mood and turn on the lights? Only experience answers that question. Fortunately, new cameras and lenses are being introduced that require lower base-light levels than their predecessors, which should allow news lighting in the future to continue to become easier and more subtle. In the meantime, one good rule of thumb for natural light interviews is to shoot when you see the whites of your subject's eyes. If there is not enough existing light to see the white areas of the eyes as white and not a dark gray in the viewfinder, then you need to add more light. Keep in mind that this is a very general rule. Once again, contrast will be your overriding factor. Contrast will determine separation of subject and background. Often the subject is too dark or too backlit against a bright background; you will be unable to see a subject's eyes clearly. You may be able to overexpose the scene but still not see their eyes. More light must be added to the scene to keep the subject from appearing corpse-like or as a silhouette—effects you do not want except in special situations. Decide what the subject of your shot is, then expose for it. If the rest of the scene is overexposed, add light to your subject so you can iris down for the overexposed portion or change the shot.

Adding a decibel boost will increase the sensitivity of the pickup device, thereby increasing the range of light in which your camera is effective. This should only be done in the most extreme cases. If a decibel

Figure 5.40 Highlighting an object in the background can be both editorial (the object is part of the story) and artistic (the object adds a dynamic to the frame design).

boost gives that added detail to a shot to be able to see the subject, then do it. Remember that every decibel boost increases the noise or graininess of the picture. At +18 dB, the picture quality is quite poor. Any decibel boost for EFP use is strictly out. Only in very desperate ENG situations should you use this gain switch for signal boosting. Choose to use it very carefully.

CONCLUSIONS

Regardless of the lighting style you choose, approach the setup with the following principles in mind:

1. Survey the available light, subjects to be lit, and lighting equipment on hand.
2. Decide on the appropriate color temperature.
3. Consider light direction and balance.
4. Light for your wide shot first, then your tight shots.
5. Build your lighting by setting one light at a time:

   a. Start with your key light; place and adjust it with no other lights on until you are satisfied with the results.
   b. Place and adjust your fill light; make sure that its placement and intensity are acceptable for the situation.
   c. Complete the basic setup with a backlight.

   d. If necessary, add background lights and/or a kicker, eye light, or special-effects lights.

By building your lighting setup one light at a time, problems surface early and can be more easily corrected without the confusion of other lights in wrong positions.

Keep in mind that turning on *any* light changes everything. You have contaminated the scene. The choice then becomes how much effort you put into rectifying the damage.

In EFP situations the script will always determine the solution. You are satisfying a client and your lighting has to do that as well. How well you light will determine how well you are communicating the ideas of the client through the script. The end justifies the means. To compete in the world of production, you need the highest skill levels you can possibly obtain and lighting will be the highest skill of all.

For news, the answers are not at all obvious. The camera light says "news crew" so the viewer knows there's a news photographer there taping the scene. But that light causes some people to act unnatural, appear unnatural, or even perform for the camera. Not using the light may yield more "real" results. Turning out all the existing lights in an office and setting up your own to selectively light certain areas for emphasis may be unrealistic but also may be a better communication of real information. Simply shooting the CEO behind the desk with a blank wall for a background may be more real because that's what's really there. What should you do? The writer gets to write selective words and edit the interview down to use only what he or she deems important or what "should" be communicated. Why shouldn't the photographer have that same ability to freely communicate what he or she feels is important, visually, to the same story? There are strong arguments for both ways of doing it. Only you and your employer can make that decision. The point of this book is to make the skills of both options available to you. (See Figure 5.41.)

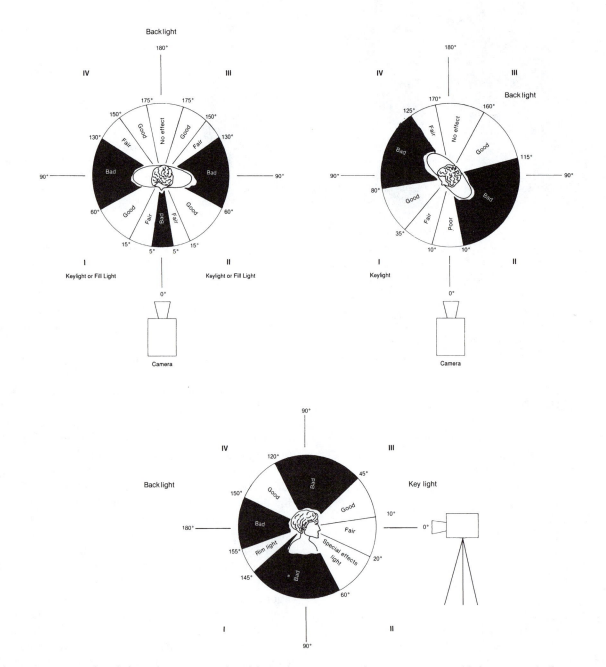

Figure 5.41 Use these lighting zones as general guidelines. They may not apply to recreating natural lighting, special effects, or creative lighting, but do deal with formal portraiture lighting.

part two

The Process

6 Scriptwriting

Many scriptwriters feel that writing for portable video is easier than writing for the studio. This opinion probably stems from the fact that the portable video scriptwriter can have natural settings and does not rely on artificially created settings in the studio. Also, the nature of portable video includes shooting for the edit, where a specific look or effect can be created by doing a number of takes with slight variations and selecting the one that matches the script best during the postproduction process.

Portable video projects can be long or short, dramatic or comical, fictional or factual, but they are all derived from a script. Scripts are necessary for ENG and EFP because they are blueprints or diagrams of the way stories are actually put together.

Regardless of style, intent, or format, video scripts have something in common: They are all written for the spoken word, that is, for the ear. Writing for video is unlike writing for the print media, which is writing for the eye. Readers of the print media can read at their own comfortable pace. They can reread words or sentences whenever necessary. This puts the burden of comprehension on the reader.

In video, the script must be written in such a way that it is comprehensible to the audience the first time it is heard (unless it is a training tape that can be replayed). All viewers see and hear the video at the same rate. Even if viewers watch a videotape by themselves and are able to replay it, video scripts should be understandable at the outset.

Writing for any script requires both common sense and talent. A writer needs common sense to realize that writing for the ear requires relatively short sentences, words, and phrases easy to pronounce and unambiguous in their meaning, and a conversational style. Writers demonstrate their talent by conveying precise meaning and selecting creative and interesting approaches to the material. This is not always easy—many scripts deal with mundane factual material, such as a piece explaining how a mowing device is connected to a tractor. A talented scriptwriter can take dull, factual material and present it in an interesting way.

ELECTRONIC NEWS GATHERING

Scripts for ENG stories are generally written by reporters involved in covering the events shown in the video portion of the story. These people are often trained in broadcast journalism and have certain conventions that they must follow. Stories involving hard news such as major fires, crimes, or elections require quick turnaround time—the story is often written the day it is broadcast or even just minutes before it airs. Features, stories that do not necessarily involve hard news and are not time sensitive, are more like EFP projects, because they can allow for more planning time and need not be aired the day they are shot. (See Figure 6.1.) Essentially, ENG stories are written to convey precise and understandable material in an informative yet interesting way. The written material should address these questions: who, what, where, and when.

The biggest difference between ENG and EFP scriptwriting is the fact that ENG scripts are almost always written after the video has been shot. After an event has been covered, the ENG writer reviews the tape and writes a script so that the raw footage can be edited into a finished story. This procedure is

Bighorn Sheep pkg

(chopper nat sound up)

Attached by a rope to this helicopter are sheep. . .Rocky Mountain bighorn sheep. . .animals that were once a natural part of the Southwest. But today, in northern New Mexico's Santa Fe and Carson National Forests. . .it is only through efforts like these that the sheep have returned to their historic rangeland.

SOT AMY in 40:19 "The operation has been an unbelievable, logistical undertaking, because this involves working in a wilderness environment, which are very unpredictable." out 40:29

Amy Fisher, who heads up the bighorn sheep project for the New Mexico Game and Fish Department, says the goal is to capture and move 20 to 30 adult sheep. . .any lambs would be a bonus.

(NAT SOT "Watcha doing, huh?")

STAND UP "Behind me is the Pecos Wilderness Area where the sheep have come from--they were re-introduced there some 15 years ago. Now, part of that herd will be headed to another Wilderness area called Wheeler Peak."

Before heading out to their new home. . .these sheep are weighed. . .examined. . .inoculated with antibiotics. . .

(NAT SOUND "respiration. . .16. . .16. . .pulse. ..)

. . .all in a very intense outdoor mobil clinic of sorts where seconds matter.

SOT "We gotta keep handling time down, we gotta keep temperatures down and pulse and respiration down. They actually could die from the handling procedure."

The sheep are driven by truck to a different forest. . .their new home. . .a place where their presence is a step toward bringing this ecosystem back to the way it was.

SOT "It represents a real gift to the state of New Mexico."

In northern New Mexico. . .Bonnie Holmes, for CNN."

Figure 6.1 This script for a news feature includes natural sound on tape (SOT), footage of sheep being transported and attended to, and a reporter's stand-up shot. Courtesy of Bonnie Holmes.

necessary, because the reporter is often unsure of what is going to happen at the event or what the usable footage will be until after the video recording has been made. (Keep in mind that a reshoot or second take of an event is often impossible in ENG.)

The ENG script is written between the time the event is shot and the time it is broadcast. This usually means that the script is written during the afternoon just before the evening newscast. The ENG scriptwriter has hours or sometimes just minutes to write the script. This is quite different from scriptwriting for EFP.

ELECTRONIC FIELD PRODUCTION

Generally, EFP scriptwriters have much more time for the process than scriptwriters in ENG. EFP scripts are often written with enough lead time to allow for a careful review and revision process. The process allows a script to be evaluated not just for its meaning and effectiveness, but also for its adherence to the capabilities of the production unit that will shoot it and to the budget for the project.

Scripts for commercials, training tapes, entertainment, and so on can be written and rewritten until the scriptwriter, producer, director, and client are satisfied. The scripts usually do not have to reflect the reality of an event or issue as they do in ENG, but they must reflect the concept and intentions of the client and/or producer.

The procedure for EFP scriptwriting is often careful and lengthy:

1. The goals for the script must be set.
2. The audience must be carefully analyzed.
3. A format must be selected.
4. A central visual theme should be developed.
5. Research must be done to learn about the concepts to be shown or explained in the script.
6. A treatment should be written that conveys the essence of the script.
7. An outline is prepared that lists in proper order all the important aspects of the script.
8. A storyboard is often necessary to help others visualize your ideas.
9. The script must be written.
10. Reviews are often made at this point.
11. Revisions are made in accordance with reviews.

Goals

Once the process of initiating a video project has begun, set your goals at a reasonable and attainable level. Attempting to present the entire history of a large corporation in a comprehensive and detailed fashion may be unrealistic in a 3-minute portion of a 10-minute video presented to stockholders at their annual meeting. It may also destroy your budget. The best way to avoid a problem like this is to set specific goals. Goal outlining should be done on two levels. First, determine the overall purpose of your project. Is it to entertain, inform, demonstrate, or persuade? Then set very specific goals.

An instructional videotape that attempts to familiarize the sales managers of a farm implement company with a new model tractor might have the following goals:

1. Provide information about the new model: size, weight, performance, cost.
2. Increase motivation to sell the new model by explaining bonuses and incentives.
3. Introduce marketing and sales procedures that will enhance sales of the new model.

Any communication may have three different kinds of effects on an audience: cognitive, emotional,

and behavioral. **Cognitive effects** are those that occur when the audience gains knowledge or information. **Emotional** effects are those that cause an attitudinal or mode change in the audience. The third effect, **behavioral change,** occurs when the audience actually changes its behavior in some measurable way, such as buying a new brand of detergent or voting for a politician. In the planning stage, these potential effects can be viewed as obtainable goals or objectives.

Many video projects do not have all three types of desired objectives. Videos made for artistic or entertainment purposes may only strive for an emotional effect. It is appropriate, however, to consider that all three effects may take place in your intended audience.

Knowing the Audience

Once you have decided what the goals are for your video, it is time to pay more serious attention to your audience. Your video project can be tremendously exciting, visually creative, and perfectly shot, but it may be a total failure if your script is not written for the intended audience. Consider the difference in a script for a feature that will appear on a local broadcast station's magazine show and a script for a video that will be shown only to volunteers for a charity at their organizational meeting. The topic may be the same, but the style would be quite different. The feature is scripted to heighten awareness about the good things being done by the charity and the need for volunteers or donors to help. The video shown at the organizational meeting would be written to raise the enthusiasm and energy level of the audience and demonstrate or suggest specific behaviors needed to help the charity.

This same charity might want to produce a video for use in elementary schools to inform children about the importance of the charity's efforts. Obviously, the language of the script and the pacing and style of the shooting and editing would be different from either the magazine feature or the video made for committed volunteers.

The more you know about your audience, the better. Demographic factors such as age, income, sex, and education level are perhaps the best starting points to help you become familiar with the audience. Information about these factors will help you to make some basic decisions about your script. You may also want to consider psychological factors such as lifestyle, attitudes, personal interests, and hobbies.

Writing for a small, well-defined audience can be very different from writing for a large heterogeneous audience.

The exhibition of the final product is also a consideration. Will 10 people see the video? 10,000? Tens of thousands? How will the video actually be shown? On broadcast TV? Cable? A private showing to a small audience using a small TV monitor? A showing to an audience of 100 or more using a projection TV? Will a frame or even the entire video be part of a World Wide Web page, Internet site, or multimedia presentation? After you have carefully considered the audience, you can move on to deciding on your format.

Format

Video projects can be categorized by their format, which refers to the overall organization of the project. Broadcast-TV programs conform to a limited number of standard formats that provide understanding of the type of entertainment and a time frame for viewers. In broadcast TV, most programs are written for 30- or 60-minute lengths. The most common formats include:

drama	situation comedy
newscast	talk show/interview
game show	documentary
sports or event coverage	highlight (sports)
compilation/video clips	magazine/features
action/adventure	

Many of these formats have been adapted to nonbroadcast situations to get attention and to increase viewer appreciation. For example, a new health benefit could be explained to employees of a large corporation by an executive talking to the camera and using an occasional chart or graphic. Another approach might have employees in a simulated game show, like *Jeopardy*, trying to give answers to questions about changes from old benefits to new. The parody of the game show format gives the writers the opportunity to inject humor into what might be very dull material. Another approach might be to have a TV talk show host interview the company executive rather than have the executive do a talking head. The show becomes more visually interesting; the question-and-answer format allows the host to represent the audience and their predictable questions.

Other formats are more appropriate for non-broadcast TV projects or those that are not program-length projects. These include:

demonstration/how-to	music video
instruction/classroom topics	video art
public service announcement (PSA)	commercial

Choosing one of these formats or a combination can give your project a structure and organization helpful to you as a writer and to your audience as viewers.

Style

The style of your writing can vary considerably, but in this context we can categorize styles of writing by how the information of your text gets into your program. You can have an announcer give information, usually referred to as narration. You can have dialogue, words delivered by two people at a time, that is either informational, dramatic, or simply entertaining. You can have a combination of either of the above with natural "sound bites" that are words delivered by a speaker in response to prompting or a question.

Narration

Narration is usually a simple, straightforward reading of the script by a narrator or announcer. The narrator is usually not on camera, nor recorded when the video is shot. Narration is also referred to as **voice-over**. It is common practice to record the narration at a recording session separate from all visual shooting.

Narration should be written to enhance the video and make it more compelling. Good narration guides viewers to a specific time and place that is represented by the video. This can be important when your setting is somewhat generic. For example, an opening shot may be of a person in bed sleeping in a darkened room; an alarm clock next to the bed reads 3:10. The audience may automatically assume that this was shot at night. Since the intention of the video is to inform the audience about the dangers of sleep deprivation and irregular sleep behavior, the narration could be used to let the audience know that it is 3:10 P.M. not 3:10 A.M. For example, the opening narrative line could be: "If it was 3:10 A.M. Ralph Salesman would not be shown in this video. The problem is, this video was shot at 3:10 P.M., when Ralph should be meeting with sales clients. Ralph suffers from 'nonsleepnia,' a condition that is characterized by irregular sleep patterns. In this video we will discuss this vexing behavioral problem and suggest proper methods of treating it." The narration helps establish the scene and leads the audience into the purpose of the video. In other words, the narration can be a necessary part of the establishing visual shot.

Narration is best when it is succinct and used sparingly. Don't use it unless it adds something to the video. Heavy narration is necessary for a training video or a video dealing with events that occurred but were not shot (for example, some historical event before the age of photography), but in all cases, avoid continuous, monotonous narration. Organize your narration in complete thoughts, like paragraphs in the print media. Don't be afraid to break up your narration with periods of silence (assuming you have good video) or to change your narrator or use "sound-bite" type material when appropriate people answer questions relevant to the topic of your video.

Because video projects are written for the ear, the style of narration should be conversational, not overly flowery or stiffly formal. Remember, your video might be viewed by many people at once, but videos are most effective when they reach people as individuals, similar to interpersonal communication.

Dialogue

Dialogue is commonly used for dramatic presentations or when situations are dramatized. It is especially difficult to write because, unlike narration, you have to write in more than one voice. Although referred to as dialogue, this style of writing often encompasses more than just two people, but usually it is written with one character addressing another character at a time. Characters come and go throughout, but most of the script is written for two people interacting at a time.

Interview

Writing for a program that involves interviews requires question preparation for the interviewer, but does not require that you write responses for the interviewee. Therefore, your task is to prepare questions that are thought provoking and answer provoking. This is most common in ENG, but also occurs in corporate video and feature/magazine programs. You want to write questions that will not be answered by simple "Yes," "No," or "I don't know" responses. Many informational programs will have a combination of narration and responses from persons who are relevant to the program. For example, a program designed to explore a company's role in preserving the ecological integrity around one of its manufacturing plants could open with narration extolling the virtues of the company's efforts at preservation, but also include sound bites from credible authorities such as biologists who respond to questions about the environmental conditions at the site.

Central Visual Theme

Your central visual theme should be stated as a short phrase or sentence that conveys the essence of your visual goal and the look of your video project. The statement should include the major visual elements of your project.

If the project is a 30-second public service announcement for the local public library, an appropriate phrase might be "Books are your windows on the world." An appropriate phrase for a 5-minute demonstration videotape of a new computer workstation could be "The new Plum III computer fits your desk, your hands, and your mind." By stating your visual idea in a short, succinct central visual theme at the beginning, you prevent further levels of script and other production complexities from obscuring your original intent. Should problems arise during the preproduction phase of your project, it may be helpful to review your initial statement.

Research

Because producers of EFP video can provide their services to many different kinds of clients, you should not be surprised to learn that the product or service that is the central topic of the video project is one that may require a familiarity with technical terms or procedures beyond the realm of the video producer's experience. Since a complete video project requires a fluency in both the video and audio portions of the project, research is often necessary to attain this fluency. This fluency can be achieved in several ways:

1. Interviews with knowledgeable individuals
2. Reading

3. Viewing other information previously prepared either by or for the client.

Interviews

Interviews with experts may serve two purposes: You may better understand the topic area and you may be able to videotape the expert and use some of the footage for your project.

Reading Material

Reading material should be available in the form of trade journals or newspaper or newsletter articles that explain the area and provide background information. Books are often available to give in-depth information for longer projects or those involving highly technical subject matter.

Client Information

Information that originated from the client is potentially the most helpful, but it is often overlooked. Press releases, marketing information, previous advertising, or sales brochures can give a quick and accurate overview of the client's goals, techniques, or philosophy.

For example, a few years ago, a sugar manufacturing company needed a videotape that would give a brief history of the company and describe the steps taken to manufacture sugar from sugar beets. The tape was to be produced for elementary schools and libraries.

After checking numerous possible sources, it was found that an old brochure gave much of the historical information and a 20-year-old film had animation sequences in it that helped show and explain the complex technical processes involved. In fact, the animation sequences were still accurate enough that some careful editing allowed them to be transferred to video and used to explain that portion of the company's operation. Needless to say, much time and money was saved as a result of the research for related materials.

Internet Search

Just about any topic, person, or place can be researched through the resources available on the Internet. If you have a good idea regarding what you are looking for, many of the **search engines** available can find very specific information for you in a very short time. Just about anything, including audio and video information, can be downloaded to help give you a better understanding of your topic.

Treatment

Presentations involving drama, characters, and a plot require a stated treatment or brief summary of the project, written in the earliest stages of preproduction to allow the creator (or scriptwriter) to tell the story and better orient the production team (even the scriptwriter). The treatment is a short encapsulation of the setting, characters, points of view, and the plot. Major events or changes in characters or characterizations should be mentioned in the treatment. While this step is required in fiction, it is also strongly recommended for nonfiction. The treatment tells the story in narrative form (without dialogue) so that the client or financial backers have a good feeling for what the finished product will look like.

The treatment not only keeps the scriptwriter on track, but it also keeps other members of the creative team *and the client* on track. The treatment provides firm guidelines for everyone to remember throughout the creative process.

For informational projects that have a nonfiction style, the treatment may be quite brief—two or three pages for a short video. This type of treatment should contain three elements: goal, strategy, and content.

Goal

The goal of the project should accurately reflect what the originator wants: training, promotion, publicity, or whatever. This should be accomplished in a few sentences or a single paragraph.

Strategy

The strategy of the production explains what method will be used to accomplish the goal of the production. If the goal is to teach salespeople how to use a new laptop computer to enter sales data, then the strategy might be a step-by-step demonstration showing the computer and the data entry procedure. If the goal is to heighten awareness of a new health benefit, the strategy might be a simulated press conference with the most commonly expressed questions asked and answered. Obviously, your strategy should logically relate to achieving your goal. Your client should not wonder how your pure creativity is going to accomplish the goal. If the strategy does not make sense to the client at this stage, you are headed for big problems later.

Content

The content need not be a verbatim script, but a general outline of what will happen and when. Being too specific is probably as inappropriate as being too vague. It is best to give yourself some creative wiggle room here. Often some of your original ideas will not pan out; leave room for slight changes to accommodate ideas that actually make it to the video intact. But if you are too vague, the linkage between content, strategy, and goal might not make sense to your client.

For most corporate video projects, a few pages specifying the treatment are sufficient. A complex fiction project with a 30- or 60-minute duration might require a 10- to 15-page treatment to help convey what the final product will look like. This type of treatment may include descriptions of the locations, characters, and some camera direction as well.

Outline

Now all the facts, figures, and visual ideas need to be organized so that they will form the skeleton for the body of your project. An outline should simply and succinctly list the points, facts, comments, and visualizations that will tell your story in the appropriate order. You can easily reshuffle your ideas to form the best story at this stage. Allowing your outline to be reviewed by other production team members, other professionals, or even the client may save hours of rewriting, reediting, or even reshooting. (See Figure 6.2.)

One convenient way to organize your outline is to use index cards. Utilize one idea, fact, or visualization per index card and include, when possible, a small sketch or photo to clarify the visual idea. Arrange your cards in a logical sequence, then try to tell your story by reading (and embellishing on) each card in the sequence. A few attempts at this storytelling will probably reveal inconsistency, improper order, and difficult or clumsy transitions that may be hiding in your future outline. Once your cards are in the proper order, construct an outline and allow others to give you some feedback.

Storyboard

The next step after the written outline is a storyboard or pictorial outline, which can be drawn up by the director, producer, advertising agency, or even the clients. The storyboard is a roughed-out drawing of every scene to be produced in the video. Special pads of paper with blank TV screen outlines on them are usually used to maintain the proper aspect ratio for TV photography. (See Figure 6.3.) With this form, each picture or scene is shown with the dialogue or camera directions to be used directly beneath it. Another format that requires more descriptive information has the description of the scene to the right of the picture. (See Figure 6.4.)

The storyboard allows all crew members to see exactly how the shots should look. This allows for all blocking, props, lighting, special equipment, and special effects to be worked out while the video is still in preproduction. Costs and time can be more closely controlled using the storyboard, and the entire crew knows exactly how the finished product should look. Storyboards help eliminate the shocked comment that occurs on showing the client the rough-cut version: "That's not at all what we had in mind."

A good storyboard can save time in the long run and help head off serious problems in the production of the piece. Even if no one involved in the production can draw, stick figures and rough drawings are better than none at all. Alfred Hitchcock never shot a frame of film until it was carefully drawn out in every detail on a storyboard. Steven Spielberg often has drawings of sets and pictures of locations for all scenes before shooting a movie.

Script

Now you are ready to write a script that will guide you in shooting the raw footage for your program. At this point your creativity and skill must be utilized. There are some guidelines to keep in mind:

1. *Visualize the items on your outline or expand the pictures from your storyboard.* Fill in the gaps between the panels of the storyboard; visualize the transitions. How do you get from one panel (or outline item) to the next? Think visually; then allow the audio portion of the script to enhance the video.

2. *Make an effort to capture your audience's interest very early in the script.* Try to "hook" your audience with a compelling audio, video, or combined shot in the introductory part of the script. You need this to keep your audience throughout your project. In a video brochure for a new apartment complex, you might have an opening shot of a terrific view of a nearby mountain peak. Your narration could say something like: "How would you like a view like this from your apartment? Keep watching and we'll show you a new apartment community where every

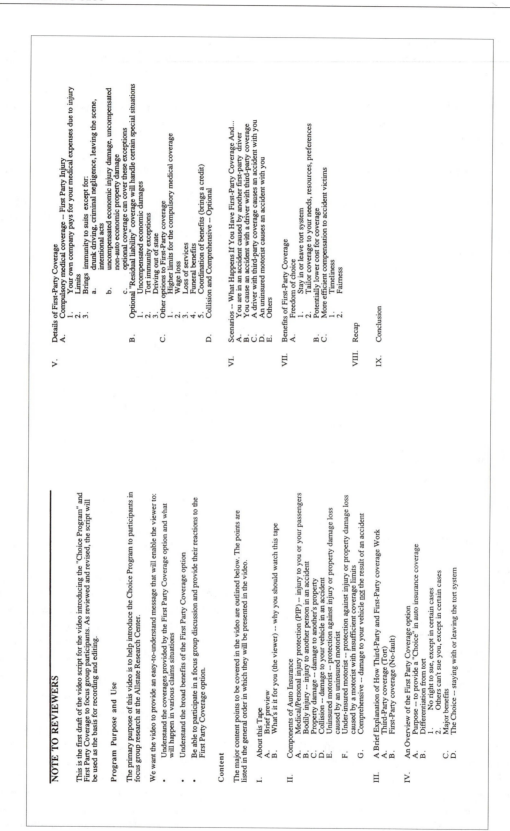

Figure 6.2 Objectives and outline for a corporate video script. Courtesy Allstate Insurance Company.

VISUAL MEDIA PRODUCTIONS

MOTOROLA INC

STORYBOARD

Project Number : ___ ___ ___ ___ ___ — ___ ___ ___ ___   Date : _____   Page _____ of _____

Project Name : _____   Contact Person : _____

Producer : _____   Director : _____   Writer : _____

VISUAL

AUDIO

VISUAL

AUDIO

Figure 6.3   Blanks used for a storyboard by a corporate video operation. Courtesy Motorola, Integrated Information Systems Group, Visual Media Communications.

Congress on Endovascular Interventions SPFX Sequence Number3 (FLAME)

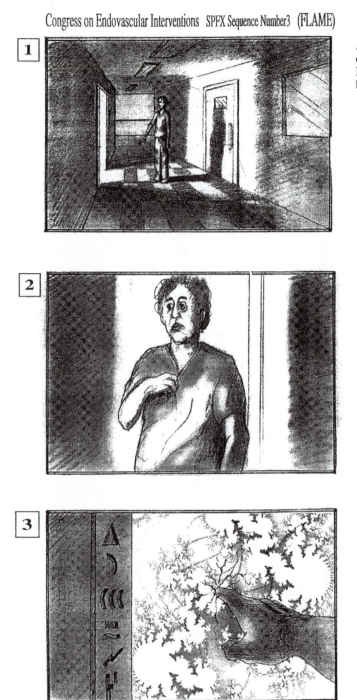

As the surgeon passes down the empty corridor, he sees a strange light emanating from what used to be OR#2..

Frightened and confused, yet entranced by the light, he moves in for a closer examination of this compelling occurrence.

We notice strange symbols on the door jam that appears to be made of an unfamiliar metal alloy or resin.

The doorway seems to be filled with clouds of swirling colored gas...oddly two dimensional in appearance.

As he touches the "barrier" he is suddenly drawn in... closer and closer... unable to break free of its pull.

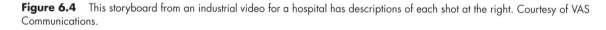

Figure 6.4 This storyboard from an industrial video for a hospital has descriptions of each shot at the right. Courtesy of VAS Communications.

apartment has a view like this or better! And if you call a number we'll give you later in this video, you may win a free year's lease!"

3. *Consider your writing style.* Do not write as if you are lecturing, writing a technical document, or a brochure. Make sure that your writing is conversational. It is best to try to create short sentences. This is the way most people talk to one another; therefore, it is appropriate in both dialogue or narration. Another suggestion is to avoid obscure or unfamiliar terminology unless the narrator explains the terms shortly before or after their use. Make sure that the dialogue or narration is appropriate for the speaker(s). You would not have the president of a corporation say, "Let's get your butts in gear," during a motivational video aimed at company workers. The statement "Let's combine our energies and talents so we can get busy solving these problems together" would be more appropriate. A 5-year-old would not normally say, "I seem to have developed an intense craving for an ice cream cone." More probably, a 5-year-old would say, "Mommy, can I have some ice cream?" or "Gimme some ice cream!"

4. *Keep in mind that regardless of the specific goal of the video project, it must tell a story.* It should have a beginning, middle, and end with an appropriate story line that attempts to meet your objectives. Make sure that your central visual theme is not obscured by an overly complex or convoluted story line.

5. *Know what length of time your video must be and write accordingly.* Assume that about 20 words equals 10 seconds of reading time. Each minute will have about 120 words. After it is written, read it out loud and time it to make sure you are accurate if length is important.

6. *Include all necessary directions that explain comprehensively how to translate the written words and ideas into video information.* The style, clarity, and completeness of the script should be such that it allows a competent director who may not have been involved with the planning or scriptwriting to take the script and shoot the program as you intended it to be shot. (See Table 6.1 for some common production terms used in TV scriptwriting.)

7. *Expect revisions of your script.* No script remains intact in its first version throughout the production process. Your script should be considered a first draft.

Table 6.1. Terms used in scriptwriting.

Camera Shots	Common Abbreviations
Long shot, wide shot	LS, WS
Medium shot	MS
Close-up, tight shot	CU, TS
Extreme close-up	XCU or ECU
Camera Movement	
Zoom or zoom in	Z or ZI
Pan (left or right)	PL or PR
Dolly (in or out)	DI or DO
Tilt (up or down)	TU or TD
Transitions	
Cut, take	—
Dissolve	Diss
Fade (in or out)	FI or FO

At this point, your script is ready for some fine-tuning in the review process. (See Figure 6.5.) If you feel that your script will be going through many reviews and edits, it may be easier to use some type of scriptwriting program to help you format and edit quickly. Although some word processors have this capability, it may be best to get a program that is designed for writing scripts for electronic media. (See Figure 6.6.)

Review

After the first draft is written, most scripts are subject to some sort of review process. For a practitioner of video art or a student of video, this review process is internal. The scriptwriter should reread the script a few days after it is written and reassess its merit. Does it depict the desired mood or concepts in the manner intended? Often some rewriting is necessary.

For scriptwriters in corporate video or any video made for a client, the client will generally want to read the first draft to see if it conveys the desired meaning. In many cases, this review process is not just helpful, it is mandatory. Production often cannot start without client approval of the script. Although it may seem tedious, this review and approval process is a safeguard for the EFP producer and scriptwriter.

Asia-Pacific Aviation Symposium • 3/6/96 • 3

VISUAL	AUDIO	

VISUAL

5. Same map with the 15 highlighted countries fading back. List also fades out.

6. U.S.A. is highlighted.

FAA logo fades in right.

7. Same graphic. Motorola logo fades in.

Reel 19 – W/S AA taking into DFW ✓
5:01:24

Fade u (M) logo

Music
Graphic Slate #1

8. **(a)** Open with modified version of the spinning globe graphic.

Super in ghosted letters:

Key Products

(b) Shot of the four CM-200 boxes: the VHF transmitter, the VHF receiver, the UHF #2) transmitter and the UHF receiver.

Reel 4 – 4:06:26

Super:

- CM-200

AUDIO

1 ...and we've won a series of

2 important contracts with the

3 United States Federal Aviation

4 Administration.

5

6 Today, every major airport in the

7 American National Airspace System

8 uses Motorola technology.

Rear ob AA plane taking off – Reel 17 1:34:31

-- SUBTLE SHIFT/FIRST SEGMENT *out to all 4*
4:10:09 – zoom out to all 4

9

#1) → 4:02:06 – Snap zoom out to 4 shot 10

11 One of our key products that is

currently in use in airports across

12 the U.S. is the CM-200 / a 19- *Dissolve*

13 inch, rack-mounted, UHF/VHF

14 transmitter and receiver system.

15

dt 16
(4:02:55 pan up to 4 shot
(4:03:09 push up to 4 shot 17

18
tilt down to CM-200 products 19

20

21

22

23

24

25

Visual Media Productions

Media, Publication Systems & Services, GSTG

Figure 6.5 A script with typical revisions. Courtesy of Motorola, Integrated Information Systems Group, Visual Media Communications.

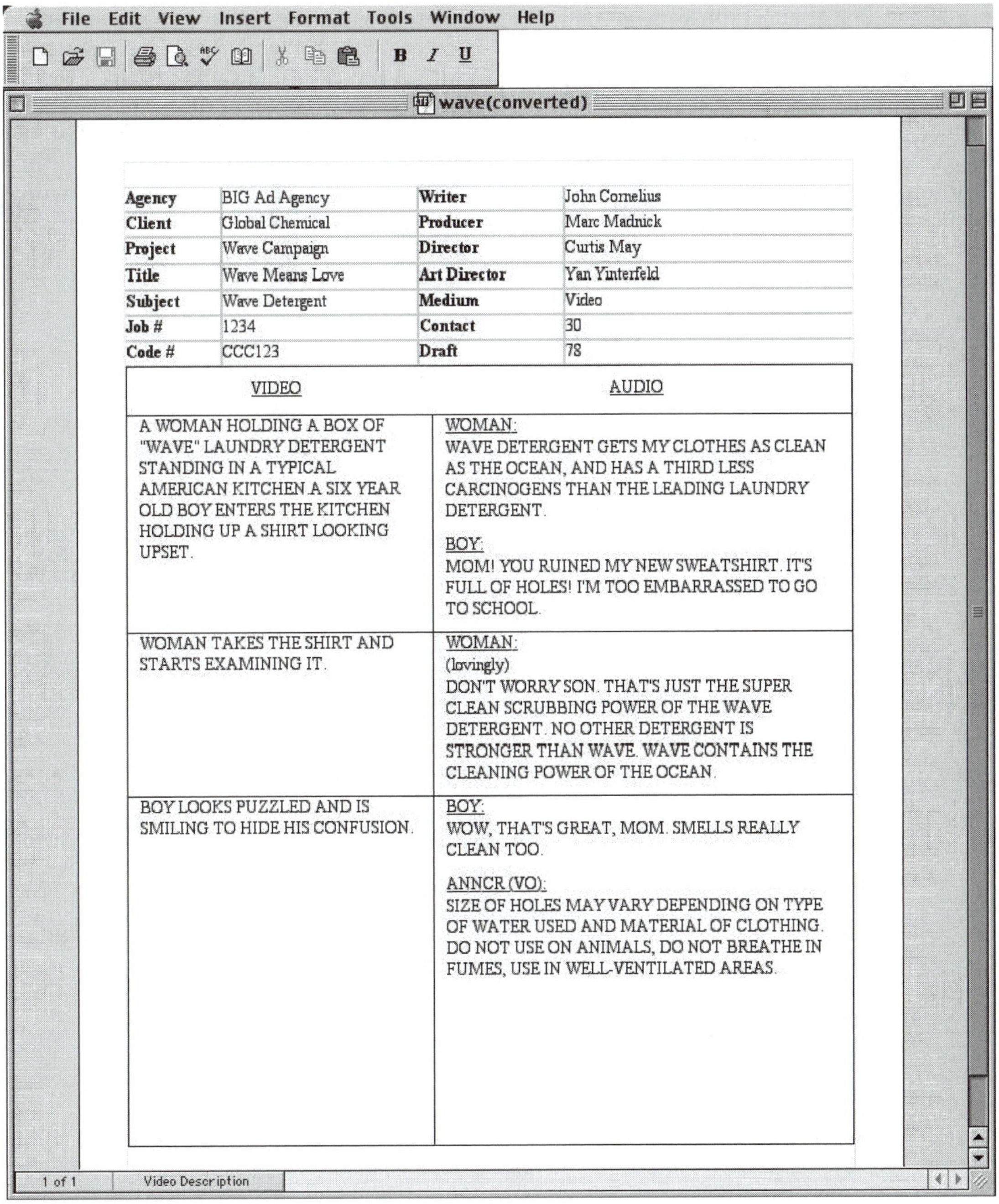

Agency	BIG Ad Agency	**Writer**	John Cornelius
Client	Global Chemical	**Producer**	Marc Madnick
Project	Wave Campaign	**Director**	Curtis May
Title	Wave Means Love	**Art Director**	Yan Yinterfeld
Subject	Wave Detergent	**Medium**	Video
Job #	1234	**Contact**	30
Code #	CCC123	**Draft**	78

VIDEO	AUDIO
A WOMAN HOLDING A BOX OF "WAVE" LAUNDRY DETERGENT STANDING IN A TYPICAL AMERICAN KITCHEN A SIX YEAR OLD BOY ENTERS THE KITCHEN HOLDING UP A SHIRT LOOKING UPSET.	WOMAN: WAVE DETERGENT GETS MY CLOTHES AS CLEAN AS THE OCEAN, AND HAS A THIRD LESS CARCINOGENS THAN THE LEADING LAUNDRY DETERGENT. BOY: MOM! YOU RUINED MY NEW SWEATSHIRT. IT'S FULL OF HOLES! I'M TOO EMBARRASSED TO GO TO SCHOOL.
WOMAN TAKES THE SHIRT AND STARTS EXAMINING IT.	WOMAN: (lovingly) DON'T WORRY SON. THAT'S JUST THE SUPER CLEAN SCRUBBING POWER OF THE WAVE DETERGENT. NO OTHER DETERGENT IS STRONGER THAN WAVE. WAVE CONTAINS THE CLEANING POWER OF THE OCEAN.
BOY LOOKS PUZZLED AND IS SMILING TO HIDE HIS CONFUSION.	BOY: WOW, THAT'S GREAT, MOM. SMELLS REALLY CLEAN TOO. ANNCR (VO): SIZE OF HOLES MAY VARY DEPENDING ON TYPE OF WATER USED AND MATERIAL OF CLOTHING. DO NOT USE ON ANIMALS, DO NOT BREATHE IN FUMES, USE IN WELL-VENTILATED AREAS.

Figure 6.6 A screen from the Final Draft A/V scriptwriting program. The program will help create scripts in a variety of formats. Courtesy of Final Draft, Inc.

It often prevents a client from complaining about the scriptwriter's interpretation of his objectives.

This review process leads to a second draft and sometimes numerous successive drafts. When a draft is finally approved, it becomes a shooting script and acts as the guide for the actual production work.

Edit

After the raw footage has been shot, producers, directors, and writers have another step in the scriptwriting process available to them that is often unavailable to those in studio TV. This step allows members of the EFP production team to view all tapes shot for the shooting script and decide if revisions to the original script are needed.

If changes are needed, the script can be rewritten to accommodate the editing process. Shot sequences may be changed, some shots or scenes may be deleted, or some new shots may be added. One of the real advantages of EFP television over studio TV becomes especially apparent if new shots are needed: Although equipment and personnel may need to be

rescheduled, costly studio space will not have to be rescheduled. The additional EFP work can be done with as few as two or three crew members.

The final version of the script, the editing script, is completed at this point. It is the last step in the production process before the final edit of the program is completed. This step usually involves minor changes to fine-tune the most recent draft of the script and the raw footage into a completed program.

7

Preproduction and Production

This chapter will guide you from the preliminary stages of thinking about a video project, to the essential steps needed for preproduction, to the day of actual production and shooting. The activities discussed in this chapter will make the difference between success and failure. Preparing for the shoot and actually performing the shoot are phases in the overall production process where most of the planning and video work is accomplished. The first section, preproduction, guides you through all of the steps you will need to plan your project in a professional way. The second section, production, guides you through the day or days of the shoot and gives you the information you need to begin, execute, and finish a professional style video shoot in the field.

PART ONE: PREPRODUCTION

Between scriptwriting and actual production of an EFP video comes the time for preproduction planning and preparation. This part of the production process should account for a majority of the total time spent on the project. Since careful and efficient planning at this stage can save time and money in the actual production phase, it is not unusual for video professionals to spend about 60 to 80% of their time in preproduction activities. The preproduction phase leads to a further divergence in methods between the ENG and EFP styles of portable video.

ELECTRONIC NEWS GATHERING

ENG style demands that events be covered as soon as they occur—leaving little or no time for careful planning. Preparations for upcoming stories are simply the experiences gained from the previous stories. Events occur on their own schedules, forcing the ENG photographer to cope with whatever difficulties are encountered without the benefit of a second take.

ENG situations call for a more bare-bones style of TV photography. The number one goal is simply to bring back acceptable quality video from every assignment, regardless of conditions or difficulty. What you can do beyond this in the way of quality and content is what makes a news photographer great. Often all the equipment needed for the entire day must be carried by you at all times during that day; you must literally wear the gear. This limits the complexity of what you can do. It does not, however, limit the creativity of what you can do. Where EFP plans for every contingency and need, ENG plans for how much use can be derived from any one item of gear. The ability to travel quickly without an overload of equipment is essential due to the many deadlines in news gathering. A news photographer learns to anticipate how the story will unfold and what equipment will be useful on any given shoot mostly through experience. The trick to is to always have what you need before you need it and not have too much when you do not need it. The ability to improvise is the number one item on the list of things to bring.

Because of the nature of news stories, everything you may ever need should be in the van or car with you every day. A return trip to the station may be impossible and you may not even know what assignments you will have for that day. It becomes incumbent on the photographer, in many newsrooms, to find out what the next assignment is. Often the information given to the photographer is little more than a street address. Sometimes the assignment may require special considerations that the photographer really needs to know about. The first of these considerations is whether the story is to be done live or not. The planning for any event or story starts when the story is assigned. This may be days, hours, or minutes before the shoot begins. More time available for planning gives news crews the opportunity to add more elements to their shooting plan and to raise the production values of the story. In the case of spot news, you may have only the time it takes to drive to the location to formulate a plan as to how to shoot the scene, how much time to spend doing each task, and how to get a live shot ready for the 5:00 P.M. news. A news photographer always has a plan waiting and ready.

ELECTRONIC FIELD PRODUCTION

EFP productions are usually shot from a carefully planned script or storyboard that gives the videographer control over much of what is shot. This preparation for EFP work is actually similar to the preproduction process in studio work, but with some important differences. As in studio preproduction, EFP preproduction includes crew and talent organization and selection; a large amount of scheduling, budgeting, graphics planning, and preparation; and the procurement of clearance on copyrighted materials. Studio and EFP preproduction clearly differ, however, because of the added tasks of location selection, travel for talent and crew, and transportation of equipment to the desired location for EFP production. (See Figure 7.1.)

PRODUCTION CREW

The responsibility for selecting the crew is commonly the domain of a person called the executive producer. This person first selects a producer who then helps the executive producer select the other major members of the production crew, including the director,

videographer, audio engineer, lighting director, talent, grip, and editor. The number of people assigned to each task depends on the complexity of the project. A small project may require only one person in each area of responsibility or even one person who covers several areas. Larger projects require several people in each area.

News-gathering crews are usually just one or two people: the photographer with or without a reporter. As market size or the demand for quality increases, a news crew can end up with the same staffing as a major EFP shoot. This is especially true in the area of documentary shooting. While technically a news-style product, documentaries are often done more like production work with large crews and several layers of creative and financial control.

Executive Producer

The production crew begins with the executive producer, who acts as a general supervisor of the project and often serves in this capacity on more than one project at a time. The executive producer initiates selection of the production crew after deciding on project feasibility, given all the financial, equipment, personnel, and time constraints. Very often the executive producer finds the money that funds the project.

A scriptwriter or project creator often seeks a person to act as an executive producer who is able to find a funding source as well as the personnel and equipment to produce the script. Once the funding is located, the executive producer often decides generally how the money will be spent. Acting as a liaison between a client and the EFP team, the executive producer frequently selects (or at least suggests) the major members of the production team: the producer, director, and talent. The executive producer may also seek outlets for the exhibition of the project, if appropriate. After initiating the project and selecting a producer, the executive producer often plays a minor role in the day-to-day operation of the project, which is delegated to the producer.

Producer

Usually selected by the executive producer, the producer is involved from the very beginning of an EFP project as the overall coordinator and schedule-maker. Although the specifics of scheduling are often the responsibility of others on the team, the producer sets the parameters for the project (for example, the completion date). Having the best overall picture of

PREPRODUCTION CHECKLIST

Client work/general feasibility conversation
Proposal w/script
Specific feasibility decision
Projections of needs: costs, facilities, equipment, personnel
Budget compilation
Preparation of script for shooting
Analysis of script into component parts for final product:
      facilities and locations—studio, showroom, office, plant
      talent
      equipment
      graphics
      props, costumes, set design
      personnel for production
      number and length of shoots required during production
      post-production needs/scheduling
Location selection, survey, analysis, decision
Facilities decision and scheduling
Talent decision and scheduling:
      Is an audition necessary?
Equipment scheduling:
      Is equipment on - hand sufficient?
      Will renting/leasing be necessary?
Graphics, music, sound effects:
      Is artwork needed? Does it require outside work?
      Graphic design or computer graphics?
      Are there any computer/digital special effects?
      Is music required? Are composers/performers needed?
      Are sound effects needed?
      Order graphics, music, sound effects.
Clearance
      Will any copyrighted material be used?
Props, costume, set elements
      Do props need to be purchased or constructed?
Personnel
      How many shoots are there and how long will they be?
      Do you have enough qualified personnel to staff a crew for all shoots?
Post-production planning and scheduling
      Can editing be done in - house?
      Can the necessary editing time be scheduled either in - house or elsewhere?
Preparation for shooting
      Are rehearsals necessary?
      Can they be done on - location?
      Are crew or staff meetings necessary?

Figure 7.1   EFP preproduction checklist.

the specific needs of the current production, the producer also knows the requirements for other projects that involve the production facility. The pivotal person on the video production team, the producer makes the decisions regarding money, personnel selection, and schedule.

For many projects done in-house at TV stations, production companies, or corporations, the team may already be on staff and simply moves from project to project. Larger companies may have many people in pools of job categories selected on the basis of availability, not ability. While this system works most of the time, it can lead to disaster. It is always better to have the production team hand-picked to get the best working relationships and the best end product.

Director

The director takes a script for a video project and translates it into a visual reality. The director is therefore an interpreter of the scriptwriter's words, a translator who takes written communication and transforms it into visual communication, or makes a storyboard come to life. The director must coordinate activities just before and during production, as well as coordinate the activities of the camera operator, talent, and lighting director during rehearsals to create the effect called for by the script or storyboard.

Once the desired aesthetic effect is achieved, the director can begin the actual taping. Because most EFP productions differ from studio TV in that EFP usually involves one portable camera rather than several studio cameras, a good EFP director should know the film style of shooting a scene. The film style of direction does not require one-take production with little or no postproduction editing. Instead, in film style, the director uses one camera to retake the scene from different camera angles and focal lengths to allow selection during postproduction and the freedom to shoot scenes out of sequence for efficiency.

The director must also be able to work with people effectively. This may involve coaching, cajoling, coercing, or otherwise persuading actors and other performers to get the desired performance from them. The director has to do this without alienating or demeaning the talent. One disgruntled actor can easily sour the efforts of an entire crew. Since field production involves smaller crews than studio work, each crew member's performance becomes essential to the success of the shoot. It is the director's responsibility to get the best possible work from the entire crew.

Videographer

The videographer in field TV has a larger responsibility than the videographer in studio TV, primarily because the field director does not sit in front of a monitor bank in a sound-isolated control room and give directions as does the director in studio TV. In the field, the director may have a portable monitor (which may be small or washed out by the sun) but cannot always give direction during a shot because spoken commands may be picked up by live microphones.

The camera directions are given before a shot and then both director and videographer work together to make a shot look its best. A good videographer takes the director's verbal commands and gets the desired camera shots and finds additional shots through the variation of camera angle, focal length, selective focus, or camera movement. This can make a scene more interesting after it is edited. If the director is working from a storyboard, the videographer gives suggestions as to how the camera can be placed and moved to match the desired effect and look.

Audio Engineer

The EFP audio engineer is responsible for accurately recording sounds on the location shoot. Unlike studio audio engineers who have the equipment storeroom within easy reach, the field sound engineer must anticipate all sound requirements of the location shoot and pack the necessary items to accommodate them. Once on location, the audio engineer must live with the equipment decisions already made.

While studio sound engineers often have large, easy-to-read VU meters and high-quality control room monitor speakers to assess sound quality, location audio engineers often cope with tiny VU meters located on a portable audio mixer and a set of headphones. Since the camcorder is designed to be operated by one person—the videographer (or news photographer)—he or she may have to assume the duties of the audio engineer. This may be fine when the production is very basic, but can be quite a burden on the videographer when the audio situation is complex. When more than one or two microphones are required, the person assuming audio responsibilities must set up the microphones with the use of a mixer and then provide one or two audio channels from the mixer to the camcorder for recording. Audio engineers sometimes record a separate sound track, called

wild sound, on an audio recorder to be added in post-production.

Lighting Director

Location shoots require a crew member who can provide lighting that will satisfy the basic needs of the camera and the aesthetic requirements of the script. While on smaller crews that job goes to the videographer but as the size and complexity of the production grows, a separate crew member, the lighting director, can be an indispensable addition. The videographer may need to start blocking and shooting one location while the lighting director and crew start lighting the next location to move the production along at a quicker pace. The lighting director should not only have a thorough knowledge of lighting techniques and instruments but also a familiarity with the specific demands of the lighting situation and the electrical power capabilities of the locations.

Grip or Utility

In the film industry, almost every member of the crew has a specific job title that has evolved over the years. Jobs like best boy, gaffer, and key grip are lumped into one title for TV production: the grip. People from a TV studio background usually call them utilities. Unlike the film industry, these grips or utilities can cover quite a broad range of jobs on the production unless otherwise limited by a union agreement.

On any given crew, one or more members function as a grip whose responsibilities are to hold, or grip, reflectors or lights, a shotgun microphone, the VCR, or any other piece of equipment that requires attention during the shoot. The grip is often an assistant or apprentice to one of the other crew members and should have a basic knowledge of the equipment, that is, he should know the equipment by name and how to handle it. Because of the responsibility of holding equipment during the shoot, the grip should be steady and capable of moving equipment in and out of location as well as the vehicle used for transporting the equipment.

Talent

Selecting talent is a somewhat different chore from selecting other members of the team. Whereas other crew members are most often employed by the same company as the producer, the talent may not be. In a half-dozen different shoots, it would not be unusual to have a different main talent for each one. This may not be the case, however, for industrial video for training and demonstration purposes, or for internal public relations programs that have a regular host.

Talent may be selected by committee or by the executive producer, producer, or director. Talent can be locally acquired on location (that is, in the city you will be traveling to) or imported with the rest of the crew. One mistake often made by beginners is to select nonprofessional actors as talent because of their voice or overall appearance. This can be dangerous. Inexperienced talent often force numerous retakes, because they may be unable to take directions to correct mistakes. Sometimes nonprofessionals look terrific in person or in rehearsal but cannot adapt to the real situation when taping. The advice here is to stick to experienced professionals whenever the budget allows.

As in so many areas of today's TV production, the better professional is more likely to be in a union or guild. This is very much the case with talent. Any professional performer sooner or later is required to join either the Screen Actors Guild (SAG) or the American Federation of Television and Radio Artists (AFTRA). A requirement of membership is the commitment to never work without a union contract, even in a nonunion production. This means you will have to pay minimum professional rates (and maybe more) to have a union professional in your show.

Editor

The editor takes the original, or raw, footage that has been shot and, with the help of a script, reassembles the program into its proper order. Often the scenes are shot out of sequence and numerous takes are available for each scene. This allows the editor to use some creativity and professional skills to produce a finished master tape that is creative and visually pleasing. However, the master tape must also follow the accepted rules for keeping the flow of the program visually and chronologically correct, while yielding the meaning intended by the producer, director, and scriptwriter.

A good editor enhances the ideas of the people who wrote and visually interpreted the script without changing either its meaning or its effect on the viewer. When hiring an editor, look for three skills: a dexterity with the editing machinery, a thorough knowledge of the software and computers involved, and, most importantly, a strong sense for how to tell a story visually.

SCHEDULING AND COORDINATING

Scheduling an EFP project is often a slow and difficult process. Since many crew members in EFP work have other responsibilities and video equipment is constantly being used for a variety of projects, getting a full crew with all the necessary equipment sometimes seems like trying to carry all of the unfolded laundry without a laundry basket. If you stoop down to adjust a scheduled shoot time for a critical crew member, you may find that you have dropped something else, such as the availability of a special camera or even the talent. Occasionally an unforeseen delay, albeit a short one, can cause a serious problem in postproduction, such as missing a scheduled visit to the editing suite of your choice.

Factors to Consider

When creating your schedule, first consider the general categories of items to be scheduled. You have people, equipment, materials, and facilities or locations. **Prioritize these items based on your lack of control over them and schedule those items first over which you have little control.** The logic here is that once you have locked into place those items that may have no flexibility, you can more easily schedule in the more flexible items. A couple of examples may help to illustrate.

First, your independent production company may have contracted to shoot a 5-minute demonstration/sales tape for a company that manufactures a farm implement that attaches to a small tractor and removes weeds that grow between the rows of soybean fields. Obviously, the first thing to do is find out what a soybean is and where it is grown. If you are not from the Midwest, you may think that soybeans grow in health food stores. Fortunately, your client cannot only orient you to soybeans and the new product but also suggest an appropriate location, such as the client's own test plots, for the shoot.

Factors such as soil conditions, weed height, soybean height, and weather may dictate whether you can actually go into the field for a demonstration. In other words, you must know the details and limitations of your location. After all of these factors are considered, a window of time (for example, the last week of May) can be designated as the best period of time for the shoot to take place.

A second example probably represents a more common situation. An advertiser requests that your independent production company shoot a 30-second commercial featuring a new line of small kitchen appliances. Since the appliances require a precise setting and lighting situation, you decide that a studio is needed.

As is the case with most smaller production companies, you do not own a studio or a space large enough to house the necessary set and lights. In this case, you must find a studio that is affordable and technically acceptable. The studio must also be available at a time that will allow you enough postproduction time to have the commercial completed before the first scheduled broadcast date. Once you have the studio scheduled, you can proceed to schedule other items.

These examples were chosen because location or facilities are often the least available and not within the producer's control. But any necessary item can have the least availability. Your talent may have only 2 days a month for shooting; the digital Betacam camcorder that you need to rent may be in high demand and short supply; your whole team may have a sporadic schedule of shots for previously scheduled projects.

As a rule of thumb, you can expect to schedule the following categories of items (listed in descending order of scheduling difficulty):

1. Location or special facilities (studio, office building, yacht)
2. Special equipment (fog machine, fireworks, special spotlight)
3. Talent or crucial crew members (a famous spokesperson or star)
4. Postproduction time, facilities, personnel
5. Graphics, props
6. Crew members for noncrucial assignments.

Keep in mind that for any given shoot, any or all of these can be difficult to schedule.

Guidelines for Schedule Making

There is no set formula to guide your schedule making, but here are a few hints that will come in handy when going about the chore:

1. *Be flexible.* Do not allow your own inflexibility to create scheduling problems. Even if you do not like starting a project on Friday, it may be the best

starting day when you consider the schedules of others.

2. *Do not schedule too tightly.* Add time for reshooting or catch-up. If your shooting will be done outdoors, make sure you include some rain dates.

3. *Consult past schedules whenever possible.* How long did the same crew take for a similar project in the past?

4. *Have contingency plans.* What is the probability of equipment failure? Are certain pieces of equipment prone to failure in the field? Make sure that equipment failure, crew no-shows, or talent problems do not prevent you from meeting your completion deadline.

LOCATION SELECTION AND SURVEY

In this phase of preproduction, the actual shooting location must be selected and investigated for specific information to facilitate the actual shoot. The script will probably guide you to a few choices for the location of your shoot. Many times the location is actually dictated by the script: for example, Disney World, a particular shopping center, or the corporate president's office. In this case, you can avoid the selection process and go right to the scouting procedure.

When the script gives only a general description of the location (for example, the backyard of a suburban home or a classroom), you have to select a few possible locations and scout them with a visit to see if they will satisfy your needs. Beyond the general look or aesthetics of the place, each location that you intend to use must meet some specific requirements. (See Figure 7.2.)

During this visit you may find it helpful to conduct a survey for later comparison with surveys taken at alternate locations. An excellent way to do this comparison is to use a Polaroid or digital still camera. Using these still shots, you can sit in the comfort of the office and discuss with other members of the team which site would be better suited to the production and what problems other members foresee. The following is a list of some of the questions you need to ask during the site survey or at least before the final decision is made:

1. *Is the location accessible?* A beautiful mountain meadow or an island in the middle of a lake may be aesthetically perfect, but if your crew can only reach it on foot, by canoe, or by specially equipped four-wheel drive vehicles, you should be prepared to pay for that or look elsewhere.

2. *Can you get permission to use the site?* The owner might let you visit but not necessarily bring your 10-person crew, equipment, vehicles, and the curious onlookers often attracted by the sight of a video camera. Permission in writing is the safest method. A check of local laws regarding shooting is necessary; a permit may be required.

3. *Can you maintain the appropriate traffic control?* Shooting on a street corner or side street may seem easy during a 7:00 A.M. visit, but how busy would it be if you shot at 11:00 A.M.? Sidewalks or even hiking trails can be full of curious people, or even not-so-curious people, who demand the right-of-way. Make sure that the owner, park officials, city, or highway police agree to let you divert traffic from your location. In many cities, permits are required to shoot on or near any public property. These permits may also require fees and proof of insurance coverage.

4. *What kind of lighting do you have?* Full sun can be as troublesome as no sun at all. You may need to add fill light to harsh shadows or shaded faces. If artificial light is preferred, can you somehow eliminate the unwanted light? Time of day may dictate your shooting schedule.

5. *What are the sound characteristics of the location?* Empty rooms without carpeting or draperies may cause echoes. In most cases, adding sound is no problem, but taking away sound is nearly impossible. A too noisy location is highly undesirable or may require highly specialized microphones. Again, try to find out what the location sound will be at the approximate time of day at which you will shoot.

6. *Is electrical power available at the location?* If not, you may merely need to pack some batteries. But if artificial light is required, you will have to generate your own AC power. This may be accomplished with a gasoline-powered generator, but this is another piece of equipment that adds its own bulk and weight plus that of its fuel. Also keep in mind that video lights require *much* power and that the generators produce noise as well as power.

7. *Is there an acceptable spot available for camera placement?* Many panoramic views available to the

(A) **MOTOROLA INC.**

VISUAL MEDIA PRODUCTIONS

LOCATION SCOUTING REPORT - Video

Project Number : ___ ___ ___ ___ ___ — ___ ___ ___ ___   Scouting Date : _____

Contact Person : _____   Phone : _____

■ **ADDRESS OF LOCATION :** _____

Directions/Parking ? _____

_____

_____

_____   FEEL FREE TO DRAW OUT DIRECTIONS

_____

■ **SPACE REQUIREMENTS :**

Number of Camerpersons : _____ Camera Positions : _____

_____

Descibe Shot/Activity : _____

_____

■ **LIGHT REQUIREMENTS ;**

Level Required : _____   Source of Light : _____

Ceiling Height : _____   Ambient Light : _____

Reflective Surfaces : _____   Sun Location : _____

■ **SOUND :**

Recording Sound : _____ ☐ Sync ☐ Wild   Potential Interference : _____

Ambient Sound Present : _____   ☐ Use ☐ Avoid

■ **POWER :**

Location of Outlets : _____   Capacity ? _____

Location of Circuit Breakers : _____   Tie In ? ☐ Yes ☐ No

Engineer/Maintenance Contact : _____   Phone : _____

Figure 7.2 Location scouting report used in corporate video. Courtesy of Motorola, Integrated Information Systems Group, Visual Media Communications.

scout may be unavailable to a cumbersome video camera with attached tripod and cables. Make sure that there is a safe spot for your three-legged friend.

8. *Does the location allow convenient loading and unloading?* Are the doors and hallways wide enough and the floor even enough to allow your crew to roll in the cases of equipment? Where can you park the equipment van? Inconvenient access can add unnecessary and costly time to your shoot.

9. *Will the location be available at any time after the scheduled shoot?* It does not happen often, but even professionals can lose, destroy, or record over raw footage before the edited master is completed. Clients or producers can change their minds about how the program should look and sometimes require a return to the location for a reshoot. Even if this is a rare necessity, it is a good idea to pick a location that allows a possible return for additional shooting.

10. *What crew conveniences are available?* Will the crew have to pack their own lunches? They may need adequate water, bathroom facilities, shade, or a cool spot to rest. Full sun for a full day or no sun at all may lead to some very unhappy crew members. If talent has been hired to be on location, they may have special needs that require special facilities, such as a dressing room trailer parked at the site.

11. *Will the shoot be sent via microwave or satellite to another location?* Can the signal that you send to the other location be seen, or are there buildings, mountains, or interferences that may require special arrangements?

12. *Is safety and security an issue?* Can you physically watch all of your equipment (and perhaps all your people) to guarantee safety throughout your stay? How cold or hot does it get at the location? Does your insurance include coverage for shooting at the location or under the circumstances?

GRAPHICS AND PROPS PREPARATION

The preproduction stage is the appropriate time to order the graphics and other necessary materials in order to have them ready before actual production begins. For most productions, this will include artwork for studio cards that do not have to be video-taped in a studio, photographic work for slides, film footage (for example, animation) or computer-generated animation, or graphics. In large production houses, most of these things are done in-house by staff artists, photographers, cinematographers, or computer specialists. Smaller production units often have to find specialists who can provide these materials as subcontractors.

This stage of the production process is the appropriate time to locate costumes, makeup accessories, set props, and other items necessary for the production. If sets or props need to be constructed, initiate the process at this point.

CLEARANCE ON COPYRIGHT MATERIALS

If you expect your video project to really be yours after it is completed, it is best to make sure that all the material you use has been created by you or people who are working for you on the project. If you or one of your coworkers uses material owned by others, you may find yourself spending time with lawyers instead of looking for more video projects to produce.

The use of other people's material without their permission is a copyright infringement; if you are caught doing it, you have created a legal problem for yourself. The problem arises very often when copyrighted music is used without permission. Four simple approaches will help you avoid this problem:

1. *If you need music for your program and the music you choose is copyrighted, contact the copyright holder* (the record company, music publishing company, or individual artist) *in writing and ask for permission to use the material.* In your request, be as specific as you can as to your intentions. Name the material, the excerpt (if appropriate), the program it will be used in, the distribution or exhibition plans, and any other relevant information. If you do this far enough in advance of your postproduction time, you may get an approval for use of the materials, or *clearance* as it is referred to in the publishing business.

2. *Use material that is in the public domain—material that has never been copyrighted or material whose copyright has expired.* Material that has not been copyrighted is probably available from your local amateur composer or music student. They may

have excellent material already composed or may be able to compose music tailor-made for your project. Material composed long ago, such as old folk tunes ("I've Been Workin' on the Railroad" or "Oh, Susanna") or classical music that could be performed especially for your project, is generally available for use since the copyright has long since expired. (Bach and Beethoven are rarely offended when you use their material.)

3. *Purchase the material or subscribe to a library service that provides music or other material such as sound effects.* These services work in two ways. One way allows you to use the material as often as you need to use it; you buy this privilege when paying for the material, and its use is at your discretion. A second type of service involves a needle-drop fee. Music library services provide you with the material, but you must pay when you use it. Hence, every time your "needle drops" on the record (those big plastic plate-like things used before CDs and DVDs) for actual use in a production, you owe the service a fee.

4. *Hire a musician or musical group that will use original compositions and perform them for you.* Once you pay for this service, you should own the privilege of using the material.

TRAVEL PLANNING

By definition, all EFP involves some type of travel. Some set procedures for travel will help you to cope with the trials and tribulations of constantly leaving your home base to get the work done. If the travel is local and requires only a reasonable amount of driving time, a minivan, station wagon, or hatchback auto can possibly serve the needs of a small crew and a one-camera shoot.

Transporting Equipment

For out-of-town shoots, your transportation vehicle should have plenty of space for backup equipment, extra personnel, extra tape, and perhaps some test or repair equipment. If your shoot is three driving hours away from your studio or office, you certainly do not want to waste time sending the vehicle back for an extra battery, cable, or mic.

A van or truck might also allow you to bring a power generator when needed. Sometimes renting the

appropriate vehicle allows you to bring all the necessary equipment and personnel along and prevents the need to hire freelance personnel or rent equipment at the location.

While EFP crews tend to carry their equipment in cases and use different vehicles for different shoots, an ENG crew usually has a dedicated vehicle with the equipment always stored in that vehicle. The typical news van has many built-in shelves and storage areas for the gear (including the camera) that allow for quick and easy access. Most ENG gear is kept as ready-to-shoot as possible because of the ever-present possibility of spot news happening. In these situations, seconds can mean the difference in getting the shot or not. The camera system has to be in a constant state of readiness; just turn it on and shoot. This also means that the gear must be in a secured state while riding in the vehicle at all times. You cannot have equipment rolling around or falling over while you are driving. Careful thought has to be given as to how the gear will be carried. The goal is to get as much equipment in the van as possible, keep it readily accessible, and at the same time keep it safe under all kinds of driving conditions. (See Figure 7.3.)

Equipment Cube

Whether you drive a car, truck, or other vehicle, you should know the volume and weight of your equipment before your shoot so that you can compare these figures with the available storage space and maximum load handling capability of your vehicle. This information is probably available in the owner's manuals for your equipment. Before renting a vehicle for a shoot, you should find out how much cubic space is needed for your equipment. Make sure that when you reserve a rental car, you don't just say, "Give me a minivan." This term means different things to different rental companies. If your cubic feet demand requires a particular brand of minivan, make sure that you request it by name and explain why it is important that you actually get that particular vehicle. If the vehicle you get is too small, you will find that the crew does not like riding to the shoot with heavy equipment on their laps.

The process of determining the total cubic feet for your equipment can be achieved by simply stacking your equipment, which has been packed in its travel cases, on the floor in a compact manner and measuring the height, width, and depth of your cube. (See Figure 7.4.) First, multiply height by width by

EQUIPMENT CHECKLIST

CAMERA

- [ ] Set up and registration
- [ ] Charged batteries
- [ ] AC power supply
- [ ] Camera control unit
- [ ] Distribution amplifier/equalizer
- [ ] Composite/component adapter
- [ ] Wide angle lens/adapter
- [ ] Filters
- [ ] Waveform and vector scopes
- [ ] Tripod w/head
- [ ] High hat
- [ ] Tripod wheels/dolly
- [ ] Boom/crane
- [ ] Steadi-cam/Tyler mount
- [ ] Suction mount
- [ ] Gyro lens
- [ ] Tripod adapter plate
- [ ] Lens cleaner and tissue
- [ ] Shipping case
- [ ] Weather protection

LIGHTING

- [ ] Open-faced lights
- [ ] Fresnel lights
- [ ] HMI lights
- [ ] Reflectors
- [ ] Silks/scrims/butterflies/flags
- [ ] C-stands
- [ ] Extension cords
- [ ] Blue gels or dichroic filters
- [ ] Colored gels
- [ ] Black-out cloth
- [ ] Grip equipment
- [ ] Sand bags/water bags
- [ ] Spare lamps
- [ ] Gloves

RECORDER

- [ ] Record/play test

- [ ] Charged batteries
- [ ] AC power supply
- [ ] Playback machine
- [ ] Color monitor/outdoor hood
- [ ] Coaxial cable/barrels
- [ ] RF cable
- [ ] Multi-pin cable
- [ ] Tape stock
- [ ] Head cleaners
- [ ] Shipping/carrying case
- [ ] Audio monitoring headsets

AUDIO

- [ ] Omnidirectional/shotgun
- [ ] Hand-held/lavelier
- [ ] Fishpole/boom
- [ ] Wireless
- [ ] Filters
- [ ] Format adaptors
- [ ] Mixer/stereo
- [ ] Cables
- [ ] Wind protection
- [ ] Sound panels

ODDS AND ENDS

- [ ] Duct tape
- [ ] Rubber mats
- [ ] Plastic tarps/trash bags
- [ ] Rope
- [ ] Contact cement
- [ ] Tool kit
- [ ] Aluminum foil
- [ ] Spring clamps
- [ ] Colored tapes
- [ ] Magic markers/pens
- [ ] Self-stick labels
- [ ] Chairs
- [ ] Food/water
- [ ] Talent make-up
- [ ] Hair spray

ADDITIONAL ITEMS FOR THIS SHOOT

Figure 7.3   Equipment checklist.

depth to find the volume. Keep in mind that most rental cars, SUVs, and minivans don't have open cargo areas but simply areas where the back seats fold down but can't be removed. The odd spaces created by these folded seats can make loading equipment cases difficult and leave a lot of wasted space. Renting cargo vans is the best solution but most of the time they are not available at airports.

This procedure may seem time consuming, but it only needs to be done correctly once. New pieces of equipment can usually be added to the list without going through the cube procedure. After you know the amount of cubic space you will need, it will be easier to select the appropriate vehicle for rental or purchase.

Air Travel

When the location is many miles away, air travel may be the only means of transportation. Because of the large expense involved, you are faced with some tough decisions: Should you bring a full crew and pay their airfare, lodging, and meals, or hire freelance professionals at the location? Should you bring your own equipment, pay for its transportation, risk its rough handling at airport loading and unloading, or pay to rent equipment at the location?

Both questions are complex and depend on the availability of qualified personnel and reasonably priced professional equipment that is dependable. Keep in mind that renting equipment often means changing equipment or brands, and operating procedures may be different. Do this only if your personnel are experienced.

Whatever your decisions, make sure that you make your travel plans well in advance of your shoot date. Nothing is more aggravating than going through your travel decision-making process only to find that the vehicle you want to rent is not available or the flight you need is booked. Air travel reservations and tickets bought in advance of the shoot date often result in discount fares, which may allow you to bring the extra crew member or piece of equipment.

Travel Tips

Here are some travel pointers to consider before traveling:

1. *Never put your camera, camcorder, recorder, or laptop computer in with the baggage or air*

Figure 7.4 For any type of travel, your equipment should be well packed in protective cases; the number, size, and weight of the cases should be carefully noted.

freight. Always hand-carry these items as carry-on luggage, and either stow them on the floor beneath your feet or in the overhead bin. Several companies make padded, soft cases specifically to take the camera/camcorder on a plane as carry-on luggage. The camera and recorder are the most important pieces of equipment you have, and you cannot take a chance on them being dropped from the cargo bay door by a reckless handler, or left in Chicago when you've gone on to Los Angeles. You must also be prepared to *shoot* tape at any time before, during, or after the flight. You should have at least one battery, a tape, and a mic—as well as the camera—with you at all times.

2. *Send all of your cases through as luggage on your flight.* Never ship any of your gear air freight unless you will not need it for awhile after you get where you are going. Air freight can take a full day or

more to get there and doesn't arrive at the same terminal as you do.

3. *Keep all your cases at a reasonable size and weight.* Any cases larger than the biggest suitcase typically used by travelers, or any case weighing more than 70 pounds, can be rejected by the airline. This may mean more cases, but at least they will all be boarding the same flight as you.

4. *Expect to pay an excess baggage fee for most of your cases.* It is not unusual to have 15 or more cases with you for production shooting or extensive news shoots. It may cost more than sending them by freight (anywhere from $30 to $75 a case), but they will be there when you are. There often is no other option, especially for a traveling news crew.

5. *Call the airline in advance to tell them what you are bringing.* The airline may be able to help in getting the cases checked through and make better arrangements for your camera on the plane. They are used to dealing with TV crews.

6. *Make sure everything is well packed and padded.* As in the determination of your equipment cube, your regular set of gear needs to go through a packing/padding determination only once. After that you should have a set of pads that you use whenever you travel. If you think that this is not important, watch how luggage is loaded and unloaded from airplane cargo holds. It will renew your motivation to pack and pad your equipment well.

7. *Make a list with brand names, model numbers, and serial numbers of everything you are taking.* Leave one copy at home and keep one copy with you at all times.

8. *Remember that thieves know what expensive video equipment cases look like.* In a large airport an inattentive photographer can lose a case or two in a split second.

9. *Have a Skycap help you whenever you can.* This costs more money, but helps prevent theft and makes it easier to haul.

10. *Get a car or van that you can work out of the whole time you are on the shoot.* If the car is just big enough to hold the crew and gear with no room to spare, you might find yourself having to dig out equipment every time you need something. It may be better, though more costly, to rent a bigger vehicle or a second vehicle to give yourself some room to

work. At least you will not be unloading the entire car at every stop.

Foreign Travel

Traveling outside the United States can be fun and challenging but also a major headache for those who are unprepared. Each country has its own way of doing things; many do not have the rights of a free press. Doing business as usual could land you in jail and, in some repressive countries, can actually get you executed. These are not things to be taken lightly. Do extensive research regarding the countries you will be traveling in to see what media restrictions may be in place. Permits may be required to do any kind of professional photography, including news. Find someone who has shot in that country before and gain from his or her experience.

Besides the political concerns that can be dangerous to your health, there are economic concerns. Most countries, including the United States, have import/export laws placing tariffs on certain high-quality photographic and electronic equipment. After going to certain countries and returning to this one, you will be asked to prove that the equipment you have is indeed yours and that you bought it here after paying the proper taxes. The best way to prove this is to have a **carnet**, a document recognized by the Customs Service that guarantees that the equipment is yours. You need a complete list of all your equipment with brands, serial numbers, purchase prices, and model numbers. You should have many copies of this list with you as you travel. The carnet requires the posting of a bond for this list of gear (up to 10% of the equipment's value). Although the document is recognized in many countries around the world, it is not recognized in all countries. The next best solution is to simply have the gear registered with the U.S. Customs Service. The carnet is for reentry to the United States, but some countries also take it as proof of ownership. If you are going to a country that doesn't accept a carnet, try to get in touch with their consulate here to make arrangements to get your gear in and out of that country. Always travel with as much documentation as possible. It is not unheard of to have gear confiscated or impounded for lack of documents. There are companies in almost every port both here and abroad that offer a customs-help service. These customs brokers are simply facilitators who, for a fee, can guide you through any customs clearance legally.

Press credentials are very useful in a foreign land. Officials at many entry points to a country are accustomed to seeing traveling news crews. Showing a press pass, even a hometown press pass, can prove effective. If your gear looks worn and has ID stickers of the station on it, few customs officials question its origin. If it is EFP gear that looks new, you will need documentation. A letter from the production company or from that country's consulate introducing you is better than nothing. Always have a return ticket with you even if it is for an incorrect date. Coming into a country with new or near new video gear and a one-way ticket can send up a very large red flag. You may find yourself trying to spring your gear from the impound cage for the next few days.

Always have a large amount of cash with you. It is amazing how many problems can be solved with the right amount of money in a foreign land. Credit cards and traveler's checks are fine in the hotel but not elsewhere. Bribery is not a nice word in this country, but it is a way of life in many parts of the world. Gratuities may be a better word, but regardless of what you call it, you had better be prepared for it. Never let anyone see how much money you have, and never keep it all in one place. A healthy dose of paranoia and some preplanning can make your trip a smooth and successful one.

PART TWO: PRODUCTION/ SHOOTING ON LOCATION

Pulling up to the location of the shoot is when the moment of truth starts. All the planning, preparation, and training is now going to be put to use. Now, more than ever, the main factors driving news (ENG) and production (EFP) are in play: *time* and *money*. News is done on a deadline and production is done on a budget.

In either case, the goal is to stick with what you have learned. You must go about the act of shooting with deliberation: a conscious attention to the details of what makes a story work, what shots are necessary for editing, how much time everything is taking, and where everything is leading. This section of the chapter contains some of the general considerations that need to be dealt with in any location shoot. Each trip into the field will be different. Conditions and circumstances will be different as will your goals. With a firm grasp of the basic elements of visual communi-

cation and the abilities of your equipment, you can execute any shooting assignment—news or production—with confidence.

The two most important points at the start of any location shooting are (1) you must have everything you might possibly need with you at the start of the day and (2) you must adjust your needs to the limitations of the site.

ENG VERSUS EFP

The differences between an ENG shoot and an EFP shoot can be enormous. The coverage of news events is largely unpredictable and short notice is more common than advance notice. Therefore, the strategy for an ENG shoot is to be constantly prepared for almost any twist and turn in the situation. A news photographer never knows if the next shoot is a plane crash or a city council meeting. As he or she pulls up to the location a mental checklist needs to be done. Sometimes, with very little knowledge of the story or situation, the news photographer must make decisions that can affect the way the story is covered. Things as simple as whether or not to bring the tripod from the car can change the way the story is visually approached. Anticipation and instinct are two very valuable traits in a news photographer. Unfortunately, both of them tend to come with experience and not from a textbook. The best way to learn news shooting is to know the basics and just get out there and do it.

Most EFP situations involve following a master plan or script. There will always be unexpected problems but, for the most part, a production shooter will know everything that needs to be done far in advance. The shoot has been planned. The difficulties during the shoot are keeping things on schedule and on budget while still achieving the goals of the producer. Much of this section is aimed at the typical EFP shoot, but all the principles here can apply to any form of shooting.

SETTING UP

One of the first skills a good photographer needs to learn on location is how to imagine the site with all the equipment in place. "Loading in," as it's called, needs to be done with an eye to the finished setup. The camera location is always the very first thing to be determined. But moving a large sofa out of the way of the camera's spot can backfire if it's moved right to the place where the key light has to go. Upon arrival, the photographer must first visualize the situation with everything set up so that equipment can be quickly placed in the right spot the first time. (See Figure 7.5.)

For EFP shoots, keep in mind that just having a crew show up for the shoot doesn't mean that anyone remembers what to do, or at least what they are supposed to do that day or on that shoot. It is a good idea to have a meeting just after making the initial on-site assessment to give out specific assignments. This division of labor will help avoid crew conflicts and also prevent people from standing around at the location. It will also help prevent having all the equipment cases piled right where you need to work. It is always a good idea to establish a staging area where equipment can be close to the final location without its being in the way.

Setting up for your shoot involves a number of individual tasks, some of which happen concurrently. Sometimes, as the scene is coming together, you will notice potential trouble spots. Before the work of the entire crew is wasted, you need to stop the setup and make adjustments. For example, a multimedia project about bicycle riding requires a mountainous terrain to help demonstrate the ruggedness of a new model mountain bike. The site survey and the pre-

production process has the bike and a rider set against rugged hills or mountains. On the shoot day the hills are hidden by low clouds. Is there a better place for this shot now that the hills are gone from view? This decision needs to be made before everything is set up.

Initial camera placement is dictated by the type of shot that you want to obtain first. If you want to prevent the busy background behind your subject from being a distraction, you could keep the camera-to-subject distance long and shoot with a long focal lens. This will blur the background. A shot that requires showing quite a bit of detail of a complex object like an old coin needs to have the camera very close to the subject.

The appropriate, preferable location for the tripod is a level area out of the way of traffic (both vehicular and pedestrian) and wind gusts or water-spray. Use of a handheld camera requires that the location also be relatively flat to allow the camera operator to move around unimpeded. Other mounting options present a more complex preparation problem. If the camera is to be mounted on a crab dolly that will travel on tracks, this dolly unit needs a flat surface and plenty of space. You also must allow enough time for constructing the dolly's tracks. Other mountings, such as those on an auto for shots of a driver and/or passengers while driving, or shots of the scenery as the car passes by, take plenty of time

Figure 7.5 Equipment for a large news or production shoot can take up quite a bit of space. Having everything in cases can make travel and loading easier.

and must be mounted carefully to avoid camera vibration while the car moves. In addition, if the car is moving at high speeds, the mount needs to be extremely strong and able to withstand high wind speeds without moving or even getting blown off the car.

SOUND AND LIGHT

Once the subject is placed and the camera location is chosen, lights and sound equipment can be added if necessary. The subject might have been placed in a location that allows the use of natural light, but often sunlight must be reflected or softened with a filter material. A light reflector will help fill in harsh shadows or simply add more light to the subject. Artificial lights may be added if the available light is insufficient. Adding artificial light to natural light may require matching the color temperature to the existing light, usually 5600 K. This can be accomplished by using an HMI light or placing a color correction gel (daylight blue) over a standard video light. Specific types of light mounts and light stands can be considered to give the desired lighting on the subject within other constraints, such as available power, available space, ability to reflect off surfaces, and so on. While lighting is attended to, other crew members can be attending to the audio needs of the production.

With any luck, a good scouting report has yielded a location selection that considers the ambient sound of that location and outside sounds such as traffic that might occur at varying times of day. A final assessment at the time of the shoot is always necessary. Things may be different. All too often small but common things, such as occasional aircraft passing overhead or the all but unnoticed rumble of an air conditioner, can escape the location scout but become an extreme annoyance when heard on mic.

Microphone selection and microphone placement are critical procedures on location. Are they or their shadows in the shot? Can framing and lighting accommodate the mic placement demands? If microphone cables are placed across a place where people must walk during the shoot, care must be taken to securely tape the cables to the ground for safety and to prevent cables from being pulled out of the recorder, or microphones being yanked out of your shot because someone or something has caught the cable. They also must be kept away from power cords to reduce the chances of audio interference hum.

LOCATION INTEGRITY

Location integrity concerns assessing and then maintaining the condition of the location at which you are shooting. Although your location scouting should give pertinent information, when you arrive for the shoot you once again have to ensure that the situation will be safe and then make sure the location is not damaged during taping. Everything from electrical shock hazards to the condition of the hardwood floors has to be considered. The shooting location has to be made safe for not only the crew but the public as well. Do any cables or cords run across pathways? If so, are they taped down? Is there sufficient distance between car traffic and the crew? Are all lights well secured and stands weighted down to avoid accidentally tipping them over? You should also consider things like slick flooring or the ability of the location's floor to support your equipment and crew. Crowding all the equipment and crew onto a small balcony to get the perfect shot of the sunset behind your talent might be motivated by aesthetic concerns, but if the balcony can't support the huge increase in weight it has to bear, the shoot could be a disaster.

One important goal in location shooting is to be able to enter the location with your crew and equipment, set up, rehearse, shoot, and wrap up without leaving a trace. It is the same kind of awareness that you would have when going backpacking or camping. You need to use the site, but not abuse it. Heavy, bulky equipment can cause damage to woodwork or even cut grooves in flooring. Hot lights set too close to delicate drapery can cause discoloration, scorching, or even a fire. Rolling or dragging your equipment across exposed wires can also create problems. It is always a good idea—if possible—to have thick blankets like those used by moving companies to place over floors and carpet or pieces of delicate furniture that are very near the equipment setups. Scratching an antique desk can take the profit right out of any shoot or stick the station with a hefty bill. That is why TV stations and production companies have insurance. Without it, your job or entire business could be in jeopardy.

MAINTAINING CONTROL

Studios are designed the way they are to allow the television producer the ability to control almost all production variables. In addition to sound, light, camera placement, and availability, the studio usually is closely temperature controlled and is considered a restricted area to people not involved in the production. When you go to a remote site for your EFP shoot, your job is to try to control as many of the production variables as you can given the crew, budget, equipment, and time frame allowed for by the project. Again, selecting the right location will help you control the variables.

In any situation where you are acting as both photographer and director (and maybe producer, too) you need to be in charge at all times. You must watch over the entire site, looking for potential problems and safety concerns. If a grip or PA (production assistant) is no longer needed in his assigned role, reassign him to crowd control or to pulling camera cables. Unless you have large unionized crews, it's best to keep everyone working on some aspect of the production or site integrity the entire time they're on location.

In ENG, control may be nearly impossible to obtain. In general, a news shooter will only have to worry about two people: herself and the reporter. And this worry is usually to just stay out of the way. That involves constantly looking over your shoulder and from side to side. Shooting inside a factory with busy forklifts zooming around the plant floor can make for a dangerous situation. Shooting in a sports arena with many intoxicated fans can be just as dangerous. In each situation, you cannot control the environment so you must have complete control of just what you are doing. Tricks like setting up with your back against a wall or fence will protect that direction of approach from unwanted intervention and danger. By using site materials (chairs or tables, for example) or natural boundaries like walls or hedges, you can usually create a little "safe zone" for your setup. The more you can isolate yourself from trouble, the better the shoot will go. Of course, at times you will have to "wade in among 'em" to get the shots. In those cases, all you can do is hold tight to the camera and make sure any cables are closely controlled and not getting hung up on anything. And nothing upsets people more than getting their head banged by the battery on the back of your camera as you turn around too quickly in a crowd. Move with deliberate caution.

BACKUP PLANS

Try not to go to any location without some type of backup plan. This may be necessary for a variety of reasons. Weather problems can force your shoot to a different location in order to tape from a sheltered spot. Last minute changes in personnel due to illness or conflicting scheduling can force you to rethink crew assignments. If your camera operator is a no-show at the last minute, who will be your backup shooter?

No matter what the plan is, in either news or production, you should always have a what-if scenario in the back of your mind. How can this shot be done while eliminating the offending element? You're set up in a good spot to get the candidate at the podium, but now the audience is standing on their chairs and you can't see the stage at all. How are you going to get the most dramatic part of this speech? You can run down to the front of the crowd, but how will you get the podium audio? Can you still see the politician from an angle that low? Never assume your first choice will work perfectly, especially in news. For EFP you will have more control—and, one hopes, more help—but you still need to have a plan ready when the situation goes awry.

SECURITY

Shooting on location means that you leave the safety and security of the studio. When you go on location to shoot, you bring expensive equipment out into the open for people to see and perhaps give those that are criminally inclined an opportunity to steal it. Not only does theft of cameras and other equipment happen, it happens all too often. Professional camcorders can be sold quickly and often transported out of the country before they can be traced to the rightful owners. There are criminals in this country who travel to newsworthy events to see if an opportunity will arise to steal equipment. ENG often requires a news crew to shoot in a high-crime area, increasing the chances that thieves may see the equipment and try their luck. Although it would be rare for a camera to be stolen right off the tripod while the crew is working around it, the times when cameras and other equipment are being loaded and unloaded are the most opportune for thieves. The most simple rule of thumb for protecting your gear on location is just don't ever let it out of your sight. If you're by yourself, that means taking the camera to lunch with you and even to the bathroom. You wouldn't leave a $10,000 diamond necklace lying on the back seat of your car while it's parked would you? Many cameras are worth a lot more than that.

Your crew is also at greater risk on location. Muggings and assaults can happen, especially when newsworthy events are occurring and attention is focused closely on a particular action, but not necessarily the perimeter where the production crew is working. In ENG work, reporters and photographers are often in danger from other people, but also from the elements of the event itself. Shooting a forest fire, hurricane, or tornado presents obvious personal danger. News events like foiled robberies that result in hostage situations can lead to shooting, bombs, and other dangers. Covering wars, uprisings, or events like the riots that occurred in Los Angeles after the legal decision in the Rodney King case can put television production people in a situation where danger can come at any time and from any direction. In dangerous situations, the job of the EFP producer is to keep his crew and equipment safe. In ENG, the crew might only be the photographer and the reporter. These people must truly "watch each others' backs" while shooting.

It is not unreasonable for producers and even news crews to hire private security guards to accompany them into the field when the possibility of danger exists. In larger cities, production crews pay off-duty police to watch over the production.

DEALING WITH THE PUBLIC

Remote shooting doesn't necessarily imply shooting at locations remote enough to be far from the public. This is especially true in ENG, where most of the stories involve people. On a large budget, EFP project crowd control is often the responsibility of a crew member such as the assistant director. Even if taping permits don't require it, that person should get permission from the appropriate authorities to barricade streets or portions of streets to keep curious onlookers away from the shots. When this is not possible, a crew member should be asked to deflect passers-by and gawkers. The vast majority of the time, these people who appear at the location are merely trying to satisfy their curiosity about what is going on.

Unfortunately, these folks and their questions (or their desire to be on television) can be time-consuming distractions and can jeopardize your ability to get the necessary shots. It is a constant job to find shorthand ways to fend off the curious (sarcastically referred to by news people as "lens lice") in order to get the work done in a timely manner. It is never a

good idea to be rude or curt with the public, no matter how obnoxious their behavior may be. It is not uncommon for people to vent their anger about the news media at you even though you may be on a production shoot. Don't argue with them. Say you're sorry for the state of affairs in TV but you're powerless to change any of it. Acknowledge their complaint but don't enter a debate. You have work to do and they have years of anger that won't be satiated in this situation. Avoid confrontation at all costs. This is one of those unforeseen factors that can change a shoot. One belligerent member of the public can shut down an entire production. You could be forced to move to another location or call the police. (See Figure 7.6.)

CHECKLISTS

Shooting on location with portable equipment is a complex task that consumes considerable time and energy. You can easily make it an even harder task by trying to memorize everything that you need to do and bring to the shoot. Instead, you make appropriate lists and notes to yourself (and others) in preproduction so that you can arrive at the shoot with everything and everyone that you need for the shoot. You can begin setup, rehearsal, and shooting without having to return to home base to get forgotten equipment, supplies, or even people. In EFP, the location shoots are often very different from each other. No two are exactly alike. Therefore the equipment and facilities that you require for each shoot are probably somewhat different. Using the facilities sheet during each shoot helps you keep track of everything that you need for each shoot on location.

This sheet has been known for years as a "fax" sheet, but now that the electronic send/receive devices common to almost all offices are referred to as fax machines and people use fax header sheets with every fax sent, it is best to rename the facilities sheet to avoid confusion with a sheet used for electronic faxing. Using a checklist for equipment needs and facilities will save you time as the shoot goes along. "A gaffer's clamp would really solve this problem, do we have one?" Check the sheet.

You should also have checklists of shots needed for the day or location. It's easy to forget the cutaway of the sign after spending so much time on the talent's blocking and lighting. Even in news, it is a good idea to have a scratch "laundry list" of shots in your

Figure 7.6 Even a simple sign can help keep the public out of your work space.

pocket. A quick meeting with the reporter at the start of the story can lead to such a list. The reporter goes off to gather facts and the photographer starts the methodical work of "knocking off" the list. There are always so many things to remember and deal with (like the public) that forgetting a very small but highly important shot can easily happen. If at all possible, make a list.

ROLLING TAPE

After taking into consideration all of the above ideas and concerns, it is now time to roll the camera. Keep in mind that all that has been discussed so far is actually there to ensure that the creativity of the shoot can happen in a safe environment free from unnecessary distractions—even if it's in the middle of utter chaos. By being acutely aware of all that's going on around you, you can now comfortably change your concen-

tration to the real business at hand: shooting. Nobody ever said TV was easy.

REHEARSING

In EFP, rehearsals can begin as the camera, lights, and sound equipment are being set. This may involve a performer narrating, an athlete demonstrating a tennis swing, a chemist pouring liquid into a test tube, or even an animal performing a trick. The person who is directing the shoot should see how the subject will perform the desired action and make sure it is in keeping with the intention of the script. This is often a judgment call on the part of the director, because it is the director who has the most influence on the visual interpretation of the words and directions contained in the script.

This is the time when many problems make themselves apparent. Lights may need to be adjusted, the mic placement changed, or the entire shot scrubbed. Rehearsals can actually start before the talent or real subject is there. If you have any idea what the action will be, have a stand-in walk through the scene. They may be the wrong height or hair color but seeing a body in the shot can get the scene closer to the final frame. There's a saying in the movie industry: "You can't light air." It means you can set up all the lights you want, but until there is an actual subject in the picture, you can't tell if everything is working according to plan.

Even in ENG, it's a good idea to rehearse such things as stand-ups or even to first walk through a handheld camera shot before committing it to tape. You may find that the shot doesn't work and you can quickly move on to something else. Many reporters never "nail" the stand-up on the first try. Especially if the stand-up is going to take place as some background action is happening, a good rehearsal can save the shot. As the complexity of the shot increases, so does the need for rehearsal. The reporter may want to do the on-camera shot just as the train is pulling into the station. Walking through the shot while imagining the train being there may look silly to the watching public but could also mean the difference in getting this one-chance shot right or not getting it at all.

SHOOTING (AND RESHOOTING)

As your finger is poised on the record button, there is one more checklist to be gone over. Is the camera white balanced? Is the focus set? Do you have enough tape left on this roll (or even have a tape in the deck)? Is the audio good or do we have a plane flying over? Are the batteries holding up? Are you comfortable? It doesn't do the scene any good if the camera operator is contorted around the camera and can't stand there for more than 30 seconds before fatiguing, or if the eye piece is not adjusted for your eyes. You should be at the point where everything has been dealt with and now, free from anxiety, all you have to do is just make the shot.

Your concentration can now turn to maintaining framing, following the action, and making sure the shot goes the way it was intended to work.

It is of crucial importance that you know what you have on tape once the shot ends. You may be surprised by how often your memory can conflict with what actually ends up on the tape. In the jostling of

the crowd, how long was the candidate in the frame? You may think several seconds but by playing the tape back it turns out to be only 1 or 2 seconds—not enough to be usable. Don't say you have the shot unless you are absolutely sure you have it. In EFP situations, you often have the luxury of playing the shot back in the field to check it. That, of course, presents another possible problem: After playing back a shot, you must make sure you recue the tape properly and don't record over previous material. In ENG you almost never have the ability to look at what you have done in the field. You simply have to know what you have or don't have on the tape. That requires a rather strenuous level of concentration, often involving counting the seconds in your head to determine the length of shots.

A constantly revolving and evolving checklist of factors, such as camera wobble, framing, anticipation of action, the best focal length to use, editing considerations, and simply choosing which subject to follow, are all part of the creative process. Once again, that's why you can't be overprepared for any shoot. And news can be the most difficult of all to plan for. In the chapters on ENG and EFP styles, more specific information is given as to what kinds of shots and techniques various situations will require.

WRAPPING UP

There are several pitfalls that you should think about when you begin to wrap up after your shooting is over. First, are you sure that you have shot everything that you will need? Less experienced videographers often make the mistake of leaving the location without getting all the shots necessary for the editor to put the story together. The shots most commonly left out are cutaway shots used to cover some bad video or transition shots. It is best to review the tape of your shots on a color monitor to make sure that all of your shots have proper color balance, exposure, framing, composition, and acceptable backgrounds. At this time it is a good idea to listen carefully to your audio. You may find that some of the audio is not clear or that you picked up some interference. This is also a good time to record some ambient sound for use in editing. After you have completed this test of your recorded material (and have reshot anything that is not acceptable) you should begin to wrap up.

Start the process by turning off all of your video lights. The less you use your lights, the longer they will last, so turn them off as soon as you are sure they are no longer needed. Also, they must cool down before they can be removed from their mounts and put back into their cases. Next, remove all tapes from recorders and check to see if all tapes are properly labeled. Do this before you cut off power to the recorders, because you cannot eject tapes without power to the machines. The next step is to turn off the camera and remove it from the tripod or mount. Put the camera in its case or in a very safe but visible place, usually on the floor. Remember not to leave the camera unattended, because this is the point in the location shooting process when cameras can be stolen. Your tripod or mount should then be taken down to traveling size and put in its case, if it has one. All connecting cables for signal and power should be properly coiled and stowed in the accessories case or bag.

At this point, it is appropriate to carefully remove all gaffer tape that you have used on floors, walls, or doors. You may have to remove any sticky residue that remains after the tape has been pulled off. Sticky residue on glass can be removed with a razor blade. Floors, walls, and desktops can be cleaned with a mild solvent, but avoid using any liquid on wood surfaces if at all possible. If your light housings are cool to the touch, they should be lowered, then removed from their stands or mounts. Place the lights in their case, but remember that the bulbs are extremely fragile, especially when they are hot or even warm. Take down the light stands or mounts and place them in their case or secure them in the vehicle. All props and set pieces should be removed and placed in the vehicle. You probably should place your camera in the vehicle last so you do not have to put heavy equipment cases on top of the camera case.

Now you should have all the equipment loaded in the vehicle, and you can conduct a very careful visual survey of the location called the "idiot check." Check around power outlets for extension cords left behind. Was your equipment placed in more than one room at any time during the shoot? This is another good reason to have a staging area where equipment can stay when not in use. Check all rooms used for the shoot. And pick up all the trash generated during the taping like coffee cups and soda cans. If the site is as clean as when you first entered it, and the objects or furniture have been replaced to their original locations, ask the contact person to look it over. Let them know you have made every effort to return the site to its original condition. If they "buy" your cleanup, thank them for the use of the location (especially important if there is any chance that you might have to return to that location) and leave with peace of mind.

Even in the hectic pace of news, take the time to restore the site you have used to an acceptable condition. Your trash can be a very ugly reminder of why many people distrust or even hate the media. Sometimes you may only have apologies to give for the trampled flowers, but make some type of effort to acknowledge your damage. Don't confuse arrogance with the rights of a free press. If you make a mess, take responsibility for it.

Postproduction: Editing It All Together

PART ONE: TECHNICAL EDITING BASICS

As we mentioned at the beginning of this book, videotape has many advantages over film in single-camera production. One of those advantages is the ease of editing. Film requires developing time, viewing time, and cutting and splicing time—a slow process often involving several different people and even different companies. Videotape can be taken directly to an editing system and quickly edited by one person. Today, there is virtually no use of film in TV news, and film used in projects for other uses are actually transferred to videotape for editing.

Video editing stands at a crossroads today. The most common form of editing, in use since the 1960s is called **linear editing**. It involves recording selected portions of a tape being played on one machine onto another. This is the way tape has been *cut* since the early days of video. But like so many areas of our lives, the computer has intervened to produce a new way of doing things. By using digital technology, the tape images are transferred or digitized to the hard drives of computers. The transferred scenes are then put together in a fashion called **nonlinear editing**, a process very similar to the way a word processor program works. The style of editing, or shot selection and pacing, is the same for both systems. While linear editing will remain in use for some time to come because of the vast investment of equipment in the marketplace, nonlinear editing will constantly grow in popularity. Unfortunately, because this is the early dawn of this technological change, the exact method-ology and systems used in the nonlinear process have not been standardized. These editing systems are changing on an almost monthly basis. The technology is changing too rapidly for an in-depth look at any particular system. Therefore, the primary thrust of this chapter is on the technique of editing and not the mechanics of system operations.

The concept of video editing is basically a process of information transfer. Information, such as video pictures, sound, and control signals, is transferred from a source or player machine to a recorder or edit machine. The source has the unedited, or raw, video-tape footage; the recorder eventually has the edited story, or **edit master**. Almost all editing systems in TV stations, corporate video centers, and independent production houses are set up so that the information flows from left to right.

In multicamera studio work, one technique of shooting is referred to as live on tape. This refers to shooting the entire scene or show without having to stop and make edits or do what is called **pull-ups** where the show is edited at a later time. This process is the same as live TV. A 30-minute show is completed 30 minutes after the show begins; no editing is required. The most obvious reason for this is economics: Studio time is saved and editing time is eliminated. In ENG, the need for immediacy in a newscast and the ability to have a late-breaking news story air quickly can also require a live-to-tape technique.

More commonly, however, in both news and production, the expectation is that the field footage is shot for the edit. In other words, editing is an expected and necessary part of the production process.

Scenes are often shot out of order for convenience. Multiple takes of the same scene or shot are done to allow the director and editor to select the shot that best captures what they intend to communicate. In portable video, the director and editor often have more time to think about and make shot selection decisions by reviewing the tapes in the edit room.

In corporate video production centers, the first skill that managers look for in their entry-level hires is editing. A person skilled in editing should be knowledgeable not only about the process of editing itself, but also about framing, composition, visual pacing, and flow. A skilled editor knows how to put it all together and is therefore a crucial member of the production team. (See Figure 8.1.)

VIDEOTAPE FORMATS

A thorough knowledge of the information contained on a videotape is a necessity in understanding the process of electronic editing or information transfer. There are various ways of recording information (audio, video, and synchronization) onto videotape, which results in a number of different formats. The formats vary in a number of ways:

1. Tape width
2. Types of information
3. Physical and electronic methods of actually placing the information onto the tape.

Some formats share the same tape width, but with the exception of Sony's standard and SP tape types of their U-Matic and Beta formats, no two formats mentioned here are compatible; that is, a particular tape format cannot be played on a machine with a different format. As digital mediums continue to enter the marketplace, even more noncompatible formats will arise.

Reel-to-Reel Format

Before cassettes came into use, videotape was wrapped on reels similar to those used for film projection. This system required a supply reel and a take-up reel.

Two-Inch Quadruplex. This tape was the broadcast industry standard for many years. Quadruplex is a high-quality format that uses four heads and records four tracks of information (hence the name quadruplex) onto 2-inch magnetic tape. The Quadruplex format is no longer used.

One-Inch Type C. The 1-inch Type C format works on a smaller machine and surpasses the quality of the quadruplex, or 2-inch, format. Type C was a breakthrough for videotape, because it allows special effects, such as slow motion, accelerated motion, and freeze frame.

The 1-inch Type C format was the broadcast industry standard for most studio production until the early 1990s. This format is currently used only occasionally in the field because of its size and the expense of the portable recording machines. Large-scale portable shoots such as those for professional sports often have large production vehicles that can house a number of 1-inch machines. In addition to using one VCR per camera for recording, one or more machines are often used for instant replay.

Videocassette Format

Cassettes were successfully adapted for use with videotape in the early 1970s. The videocassette allows the tape-supply and take-up reels to be housed inside a plastic case. Since videocassettes are self-threading, physical handling of the tape is not necessary. When housed in a videocassette, the videotape is better protected from heat, moisture, and dust than on reel-to-reel tape.

Professional. Generally superior in performance to those used by consumers, professional videocassette formats are used by professional broadcasters, networks (both cable and broadcast), independent production houses, and high-end corporate video users. These formats provide more lines of resolution and better color reproduction than most consumer formats and have less signal loss during editing and duplication.

Three-Quarter-Inch U-Matic and SP U-Matic. From the late 1970s through the 1980s, the 3/4-inch videocassette was the standard for most broadcast news operations, educational, institutional, and corporate video production units. Within U-Matic there are two different subformats. Regular U-Matic has been commonly used since the mid-1970s. An improved version of the U-Matic format called U-Matic SP, introduced in 1986, has better resolution (330 lines compared to 280) and less ringing (distortion) of both the luminance and chrominance signals. In addition, the format also features a noise reduction

Figure 8.1   The top picture shows a simple ³/₄-inch U-Matic editing system with a remote edit control panel. The bottom picture shows an A/B roll-editing system with two player VCRs that send the signal through a TBC and switch and then to a recorder; the switch receives video from the two player VCRs, an effects generator, and a character generator.

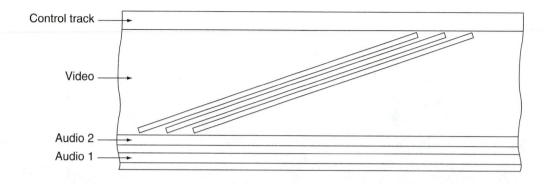

Figure 8.2 Video and audio track pattern on a section of 3/4-inch U-Matic cassette tape.

system for its audio channels, a time code that is part of the video signal, and less generational loss. A third-generation SP tape will look almost as good as a first-generation regular U-Matic recording. Although the U-Matic format is one of the oldest tape systems to be used, it is also one of the most popular. Because of the enormous libraries of 3/4-inch tape and the number of machines still in service, this tape format will be around in some form for some time. (See Figure 8.2.)

Half-Inch Betacam, Betacam SP, and MII.

In many professional production operations, especially broadcast and high-quality independent production, the format of choice is professional 1/2-inch Betacam, Betacam SP, and to a much lesser degree, MII. Regular Betacam recorders are no longer manufactured, although they are still extensively used. The process of encoding information on Betacam SP and MII is radically different from the original consumer formats. This style of encoding information is called **component video.** Component video recording utilizes different tracks on the videotape to record the luminance and chrominance information. The procedure used by earlier formats is **composite video,** where the luminance and chrominance information (along with the appropriate synchronization signals) are combined on one track per video field. In component video, two tracks are required per video field. These tracks, the Y track for luminance and the C track for chrominance, are combined for replay to yield one video field. (See Figure 8.3)

The advantage of using component video recording is that the higher frequency information in the luminance and chrominance signals is not lost when combined as it is in composite recording. The quality of component video surpasses the 1-inch C format

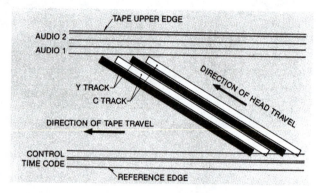

Figure 8.3 Video and audio track pattern on a section of 1/2-inch Betacam SP videotape.

video and, because of the advantages of these smaller and less expensive videocassettes, recorders, and players, the 1-inch format is slowly fading out. Of the two formats, Betacam (now Betacam SP) enjoys enormous popularity with the high-end portable video users and would be considered the standard of the industry.

Digital Video. The videotape formats discussed to this point have utilized an analog procedure to encode and decode video and audio information that does have some drawbacks. The analog process is a process that reads a video signal and then approximates it in reproduction. This becomes especially apparent in duplication. In the process of duplicating a signal from one tape to another, a small amount of information is lost. After several repetitions of this process, a tape that is a copy of a copy of a copy has noticeably less sharpness and may have smeary and inaccurate color. The amount of signal lost depends on the format; professional formats such as SP Beta lose less information per generation than other formats such as U-Matic and the home video formats. Because of the nature of the way the signal is encoded onto tape, digital video recording allows for no signal degradation from generation to generation, as long as the signal transfer is done properly. This means a tape can be copied and copies can be made of the copy without noticing which is the original. Digital video also has superior video and audio signals as compared with all other formats. Specifically, the video signal has a very high signal-to-noise ratio and avoids the moiré pattern problem (a herringbone distortion when sharp focus, fine detail patterns appear) common to all analog formats. The audio is exceptionally good—similar in quality to an audio compact disc. Four audio channels are available for recording and editing. (See Figures 8.4 and 8.5.)

Consumer. Consumer videocassette formats were developed to be easy to use, inexpensive, and of good quality. Consumer formats generally have fewer lines of resolution and poorer color reproduction than professional formats.

Betamax and VHS The first home video format, Betamax, has become essentially obsolete. Although there are many machines in homes throughout the country, video stores that rent Betamax tapes are becoming quite scarce. Camcorders and editing systems for Betamax are no longer in production. The format is technically superior to the VHS format but has less recording time per cassette. The VHS format has flourished significantly in the last 20 years and enjoys enormous popularity. Camcorders using both the

standard size VHS cassette and the smaller VHS-C cassettes and editing systems abound in the marketplace. In fact, editing systems have become quite good for VHS tape and are common in educational, governmental, institutional, and independent video production facilities. Perhaps the greatest growth has been in home video, where large numbers of consumers have purchased camcorders and are now starting to purchase editing equipment.

S-VHS This format is referred to as Super VHS and is another derivative of standard VHS, but is not compatible with standard VHS VCRs. The benefit of the format is increased resolution and elimination of some of the color interference of VHS recording. The

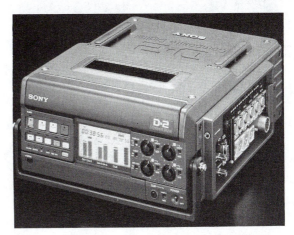

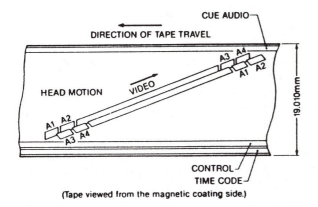

Figure 8.4 Video and audio track pattern on a section of digital video tape. A1–A4 refers to the four audio tracks.

Figure 8.5 Digital video recorders for (A) studio and (B) portable applications. Courtesy Sony Corp.

resolution is greater than 400 lines (as compared with 260 for standard VHS), thus allowing the picture to have a professional appearance. A larger bandwidth for more video signal information (similar to professional formats) makes this high resolution possible, but it requires a special output cable that separates the luminance or brightness information (Y) from the chrominance or color information (C). This cable features a special connector referred to as an S connector.

Eight Millimeter (8mm) and Hi8   In the late 1980s, a videotape format was introduced that utilized a tape width even narrower than the 1/2-inch formats. The videotape for this format was only 8mm wide, or roughly 1/3-inch wide. Despite this diminutive size, the quality of the format is comparable to the existing consumer formats of VHS and S-VHS. In addition to good-quality video, this format offered two different kinds of audio recording. Two standard linear audio tracks are available that are comparable to that of other formats. In addition, a **pulse code modulation** (PCM) system is utilized that yields two tracks of near-digital-quality audio. This type of audio recording yields a larger dynamic range and frequency response superior to existing analog audio-recording methods. (See Figure 8.6.) One important problem with these formats lies is the fact that neither can accomplish audio dubs easily.

The 8mm format, despite being designed for nonbroadcast use, comes with the capability of encoding time code on the tape. This time code, though incompatible with the time code on professional formats, helps make the editing process significantly more exact by putting a permanent address on each frame of video.

Just as VHS was improved with S-VHS, 8mm received a significant upgrade with the advent of Hi8. By increasing the bandwidth for the luminance signal, a horizontal resolution of more than 400 TV lines is possible in this format. The video signal-to-

noise ratio (S/N ratio) is also improved, yielding a clearer picture with less interference. Like S-VHS, it requires a special output cable, an S connector, to separate the luminance from the chrominance information to fully realize the quality when viewing the tape on a TV or when making copies. Another feature of the format is that it can reproduce images in the slow-motion or still-frame mode without distortion or interference.

Digital Tapes   Like the professional formats, consumer systems will eventually become digital. These new formats are giving consumers and low-end professionals digital tools that more effectively interface with the computer world. Also, as in the professional world, the competition to set the standards for compatibility is fierce. There is likely to be only one winner. Just as VHS overcame Betamax, only one format may still be in use several years after many were introduced. Which one that will be is anyone's guess. But one thing is certain: In the not too distant future, all videotape formats will be obsolete in favor of some other digital storage medium.

Two major digital formats are currently available to consumers and industrial users. These formats are Digital 8 and Mini DV. Digital 8 was introduced by Sony in the late 1990s. It was designed for use by people who had previously used Sony's 8mm or Hi8 formats. These camcorders allow users who have stocks of 8mm or Hi8 tapes an opportunity to use a computer to edit these tapes in the digital environment. The Digital 8 camcorder plays both 8mm and Hi8 analog tapes and will convert the analog information into digital information and then send it to a digital editor through a FireWire port.

Mini DV has become the digital format of choice for serious amateurs and many professionals. The audio and video recording is excellent and tape dubbing has no generational loss. The format features a very small videotape cassette, thus allowing very small camcorders. Video resolution is 525 lines (compared to the 400 lines available from S-VHS or Hi8). Some users have reported that the format has some visual distortions, often referred to as artifacts, that may appear in the picture occasionally. This is caused by the way the format compresses the video to make the data handling easier and this is considered a minor problem by most users. Mini DV contains the typical information tracks— audio and video—but also has a subcode track and an ITI track. The subcode track (actually an area on the videotape) contains information about time code, date, time and

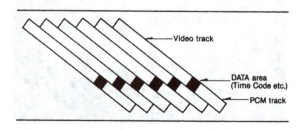

Figure 8.6   Video and audio track pattern on a section of 8mm videotape. Courtesy Sony Corp.

track numbers. (See Figure 8.7.) The ITI area contains information that allows video insert editing. Audio information is stored in two ways: One way offers CD-like quality, while the other option allows audio dubs after the original video is shot.

Oxide and Metal   The last point to note in the differences among videotape formats is what type of material coats the tape itself. All of the older formats use an oxide coating to create the recording medium. This material was found to limit the ability of the surface to record the higher frequencies necessary to give a high-quality product. All of the newer formats, such as Beta SP, S-VHS, and Hi8, use a metal-particle-coated tape, often referred to as simply metal tape. Certain machine models within each format may not play or record on oxide tape or may *only* work with metal tape. Whatever machine you happen to use, make sure you know exactly which kind of tape it will take.

New Formats   At least two new formats for videotaping with camcorders are on the horizon and should be available soon in this country. Sony expects to have a camcorder that will store images on a Mini-Disc in MPEG-2 video with four high-quality audio tracks. This camcorder also has the capability of editing within the camcorder. Hitachi is now offering a camcorder that records video on a removable DVD-RAM disc, also storing as MPEG-2 files. This camcorder will feature long recording times and high-quality audio and video. The exciting aspect of these new formats is that they will not utilize videotape and therefore not be subject to tape deterioration over time and other storage and recording problems common to videotape.

TYPES OF EDITS

On linear editing systems you need to be familiar with two types of edits: the assemble edit and the insert edit. Choosing between these two types of edits is often the first decision that you will make when beginning to edit your story or project.

Assemble Edit

An **assemble edit** transfers all information from the source machine to the edit machine. Specifically, it transfers the control track, video track, and both audio tracks to the edit machine. In other words, it duplicates the information from the source tape onto the edit tape. When placing an entire program or long segment onto a new videotape, an assemble edit is usually appropriate. This process is similar to a straight dubbing, or duping, process that can be accomplished using two tape machines and no editing controller. Pressing "Play" on the source machine and "Record/Play" on the edit machine will achieve the same thing as an assemble edit.

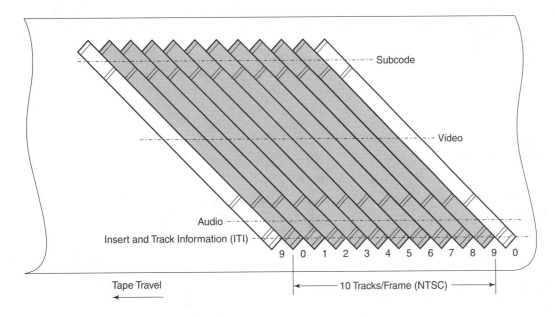

Figure 8.7 Track pattern on a section of Mini DV tape.

Assemble edits have two disadvantages:

1. This edit is all or nothing. All information is transferred, erasing anything on the edit master tape. Everything, including all audio and video, is laid down in one edit.
2. At the end of every assemble edit, a few frames of snow or a glitch appears on the tape. This is a result of transferring the control track. The erase head of the recorder precedes the record head by several frames. It erases everything on the tape in an assemble edit and thus leaves a hole at the end of every edit.

This presents no problem if you are duplicating an entire program, but if you are trying to place a video segment into an already existing story or piece on your edited master tape, you will then have an annoying (and technically unacceptable) glitch in your final edited master. You can avoid this problem when editing a piece consecutively, one segment at a time. After each segment is recorded on the edit machine, you must back up the tape and start your next segment before the glitch. (See Figure 8.8.)

Insert Edit

The insert edit allows you to select either the video track, audio track one, audio track two, or any combination of them to be transferred to the edit master. An insert edit does not cause a glitch at the end of the edit, because it does not transfer control track information. If you select only the video portion of the playback tape to be transferred, an erase head on the recorder will eliminate any picture where you have chosen to put the new picture, leaving the audio channels untouched. Since insert edits do not transfer control track, no erasures are made on the control track of the edit master tape.

One requirement of insert editing is that the tape you use to edit onto must have a good control track before you attempt an insert edit. If you use a tape that already has any type of video recorded on it, there is no problem as long as the control track has no breaks in it. If you use a new tape as the edit master (as is common when you have an important story or program to edit onto the tape), you must put a control track on it first before editing.

The most common procedure for doing this is called **black bursting** the tape. This is a procedure that requires you to record your videotape with a steady black-only signal (that is, with no other picture information). This can be accomplished using a signal generator that generates video black (a steady black picture) or by connecting your tape deck to a camera and recording the tape with the camera on, but with the lens capped. Some editors choose an alternative to the black-only signal and use a color bar pattern from a signal generator or camera instead of black. This method prevents the possibility of unedited spaces within the edit master slipping past a hurried editor's eye. Black frames can remain in the edit master when inaccurate editing leaves some missed spaces. If the tape is color bar burst, these unedited spaces show the bright color bars and are easier to spot and cover with corrected edits.

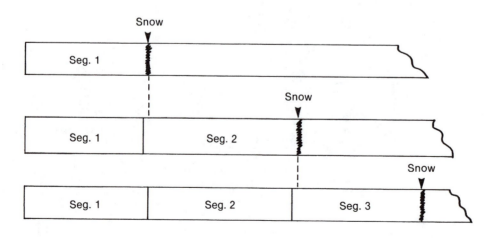

Figure 8.8 When assemble editing one segment at a time, backspace to a point before the glitch and start the next segment there.

TECHNICAL CONCEPTS

When working with videotape, you can gain a better understanding of the editing process by familiarizing yourself with some key terms and concepts that explain the videotaping process. A solid understanding of videotape recording fundamentals should provide a good context for understanding the videotape editing process.

Scanning

NTSC video is created by a scanning beam that traces out 525 lines on the face of a TV monitor. It does this in two moves. It first scans the 262.5 odd-numbered lines, and then the 262.5 even-numbered lines. This entire scanning process occurs 30 times per second, fast enough to allow our eyes and brains to believe that we are seeing a solid, constant image.

Fields, Frames, and Segments

The complete scanning of either the odd or the even lines forms a half-picture known as a **field**. Two fields, when combined or interlaced, form a **frame** or complete picture. In some formats (for example, the 1-inch type C), a frame is encoded onto tape in one continuous line and is called a **nonsegmented format.** Other formats (for example, the 1/2-inch U-Matic) that encode each frame on a separate line are called **segmented formats.** The nonsegmented format allows for some special effects, like noise-free slow motion or freeze-frame without using a time-base corrector, while segmented formats do not.

Fields have a definite order to them: They are recorded and played back in sequence—the first field then the second in order to make one frame. Editing systems must be able to distinguish between the first and second fields when edits are made. If this distinction is not made and an edit is done between fields one and two (in the middle of a frame), it will cause a glitch, picture breakup, or simply a bad edit. Editing systems have a special circuit built in called a **frame servo,** which prevents these bad edits (also known as wrong-field edits) from occurring.

Tracking

When a videotape is recorded on a VCR, it is recorded at a particular speed with the information placed onto the tape at particular locations. Thus, each VCR is slightly different from the next. This slight difference between VCRs is called tracking, and VCRs generally have a control that allows the playback machine to track very closely to the way the original recorder has placed the information onto the tape. Older videotape machines required you to set the tracking control (measured by a small meter) on your source or playback machine to optimize your tracking. If your playback machine tracks much differently than the machine originally used for recording, a poor-quality picture with snow, wrong colors, distortion, or bad audio will result. More up-to-date machines have auto-tracking functions.

Control-Track Editing

All formats of videotape include one track of information called the control track. This track is crucial to the editing process, because editing systems rely on the control track for synchronization. The control track is analogous to the sprocket holes in film: It conveys the information that keeps the tape playing at the right speed.

If your control track is damaged or partially missing, your videocassette deck will not locate the video information and you may have a total loss of video on the screen. The editing system will only make edits when it can read the control track of your source machine. You can think of your control track as the clothes rod in your closet; without a good strong clothes rod, you can put your clothes in the closet, but they will probably fall down. If you edit with a poorly recorded or missing control track, you may think that you are making an edit, but your video will fall out of sight.

Time-Code Editing

All professional editing machines make extensive use of time code in the editing process. If the control track is analogous to the sprocket holes in film, time code is like the edge numbers on the film uniquely identifying each frame. Time-code numbers are used by the producer or editor to keep track of which shots they want to use as the tape is being shot or while viewing the tape on a machine with a time-code reader. The editor can quickly find any shot on the tape if the time code for the start of that shot is known. Edit machines can use either control-track reference or time-code reference to perform edits. Both appear as numbers in the timer display on the edit machine and a switch tells you which you are using.

For control-track editing, the timer can be set at any number and changed at any time during the edit process (but not during an actual edit). Time-code display will always show the number that is recorded on the tape. Professional editors always edit with the machines in time-code mode because the edits are more accurate (there is less chance that a control-track error might cause the edit to miss by several frames) and easier if the editor is working from script notes or even making notes for further work to be done on the piece. Time code is not transferred during the edit process. This means that the black-burst edit master tape must have its own time code already on it. These tapes are generally blackened on a machine similar to the edit VCR (if not the same machine) and the time code would be put there automatically. It does not matter what the time-code numbers are on the recorder, but often the code starts at all zeros at the beginning of the tape. In EFP edit masters, where only one finished piece will be put on a single tape, many editors like to black burst the tape starting with 00:58:00:00 and begin the first shot of the piece at 01:00:00:00, leaving the first 2 minutes of the tape for color bars, test tone, and countdown.

Time-Base Correction

Although most video recorders marketed today for professional ENG and EFP are high quality and manufactured to very strict standards, slight variations in their performance often occur. In other words, each helical scan videotape recorder has slight differences. Even if two recorders are capable of identical performances, new, subtle differences become apparent over time because of different wear and other factors.

These subtle differences cause slight timing variations or errors when tapes are recorded on one VCR and played back on another. The answer to this problem is a **time-base corrector (TBC)**, which takes the output of a helical scan VCR and corrects the signal by making the necessary adjustments, line by line, to that signal. Time-base correctors often have a second device installed within them that allows for manipulation of the video level or gain, the black level, the color phase or tint, and the chroma level or amount of color information of the signal. This device, known as a **processing amplifier,** or proc-amp, is often built into the time-base corrector.

Virtually all professional videotape recorders have TBCs built into them. However, the processing amplifier portion of the TBC should not be used without a waveform monitor and a vectorscope. Without these two monitors, you cannot see the effects of any adjustments you make on the processing amplifier. Older systems that make use of machines without TBCs still work, but before any tape is played over the air or transmitted by any means, you must have a TBC.

Newer videotape recorders designed for the professional market now have circuitry that provide "time based stability." The major issue of time based correction becomes a minor issue because of the nature of digital formats. While analog format required precise synchronization that was beyond the ability of analog VTRs, the digital VTRs provide enough stability to make addition of a time based corrector unnecessary. Therefore, most professional digital VTRs can be used to feed editing systems without additional synchronization. (See Figure 8.9.)

EDITING MACHINES

Most editing machines, and even some nonlinear systems, follow the same approach to performing an edit. Besides the basic FAST FORWARD, REWIND, PLAY, STOP, PAUSE, and RECORD features, there is a variable-speed control on the machines called SHUTTLE/JOG/SEARCH that allows the operator to cue the videotape to the precise frame at which to start an edit. There will also be some means of entering the edit points chosen by the operator into the edit console memory. Usually, the ENTER button is used in conjunction with the IN and OUT buttons to give that message to the recorder. All of these func-

Figure 8.9 This DV player/recorder has time based stability and is used to feed digital nonlinear editing systems.

tions are on the face of the tape machine but can be on a separate unit called an edit controller that connects the record machine with one or more playback machines.

Most recorders allow the editor to shift the edit mode from assemble to insert as well as preview the edit, without actually performing it, with the use of the PREVIEW button. To make slight corrections in the edit points that are already entered in the console, there are usually two buttons, (+) and (−), for edit-point shifting or trimming. When an edit console is in the insert edit mode, you must choose whether you will insert video, channel 1 audio, or channel 2 audio. You can choose one or more in any combination. (See Figure 8.10.)

Video Controls

Besides the controls for performing edits, some older tape machines have other controls relating to input and output. The **skew knob** (which controls the tension in a videotape) is generally not used by the operator unless there is some major problem with the tape in the machine. **Video level control** (which measures the amplitude of the video signal) is also not usually used by the operator unless a waveform monitor is hooked up to the output of the tape machine. Without the scope, the video level knob should be left centered in the notch, or automatic, position.

The operator may have to adjust tracking control on the machine used as the player. Leave the **tracking knob** on the recorder in the notch (usually the 12-o-clock position) during the editing. Adjust the tracking knob on the player while the tape is being played. Each time a different tape is played in the playback machine, adjust the tracking knob so that you can achieve optimum tracking.

To set the tracking for the tape to be used in the player, play any portion of the tape and rotate the tracking knob until the needle on the meter reads as

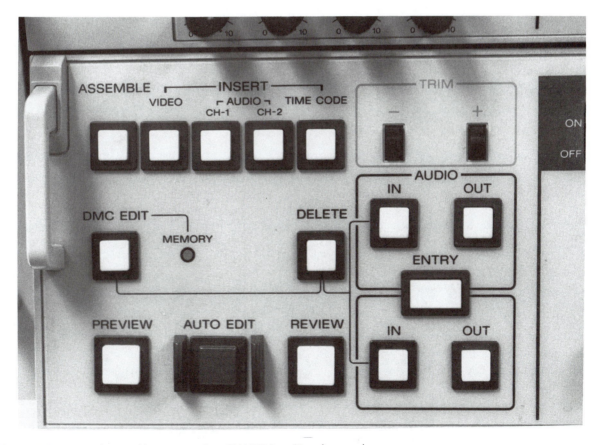

Figure 8.10 The edit control buttons on a Sony BVW-75 Beta SP studio recorder.

high as it can in the positive direction. The knob can stay in that position as long as you are using that tape. If you should switch to another tape in the player, then the tracking will have to be readjusted. New machines have automatic tracking.

Audio Controls

The audio controls follow basic standard practices. There is usually an **audio limiter** switch, ON or OFF. The limiter helps when editing is being done under deadline pressure and there is little time to make critical adjustments. Most of the time it is best not to use it.

Most newer tape machines have separate **record** and **playback controls** for audio. In general, for both playback and recording levels, the controls should be set for the loudest peaks of the audio signal. A peak should deflect the needle on a VU meter to at or near 0. The VU meter measures volume units; its scale goes

from −20 to +5. A good range for average needle deflection is between −7 and −2. (See Figure 8.11.)

The best way to calibrate audio levels is to use a standard or known source, preferably an oscillating tone from an audio mixer. From this source, the audio level should be set at 0 dB. Feed this signal through the player and into the recorder. The playback levels on the player should be adjusted to read 0 dB on the scale, and the record level on the recorder should be set at 0 dB.

To maintain the calibration of the audio setup, do all audio mixing in only one area, in most cases, at the playback source. Leave the record levels untouched for the entire editing process. Many edit setups will have a separate audio mixer between the player and the recorder to give better control over the audio or to allow the mixing in of audio sources other than those on the tape machines. Again, calibration of all audio controls before editing is very important.

Figure 8.11 Audio VU meters with volume controls and a video meter with tracking and level controls for a Sony VO 5850.

Most edit-capable machines also have mix select switches of some type. These can route the audio input and output. They indicate which channel of audio is coming from a machine, to which channel it is going, and which channel is being fed to the audio monitor. The way one machine is wired to the other can also determine how the routing of the audio can be controlled. If you familiarize yourself with your audio setup, you should be able to mix or isolate any channel of audio and have the playback levels set in the calibrated positions so there will not be any surprises in the audio of the finished product.

On the machines that can record metal tapes, such as Beta SP and MII, there are four channels of audio. For the most part you will only be using the two linear channels (channels 1 and 2) for all your audio needs. As you progress into more professional situations and stereo audio recording, you can make better use of the other two channels. This book limits discussion to only the linear channels.

Video Connections

Cable hookups between machines are a key to understanding the operation of any editing setup. The most important cable between the player and recorder is the edit control cable. If a separate edit console is required, then this cable goes from each of the decks to the console. The edit control cable is a multi-pin cable that allows the two machines to talk to each other via the edit controls. Both the player and the recorder have several video inputs and outputs.

In most TV stations and production houses, editing packages are on a video routing system. The video cable from the routing system goes into the VIDEO IN connector on the recorder. If the edit machines are on house sync, then a video line with that sync goes into the SYNC IN connector.

Video-Routing System.
A video-routing system is like a cable TV system. Multiple channels of audio and video (not a combined RF signal like cable, which combines audio and video and transmits it at a frequency similar to radio or home cable TV) from a central distribution center are sent to each editing setup or edit bay. Almost any video output in the building can be put on the routing system. Such things as color bars, black video, character generators, switch outputs, studio cameras, satellite reception, other tape machines, and even broadcast signals from other TV stations can be on the routing system.

By dialing the number of what you want to see, you can feed the video of the router to the player of that edit bay. The player machine can pass it on just like video and audio from a tape. Most of the time the machine should be fed black video from the routing system.

Synchronization

A synchronization pulse or reference signal, called **sync**, is the time reference that allows the electronics of two or more tape machines or cameras to work together. Although a VCR or camera has internal synchronization if two machines are hooked together (such as multiple cameras feeding into one switcher or two VCRs in an edit bay), only one sync source can be used. Any two machines designed to edit always allow the player machine to be the source of synchronization for the recorder as part of their edit functions.

Cameras, like edit machines, do not sync to each other without being connected to each other. They must be fed a reference that can be common to all of them; this is called **gen-lock**. Edit machines and cameras can be fed an external reference sync from the main sync generator in the station or studio. This **house sync**, as it is referred to, is more reliable and enables the machines to perform at their peak. An editing system works without either a routing system or external sync, but both are a great advantage. (See Figure 8.12.)

On the player, there will be two VIDEO OUT connectors, one to be cabled to the recorder's VIDEO IN and the other to the monitor's VIDEO IN. If you are using a monitor that can interface with the player via a multi-pin monitor cable, then the simple video-only cable is not necessary.

As with the player, if the recorder is running on house sync, then the sync cable will go into the recorder's SYNC IN connector and the switch at both the SYNC IN connectors should be in the EXTERNAL SYNC position. If the edit bay is freestanding (not on house sync), the switch is in the INTERNAL SYNC position. Newer edit machines not only have internal sync but also an internal black generator.

Audio Connections

The audio connections can be much more complicated than the video. For the player, if the edit unit is on a routing system that delivers sound to various

Figure 8.12   The back panel of a Sony BVW-75. On this machine the synchronization inputs/outputs are called "REF.VIDEO" and can be switched from external to automatic select.

locations, then the audio from that system goes into the AUDIO IN connector. On some machines it may be necessary to have a Y cable made to get the audio onto both channels of the audio input. The output of the machine should be from channel 1, channel 2, and monitor AUDIO OUT. If you are using a multi-pin monitor cable then you will not need the monitor AUDIO OUT.

The audio lines can go to an audio-mixing board or straight to the recorder. If the lines go to a separate mixer, you will have maximum control over the routing and volume of the audio signals. If you are using a mono-mixer, the single audio line out from the mixer output can be split into a Y to feed both channels of the recorder's AUDIO IN, because all mixing is done at either the player or the mixer.

Even though there probably is different audio on the two channels of the finished product, they should be premixed to the proper volumes. In other words, the two channels on the recorder are for receiving premixed audio, and their playback and record levels should never be changed from their calibrated posi-

tion. The two channels of audio play together with no need to monitor the volume of one versus the other. Each audio input should have a switch for line- or mic-level input/output. Set the switches for the signal level you are using.

Video Input Switch

Another control for older VCRs is the VIDEO INPUT. The switch usually has two inputs, line and dub. For the player, the switch is usually in the LINE position. When the player is hooked up to a routing system, the LINE position allows it to be fed whatever is coming off the router; for editing, the player should be fed black video. If there is no router, the machine is not receiving any source and the position of the switch is unimportant for the player.

The recorder's switch should always be in the DUB or EDIT position. This switch commands the recorder to look to the other machine for its reference control (very necessary information for the editing process) and for its video source. If you are using a multi-pin cable with your monitors and your machine has a VIDEO INPUT switch for TV, that position feeds the machine whatever is on the TV tuner of its monitor. In other words, you can record off-air anything that the TV set can pick up.

The VIDEO INPUT switch on newer component VCRs is somewhat different from the one on the older U-Matic machines. There are often three positions for the switch: Y/R-B, composite, and CTDM. In general the player machine is in the composite position, and the recorder is in the Y/RB (component) position. The setup may vary from format to format and according to how the machines are tied into the house system or type of edit controller. Like any complicated piece of machinery, it is best to read the operator's book thoroughly and check to see exactly how the machines are hooked up. With so many formats and composite/component translations, it is easy to become confused, especially when machines of different formats are connected as part of an edit system. In most TV stations and many production houses, an edit station will have several formats interconnected to be able to make use of the vast tape libraries that contain a broad range of tape types. And now with digital tape formats added to the mix, the connections will be a nightmare.

UNDERSTANDING THE EDITING SYSTEM

It is not possible for this book to cover all the combinations of formats, manufacturers, and wiring hookups. The following sections concern the basic functions of edit machines in general. While machines may vary by brand and format, the process of making a simple edit remains almost identical.

Performing an Insert Edit

Here we discuss a sample edit on a Sony BVW-75 editing system. The tape you are editing onto should be black burst or have some type of video signal already on it. You can burst the entire tape or just enough of it to give plenty of room for the length of your finished product. This gives the record tape a control track that allows you to do insert editing right from the start of your project.

Assume you already have a countdown or leader on your record tape and you are ready to lay the first shot down. With the raw material in the player and

the edit tape in the recorder, both machines should be in STOP. The control panel of the recorder controls both machines by using the PLAYER/RECORDER switch to designate which machine is being commanded. (See Figure 8.13.)

The PB-PB/EE (playback-playback/edit entry) switch allows you to play the audio and video through the recorder while the recorder is not in the RECORD mode but merely in STOP. PB lets the machine act as a normal VCR. PB/EE feeds video and audio through the meters to the record heads while the machine is in STOP. This allows you to use only one video and audio monitor for both machines if necessary, without having to eject the tape in the recorder or put the recorder in record mode to look at the output of the player.

With the PB-PB/EE switch in the PB/EE position on the recorder, change the control designator to PLAYER and push the SEARCH button. This allows you to move the tape by means of the SEARCH knob in either direction up to 10 times the normal speed. Using the SEARCH knob, shuttle the tape to the point you would like to have as the beginning of the shot. By pushing the ENTER and the IN buttons at the same time, you have given the edit control memory the in-point.

Switch the designator to RECORDER, and do the same procedure to line up the spot on the record tape where you wish the edit to begin. Give the recorder its in-time. While still on the RECORDER designator, push the button marked PREVIEW and view what the edit will actually look like. The machines will go through the editing process but will not actually transfer the video.

The edit will continue to run until you give it a STOP command. There are two ways of doing this: by pushing the STOP button on the recorder, which will leave no memory of an out-point in the edit control, or by pressing ENTER OUT on the recorder, which will be placed in the memory.

If this preview edit appears satisfactory, press the EDIT button and the machines will perform the edit by the in-points you have given them. If an out-point has been entered (you need to enter an out-point only on the recorder), then the edit will run only to that point. When the edit is finished, the recorder and player will cue up their tapes on the last frame of that edit and erase all previous in- and out-points in the controller memory.

If you stop an edit by simply pressing STOP on the recorder, the edit will instantly stop but the machines will still have the memory of the in- and

Figure 8.13 The PLAYER/RECORDER control.

out-points last given because you have interrupted the edit. The machine thinks it must redo the edit from the beginning. The only ways to erase those times are to put in an out-point and let the edit run its course, enter new points for both machines, or, if you are using the control-track editing method, reset the timers on both machines, which will erase the memory of any in-points or out-points previously given.

If you should wish to change an edit point slightly, say, either an in- or an out-point, you can use the TRIM button on the control panel. Use the machine designator to shift control to the machine that needs the edit-point changes. By holding down the IN button, press the + or the − button once for every frame of video you wish the edit point to be moved forward or backward. The same can be done for the out-points, and this can be done for either machine.

Once you master what the buttons do and how to use them to their best advantage (and you will find many shortcuts), you can edit swiftly and accurately. Study the user's booklet that comes with the machine you are using.

On-Line and Off-Line Editing

Edit systems are often divided into two categories: on-line systems and off-line systems. Off-line usually refers to rough cut systems where the edit master is used for viewing or evaluation purposes only and not for broadcast or release. These types of systems are generally of low quality and accuracy. Until recently, the off-line editor was an older edit system like an analog 3/4-inch U-Matic or consumer VHS system. Although analog systems are still common at post-production facilities, digital systems are also being used for off-line work.

Lower priced, lower quality nonlinear systems are available that are also used for off-line work. An example of this type of system is the Casablanca Avio system. These systems can digitize input video at a low resolution and make it available for quick and easy editing.

Higher priced editors can also be used for off-line work. When an off-line edit session is required, the video is digitized at a lower resolution to consume less space in storage and generally cut down on processing time. Simple rather than complex effects are used for the purpose of putting the project together. The main product of the off-line work is to create two very important lists. The first is the list of video segments and lengths of segments that will be used in the final edited version. The second is the list of edits and special effects that need to be made and the edit points at which they will be made. The list, sometimes known as an edit decision list or EDL becomes the blueprint for the on-line editing work.

On-line editing is performed on machines or systems capable of producing a high-quality or broadcast level edit master. Work completed on the on-line editor is expected to be a finished product ready for broadcast, CD-ROM, or other distribution medium. Many on-line editors are in use today that are analog, however most facilities are moving toward computer-based digital editors for all of their on-line editing needs. Even older analog on-line edit systems have used a computer interface that takes the edit decision information gained through off-line work and translates that information into on-line postproduction work. (See Figure 8.14.)

The Digital Environment

Much has been written and said about the fact that many things in our technological society are a part of the digital environment. Since all computers use

Figure 8.14   An editor operates the controls of an older analog on-line multi-machine edit system. Player or source machines are mounted in the rack to the left. The edit controller, video switcher for special effects and keys, and the audio mixer are mounted in the console. The record machine is in the rack to the right. Photo by John Lebya.

digital information to perform the many tasks they are capable of performing, understanding how information becomes digital and how it differs from the analog environment is both important and useful.

Analog versus Digital

Analog and digital are two ways of encoding information onto a storage medium. Conceptually, the difference between the two may be understood by considering analog to be a continuous process while digital is a discrete process. **Analog** videotape recording occurs when the recorder receives a signal and continuously tries to make a copy of that signal. **Digital** encoding breaks the signal down into small "pieces" or **bits** and assigns a numeric description of the signal using 0s and 1s. Digital encoding processes for video are being constantly refined so that digital encoding for recording is now at least as good as analog recording. In addition to random access, digitizing affords other opportunities. Once a frame of video is digitized, it can be more easily manipulated than analog video. In fact, many digital editors now have the capability to produce special effects that were until recently available only through the use of expensive equipment like digital video effects machines (known as DVEs).

Linear and Nonlinear Editing

The introduction of the computer to such mundane tasks as typing a letter forever changed how we deal with written text. When using a word processor, inserting material into a document was no longer problematic. We could find the spot to enter the additional information and just enter it. The program automatically adjusted everything from that point on to the end of the document without problems. The program created a "working document" in the active memory that was flexible as to length and content. Changes were easy and very quick once the proper commands were used. Not only could extra letters or words be added or deleted easily, but additional documents could be inserted into the document being created. Length could change dramatically with a few keystrokes. Documents were created in memory and printed out as a finished product when it met the satisfaction of the author.

The differences between using typewriters to create documents and computers with word processing programs are very similar to the differences between editing video with a linear editor and a nonlinear editor. Linear editors use videotape and create programs segment by segment, end to end, just as we do when we write a paper on a typewriter. Small corrections are possible and relatively easy. If we want to insert 15 seconds of new material into a program that is already created, we can do so if we are replacing 15 seconds of video already in the program. The problem occurs if we want to insert 30 seconds of video into a spot in the program that was originally 15 seconds long. Doing this would require everything after that point in the program to be reedited. In addition to this problem, linear editing has some other drawbacks. Because shots are recorded on linear videotape, finding the shots that we want to insert into a program requires shuttling the tape backward or forward to physically locate the shot. This has two drawbacks: First it is a slow process, limited by the speed of the search modes of the videotape machine; and second, constant playing and replaying of the tape can cause some physical wear on the tape that can degrade the image. Because of the difficulties in reediting within a show, and the slowness of finding shots for use in the final program, linear editing often results in just one version of the program or project. Additional versions become too costly both in time and money. Just as word processors have helped writers to become more prolific, nonlinear editors have helped people who work in video to become more prolific. The ability to rework sections of a complete paper helps writers; the same flexibility allows editors to rework already completed sections.

Nonlinear editors do not have to shuttle tape to find desired shots. Like word processors, shots can be stored in memory as individual files and can be accessed in any order without having to "shuttle through" other shots. This is just how a word processor stores previous documents or files. This style of storage and easy retrieval is referred to as **random access**. This ability to randomly access shots regardless of the order in which they were shot is not new to visual editing. Although motion pictures are shot on linear film, the negatives are usually cut into segments or shots and stored for easy, direct access. Motion picture editing has almost always been nonlinear. The nature of how video is encoded onto videotape has prevented video from being edited in a nonlinear way. This has now changed with the availability of nonlinear digital video editors. Nonlinear editors also have the capability to integrate other media that has been digitized, such as digital audio or still pictures that have been scanned. These editors can take all of these other media and seamlessly combine them into an edited master.

Digititalization

Before video that has been shot in analog tape format can be edited on a digital editor, it must be converted. This conversion is referred to as the analog-to-digital conversion or **digitalization**. This is usually a simple procedure similar to dubbing from a playback machine to a record machine. The device that accomplishes this task is called a **codec**, because it is a **coder** and a **decoder**. The information transferred is usually the video information, the audio information (which can be one or more channels), and time-code information. The analog information is converted into binary information consisting of 0s and 1s. This process would be very simple except for the fact that each frame of video requires almost 1 megabyte of storage space. One second of video requires almost 30 megabytes. This has long been a problem with analog-to-digital conversions and digital recording in general. Another problem lies in the fact that the digitalization process occurs in real time. In other words, if you need to digitize 15 minutes of analog video, it takes 15 minutes of time to do it. The tape plays at its normal speed and as this occurs, the analog signal is converted to digital. Therefore, the time-saving features of nonlinear editing really begin *after* the analog tape is digitized.

The storage space required for digitized video is huge. As computer technology advances, so does storage space technology, making storage of digital video easier. But a quicker and somewhat more practical solution is used by many digital editors. This solution is to **compress** files to allow more information to fit into a small amount of storage space.

Compression

After digitalization, the video, audio, and time-code information can be compressed to allow a large signal to fit into a small amount of storage space. The actual compression is achieved through a series of steps that eventually reduces the information by 98.5%. In other words, information that once occupied 100 units of space only needs 1.5 units of space after compression. This is a very sophisticated process and relies on facts like the perception of humans. Humans see little detail in moving objects,

therefore some of the information in moving objects can be removed. A second reality of human perception is that humans perceive brightness more readily than color information. Color information is reduced from three colors to two and information that is redundant from frame to frame is also removed. The result is a signal that may be compressed enough to only take up 1.5% of its original space.

A number of different compression systems are available for compressing video. New systems are constantly being tested to improve video quality while decreasing the space it requires after compression. The Avid editors use **Motion-JPEG** (Joint Photographic Experts Group) for compression. Several systems under the **MPEG** acronym (Moving Pictures Experts Group) are in use and under further development. Currently, **MPEG-2** is a standard used for broadcast-quality compression. This standard reduces video to about 20% of its original size. Most professional nonlinear systems have a variable rate of compression that allows for different levels of quality. A high compression mode is used for doing off-line edits, which increases the speed of the process and reduces the amount of storage needed for the digitized video but greatly lowers the quality. A low compression mode is used for on-line editing where the edited master file can be output to high-quality tape or directly to air in some situations. This method requires a great deal of storage space in the computer. It is realistic to predict that a compression system economical enough to be included in personal computers will soon evolve that will allow broadcast-quality editing.

Editing in the Nonlinear Environment

Editing in the nonlinear environment involves editor configurations that are a bit different than they were in the analog environment. Digital machines, depending on their capabilities and their applications, are configured either as stand-alone systems or as part of a workgroup network. Although the conceptual process of editing is similar in both the analog and digital environments, the process of nonlinear editing differs from analog editing and requires slightly different procedures.

Stand-Alone Systems versus Workgroup Networks

Two models are emerging for editing in the nonlinear environment, stand-alone stations and workgroup networks. The stand-alone station is just that—an editor that is self-contained and can be used to edit all images into the finished product. Once all information and files are available at the station, a finished product can be put together by the operator. Stand-alone stations do not require network connections with other equipment and therefore there is no need for network compatibility. A stand-alone system usually includes the editing system, which consists of the computer editor, monitors, keyboard, mouse, and other peripherals for input and output of information. One important requirement is that the system is able to receive video information from some type of outside source. The source is commonly a VCR that is dedicated to that station or a video signal sent to the station via some type of video and distribution system. Inputs to the system for graphic material or audio can also be entered by DVD, CD-ROM, or floppy disk. Edit stations should also be able to accept video that is input from a variety of cameras, both analog and digital.

Workgroup editing networks are workstations that are interconnected by some type of local-area network. Audio workstations, graphics stations, digitizing stations, logging stations, character generation stations, and special effects and animation stations are all connected to allow access to a centrally stored data bank with raw video or the transfer of work to the editor for final editing.

Nonlinear edit systems that are affordable and easy to use are available now for off-line editing. An example of this type of editor is the MacroSystem (formerly Draco) Avio editor, a computer-based turnkey editor that is available for less than $2000. This editor is a storyboard style editor that edits video by putting video clips together on a storyboard type interface. Commands are entered by using a trackball to make selections from simple menu screens.

A Sample Nonlinear Editing Session

Using the main menu (see Figure 8.15), set up the editor for your session by selecting System Settings, then the language to be used on the menu itself. The speed of the trackball can also be set. Project settings involve selecting the right quality level for your video and audio. Since quality is directly related to compression, you will find that the higher the compression, the lower the quality, but the more video you can put into a small space on the hard drive. If your

video is shot on Super VHS tape it would be best to use this level of quality or lower for off-line purposes.

Video Settings
Most editors have some type of processing amplifier that will allow you to adjust various aspects of the video that you want to digitize. On the Avio, you can change the settings of the brightness, saturation, and contrast of the video you want to digitize for editing.

Recording (Digitizing)
Move the trackball indicator to the record button and left click to enter the recording mode. At this point, you should have a VCR connected to the editor and a tape cued. Start recording by starting the VCR and then left clicking on the record button. When you have recorded at least as much as you need of that shot, scene, or sequence of scenes, move the trackball indicator to the stop button and left click. You will now have created a "scene" that will be available for editing. Continue through your raw footage until you have digitized all scenes that you will want available for editing. Return to the main menu

Trimming
Since the recording of the scenes onto the editor is somewhat inexact, you may have to trim scenes to eliminate shots or frames that will not be needed. Move the trackball indicator to Trim and left click to enter the Trim mode and display the Trim screen. (See

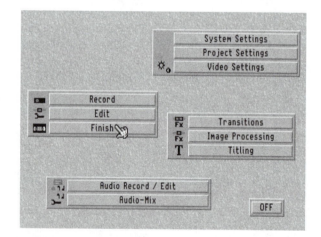

Figure 8.15 The Casablanca Avio Main screen presents all of the elements of video editing in logical blocks, from system, project, and video settings (upper right) to audio editing (lower left). Clicking on an item brings the user to a screen dedicated to its particular function.

Figure 8.16.) Remove frames from either the beginning or end of the scene by using the IN and OUT buttons and scrolling with the trackball. By slowly moving the trackball itself, you should be able to scroll from the beginning toward the end or the end toward the beginning of the scene. Left clicking on the trackball button while the IN or the OUT button is depressed will adjust the length of the scene. The scene is then trimmed for editing. Note that the trimming is not permanent; if you change your mind, you can restore the scene to its original length.

Editing a Program

Splitting

When you have recorded scenes that are too lengthy for easy editing, you can split them into two or more pieces. Left click on the Split button on the Edit screen. Left click on the Split Position button to allow scrolling through the scene to get exact start and stop points. You can click either Use to create a new scene or Drop to remove the footage up to the current frame. Splitting scenes does not affect the original scene because splitting makes a copy of the original scene and then performs the splits.

Effects

By clicking on the Special button in the Edit menu, you can change the video in any of your scenes. Effects like reversing the direction of the scene, slow motion, quick motion, still scene, and strobe are available by selecting the effect and clicking on it. Many effects provide a variety of options. For example, the slow and quick motion effects let you decide how slow or how quick to make your scene. You can layer an unlimited number of effects on scenes in the Edit window.

Putting Scenes Together

While in the Edit window, you can select scenes to be placed in the storyboard to be included in the final project. (See Figure 8.17.) Click on a scene to select it then click on Add. The scene is then copied and placed in the storyboard. Continue this procedure for more scenes to add to the storyboard. Scenes can be removed by placing the scene to be removed in the Workbox, in the center of the storyboard, and then clicking on Remove.

Transitions

A fun part of nonlinear editing is the wide array of transitions that you can add to your project simply by selecting them from a menu. Once you have some scenes put together on a storyboard, you can go to the Main Menu and click on Transitions. The Workbox now shows two scenes instead of one. If you choose a transition, it will be placed between those two scenes. Select a transition from the list. Real-time transitions take effect immediately. You can preview the other

Figure 8.16 The Trim screen lets you scroll a trackball to select the exact points at which the scene begins and ends, accurate to a single frame. The numbers display the minutes: seconds: frames of the current in- and out-points as well as the scene's duration.

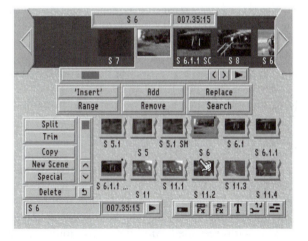

Figure 8.17 The Edit screen presents the image scenes (sometimes called "clips") that have been recorded (or digitized) onto the Avio's hard drive, represented by the first frame of each scene. The upper half of the window shows scenes on a "storyboard" in the order of their appearance in the project. The lower half shows the scenes available for the project, and provides Split, Trim, and other functions.

transitions in a small screen after your selection. At this point you can really enjoy nonlinear editing. If you do not like your first selection, make another by clicking on the type of transition you would like to try. For non-real-time transitions, your selection is temporary until you tell the editor to "render" the transition. The Create process merely tells the editor to proceed with rendering the transition so that it can be viewed in the full frame. Rendering can be instantaneous for short-duration effects like transitions. Other kinds of effects like 3D effects take more time. Rendering can take a few seconds or even a few minutes. Once you gain experience with this process, you may choose to wait until your project is completely edited to render all effects at once, just before you record your project back onto videotape.

Titling

Nonlinear editors have the capability to add titles and graphic material to your video. Choose your font, size, scroll motion, fades, colors, and so on. The speed of crawl can also be adjusted.

Audio

You can add audio to your project during the editing process if the audio on the videotape is not sufficient for your needs. If your off-line editor is a stand-alone unit, you will need to be able to input an audio signal to the editor using a tape deck, CD player, or other audio source. On the main menu, click on Audio Record. Start the audio you want to record and click on the record button on the screen. You can adjust the audio level and also name the audio clip.

The Audio Mix-Dub menu allows you to select the audio clip that you have recorded and insert it into an extra audio track used for background audio. Click on the Insert button. You can fade the audio selection in or out by clicking on the Fade In or Fade Out sliders and setting the timing for the fade.

Finish

Complete your off-line project by clicking on Finish from the main menu. Select record to VTR. You can then render all special effects. The editor will prompt you to start your VTR, then play back your completed project as it is recorded. After that, you should have a completed off-line project recorded on videotape.

Editing on a Nonlinear On-Line Editor

The concepts of editing in either off-line or on-line editors are basically the same. The operation and the quality levels are different. On-line editors provide an immense array of transitions, special effects, character generation, and even some animation to create "broadcast-quality" projects that can be shown on television or stored for later duplication or exhibition.

A Sample On-Line Editing Session

On-line editors are usually powerful computers with special hardware and software added to allow rapid editing, complete with transitions, special effects, graphics, and even some animation. On-line editors are often workgroup networked to allow the easy importation of materials produced on audio editors, animation stations, or high-end graphics-producing machines. The product generated from an on-line editor should be good enough to broadcast on a television or cable station, or be used as an edit master to produce DVDs or CD-ROMs. The following is a sample edit session using a Media 100 editor.

Preferences

The Media 100 gives the editor the opportunity to select several software and hardware preferences. Using this first dialog box (see Figure 8.18), you can select Backups and choose to keep backups of bins with video clips in them and previous projects and to have deleted media files sent directly to the Recycle bin. A hardware setting dialog box allows the editor to make video (e.g., NTSC or PAL), audio, and device control selections. The Media Settings dialog box allows selection of image quality settings (e.g., KB per frame) for video, effects, and graphics for the project. These settings affect the amount of disk space the

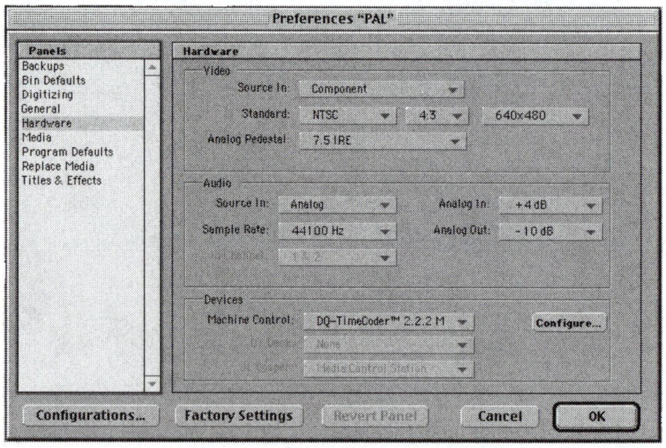

Figure 8.18 The Preferences dialog box allows changes to settings in the areas listed at left.

media you use will take up on the hard drive. At this point, the Audio Window Settings dialog box should be opened and audio preferences should be set.

Bin Window   After all of the needed footage is digitized onto the hard drive of the editor, you can start to make a tentative list of video clips to be used in the order in which they will appear in the finished program. The Bin window will show all of the video and audio clips available for editing. Each clip is represented by a pictorial keyframe, similar to the picons (picture icons) used by the off-line AVIO system. The clips can be sorted by type: Video-only clips are shown as small pictures only; audio clips are shown as a speaker on a plain background; video clips with synchronized audio are shown as pictures with a small speaker icon in the upper right corner.

From this bin you can select (by double clicking) on a keyframe to move it to the Edit Suite window. Click the Play button to view the clip. If additional clips are needed, such as still images for credits, they can be imported by clicking the Bin window to make it active. (See Figure 8.19.) Choose File, then Import.

Figure 8.19   A view of a bin window with pictorial key frames.

Open the appropriate bin folder and select the clips to be imported, being careful to describe the type of file being imported (e.g., Macintosh PICT file) to enable the editor to convert or store them properly. Click Import again and the file will be sent to the appropriate bin for use in the program.

Create a New Program   Resize the Bin window, Program window, and Edit Suite window to allow all of these windows to be viewed at once on the screen. (See Figure 8.20.) Select the desired clip, then drag and drop it onto the time line at the location at which you would like to have it in your program. Repeat this process until you have a rough version of the program with the clips arranged in the desired order. Remove gaps that might exist in the time line. These gaps occur normally as part of the drag-and-drop editing process and are easily eliminated. Play the program by moving the cursor to the beginning and then hitting the spacebar. The program will appear in the Edit Suite window. If the program is properly constructed, save the program.

Trimming   This function allows the editor to fine-tune a clip before it is added to the new program. In the Edit Suite window, select the clip to be trimmed. The clip's first frame will appear in the window. If footage is to be trimmed off the end of the clip, drag the Out trimmer to the left until the time code reads the desired out-point. This time-code value can also be typed in for trimming. In like manner, if footage is to be removed from the beginning of the clip, use the In trimmer button. Click Apply for the desired changes to occur.

Add Music for Background   Select Track then Track Setup. This shows the available audio tracks in your program. Select an empty track (e.g., A3) and the

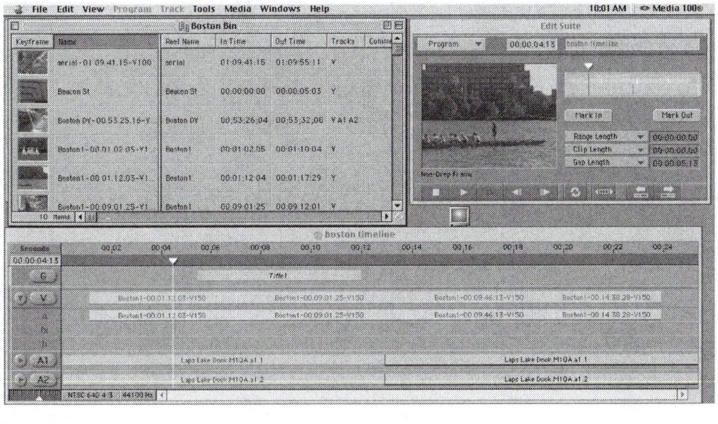

Figure 8.20   This screen shows the Bin window, Edit Suite window, and Time line to facilitate selecting clips for placement on the time line.

Program window will display a time line version of the track. Select this track and place the cursor at the point for the insertion of audio. Select the music clip from the bin and drag and drop it to the selected edit point. Play the program with the new audio. When satisfied with this edit, save the program.

Ripple Edit   This type of edit allows the editor to insert a video or audio clip that will change the length of the program. As mentioned above in linear editing, inserting into an existing program changes the length and requires reediting everything from that edit on to the end of the program. The ripple edit inserts audio, video, or both types of clips into the program and moves all the following material down to make the length change without having to make any additional edits. To accomplish this type of edit, click on the "v" track (for video). Click on the blue Operations box. Locate the cursor at the point at which the video is to be inserted. Drag and drop the video clip. This will automatically shift everything after this edit "down" to make a longer program. In situations where you want to expand the one track but not the others, the other tracks can be locked and they will not change.

Transitions

To create transitions at a number of points in your program, one method is to first "stagger" the video into A and B tracks. (See Figure 8.21.) This process creates a "virtual" effects (FX) track on the time line for the purpose of giving the editor a place to insert the desired transition. Shot 1 would be placed on the A track, shot 2 on the B track, and so on. Drag a transition to the FX track at the appropriate location between two shots and then drop the transition.

A second method for creating transitions is to use the Transition mode, where a third clip is created to overlay the two clips being combined with the transition. The clip takes the last few frames of the first shot and the first few of the second shot and then adds the transition to it. This third clip is then added to the video at the insertion point.

Special Effects

Nonlinear editors can perform amazing special effects with just a few mouse clicks. To accomplish a special effect like video that has been slowed down or sped up, select the clip that will be changed. To slow a clip down, select the Expansion button. Type in a "slowdown factor." To slow down a clip to one-half of its original speed, type in "50" for 50% of normal speed, which will double the length of the clip. Then be sure to click on the Smooth Motion check box to make sure that the motion appears smooth to the viewer. Preview the change in speed. If you are satisfied with the result, click Render in the MotionFX panel. This creates a new clip in the bin that is labeled with the percentage of reduced speed (50% for this example). This new clip must be used to replace the old one in the program time line. Find the insertion point for the new clip and drag and drop it over the old clip. Delete the old clip. Effects that change color or some other aspect of the video clip are performed in a similar way.

Importing and Exporting

On-line editors are designed to allow images and audio information to be imported and exported. Basically, the editor allows bringing in images and audio from a wide variety of programs and sources for use in editing. When a project needs special work, it can be exported to another software program, such as After Effects, that can further manipulate the project to create the desired final product. A critical factor in this process of importing and exporting is the on-line edit machine's ability to accept and send files in a variety of formats.

Figure 8.21   This time line is staggered to show where transitions can be added between shots.

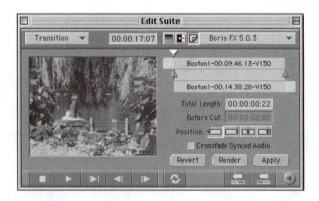

Figure 8.22   In the Transition mode, a third clip is created to overlay the two clips being combined.

The Last Step

Just as you would when word processing, the last thing you should do after editing is save the program and therefore all of the recent changes that you just made. This is especially important when your editing of the program takes place over several edit sessions. Make sure that your hard work does not get lost by using "Save Program" after each editing session.

Keep in mind that the above edit session is directly appropriate for using a Media 100 editor. As mentioned before, most high-quality nonlinear editors are similar in process for creating video programs. Variation in what preparations have to be done, what buttons to push, and the order in which all things must occur varies across brands and edit machines. The important thing to remember is that all nonlinear editors work in conceptually the same way: They require digitalization of the raw footage, organization of the clips in a bin, selection and placement of the clips onto a program that is being constructed, and proper insertion of transition, special effects, and titling.

Current Disadvantages

Although specialized uses for nonlinear editing continue to grow, many problems still exist that are preventing the quick demise of analog systems. The primary reason, mentioned above, is storage space and compression. To get the very highest quality that analog can give, digital still requires much more space than most small computer systems have available. Occupying that much space also creates another problem: speed. The larger the files, the longer it takes to manipulate them. For example, it is possible to do many of the digital special effects on most nonlinear edit systems in a process called rendering. Each effect is manufactured in the computer and stored in the project file. The time it takes to render a complicated effect can be measured in minutes. In a news or a tight-budget production environment, that can add up to costly delays.

Time is also the critical factor in digitizing material from analog into the computer. Again, in a news environment, that time simply isn't there because of intense deadline pressures. Until a medium is agreed on to acquire material in a digital form, or hybrid edit systems designed to incorporate multiple formats of analog and digital sources are commonplace, most

analog-acquired material will continue to be edited on linear systems.

PART TWO: CREATIVE EDITING BASICS

Once you know how to operate an editing machine, the next step is starting the creative editing process. Each shot of the video must be thought of as a sentence or phrase. Just as we use proper grammar when using language, a grammar of sorts exists in the assemblage of shots on the way to forming stories. Too often the pieces can appear as nothing more than laundry lists of shots.

Everything in an edited piece should have a purpose and a relationship. Every shot is there for a reason; every sound is there for a reason. Every shot should be related to the shot before it and after it; every sound related to the video over it. Everything should work together to tell the story so that the product is greater than the sum of its parts.

Each shot must be in its position for a reason; the story line must be advanced by the constant progression of pictures or images. Editing is not just the butting together of shots, it is the creation of a story with a beginning, a middle, and an end all working to communicate an idea or show an event.

SEQUENCING THE SHOTS

Ideally, every grouping of shots, or **sequence**, should have an overall statement or idea. The viewer should come away with more than just the experience of seeing a collection of pictures—a slide show. There should be an understanding of the idea just expressed. The idea may be as simple as a blood shortage at the Red Cross, but a random collection of shots on this subject adds nothing to a viewer's perception of the shortage. On the other hand, a well-thought-out ordering of the proper shots can convey much added information and understanding for the viewer.

Instead of random shots of the interior of the blood center, a careful selection can show the viewer what the script is conveying. A good three-shot segment on the blood shortage might consist of (1) an opening shot of a nearly empty room of donors giving blood; (2) a shot of a blood bag being filled at the end of a tube; and (3) a closing shot of a technician stacking filled bags in a large but empty cooler. This series shows how few people are giving blood and demonstrates that very little blood is on hand to give to hospitals.

Basic Sequence

A basic sequence is made up of a wide shot, a medium shot, a tight shot, and a cutaway. This is the minimum sequence, but the idea usually stays intact within many variations. This basic sequence translates into the following:

1. Establish what the viewer is looking at.
2. Develop that idea by giving more detailed information.
3. Emphasize the details.
4. Add any related but nonessential information to, if necessary, break the thought and prepare for the next sequence.

Preparing for the next sequence, in most cases, simply means allowing for an unnoticed bridge of time in the telling of a story.

Sample Script

Consider the following script:

> *Here at the ACME trade school, former workers of the now closed auto factory are being retrained for a new career in the field of microelectronics. Assembly line workers have traded their wrenches for textbooks in the battle to stay competitive in the fast-changing job market.*
>
> *Each member of the class hopes the new skills learned here will help land a job in the expanding high-tech work force. Locally, almost 300 new jobs were created in the last year, but none of the former Cal-plant workers were able to land any of those jobs. (Take sound-bite of student.)*

There can be two story lines here; the written story as it appears, and a visual story that can add even more information to what is being said. Read the script over to determine:

1. The amount of on-air time you have to cover.
2. What specific subjects must be shown.

3. What picture information can be added to enhance the story.

The first paragraph of the script is about 14 seconds long. You can use approximately four shots to cover that paragraph using classroom, individual students, and textbooks. You will be visualizing the size of the class, the type of elements currently being studied, and so forth.

Each story for a TV newscast should start off with about 1 or 2 seconds of video with natural sound if possible. Since the news is live, timing errors can be made on roll cues, which can result in the first second or two being cut off before it goes out over the air. It is better to lose some natural sound than part of the reporter's audio track, which is essential to understanding the story.

The First Sequence

In our example, a good opening is a wide shot of the whole room from one of the corners. The first 2 seconds are the sound of the teacher telling the class about the subject of the day. As the teacher's audio quickly fades down to a background level, let the shot run for several more seconds. At the point where the teacher's audio starts to fade down, lay in the reporters narration, most often called simply **track**. The standard location for audio in any field-produced audio (all natural sound, subject sound bites, and reporter stand-ups) is on channel 2, while reporter track is placed on channel 1. You now have the first shot, its sound, and the reporter's track for the first section (up to the first sound bite) laid in. You can start to cover the rest of the section with pictures and background sound.

A logical place to start the second shot is at the end of the word "factory" in the first sentence, because the subject has been established. We are dissecting the first sentence visually in a fashion similar to how a grammar teacher would dissect it in an English class. The cut is here because the subject of this visual sentence has been illustrated by the wide shot.

The next shot is a medium shot of a group of students listening to the teacher. It cuts best at the end of the first sentence. Just as the body of a paragraph is used to expand on the idea expressed in its topic sentence, the medium shot gives a more detailed view of the situation illustrated in the wide shot.

The next shot is a tight shot of one of the students ending on the word "for" in the second sentence, and then a cut to a tight shot of a textbook and a student's hands taking notes on the paper next to it. This shot goes until the end of the paragraph. If you have the right shots with which to work, you should be able to see how the combination of shots works to punctuate the script and round out the information the story is conveying. This is one sequence. Depending on the amount and quality of the raw material there is to work with, there can be many versions of this first sequence.

The Second Sequence

Like the script, we begin a new sequence (paragraph) at this point. Again the paragraph is about 14 seconds long. This time, however, there are few specifics to show other than the students. This is a good place to use the video to advance the story in a different but parallel course. This new paragraph gives us a chance to explore another aspect of the classroom. To enhance the feeling of positive emotion on the part of the students, we will show them in their efforts to learn.

The opening shot of this sequence is a wide shot of the instructor helping a student who is soldering circuit boards. This shot ends at the word "here" in the first sentence. The next shot is a very different angle of that same student working. The student's position and movements should be similar to the wide shot containing the teacher in order to avoid a jump cut. This shot ends at the word "force" at the end of the first sentence.

Even though the script begins a new sentence, our visual sentence is not done. The next shot is a close-up of the student's hands working on the circuit board ending on the word "year" in the second sentence. A tight shot of the concentration in the same student's face is the next shot and ends on the words "workers were."

The last shot of the sequence and the paragraph would be a shot of the board the student is working on. This time, however, it is an extreme close-up of the soldering, showing the smoke rising from the hot solder. From this shot you can cut to anything, in this case it is a sound bite that would be nice if it were from the same student we just saw working. This is a place where good photographer/reporter coordination in the field can pay off in the edit room. By shooting sequences of the characters interviewed, the edited story can develop those characters—however minor—leading up to their bites.

Think about these shots, cut on these words, and see how they fit with the script without matching it word for picture. We have captured the feel of the script but also added to it by showing more of what these students are learning as a new career. By focusing on one student in particular, it is easier to build a sequence and help the viewer follow what all the students are doing. Use the visuals to punch up a story, give emphasis to what is being said without stating the same thing, and, above all, to give more information.

The pacing just discussed is just one possible way to cover this script. As you work with the shots in the edit room, you may find that some will look better when allowed to run longer and others when used very briefly. No two editors will cut the story the same way. In effect, there is no one right way of doing it. The only common denominator is that it should feel right when viewed as a whole.

Match-Action Cutting

Within sequences of this type, there is a method called match-action cutting that can really make a sequence come alive. If the video was shot with this in mind, or if you as editor are clever enough to see it in the raw material given you, match-action editing can help give dynamics to a story. The idea is to make it appear as though more than one camera is taping a scene and it is being edited live on tape (as if switching between two cameras the way a director does in a studio).

To perform match-action editing in ENG or EFP, the photographer must separate the action into the different parts and then shoot each part separately. A good example is a factory assembly line. A sheet of metal is taken from a stack, put into a drill press, drilled, removed, and put on a new stack. Each part of the process is broken down into different shots, each from a different angle and with at least some variation in focal length.

The shots are edited together so that the viewer follows the sheet of metal through the drilling process but from many vantage points instead of just one. The worker removes a sheet from the pile in a wide shot and on his action of swinging it into place on the press, you cut to a medium shot taken from the side of the press to see the sheet (it wouldn't be the same sheet, but they all look alike) slide into position, and so on. The edits must be precise so that the action from one shot to the next is smooth. If things are taking place quickly, each edit must be very accurate with respect to the action or it will look like a jump cut. The assembly line example is an easy one because the same thing takes place over and over. It is harder to get the shots necessary for match-action editing when you have no control over the situation and things are not following a set pattern.

A good photographer always looks for things that can be built into a matched sequence. It may take some thinking and patience, but a better looking product is always worth it. If you are shooting in an office and one of the subjects answers the phone, talks, and then hangs up, perhaps another call will need to be answered. For this shot, choose a different angle and/or focal length. For example, you could match-cut a tight shot of the phone ringing to a wider shot just as the person picks up the receiver. A good editor sees the sequence and cuts it together to put life and interest in an otherwise dull office sequence. And this can be done without staging the events; simply look for repeated actions on the part of the subjects and anticipate where best to place the camera.

Match-action cuts exist in most things you shoot—look for them. Even in interviews, the establishing two-shot can have the interviewee in the exact same position saying something similar to the beginning of the sound bite. The edit from the two-shot to the talking head shot can be made into a match-action edit. It looks sharp, but it has to be done correctly. Watch the movies and see how they use matched action and then look for examples of it in TV news.

MAINTAINING CONTINUITY

Even in news shooting, like movie making, the visual story is often done in bits and pieces to be assembled later. The continuity of the finished product determines how well the viewer will be able to follow the story. There are several aspects to maintaining good continuity when it comes to choosing camera angles and shot choices in the editing process. (See Figure 8.23.)

The 180-Degree Rule

The main element of continuity is the 180° rule. A simple example of this is an interview for TV news or any two-person conversation in production or theatrical settings. In the theater, the audience stays on one side of the subjects. When you are shooting, the camera replaces the audience and therefore should always stay on one side of the action. Draw a line between the two people involved in the interview or conversation. All camera angles should be taken from one side of that line or the other. You choose which side of the line to shoot from, but you must stay on only one side.

This line is sometimes called the **line of interest**. The direction in which a person is looking determines a line of interest, such as two people in an interview (they look at each other creating one line). All your camera angles should be looking either up or down one side of that line.

For ENG and EFP photography, a line should be established in most shooting situations: meetings, speeches, concerts, protests, marches, sports, or simply any place where there is movement. If the subject does not determine the line, draw one where you will have the best background or lighting conditions and stick with it. Your wide shot not only establishes what you are looking at but also the relationships among the objects in the picture. These relationships must be maintained. The line rule keeps the relationships constant throughout your sequence of shots no matter how many shots you use. (See Figure 8.24.)

A speaker delivering a speech shot from the left side of the room (as you face the speaker) will be facing screen-right. Through the rest of the piece the speaker will always face right. A line of interest is drawn between the speaker and audience. The audience will always be facing screen-left. If you shoot all your shots with this in mind, any combination of shots can be edited together and the audience will always appear to be facing the speaker and vice versa. The viewer is never at a loss to identify the relationships among the subjects.

Crossing-the-Line Editing

These points work well when the shots are done correctly and in a controlled situation. What if the shots were not done correctly or the situation was uncontrolled and no line was ever established? The editor still must maintain continuity for a good, understandable flow of shots. By letting the line float but always keeping it in mind, the editor can move the camera angles anywhere if she does it carefully step by step.

The key to continuity is movement or direction, both actual and implied: the actual movement of a basketball team on the court or the implied direction

Figure 8.23 This series of photos represents the shots needed to maintain continuity in a simple action sequence. The actions of the subject are broken down into their individual parts and shot separately. Action shots, such as walking and chopping, can be combined in matched-action editing. Each of these shots can be done at various focal lengths (wide, medium, or tight) to allow the same action several times but never the same shot twice. This variety of shots as raw material also allows for contracting or expanding the edited length from a quick 10-second piece to a leisurely 2-minute sequence.

of a person sitting on a park bench. As long as it has movement or direction, any shot you start with defines your first continuity line, your line of interest. A good rule of thumb to get to the other side of that line in editing is to "turn" on one of these types of shots: (1) a shot straight down the line of interest, (2) a close-up shot, or (3) a wide shot that cuts to another wide shot with a different line.

In the example of the speaker and the meeting, a shot straight down the line of interest would come from the center-back of the room and have no movement or direction. This type of shot destroys the line started from the left side of the room and gives you freedom to reestablish a different one. If you choose to turn using a close-up, shoot a tight shot of the speaker facing left, then cut to a wide shot from the other side of the room so that the speaker is now facing right. You have crossed the line but not confused

the viewer because the speaker (the reference point) is in both shots. The dramatic change in focal length will mask any jump in speaker's position or posture. If you want to turn using two wide shots, you can shoot one from the left rear of the room and cut to a wide shot from the middle of the right side of the room. It is possible to turn and not confuse the viewer, using wide shots, because all the elements of the scene are present in both shots while still being very different.

For this crossing-the-line editing to work, the line cannot be crossed very often or the continuity is lost anyway. As always, when you sit down to edit, look at all the shots available to you, not only for content but also for continuity. You should be able to separate shots into sequences by continuity, grouping shots with common lines of interest and identifying turn shots to cross those lines if necessary.

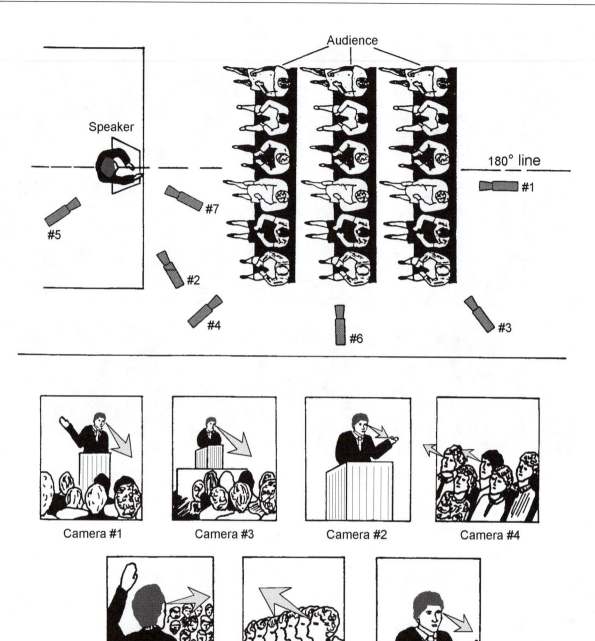

Figure 8.24 Camera placement and several sample shots for covering a typical speech.

Continuity within Sequences

Each visual sequence, like a written paragraph, must stick to one subject. To allow the viewer to fully understand that subject, each shot in the sequence must flow easily to the next shot. Each aspect of continuity must be maintained within the sequence.

Movement   Continuity can be changed at the end of a sequence but not in the middle of one. Within a sequence, every subject that has movement or direction must maintain that direction. If the subject's direction or movement is to the right at the beginning, it should always be to the right throughout the sequence. Watch a good action movie and look for the direction of the subjects (cars, people, backgrounds). Look for the 180° rule and study how it is used. The continuity is usually very good in action movies. Also watch for how they use turn shots to change the line.

Details Continuity also refers to other elements in the picture besides movement. Not only must directional and spatial relationships be maintained, but also the details within the sequences. An obvious example is the clothes a subject is wearing. If the subject has on a green shirt in one shot and a blue shirt in the next, but there is no implied change in time or place, then there is an obvious break in continuity. This also applies to the details of position and tone. You can't cut from a medium shot of the mayor slumped in his chair on the phone to a wide shot of him leaning forward drinking coffee, or from a tight shot of the councilwoman's angry glare on the podium to a medium shot of her laughing. They just don't fit together.

Background Objects in the background cannot move from one shot to the next because there will be a disruption in the sense of reality (for example, furniture in a room must stay in the same arrangement). Continuity means that elements such as these must remain the same within the framework of the story line. For ENG and EFP, many elements are not controllable, but you still must avoid the very obvious breaks in continuity. In a story about a family moving out of their house, you would not show a scene with the father packing the last box in an empty room then cut to the mother packing a box with that same room half full.

Lighting The lighting within a sequence must also remain the same, particularly outside. Shots taken on a cloudy day cannot be intercut with shots in full sunlight. A dusk-to-night outdoor concert should not show the group playing at full darkness cut with shots of the audience in sunset lighting. The time difference is too great and noticeable to even the least discriminating viewer. TV viewers are all professionals at TV watching—they have been doing it almost all of their lives.

ESTABLISHING A STORY LINE

Most finished products in ENG and EFP tell some sort of story. As a photographer or editor, it is your job to make that story come alive and make it understandable within the confines of the script and the time limit. Many news pieces and commercials have no real visual story line, just a sequence of shots that

show a particular subject. But whenever any action occurs or time obviously passes during a shoot, it can be put into story form.

In TV, the script determines most, but not all, story lines. Whenever you shoot or edit, your goal must be to establish a good story line, even in the presence of a bad script. A basic story line is very simple. Just like a story in literature, there should be a beginning, a middle, and an end.

The Beginning

Each story must start somewhere, so why not at the beginning? What happened first? Where? How? Generally, you can think of the beginning as the wide shot—the shot that establishes the content of the story, the relationships among the elements, or the feeling and tone of the topic. Most things happen along a time line; you would not show the outcome of the race and then show some of the racers still running or even starting. Things should be shown in the order in which they occur.

There should be a sense of positive time flow within the editing, as if we are seeing an encapsulated version of what took place. The beginning should initiate the story and make the viewer want to see more of it. Aim to spark a viewer's attention, or at least enhance it, by the opening sequence of the story line. The question "What's next?" should always be present. Try not to lose the viewer's attention; the audience should always be anticipating the next element of the story.

A good way of securing a viewer's attention is to establish a sequence of action to follow. A story about a school building that is going to close need not be a collection of building shots. Instead, you can open the story with a shot of kids entering the building. By doing this, you have the wide shot of the building, but the added element of kids entering the building within that shot has now started a story line. Very simplistically, you have posed these questions: Where are the kids going? What are they going to do? These are questions that you as editor and photographer can answer visually.

In this example, these questions would not be pressing in the minds of viewers, yet they establish a basic story line. Try to present a situation that needs further information or investigation to satisfy the viewer. Show the subject doing something or moving so that the activity or direction can be explored more fully. The start of a story can have a symbolic opening. The big fire piece could start with the sound of screaming sirens over a tight shot of flames. The scene is set with the elements: fire and firefighters. And audience interest is piqued: What's burning? Cutting to a wide shot answers the question and gets the story moving. A beginning must always appear to be headed somewhere. Invite the viewer to follow your lead. Make the viewer consciously or subconsciously ask "What's next?" "Why?" or "How?" and then proceed to answer the question. The beginning has to be the grabber. If you lose the viewer's interest at the beginning, then the viewer will never make it through the middle.

The Middle

The middle is the guts of the story, the development of the idea started in the beginning. Once the race has begun, how is everyone doing? As the wide shot is to the beginning of the story, the medium shot is to the middle. The elements established at the start are now explored in greater detail and examined as to how they can further the story.

In our school-closing story line, showing the reasons for this closure would make up the middle. Possible medium shots are half-full classrooms or students sitting amid dilapidated surroundings. The middle is obviously the longest segment of any story. The middle develops the ideas being expressed by the writer. There may be characters for the audience to learn about, situations to understand, or motivations to feel. Therefore, you must have very descriptive shots to build the best possible sequences to keep moving the story forward.

The End

Every story should come to some sort of conclusion. Whether it actually comes to an end, or the sun simply sets in the last shot, the story must finish in some way. In the race analogy, the end is simple: The winner crosses the finish line and receives the trophy. In the school-closing story line, the end may be the kids leaving the building and the doors closing. A story about taxis could be ended on a shot of a cab pulling away from the camera and driving off down the street—the old riding off into the sunset idea (negative motion). Even if there is no real conclusion or end, the appearance of one is desirable.

Hopefully, the idea started at the beginning has now been brought to an end. The end may be displaying a finished sculpture, sealing up a box, closing a door, the crowd applauding, a skyline shot of the city, or anything that says "The End." The more thought put into how the story will end, the better the chance the viewer will come away with a feeling that the story is complete.

Visualizing Paragraphs

No set length or number of shots makes up any segment. The beginning may be just one shot or many. The total length of the story usually determines how long each segment will be. A 90-second story probably will not have a 30-second opening sequence. Sequences are like visual paragraphs. Each part of the story can have one or more paragraphs. Once you have established a story line in your head or on paper, break it down into the beginning, middle, and end. Take each part and look for the visual paragraphs that make up that part. By organizing yourself before you shoot and edit, these visual paragraphs should come together in a flowing, descriptive story with a beginning, middle, and end.

In many TV scripts, it is impossible to establish much in the way of a visual story line. Many pieces end up being laundry lists of shots or *wallpaper* jobs. The script has no real visual interpretation, except for the very literal. A story about banks that are in financial trouble may be made up of exterior shots of the banks named in the story. The photographer and editor have little creative input on the story line. If the writer and photographer can work together as much as possible, some of these situations can be avoided or worked out but not always.

The point is to always strive for good TV—that mesh of good audio and good pictures that communicates the maximum information to the viewer. In following the script, strive for the best sequencing and story line. You have a good chance of communicating something if you can visually hold the viewer's interest. Sometimes pretty pictures are the best solution to the story line problem if you cannot obtain sequencing within the confines of the script. In this case, each shot should be able to stand alone as a complete idea or picture.

Shooting without a Script

The biggest difference between ENG and EFP is the order in which the product is assembled. For EFP, you are shooting to a script and it is easy to get what you need to cover that script. You go out knowing the pictures to get. For ENG you are shooting for a script that has not been written yet. It is hard to second-guess how the final story will be structured, what parts will be included or left out, and what specifics will be written about. You must shoot to maximize the editor's latitude when the piece is edited. At the same time, you cannot provide too much material because there will not be enough time to go through it all within the usual TV news deadlines.

Sometimes you must shoot for two or three different story lines because the outcome or direction is unclear as the story develops before you. At a certain location, the story may be the crowd at the beach, the heat, the traffic, the troublemakers, or people being turned away because the park is full. All of these elements, or only a few, can be included in one story, or you may concentrate on just one. The final script determines the kind and amount of material that should be shot, but the final script does not materialize until long after the shooting is over. How do you cover all the possibilities and still come up with good sequences and story lines but not overshoot?

The writer/producer is often not present when you shoot the video. However, if you follow the basic guidelines regarding what kind of shots to get and keep in mind what it takes to edit a story, you should have the material for any good basic piece. If you look at each situation as a mini-story (beginning, middle, and end) and shoot each situation as though it will be sequenced together (wide shot, medium shot, tight shot, and cutaway), then you have covered all the bases.

By getting the minimum number of essential shots, the photographer has covered the story and given the editor the basis for cutting to almost any script. Get the basic four-shot sequences first, just in case that is all you get. Extra shots or artistic shots can be taken only after the basics are on tape and time permits. If the editor is in a hurry, there must be places on the tape where the basic shots can be found without much searching through shots that may be good but of lesser interest or importance to a basic story line.

PACING

The last element in the relationship among shots in editing is the pacing, or timing, of the shots. The timing of each shot helps determine the mood of the piece. As a general rule, a shot less than 2 seconds long will not be consciously perceived by the viewer unless it is a very graphic or aesthetically simple shot. A shot longer than 7 seconds with no movement is usually more than the attention span of the viewer. A zoom, pan, tilt, or action in the picture can allow a shot to run almost any length depending on the mood you are trying to capture.

Editing for Dynamics

If all the shots are static with no camera moves, then the pace of the edits will generally be quicker than if there are some camera moves or action shots. If you are cutting several static shots together, try not to make the edits on a predictable beat. Vary the time between edits to give the piece some dynamics of its own. Let wide shots stay up longer than tight shots. It is easy to see what is in a tight shot, but a wide shot usually contains more information that takes longer to perceive.

Zooms and pans must be allowed to run their course. Cutting in the middle of camera movement is most often uncomfortable to the viewer. By their nature, these types of shots should be going somewhere and cutting out early makes them unfulfilling to the viewer. Anticipation is created with no real payoff.

If movement is needed but the entire shot is too long, it is better to start in the middle of the movement than to end in the middle. Let the shot finish. It is usually easier to see where the shot was coming from than not to know where it is going. It sometimes works to use just the middle of the movement, no start or finish, as long as you can tell what it is you are looking at, such as a long pan of rows of books.

A camera move shot has a certain mood to it that may not fit with the rest of the piece. They are most often used to add dynamics to what editors and producers see as dull pieces. There is a fine line between adding editorial interest and false excitement. Camera moves can add much complexity to your piece, which you may not want, by literally distracting the viewer from the subject at hand. That is why most new photographers are asked not to use zooms and pans until all other basics have been mastered.

Avoiding Predictability

While staying within the sequencing, story line, and continuity guidelines, try to vary the pace of the shots enough to avoid any predictability. The worst case is when the viewer can tell when the next edit is about to occur. The viewer should always be expecting more information (until the end of the piece) but should never be able to guess how or when it will come. As long as this anticipation is satisfied and the viewer cannot predict the next edit, the edit pace is correct. A fast-moving story requires faster edits. A slow-moving story requires more time between edits. A good action piece can have quite a few short shots if they are advancing or enhancing the action. In a fast-paced sequence, the shots may be shorter than 3 seconds, as short as 20 frames, but they must still be aesthetically clean enough so that there's not too much information and the viewer can perceive what is in the frame. This usually means using many close-ups and extreme close-ups.

Editing to Music

Cutting to music is a good example of following a preset pace. Most of the time it does not look good to cut on the simple beat of the music because it is too predictable. You will have a better flowing piece if you cut on the back beat, but even then not on every beat. Use the edits to emphasize or punctuate the music, so that the cuts are not simply a tapping foot, blindly following the lead of the music.

Picking out one instrument to follow with the edits can give the edit pace a nice tie-in—it will flow with the music but never be predictable. Sometimes switching from one instrument to another for different parts of the song can add to the interest of the pacing. With the current abundance of rock videos, there are many examples of good editing to music. Take a close look. If you turn down the sound and watch the edits, you can get a feel for the dynamics of the editing without the music. Learning to feel the pace without audio clues is a good way to learn any style of editing.

Varying the Editing Speed

By changing the pacing of edits you can change the whole mood of the piece. Switching from long-running shots to quick edits can heighten tension, action, excitement, or anticipation. Slowing down the pace can give a more relaxed feeling, an easier flow, or an emotional touch with the feeling of relaxation, serenity, or even sadness. Sit back and watch how your piece plays after you complete each segment. Do not just watch how the shots fit together, but watch how the piece feels as it moves along. Is it too fast or too slow? Does it convey the wrong mood? Does it flow as one unit, or is it simply a slide show?

Ask another editor to take a look at your piece. Sometimes you can be too close to your own work to give it an objective critique. Bad pacing can make a piece drag on forever or seem as choppy as rough seas. Good pacing can make a piece fly by while generating much information or touching the hearts of the viewers by its warm flow of images.

Comprehension

One of the biggest and most common mistakes made in all forms of video production is failing to perceive the finished product as a viewer would. The mistakes are often most noticeable in news stories. In the drive to make pieces exciting and dynamic for the viewer, the editors make use of every trick to keep the flow of images coming at a blinding pace. Fast cuts, zooms, and special effects abound. The music videos of MTV would seem to be the standard by which stories are cut.

The problem with the MTV style is basic: comprehension and the lack of it. Music videos are cut the way they are so kids can see the same video dozens of times and still get something new out of them each time. The satisfaction of a single viewing is extremely low for that reason: The producers want you to see it over and over. The typical news story is just the opposite. By far the majority of the audience will only see this story one time and one time only. If there are any distractions at all while viewing the already short presentation, the entire comprehension will be thrown off. If there is no time allowed for absorption, what chance does the viewer have for understanding?

It is important that you as the photographer/editor make sure the edit pacing is right for the comprehension of the story as well as the dynamics of the story. Sometimes the rapid assault of images effectively conveys the emotion and content you are striving for. But if there is more to communicate than that, make sure there is breathing space for the audience to take it in.

ADDING POSTPRODUCTION VALUE

Up to this point, we have been addressing what used to be called butt-splice editing: edits made without any special effects, in which the last frame of the shot butts up against the first frame of the next shot. Now it is simply called a cut, or a machine-to-machine edit. By adding a video switcher with an effects bank, however, it is possible to add another dimension to your editing. The most common effect is the mix or dissolve, but such effects as wipes, squeezes, and digital processing are now available on most switchers. Almost all nonlinear edit systems have built-in switchers that do a wide array of effects.

In the early days of TV, most news stories were cut on A and B reels (or rolls). The A reel had all of the pictures with the sound: talking heads, sound bites, stand-ups, and so forth. The B reel had all the cover footage to be used over the reporter's voice track. The piece would then be assembled live on the air. It required the technical director to switch from one film machine to the other and back at the proper times so that there was always a picture on the air. Needless to say, the process often became mixed up. If the piece was not timed out correctly by the editor when it was put together, or the director called for the wrong reel, things could look pretty bad. The same principles are used to create effects with video today, but they are not done live on the air.

Many edit controllers can operate three or more machines. To make an effect such as a simple dissolve, two playback sources need to be running at the time of the edit. The playback machines are lettered just like the reels in film editing. Machine "A" is the primary source of video, and machine "B" is for the shots used in the effect. Unlike film, where the individual shots are chopped up and laid out before being glued back together in the proper order, the video cassette remains intact. This necessitates that you make a copy or dub of the material you wish to use for any effects, if the shots to be combined are on the same original cassette, in order to create the "B" reel. This causes a loss of a generation for one of the two shots, but with high-quality equipment, this shouldn't be noticeable. With digital equipment it is not a problem at all.

As of this writing, hundreds of different special effects can be used in video postproduction. As the video industry continues to progress by leaps and bounds, the number of effects available to the editor will continue to increase, even on the simplest of systems.

The Dissolve

Special effects can allow an editor to explore a whole new area of pacing and mood creation. The dissolve or mix can be a boon or bust to the finished piece. The dissolve is an excellent way of showing the lapse in time from one shot to the next. To go from the city in daylight to the city at night with a straight edit (or cut) would be rather abrupt, but a dissolve can make the transition smooth and even artistic.

In many pieces, this way of showing the passage of time can aid in the telling of the story, since fewer shots are needed to make the transition. You can take a subject from one location to another with a simple dissolve instead of transition shots. In a long piece, it is a good idea to use both transition shots and dissolves for variety.

When a piece calls for a slow-edit pace, a dissolve adds to the relaxed feeling and to the flow from one shot to the next. Going from static shot to static shot, such as shots of photographs from an old family photo album, the dissolve takes the hard edge off the edit and gives that desirable fluid transition. For the artistic piece, the fall-colors story or the day-in-the-life of a nursing home, the dissolve can add to the beauty of the shots or give that feeling of sensitive compassion.

The basic rules of editing should still apply, however. You do not dissolve between two shots very similar in composition. You still try to give variety to the shot selection and follow basic sequencing patterns. For a solo dancer on a stage, dissolves are desirable, but each shot should be as different as possible from the next. If the dancer is framed screen right in a wide shot, the next shot could be a medium shot with the dancer in the left part of the picture. In other words, do not overlap similar images.

Let the mood and pacing of the piece determine how long a dissolve should last. A duration of 30 to 40 frames seems to look best for most uses. The slower the pace, the slower the dissolve. You must keep in mind, however, that making all edits into dissolves can make the piece boring and predictable. Try to have a good practical or artistic reason for each dissolve and any other effect you use.

The Wipe

Wipes come in a great variety; the standard left-to-right straight edge is the most common. With digital effects, wipes can be as wild as you can imagine and the effects just as varied. Most of the literal graphic ones, like spinning stars or heart shapes, have little place in ENG but have some application in EFP. The straight line wipe is used in live newscasts to go from one story to the next without having to cut back to the set for the transition.

You very seldom see a wipe used in a produced news story. The use of a wipe for ENG stories is similar to its use in the newscast itself: to go from one thing to something totally separate. If several pages of written information are to be put on the screen, a wipe is used to go from one page to the next, such as in election night tallies. Digital wipes, such as **page** or **cube wipes,** are very popular for this type of transition. The different types of wipes are often used in entertainment programs and commercials to give the production variety and a jazzy look.

EDITING SOUND

For the most part, sound editing has never been as complicated for TV as it has been for the movies. The poor quality of most TV speakers and the conditions under which most people watch TV have reduced the need for good sound, although this is changing. Picture quality and technique have come a long way, but sound quality and mixing have lagged behind. This is evident in many TV news markets in which audio is still sometimes completely absent from ENG tape.

Accurate Representation of the Event

The two sources of audio in ENG are the audio of the talent (news anchor or recorded reporter) and the sound accompanying the pictures. Because most TV news is loosely based on journalistic standards, the addition of any other audio is frowned on. The addition of music is the only exception, although in some cases it is not desirable. Adding sound can be misleading, deceptive, and sometimes downright dishonest.

The most you can do in ENG is move the sound around from one shot to another, but the sound must accurately represent what you would hear if you were there. An example is a shot of a mine with a whistle blowing; the next shot is of miners filing out to go home. The sound of the whistle may not have been recorded at the same time as that shot of the mine, but it did blow while the crew was taping and it did signal the end of a shift. The sound was used correctly.

An example of sound used incorrectly is a shot of people at an accident scene and the photographer running up to the injured on the ground while a siren is heard. The siren in this case was taken from a story shot last week and used to add a feeling of breaking news to the piece. The photographer had actually arrived late. In this case, the siren should not have been used at all. It made the story into something it was not. If you did not get the sound at the location, you should not manufacture sound to make it appear as though it came from the location. If it makes the pictures seem different from what they really were, then the sound should not be added. Sound needs to accurately depict what happened.

Adding Sound for Effect

If you photograph an explosion from a mile away, it can take the sound of the explosion several seconds to reach the camera. Do you move the sound? For EFP the answer is simple, because any sound is fair game if it enhances the idea you are trying to get across. You would have to get very far out of line to violate the "truth-in-advertising" law.

For ENG the question is harder to answer. Years of Hollywood conditioning have made audiences expect to hear the sound at the same time they see the explosion. In real life, however, the sound and picture do not match. What do you do?

You can assume that sound and picture are in sync at the point of origin (the explosion site). The audio can be synced back up in editing if the shot contains the explosion as the only audio source. If, however, there are people in the foreground reacting to the explosion as it happens, their audio, and therefore the audio from the explosion, cannot be moved. Moving the explosion's audio would distort the people's reaction to it.

There is, nevertheless, room for creativity when it comes to audio in ENG. You can add sound where it is obvious to the viewer that the sound is added for effect. Shots of an abandoned school house with the sounds of a school bell and children playing can give a powerful emotional touch to the scene. It is obvious that no children have been there in decades, but the audio implies the rich history of the once thriving school.

Imagine a reporter doing a stand-up in front of a roaring water pump with a mic that does not pick up the sound of the pump because of its placement. You see the pump, but you do not hear it. By adding the background sound of the pump in editing, the shot seems to come together better. All the pieces fit and work together for the overall effect. These are just a few examples of adding sound to enhance ENG work, but you must use sound carefully. It is a fine line that separates enhancement from deception.

Avoid Abrupt Edits

In general, avoid abrupt starting and stopping when editing audio. Even when audio must come in very quickly, a fast twist of the volume knob is better than a flip of a switch. A cut made in the middle of the bell's ring doesn't sound right. Either a quick fade-up or finding the natural starting point for the sound would be preferred. Audio cutoff is the same. Find a natural end for the sound or fade it out quickly to get out of it. Background audio can come and go with the edit points as long as the audio is truly in the background. Every picture has a sound unless it is a graphic or a freeze-frame. There is background sound for just about everything.

Natural Sound

A good news story opens with a picture that begins to tell the story or captures the viewer's attention. A reporter stand-up opening is often boring and gives the viewer little to look forward to. It looks like more news anchor and not more news. With an opening shot, there should be some good natural sound.

Use with Opening Video　A story on flooding may open with a shot of water flowing over a dam. The roar of the water is heard for a few seconds before the reporter's voice comes in. It breaks the constant flow of talking and can spark someone's interest to look at the TV instead of only listening to it.

Not only must the pictures be good, but the sound must also be good enough to make someone want to watch the pictures. Good use of natural sound can draw the viewer into the story and give the pictures that "you-are-there" feeling. This means you should open a story with the best picture you can as well as the best sound.

Use as a Transition　You can use the natural sound of the pictures to break up paragraphs in the track, get into or out of sound bites (talking heads), and bridge a gap from one part of a story to another. To move from talking about people buying new homes to discussing the number of new homes being built, you could make the transition on a shot such as an electric saw (with the sound up full) cutting a board in front of new construction. After a couple of seconds of the saw, the reporter continues the story, now talk-

ing about all the new construction. Time limits can make this type of editing difficult, but if the story is well thought out, and the reporter and photographer work together on producing it, the end product will show the effort and have a greater impact on the viewer.

The "L" Cut

A popular form of creating an audio transition is to start the audio of the next shot (usually the beginning of a new sequence) under the current shot. This is called the "L" cut. For example, we see the planner looking over the drawing for the new housing development as the reporter's track about the project comes to the end of a paragraph. While the planner is still on screen we hear the sound of a buzz saw ripping through wood for about 1 second or so before the picture of that saw pops up and starts the next section of the story about construction. The audio pulls the viewer into the next sequence and softens the transition from one location to the other.

Room Tone

One thing professional editors will always ask camera crews to get while recording interviews on location is room tone: the sound of the location without any of the subjects talking. In high-quality editing where two sound bites are to be edited together, there may be a difference in the background noise from one bite to the next. To disguise that difference, some of the ambient sounds of that location can be laid in under the edit point bridging from one shot to the next. This makes the audio edit sound more seamless.

Multiple-Source Audio Mixing

Every edit system has at least two channels of audio with which to work. One channel is usually designated for the reporter's audio and the other channel for all natural sound and sound bites. When you use music, however, it becomes difficult to incorporate natural sound (**natsound**). The music has to have a channel of its own if it is to last the entire story. This leaves only one channel for the reporter's track and any natsound, which translates into no natsound when the reporter's audio is there. It is possible, however, to carefully mix in the natsound and fade it in and out to obtain a good blend of natsound and reporter audio on the same channel.

Laydowns and Laybacks

The methods of combining more than two tracks of audio in a dual-track audio system are known as **laydowns** and **laybacks**. In our example above, the editor would decide which two audio sources were most important for determining the pacing and shot selection for the story. The story would be edited with just those two sources all the way to its conclusion.

For this discussion, assume it is a reporter's voice track and the natural sound of the pictures that are laid down first. Wanting to add a music track under the entire piece, the editor would first take one or both of the audio tracks of the finished piece and do a laydown onto a work tape of some sort. This work tape would then be synced back up with the original story and laid back to either a single track or mixed across both of the previous tracks while mixing in the music from a second playback source. Of course, you have to erase the original tracks on the edit master to do this. The obvious requirement here is that the layback be in sync with the story it was lifted from. While this process can be done on any edit system, it is usually done on an on-line system using a multi-track audio recorder tied to the edit computer by a time-code reference. The on-line computer can keep the layback in sync no matter how long the piece is. If you are trying to do this process without the aid of the computer, you should not try it on long-running pieces.

Editing Methods

Unlike working with a computer where audio and pictures can be added or subtracted at will, once a shot or a sound is laid down on tape in linear video editing, it can be a nightmare to change it later. Adding a longer or shorter video or audio clip in the middle of a finished piece necessitates reediting the rest of the story to make up for the time difference. Or, at the very least, you must do a pull-up: Dub the piece off to another tape as you add or subtract the changed material to create a new edit master tape that is now one generation further down. Before you start to edit, you must have a clear idea of where you are going, and what the finished product will be, to avoid this problem.

Advance Planning   The best way to avoid audio problems is to plan the editing well in advance. With script in hand, decide what shots you want to use and where you will use any natural sound. If your plan-

ning is good and you can stick with your decisions, edit all the sound-up-full parts first, then lay in the rest of the cover video. This means lay down your first shot with its sound up full, fade it down at the right point, lay in the reporter's track, lay in any shots with natsound up full, then the sound bite, and so on.

When you have completed this, go back and fill in all the black areas with the proper shots and their audio to complete the story. This method only works if you never change your mind after you have begun to edit and if your planning is well done and all the sequences fit. With the audio already down, you have no room to change anything as you begin to lay in your video.

Section by Section   The other method, which is just as fast, is to edit one section at a time. This allows you to fine-tune each part of the story as you go, gives you the freedom to change any parts of the story as you come to them, and, in the case of a real-time bind, allows you to skip over parts of the story and go straight to the end to finish it in some form so it can be on the air in its scheduled time slot.

Sometimes a visual sequence needs just one more second of space to have it look right. If you are editing section by section, you can make these changes without affecting anything after that part. It is very important to plan ahead. Know where you are going and what you have to work with. If you edit section by section, you keep your creative options open until the last second. Even if you are working under deadline pressure, section-by-section editing can greatly enhance the quality of the piece.

Music Editing   When using music, it must be laid down first if any of the video is to be edited to the music. If nothing is to be in sync with the music, then it is best left until last, so it is easier to mix it with other audio. Again, planning is the key. To cut to music, time out the script as to where and for how long the music and other audio is to be up full. These times must be set in advance.

Start by laying in the music and mixing it up full or just at background sound levels. You must do this according to the prearranged times decided before the editing begins. Next, lay in all the other audio that is to be up full (reporter's track, sound bites, and natsound with pictures) in the proper place. Finally, insert the rest of the shots, editing them to the music and any natsound, if appropriate or needed. If planned properly, this method lets you edit to the music without affecting the placement of the rest of the audio, so that the finished piece has all the elements timed perfectly.

SUMMARY

Editing can be every bit the creative challenge of shooting. Although this book places the greatest emphasis on photography, it is hard to separate the two. The best shooters are the ones who learn how to edit. Just as a shot can be improved by moving the camera just a few inches, an edit can be improved by changing the timing just a few frames. The goal of the editor is to take the material at hand and make an understandable presentation. The methods and varieties of solutions are as expansive as the number of editors.

By following the rules and guidelines put forth in this chapter, you can get started on any editing project. Just as in photography, however, every rule is made to be broken. And the easiest way to break the rules is by first understanding them. Learn the language of the edit and then branch out to the creative "writing" of visual communication.

part three

Styles and Applications

9

Electronic News Gathering Style

PART ONE: TAPED COVERAGE

The decisions you make in the field while shooting any story begin to give your video a look or a particular style. Because no two people see the same scene in the same way, your vision of what is possible with the camera is what becomes your style. Within the world of TV news, documentary work, and reality-based programs, you must operate under certain constants while shooting. These constants help identify for the viewer the type of story and also act as an overlay to your individual style, not replacing it but limiting it to certain parameters.

In electronic news gathering, stories tend to fall into one of several categories: spot news, general news, feature news, and sports news. Each of these areas requires a unique approach on the part of the photographer, and each has its own guidelines that define a certain look. When a story is assigned to you, the nature of that story sets up certain expectations about how it will look and how you will approach the shooting.

SPOT NEWS

Although spot news is the reason most photographers come to TV news, it is the hardest ENG style to master. It is truly what shooting news is all about. Whether it's a gun fight between law enforcement and a cult group, a raging war in the Middle East, or the attempted assassination of the president, you—because of your presence—are recording history. Even the most mundane event can suddenly become a moment in time that will live forever.

How well you do your job will also live forever. If you fail, generations to come will miss seeing that dramatic moment. Think for a moment how many events in history you remember by the pictures you saw; think how much less impact the events would have had if they had not been recorded on film or tape. If we never saw an atomic explosion, would we be as awed by its power? If we had not seen the war in Bosnia every night on the evening news, would we really grasp the death and suffering involved there?

News photography lets the viewer see and hear things as if he or she were actually present. (See Figure 9.1.) An ENG photographer's job is to bring the event to the viewer so that the viewer can react to what is happening.

It is not the photographer's job to tell someone that a war is immoral but rather to show what a war is like, what is taking place, and the effect it has on those involved. Most ENG photographers will never be in a position to record a major part of history, but some will, often solely by the luck of being at the right place at the right time. Therefore, each photographer must be prepared to rise to the occasion.

When shooting spot news, the photographer will be in one of three situations: (1) in the middle of what is happening, (2) in the middle of the aftermath, or (3) stuck on the perimeter while the event is happening or just after it has happened.

Figure 9.1 An ENG Photographer shooting a story on a city street.

Shooting in the Middle of the Action

One of the most famous examples of this situation is the assassination attempt on President Ronald Reagan in the early 1980s. The camera crews assigned to shoot every move the president makes had no idea what was about to occur on that fateful morning. Within a few seconds, the calm scene was transformed into one of utter chaos. The photographers had to operate on instinct and training to capture that moment of history. Some did better than others at capturing the event. The best shooting came from an NBC cameraman, who held his shot wide until he could tell what was going on and then decided what was most important to show. He moved the camera and used the zoom lens to take viewers from one horrible section of the scene to the next, pausing just long enough to show what was happening before moving to the next area of action. No shaky zooms or wild pans whipping around to distort what the picture contained. The cameraman found and held the shot on each element in the story in the order of its importance.

You can imagine the amount of self-control it took to do his job under these circumstances. Not many people could have done it, but this is the situation you must always be ready for if you work in news. It does not have to be the president; it could happen at a simple court hearing or as you follow a mail carrier on his route. Sometimes unexpected events happen when a camera is there. A simple demonstration by a student group may escalate into a full-scale riot with you at the center.

If you find yourself in the middle of a situation while it is happening, keep your lens at its widest setting and keep your videotape rolling. It sounds simple, but it is surprising how many good pieces of news have been lost because this rule was not followed. If the story is breaking around you, you must shoot it as you would see it. Don't zoom in to one element and exclude the others that are still happening. Pan if you have to, or walk to a better vantage point, but save the zoom for later when you feel more in control of elements.

Keep Rolling   Above all, keep rolling. From the moment the camera is turned on, roll tape and don't stop for any reason. (After things settle down or you gain control of the situation, you can be more selective about rolling tape.) White balance while rolling, run from your car or van while rolling and try to make every second of the tape viable. Even when you are running with the camera to get a better position, keep the camera on the action and as steady as possible.

By keeping the videotape rolling continuously, you cover yourself in the event something unexpected takes place while you are on the location. Many times the biggest moment of drama comes from seemingly nowhere. That fireman bursting from the front door could be the best or most important element of the story.

Keep the Lens Setting Wide   The previous point is one of the reasons to always stay wide. Camera movement is less noticeable when the shot is wide, and you also have a smaller chance of missing some important action. These are not events you will be able to get later on; once they are missed, they are gone forever. Use the camera as you use your eyes—let the viewer see as much as possible of what you see. Let it all take place before you. Use the zoom only to maintain the field of action. Go in only as tight as is necessary to eliminate areas of "dead" space.

Look as You Shoot   It may seem silly to say this, but you have to tell yourself to look up once in a while. With the lens wide, you can easily take your face away from the viewfinder and look around as you shoot. Watch your back. Look out for danger or getting in the way of emergency personnel. Above all, look for any elements you may be missing because your eye is glued to the ones in the viewfinder. When covering an event such as the Los Angeles riots, this technique could save your life.

Hold the Shots   You must learn to count in your head while you shoot. In the middle of a breaking story, time will become very distorted. When you think you have a long enough shot of one particular element, you probably do not.

Ten is a great number to use. Unless you must change shots in order to capture something that is leaving the scene or providing a more dramatic element, count to 10 before making any changes in your shot. This allows the viewer time to perceive the shot

and gives the editor the ability to cut out pans and walking shots to condense the event for presentation.

Get Static Shots   Don't forget to get **set shots** or **statics**. If the action slows for a moment, look for a good composition that you can make near where you are positioned. Don't stop rolling, but slide to the next camera angle and hold the shot as if on the tripod. Try to find the most dramatic angle you can—one that shows the totality of the event either literally or symbolically. Use this moment to catch your breath and organize your thoughts as to where you should be next. Just take in the scene, read it, and try to anticipate the next area of likely action. These statics will probably be some of your best shots.

Check Your Gear Often   Don't panic in the middle of an action scene. Move to your first shot and count it out, go to the next shot and count it out, and keep that tape rolling. Check the tape often to make sure it is indeed rolling, and check your audio often to make sure the sound is there and not too low or overmodulated. Stay wide, keep rolling, time your shots by counting in your head, and look for the most important elements to photograph. Stay with the action, and check all of your systems as often as possible.

Shooting in the Aftermath

The second example of a spot news situation is one in which the main action is over and all that remains is the aftermath. For example, you arrive at the scene of a gas explosion shortly after the firefighters have begun to aid the victims. This situation can also be very intense with quite a bit of pressure, but for the most part things are under control. While you should still follow many of the same principles as when shooting in the middle of the action, a situation like this usually gives a photographer more time to make shots. Shooting in the aftermath is the most common type of spot news. It still requires much hustle to get all the elements, but nothing new is going to happen. All the fire equipment is in place, the medical personnel are attending the injured, or the police have subdued the gunman.

In this type of aftermath situation, you do not need to roll tape the entire time, but the situation does demand fast decision-making nonetheless. You are still trying to present the story as the viewers would see and hear it if they were present. Because the events are under more control than in the first situation, your shooting can be more controlled.

Look for a Variety of Shots   Look for a good opening wide shot, and try to stay wide for most of the action shots. Because things are not moving as quickly, you have the time to look for medium shots and, above all, close-ups. With the zoom lens, you can pursue the tight shots of faces that really tell the story of the individuals involved, without fear of losing other elements of the story.

Look for the Action   With your knowledge of sequencing and storytelling elements, you should know what shots to get and be out there getting them while staying out of the way. The key is to always look for the action: Shoot what moves but keep with the story. Do not get sidetracked with unimportant things like shooting the crowd of onlookers. As when shooting in the middle of the action, this type of shooting is often off the shoulder, so use your feet as much as possible to get close to each element.

Focus on the Story   Do not include extraneous shots in what you shoot; you are merely wasting time and tape. If the crowd of spectators is not part of the story, do not shoot them. If the police are having a hard time moving them back, then they are part of the story. If the story has enough action in it, then there is no need for a cutaway and you should look for transition shots instead. By varying angles and focal lengths, the piece should fit together without the useless shot of uninvolved people watching.

In many cases it will be obvious that the main element of the story is happening when you arrive. It may be as simple as flames shooting from a building's windows or as subtle as a single person lying on the ground surrounded by a few people. Generally, a quick look around at the people involved will give you a clue as to where the main action is. If firefighters are rushing to the back of a building, maybe you should, too, if you can. The thing you must never forget is to focus on the people involved. If there is a rescue unit at the scene of the fire, then look for the injured. Stop by the ambulance first, as it will soon be leaving for the hospital; the building will be there for quite awhile. You may miss some of the best flames, but without the people the story would be lacking even more. A quick sound bite from a victim on the way to the hospital, describing a narrow escape, can sink the competition's shot of the flames you missed. Do not spend too much time on any one element. Keep moving. Look for those small but potentially powerful human elements that can take your story above and beyond the rest. Look for the elements that will not

last long and get them as soon as you can. Decide which things will move and which will be there later when things are more calm or you have more time.

As the story is winding down, look for a good closing shot. The typical one for a fire story is that of a lone firefighter sitting on the curb, with smoldering ashes in the background, removing an air mask and wiping away the sweat. Or, it may be a person quietly grieving at the site of the fire or the water to the hoses being turned off. It may also be symbolic, such as a tight shot of the police yellow or red tape blowing in the wind. You want to leave the viewer with a sense that the story is over. It can also be the shot of the ambulance driving off, but whatever it is, it should say "The End." If the story is only going to run as a 20-second voice-over there will be no air time to use such shots. For this type of presentation, you simply need the best 20 seconds of the event with the most action possible and that all-important human element. (See Figure 9.2.)

Shooting on the Perimeter of the Action

In the third example of spot news, you are restricted from close access to the action. If you are held blocks away from a chemical leak or hostage situation, you must be prepared to use the tripod and shoot at the longest focal length possible. This situation is the reason most cameras have a lens with a $2\times$ extender (which doubles focal length). It is impossible to shoot at those focal lengths from off your shoulder—they're just too shaky. If the tripod is not available, rest the camera on the ground or on anything else that will steady the picture.

Look for Movement   Because of the distance you may be from the location of the actual event, you need to keep a sharp eye peeled for any movement. The action may be simple, such as people moving around police cars or fire engines, but any movement is better than none at all. In this situation more than any other, you need to shoot anything that moves: additional equipment arriving at the scene, officials talking on two-way radios, or SWAT team members suiting up. Any movement can become symbolic action.

Remember the Edit Room   You may encounter a situation in which you will not get a shot of the real story, but you must have pictures of some sort to show on the air. In this case, you must come as close as you can to depicting the story with your shots. Sometimes

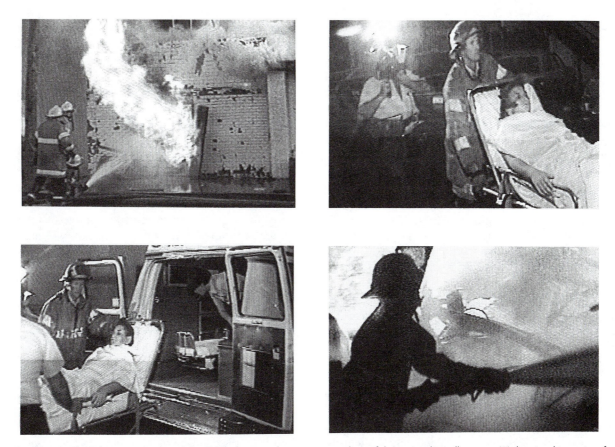

Figure 9.2 When shooting spot news, the ENG photographer tries to get shots of the action that tell a story: (1) the visual intensity of the fire; (2) and (3) the human element—how the fire affects people; and (4) the action taken by the firefighters to bring the fire under control.

this means just a shot of the police tape used at a crime scene to keep out unauthorized persons and a police officer standing next to it. Or it may be just the police car used for the roadblock keeping you out.

Never walk away from anything without enough video to cover a 1-minute story (without shooting the same shot over and over). This may really tax your creative skills, but you have to think like an editor: What I am going to use to cover this script? In a situation where the pertinent pictures are few and far between, a shot of onlookers could be useful; they still have nothing to do with the story, but they can help pad a piece that is already visually weak.

Stay Near the Center of Information   In most cases in which you are restricted from the scene and held far from any direct action, you will usually be able to be at or near the command center set up by the controlling agency. This will become your major source of pictures for the story. You may get better shots later

on, but you cannot count on that. This is why you should shoot everything you can until you have exhausted the possibilities. Police officers looking at a map, conferring with each other, or even just walking from one place to another will do. If the event goes on for quite awhile, the station will either ask for some tape to be fed back or ask for a live update with a tape insert. You had better have some tape to give them, and you certainly better be carrying more than one tape with you.

Don't Overshoot   When real pictures are scarce, be selective in the amount of tape you shoot. After you have that initial group of shots to cover a short script, fall back, observe, and conserve batteries and tape for the chance at some real action. You shouldn't have to use more than 4 to 6 minutes of tape or less if you are making every shot really count. There is no point in getting volumes of generic video that will quickly all look like the same shots over and over.

Use the Tripod The sticks allow you to use the longest focal lengths to visually reach into any scene to pick out shots your shoulder-mounted competition cannot get. They may also be the *only* shots you can get. Without the tripod—and with 2 to 3 hours of waiting—your shoulder will not be able to perform later when you might really need it. If you're on the sticks, you can always pull the camera off them quickly and run with it should the need arise.

Dealing with the Authorities

Before shooting any spot news, you should have a **press pass**, or ID card, issued by the law enforcement agencies of your city, county, and state. This identifies you as a bona fide member of a news organization. Without this pass, shooting spot news can be a risky and sometimes impossible job. A press pass sometimes even gets you across police and fire lines to gain better access to the event. Sometimes the pass is worthless, and at other times it can get you into more trouble than it keeps you out of. However, without it you do not stand a chance. The press pass involves some serious responsibilities. If the authorities let you into or close to the scene, you cannot interfere with what they are doing or disobey any special requests they have. Such requests may include not showing a certain area of a fire scene that is part of an arson investigation, or showing the face of an undercover agent. If you violate the trust given you, your future dealings with that agency are jeopardized, as well as those of your employer and other members of the press, not to mention the harm it may do the agency or the investigation.

It is not a good idea to try to outwit the authorities. It is quite impossible to shoot the rest of the story from the backseat of a police car. In some cases, the risk involved in going around authority can be life threatening. You would not want to be in the line of fire of a deranged sniper. Police/media relations are always strained at best, but the only good course of action is to play by the rules. Often there will be a need to circumvent the authorities to get at the really good pictures of the story. These decisions can only be made on a case-by-case basis and must be made with the clear understanding that what you are doing is illegal and may harm you or someone else—just like combat photographers, if you are willing to accept the ultimate responsibility, then you do as you think best. If you do get into trouble disobeying an authority, your employer will most likely *not* help you out of it. This is similar to getting a speeding ticket on your way to a story—you are on your own when breaking the law.

Going Live

On any major spot news story there will be a voice on your two-way radio screaming for a live shot even before you arrive on the scene. The pressure to get on the air first can be so great that actually shooting the story becomes a secondary consideration. Oftentimes the situation will require you to be in two places and doing two things at the same time. You will have to decide what to do. Shoot the pending dramatic rescue, or pull cables for the live shot? This may seem like a simple choice, but the voice on the other end of the radio can make it a very hard decision. Most of the time you'll know what to do by instinct.

You will also most likely not be alone for long. Any big story is going to have all the resources of the station thrown at it. You may be able to shoot tape because the second photographer arriving will do the live. Try to coordinate on the radio even before you get to the location. If you're the second to arrive from your station, you should be thinking *live shot*. Let the first in be the primary for shooting tape, and you can set up the system for getting the tape out to the world. The assignment desk may coordinate all this, but in any leadership vacuum, be ready to step in with a plan to get the story on the air with the best coverage you can and the quickest way you can. That *is* spot news.

Be Prepared

Spot news requires instinct and a great deal of luck. You can increase the luck factor by always being prepared. If your equipment is organized, easy to get to, and well maintained, and you know what is required to make a good story, then when the big one comes your way, the Emmy is yours. Shoot with both eyes open, always looking for the next shot or danger, or for what else may be about to happen. Keep your eyes moving but your camera steady. And check your systems: If you aren't rolling tape, you won't get the shot; and if you don't have audio, that's what people will remember about you for years to come—"So-and-so had the pictures and not one peep of audio; it could have been a career-making story."

GENERAL NEWS

This category of news stories is, as the label implies, very general. Most stories fall under this heading. These are the stories about the city council, the plans to build a new housing development for the elderly, or the strike by local bus drivers. Most storytelling techniques apply directly to this form of the news story. The main concept in general news, sometimes called hard news, is to communicate ideas or information to the viewer. The story must be very understandable, with a good beginning, middle, and end. It is on this type of story that reporter and photographer must work closely to produce the maximum impact on the viewer.

Presentation is of utmost importance. The subject matter might be the dullest in the world, but if the information is important (or if the boss demands the story be done), the story must be done and done well. As they say, "There's no such thing as a boring story, only a boring approach." The idea is to never lose a viewer; never give a viewer the opportunity to say "so what" or "who cares" to what you are presenting—or, worse yet, switch channels.

Get a Good First Shot

Always make the first shot of the story count. More than likely, it will be your best shot and it should be. Grab the viewer's attention immediately to get them into the rest of the story. As a general rule, it is bad form to open a story with a talking head or a reporter stand-up. This opening looks too much like the people on the news set; that is, a person talking without showing you anything. If it starts to become the same as radio, why watch?

Sound is also important in the first shot. A natural sound clip is a good opening for almost any story; a dramatic sound bite can also be a good opening, but good ones do not occur that often. In an opening shot of a street construction story, the sound of the jackhammer (if one is in the shot) up full for about 2 seconds can set the story's tone and topic right there. "Get ready, Seattle, the streets are being torn up."

Create Visual Sound Bites

The worst thing about general news stories is the lengthy talking head shots that can make up the bulk of the video. While interviews are the bread and but-

ter of TV news, they do not have to be the most boring part of the story. Like anything in TV news, the talking head can be overused. Most reporters use two basic styles of talking heads: one to make the story they have written more credible, and the other to let the subjects tell their own story. The former is more of a traditional journalism style where importance is placed on the reporter's ability to interpret and analyze, and the latter is a style of simply allowing subjects to present their points at length with little additional comment from the reporter. Both styles have their place, although letting subjects tell their own story is better suited to feature reports.

In either case, the talking head should be well shot. If the subject is to be on camera for a long time (maybe as much as 2 minutes in a 3-minute story), then the interview shot had better be pleasing and interesting to look at for the entire time. (See Figure 9.3.) By shooting each answer during the interview at a different focal length (changing focal lengths during the question) or maybe doing some answers in a reporter/subject two-shot, the parts used for the edited interview may vary enough to add some interest beyond nice framing.

You may sometimes opt to do parts of the same interview at different times and at different locations. If the same subject is to be heard many times within the story, it may be possible to shoot in more than one location. One bite may have the subject behind a desk; another may come from a walking conversation with the reporter; and still another may have the subject on a balcony overlooking the factory. It takes a little more time to do the interview, but the results are far better. Another way that can work in certain situations is simply different angles within the same basic setup. By moving the camera to different points of view within the room for different sections of the interview, the edited piece can look like a multi-camera shoot. Work with the reporter or producer to find creative ways of avoiding long stretches of static talking heads.

Cover Long Sound Bites with Video

When a piece does have long stretches of talking heads or long sound bites, try to cover as much of them as possible with "B" roll, such as shots of the subject matter or even cutaways. If you are going to use several bites or one long-running bite from a subject, the audience only needs to see that individual for

Figure 9.3 By placing this subject on the opposite side of his desk for a better background and using the table lamp and foreground, this one-light interview becomes much more interesting.

about 5 seconds. In that time, the voice is established with a name and a face so the picture portion is free to show what he or she is talking about.

A 20-second sound bite with the builder of a new housing project could have the last 15 seconds or so covered by related video (plans of the building, construction under way, and so forth). Try also to make this video lead into the next audio, whether it is another talking head or reporter voice-over. The sequence you started over the interview continues, if ever so slightly, over the beginning of the next section of script.

The same can be done in reverse. If the reporter's track is about housing construction, and it leads into a sound bite from the builder, let the video of construction overlap the first 5 to 10 seconds of the builder's 20-second bite. The builder's face will appear and connect with the voice, but the length of the talking head has been reduced in favor of more interesting video.

If the builder is to appear twice fairly close together in a piece—two bites separated by a short reporter's comment—the second bite need not have the builder on camera at all; that entire bite can be covered by "B" roll. This assumes that you have enough video to cover all the sound bites and that your video is appropriate to go over the audio.

Keep the Story Moving

Often you will not have enough video (or any appropriate video) to use in or around talking heads. Say the construction project story is done on a day where the workers are off. In these situations, you need to provide a large variety of two-shots, cutaways, and setup shots to help fill the time. Remember, any story looks better when people are in the shots. Instead of using only unpopulated shots of the site, try to find a variety of ways of working in the subject and the reporter—the only people you have. An example of a setup shot getting into a sound bite might be a zoom-out from the plans on the wall to a wide two-shot of the builder and reporter talking, or shots of them walking around the site. Taken from many angles and distances to them, you can use these shots to cover both the script and long sound bites. Shots like these fill the time and keep the video moving.

Illustrate the Topic

The hardest thing to do in general and hard news stories is to find pictures that go with the topic. If the story is about illegal campaign funds, the challenge will be there to find the pictures. By working closely with the reporter or producer, a photographer should begin early in the shooting process to visualize the unfolding story. There may be nothing to shoot but leaked memos that are nothing more than pieces of paper. If that's the case, make them into a piece of art. Place them on a desktop, light them up nicely (perhaps use a gobo pattern), and try some slow pans or tilts. (See Figure 9.4.)

Whatever the topic of the story, you must start thinking of how to cover the future script with video. Be creative. Think symbolism. A story on the hay fever season might make use of tight shots of pollen-producing weeds blowing in the breeze. Better yet, use tight shots of them in the foreground with people in the background. Or, try just a tight shot of a Kleenex box with a hand pulling out a tissue. The shot is symbolic of the sneezing that's associated with the pollen without finding someone doing it or staging the shot (a big no-no). The bottom line is, every story has pictures. The earlier you start thinking about which ones to get, the better.

General news stories are serious and business-like in subject matter and approach. Your photography should also reflect the same characteristics. There is no staging of events or the subject's actions. Your job is to simply and clearly represent the subject or event as accurately as possible while at the same time making it interesting or at least pleasing to watch. This type of story can be the greatest challenge to the news photographer. It is the place where

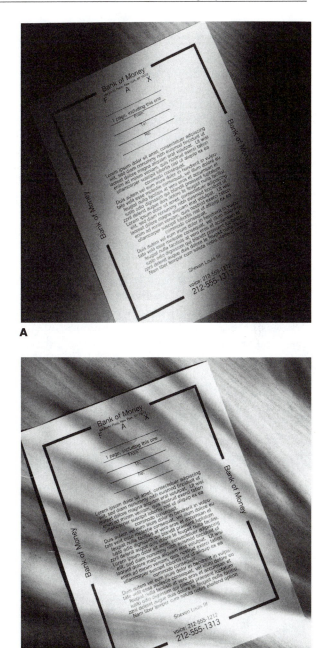

A

B

Figure 9.4 Two alternatives to shooting this document square and flat: (A) The paper is at an angle and highlighted with a shaft of light; (B) the light is shining through a water glass to create a pattern across the paper.

names are made in this industry. If you can make a city council story come alive and be as visually interesting as a feature without staging the shots, then the rest of what you do in this business will be easy.

FEATURE NEWS

This category is perhaps the most free form of all. Feature stories are usually light-hearted looks at people and events, or involved pieces on lighter or more personal, intimate subjects. They are not hard news by any means; rather, they are referred to as **soft news**. That doesn't mean they are comedies but simply stories told more like essays than news reports. The stories in this category should entertain or touch or somehow connect with the viewer on a personal level. Approach feature news with an emphasis on creativity; this type of story is a rare chance for both reporter and photographer to be as wild and imaginative or as inspiring and engaging as possible.

Music usually adds lightness or emotion to feature stories and allows the editor to do some creative cutting. While there may be only one such story in a newscast, the feature piece can be the most memorable in the show. In what can be a very depressing news day, people like to feel good about something or feel touched by another human being's experience. The feature gives viewers the chance to end the news time on a spiritual high note.

The story may be a picture essay on a skydiving contest with no reporter, or a simple story about children picking out pumpkins for Halloween. Almost any positive or good-news subject can be made into a good feature if a creative approach is used. Do not treat the feature as a nonstory and therefore a throwaway, even if it seems like an ad for some company.

The audience feels this type of story is important. It is your job to make it work creatively. The feature can also be a profile of the town's oldest volunteer, struggling to teach poor kids how to read. Or the personal story of one mother's fight to change the laws after losing her only child to a drunk driver. Whether you are showing a 2-year-old rolling a pumpkin home, or the tears of one person's crusade for a better society, the feature aims at the heart of the viewer.

It can take a whole day, a week, or even a month to do a good feature story. Or it can take an hour. The idea can be mapped out well in advance and shot a little at a time until the piece comes together. Features needn't be timely, so they can air at any time. This allows more work to be put into them. However, you will not always be given that time.

Try Different Techniques

Feature news provides a chance to use all the tricks of shooting and editing: odd angles, dramatic camera moves, unusual lighting, quick edits, wipes, and other special effects. (See Figures 9.5 and 9.6.) Features are the perfect place to use dissolves. No approach or technique is too unusual for the feature story as long as it *fits* the story. Try whatever you can to make your piece stand out and touch your audience. Good lighting, beautifully framed shots, slow zooms, dissolves, and symbolic images can come together in a feature story to touch even the most hardened news watcher. If you can feel with your camera and your editing,

Figure 9.5 Shooting XCUs and layering shots like this frame from a feature story on hummingbirds can enhance the visual experience.

then the viewer will also feel. The audience should come away from the piece affected by what you have shown them.

Many feature stories take on the air of a Hollywood movie. They may be a parody of a harder story, such as a tongue-in-cheek piece on a professional baseball league strike. The production of the story may become just as involved as any commercial shoot. The thing that separates pure journalism from this style of TV news is its goals. A general news story on the success of the Rubik's Cube (a popular puzzle toy) would discuss its inventor, sales, and so forth. A feature on the Rubik's Cube may simply be about a character (perhaps the reporter) trying to solve the puzzle with no luck, and then listing other uses for the toy, such as a door stop, and ending with the toy being run over by a steamroller. The first piece informs; the second entertains with little regard for information other than to point out that the toy is popular. Do not mislead the viewer. If the piece is to entertain, make sure it is obvious that's what's happening. Blending fact and fiction can be a dangerous game. Make sure that what you are doing has clear-cut goals and that facts are never lumped in with staged material—keep them separated in the viewer's mind. A feature on a new private fishing lake may be mostly fact, but a shot of the reporter pulling a three-foot shark out of the water may lead some viewers to think sharks are in the lake. Make sure there is only

one possible interpretation of what you are doing in the story and that any jokes are clearly understood to be just that.

SPORTS NEWS

It may be a stereotype, but it seems that most male photographers love to shoot sports. If there is a slot on the staff for a full-time sports photographer, it's never without a waiting list to fill it. Shooting sports has become an art form all its own. Sports video falls into two categories: features and competition.

Features

The ENG photographer shoots a sports feature much like the news feature—with the maximum amount of creativity and involvement. If you are doing a piece on a boxer training for a fight, get in the ring (if they let you) and have the boxer spar right at the camera lens. This type of involvement can bring the subject up close for the viewer and give a perspective not available during a match.

You can do something similar for any sport. Use the fact that it is only practice to get the camera involved in places where it normally is not used. Gymnastics is a good sport for features: put the camera under the gymnasts, let them jump over the camera,

Figure 9.6 The framing of this audience member at a memorial service uses selective focus and foreground to give added emphasis to tears on her cheeks.

or put the camera right on the balance beam. Make these stories fun to do and fun to watch, while trying to show the hard work taking place.

Competition

As a news photographer, you will videotape sports competition mainly for highlights or to capture a very short portion of the event, whereas competition coverage for EFP is often live coverage of the entire event. Almost all sporting events should be shot from a tripod, unless other footage is being obtained from the company covering the event. Choose a good vantage point where all the action is visible.

The public is used to seeing sports shot with many cameras. Most of the time you will have only one camera but be required to do just as good a job and not miss any of the action. The best location for almost any sport is from above and as much to the center of the action as possible.

Basketball and Football   For basketball, the ideal location is about one-third up the rows of seats and on the half-court line. Floor angles are nice, and you should get some if they let you, but if a major play is at the far end of the court you stand a good chance of missing it or having your view blocked by the referee or other players. The high shot gets all the action clearly and allows you to zoom in or zoom out to include as much of the action as you want. The same is the case with football. Field-level shooting is very exciting, especially from the end zone, but the best view is always from the press box or the equivalent.

If many plays are to be used as highlights, it is impractical to use a cutaway between each of these plays. Good football plays usually end with a long run, or pass, or the score itself. The ending shot will look sufficiently different from the beginning of the next highlight, and there is little worry of a jump cut. In basketball, the field of action is much smaller, and therefore most of the players tend to be in the shot most of the time. For this sport it is a good idea to zoom in on the play-maker just after the points are scored. Besides emphasizing that player, this technique allows the editor to cut from that tight shot to the next highlight (which may be at the same end of the court), or to allow time for the reporter/anchor's voice-over to talk about that player. Even in football, it is a good idea to zoom in to the key player as the play ends, unless you are already on a tight shot of that player.

Sideline photography, usually done off your shoulder, is a way to add a closer, more dramatic feel

to your highlight shots. Field-level perspectives can really distort distance and speed (remember the half-the-distance, twice-the-size concept). The big risks are missing something or being run over. If you are covered by being able to take video from another source, such as the company broadcasting the game, then anything you may miss on the sidelines can be obtained elsewhere. The biggest problem with ground-level shooting is the perspective of the camera. It is hard to tell relative distances between players, which makes some plays actually look rather nondramatic. When you are learning how to shoot these two sports, it is better to master the high shot before moving to ground level.

Baseball   This sport is difficult to shoot with only one camera. Action is taking place in two areas at the same time and it seems you should be following both the ball and the runners. Usually it is best to follow the ball until it is caught, then you can pan quickly to the runners. Just following the ball will often give you all the action anyway, but if it is a long double and a runner is headed for home, it can be difficult to show both. Do not take the easy way out and just go wide to show the whole field. A TV screen is too small for any of the real action to show up at all. If you miss the runner scoring, you can use a shot of the runner walking to the dugout as the run-scored shot.

If you are above and directly behind home plate, you should see all the plays nicely. Start on a two-shot of the pitcher and batter (top and bottom of the picture from this camera position), and zoom in to follow the ball when it's hit. If you lose the ball, zoom out wide and pan in the direction it went until you regain sight of it. (You will see the players running to where it is going.) Stay with it as you use your left eye to scan the infield for other action. If a runner is making it to home with little chance of being thrown out, quickly pan to that shot. Otherwise, stick with the ball. By making all of your moves as smoothly as possible, even when you lose sight of the ball, no one will notice any errors on your part.

Golf and Hockey   Golf balls and hockey pucks are difficult to follow: A golf ball is too small and a hockey puck moves too fast. Staying fairly wide in hockey is the best way to avoid missing the play entirely. As you become familiar with the game, it will be easier to anticipate where the puck is going. For golf, it takes a lot of practice to keep your eye glued to the ball.

Hockey is similar to basketball in how it is shot except that it moves much faster. A good sports photographer can shoot hockey fairly tight, but most people cannot. It is best to be high up and at center ice to do the shooting and again zoom in to the play-maker at the score. Golf is obviously a much slower game to shoot but can be the most strenuous to do because of all the walking between shots. It is best to be either directly behind or directly in front of the golfer. In front means way down the fairway, farther than it is possible to hit the ball. From behind, you can start wide and zoom in to follow the ball; from in front, you can start tight on the golfer and widen out to keep the ball from leaving the frame. Trying to **whip-pan** (pan the camera very fast) with the ball as it flies by you is not a good idea.

General Sports Tips

A good rule of thumb when shooting any sport you are not accustomed to is to stay wide at first and slowly shoot it tighter as you become more comfortable with the game. Shooting too tightly at first can leave you faked out, causing you to miss the play, so choose your focal length carefully. If too many plays are getting away from you, widen out until you have better control. Above all, make it smooth. Do not jerk the camera or hesitate in a zoom or pan; make every movement seem like it is purposeful whether it is or not.

Watch network or cable TV's coverage of the sport that you are going to shoot. See how the experienced professionals do it; see the kinds of shots they get and how they follow the ball. Try to take what they are doing and adapt it to a one-camera shoot. The cuts that are done live on the network may have to be done in editing for you, but if you get the right elements on tape, you can make it look pretty close to network coverage. The main thing is to follow the ball or stay with the leader. It takes practice and much concentration, but it is the only way to get professional results.

SUMMARY

Understanding what's expected of you for any assignment is a great advantage. By knowing the type of story you are assigned, you have a head start on achieving what's expected. Like many jobs, TV news is fairly predictable in the type of work that is done. The story on the city council meeting has been done the same basic way for decades. Making a radical change in that approach may not go over big with the boss or the public. Adding a touch of your personal

style and a little creative thought, however, can garner the attention of the above two benefactors. Communication is always the number one goal, and with a good working knowledge of how each type of story is done, you can carefully take the viewer to your personal vision of that story.

PART TWO: LIVE COVERAGE

LIVE TV

One of the greatest advantages that video has over film for TV is the use of portable cameras to produce live coverage from just about anywhere. It is one of the reasons that TV news has soared to such a high level of popularity. Just as an earlier generation listened to Edward R. Murrow giving live accounts of the bombings of London during World War II, today's generation has *watched* U.S. forces under missile attack live on CNN. There can be no greater drama and no greater use of the medium than to see history being made live on the screen. The fact that countless millions of people everywhere in the world can view this makes an even greater impact on world society. Marshall McLuhan's fantasy forecast that the world would become one giant global village because of TV has now become a reality. The Gulf War, the crackdown in Tiananmen Square, the dismantling of the Berlin Wall, or a white Ford Bronco driving down a freeway are all examples of the power of live TV to captivate viewers all over the world.

Even on local news stations, the use of live TV has led to the same mesmerizing effect on viewers during events of great importance or curiosity. An earthquake in San Francisco, a plane crash on the Potomac, a shootout in Watts, or a baby girl stranded at the bottom of a well have all riveted local audiences as living dramas unfolded before them just as for the people actually present.

Live TV has power of enormous proportion, which is accompanied by social responsibility. The use of live TV during the Gulf War was criticized both for elevating the reporter's personal experience above that of the overall events and for revealing too much information of possible use to the enemy. The only certainty was that everyone was watching. A single reporter panicking or giving misinformation during a major story could have had a profound effect around the world. On another level, local TV news has reduced live TV to just another gimmick to attract viewers. Despite its drawbacks and misuses, live TV is the pinnacle of broadcast journalism when news breaks out anywhere in the world.

Live TV can also be of considerable importance to the business world through teleconferences. Just as local news stations use live cameras to hype ratings, companies and educators can use live TV to add a new sense of immediacy to the information they are trying to convey. This section discusses the tools of live TV, its typical formats and uses, some tricks of the trade, and some common problems.

GETTING THE PICTURE OUT

The starting point of live TV transmission is the camera. Any broadcast-quality video camera with a composite NTSC output can feed a transmitter. Often the output of the camera is fed through a **distribution amplifier (DA)** to maintain proper video levels. A low video signal may not transmit well and will come across muddy with increased noise or poor color. A high, or hot, video signal may transmit as a washed-out picture, possibly causing a breakup in the transmission or noise in the audio portion. The most common faults in these two examples are either an improperly exposed camera or signal loss due to a long cable run from the camera to the transmitter. If these problems are not too extreme, the DA can correct them by its gain and equalizing functions. To operate, the DA must be connected to a waveform monitor to display the effects of any adjustments.

The four basic ways of transmitting a live picture from the field are by means of (1) telephone lines, (2) fiber optic lines, (3) microwaves, and (4) satellites.

Telephone Lines

The local telephone company can set up a video-feed point from just about anywhere using a balanced line (different from a regular phone line). Because of the time necessary to set up this type of transmission, it is rarely used except for events such as election returns where there is plenty of lead time for installation. Because of deregulation in the telephone industry, it may be a challenge to find the right company or unit to deliver such a line, but most phone companies have experience with this method of delivery. The lines can be run to just about anywhere that has phone service.

Fiber Optic

Similar to regular phone lines, newer phone systems have light transmitting cables already in place. These fiber optic lines carry encoded video and audio information to distant distribution centers with little loss of signal. This system's benefits are best seen when using digital signals. Special encoders and decoders are needed at each end of the fiber line to change video and audio signals into laser light and back again.

Microwaves

Microwave equipment is relatively small and usually owned by the TV station using it. The most common placement of a microwave system is in a van (sometimes called a live truck, RF truck, or feeder) that has an antenna at the top of a telescoping mast that may go as high as 50 feet. (See Figure 9.7.) The truck usually has a reel of multi-line cable (two video and four audio lines in one cable) that can stretch about 300 feet. A normal video cable allows up to a 1000-foot run before the loss of signal becomes too great for the DA to compensate.

Microwave transmitters work in a spectrum of radio-frequencies measured in gigahertz (GHz) and have specific channels assigned by the Federal Communications Commission (FCC). The standard ENG channels have always been 2, 7, and 13 GHz. Each channel can be subdivided further into parts simply called A, B, C, D, and Center, with the option of the microwaves going clockwise or counterclockwise. These variations allow many stations in the same market, or many transmitters at one station, to transmit at the same time. With the increased use of this technology, more channels have been opened up to include 2.5, 6, 6.5, 10, 12, and 40 GHz. Generally, the lower the channel number, the easier it is to transmit over long distances. A microwave link can transmit up to 50 miles if there are no obstructions. Microwaves need a clear line of sight from transmitter to receiver to work. This is why the antenna (either a dish or golden rods) is on a mast and the receiver is usually on a mountain top or the tallest building; it can then go from there to the station by a secondary microwave link or hard line (telephone lines). Because the microwave beam is very narrow, it is essential that the transmitting and receiving antennas be pointed precisely at each other. (See Figure 9.8.)

Figure 9.7 Satellite and microwave trucks (feeders) were a common sight on the street at the O.J. Simpson trial in California.

Figure 9.8 Microwave truck with mast extended.

When they are many miles apart, this is not an easy task. Experienced people at each end can accomplish this in a very short period of time, sometimes in seconds if the operators are very good.

While the truck-mounted microwaves are usually on channels 2 or 7, a portable system called a mini-mic uses channels 13, 18, and 40 GHz. This shoebox-size transmitter can be placed in a backpack for the camera operator to wear; it can also be mounted on a small tripod near the camera to take the place of what might be a hard or impossible cable-run back to the live truck. Because the range of this small transmitter is limited, a mini-mic is primarily used in sports coverage or to replace a cable where mobility is the critical factor (for example, from a high floor of a skyscraper). The receiver would be at the live van where the signal would be retransmitted to the station.

Satellites

The late 1980s saw a revolution in the cost and availability of satellite time. With so many satellites in orbit, almost anyone who had an uplink (a ground-to-satellite transmitter link) could buy time. (See Figure 9.9.) Because of such factors as CNN's 24-hour news channel, transmitting breaking stories live to the whole country became a must. While microwaves are limited to less than 50 miles and line of sight (although they can be relayed or hopped to greater distances), a portable satellite uplink mounted on a truck can go anywhere there is a road and sky. (See Figure 9.10.) Today, most stations in the top 100 markets have satellite trucks.

No one can forget the dramatic and historic pictures of CNN's Peter Arnett broadcasting live from

Figure 9.9 Satellite news gathering (SNG) trucks make it possible to feed live pictures, reports, or videotape from virtually anywhere to anywhere.

Baghdad during the Gulf War. (See Figure 9.11.) He was using an uplink system called a fly-away that is small enough to be folded down and shipped as airline baggage. Powered by batteries, a fly-away system can be used in any remote area without any utilities. The batteries can be recharged by solar devices if necessary. Live TV can literally be done from any spot on the face of the earth as soon as the crew arrives and sets up. Travel time is the only limit to getting it on the air.

COMMUNICATIONS

None of this would be possible without a top-rate communications package. This usually means a good two-way radio system or a cell phone or both. As mentioned earlier, it is critical that the transmitter and receiver of both microwave and satellite systems be pointed directly at each other. Being off by as

much as 1 degree can mean the difference in getting the signal or not. Microwave systems are one-way transmissions. When you are in the field, you cannot tell if you are lined up with the receiver; someone at the receiving point must tell you when you have it right. Microwave receivers are generally controlled remotely from the TV station by an ENG coordinator. He or she watches a digital readout of the incoming signal's strength, pans the receiver to get the strongest reading, then has the transmitter operator pan the truck's antenna until the strongest signal is found. The truck operator usually has a map with the receive site(s) on it and can aim the antenna fairly accurately with a compass or a good guess. The fine-tuning should be an easy process with good communication.

Satellite setups are much more technical but can be done without talking to anyone. Because a satellite also sends a return signal, it is possible for the operator to see the quality of the signal as it is returned and

Figure 9.10 This portable live transmitter (uplink) allows live ENG video to be sent from almost anywhere in the world to a network or news-service receiver (downlink). Courtesy CNN. All Rights Reserved.

tell how well in line the two are. The concern here is knowing which satellite, which channel, and what time to set up. Since people from all over the country may be trying to use the same satellite, there has to be a coordinator who tells each uplink what to do and when. Unlike a microwave system, this coordinator is usually at the headquarters of the satellite company, which may be on the other side of the country. Having a cell phone is sometimes the only answer, but having some type of phone is mandatory.

The receiver dish must be lined up with the satellite in use and tuned to the channel of video and audio; these are two separate systems within the transmission. The exact times of transmission must be confirmed. Satellite time can be bought on the spot or can be arranged in advance to ensure availability. Satellite time is purchased in multiples of 5 minutes and often cannot be extended. If you buy 5 minutes of time for 12:00:00 P.M., at 12:05:02 P.M. you are

off the air; the satellite owner pulls the plug. For ENG work, this means you either buy more time than you think you need, or have someone on the phone constantly with the satellite company to okay purchasing more time if it looks like the shot is going to run long. It is also possible that the next time block has already been sold and is unavailable to you. For major news events, a network may buy up all the time available and share the time with others, using a local coordinator at a single feed point. The coordinating network feeds their material first, and all others literally line up on a first-come, first-served basis to feed their material. Because of the time factors involved with satellites, most taped material is edited before sending, and live shots are locked in to specific times so local producers must slide everything else in their program to accommodate the satellite. This is one reason most satellite trucks have edit systems inside them.

The use of satellite trucks for EFP is generally much less hectic. These situations are usually planned well in advance, and the satellite time is booked with much spare time to work out any bugs or in case things run long.

INTERRUPTED FEEDBACK (IFB)

Interrupted feedback (IFB) is just as essential as the communications needed to set up the transmissions. The on-camera talent needs to be able to hear the cue that they are on the air.

Portable TV

The most primitive way of doing this in live news is to have a portable TV set tuned to your station; the talent can simply see when they are on the air. An earphone run from the TV set lets them hear the introduction and any questions that may follow. The camera operator usually has the same two-way radio used to set up the microwave signal with an earphone to listen for any instructions from the station. If the regular speaker in the TV is used when the reporter's mic is live, it may cause an audio feedback (a high-pitched screech) that would ruin the shot. (See Figure 9.12.) Using this type of IFB setup does not have the interrupt part of the system since the audio is right off the TV. Any instructions from the show director, producer, or assignment desk must be relayed to the reporter by the photographer listening to the two-way

Figure 9.11 Peter Arnett's coverage of the Gulf War from Baghdad, Iraq, was a riveting example of how important live TV coverage of a news event can be. Courtesy of CNN. All Rights Reserved.

radio. It is a good idea to be sure everyone understands the basic hand signals of TV production in case things need to be communicated while on air.

Mix-Minus

The more common form of IFB is a separate off-air audio feed called **mix-minus**. This feed is from the on-air audio board with the audio from the remote or live shot taken out or subtracted. The talent may be annoyed by their own voices coming back in their ears while they are talking. Because of the time delays involved in the signal transmission, particularly with a 2-second satellite delay, the talent hear their voices as strange echoes. A mix-minus feed is usually patched into a telephone line or a two-way radio. Some TV stations have a radio channel dedicated to

broadcasting nothing but off-air or program audio 24 hours a day. In this way, an IFB system is always in place. Other stations with multiple channels on their two-ways may simply give one channel over to IFB for the short time needed to do the shot and use it for other traffic the rest of the time. This mix-minus system allows the producer or other needed participants to interrupt the program audio and give special instructions, cues, a countdown to hit a sound bite, or whatever else is necessary, over the radio or phone IFB (hence the name interrupted feedback). Just like the dedicated radio channel for IFB, many stations have dedicated phone lines that when called automatically hook up to the mix-minus feed. In large markets, where there can be as many as six or seven different live shots back to back, the radio and phone systems can be quite complex.

Figure 9.12 Reporter and photographer doing a simple live shot on the street. IFB is transmitted to a small receiver worn by the reporter.

FORM AND STYLE

Essentially, live shots are just like stand-ups. They are generally short and done in a controlled manner. The biggest difference is that they occur at a very specific point in time and there can be no second take.

Live Spot News

In this age of instant information, the ability to go live from any major breaking story is essential. Common breaking stories that usually get live coverage include major fires, earthquakes, plane crashes, and shootings. Most stations have extensive plans for how to cover big stories such as these, but they all follow some basic rules. If more than one crew is being sent to the event, the first crew is responsible for shooting tape to document the event, and the second or next crew on the scene is there to set up for the live shot. If only one crew is available, it will quickly shoot enough tape to air about 1 minute of edited video, and then return to the van to set up the live shot. The pressure to do two things at the same time can be intense; the desire to cover the story has to be weighed against the need to get the story out first to beat the competition. This is one of the great moral dilemmas in TV journalism. The ultimate success or failure to balance these two concerns rides on the location of the live van at the scene. If the photographer can anticipate the situation on arrival and know whether any particular parking spot will allow for a signal to be set up, then the story can be shown live or taped from the same location. The ideal situation is to set up where you can see the event or disaster area and leave the camera on the tripod rolling tape while you set up the signal and run the cables. Even though this is a two-person job, most stations only staff a live truck with one photographer/engineer. Once hooked up, the camera feeds the event live to the studio where it can be recorded as well as taken live at the producer's call.

If the van is parked under power lines, or thick trees or a tall building is between it and the only receiver available, then the station could be at a serious disadvantage. In extreme cases, jobs could be lost over the failure to get a signal out. The greatest pressure in all of TV comes during setting up a live shot from a major spot news story. Without a clear battle plan as to how to pull it off, the story can turn into a nightmare. On the other hand, if you can get it set up in record time and get good pictures as well, then you will most certainly be a hero.

The other concern in the location of the van is proximity to the story. You need to ask yourself questions such as these:

- Can I safely raise the mast from this spot (any overhead power lines)?

- If I have only 300 feet of cable, can I get the camera to a good vantage point?
- Am I blocking a roadway or emergency vehicle route?
- Am I too close and likely to be caught in a dangerous situation (such as a brush fire) and have to move quickly?
- Are the authorities going to let me stay here?

The wrong answer to any of these questions can ruin your shoot or even cost you your life in the case of the power lines; always have a backup plan.

What the producer wants to see is the event or location itself. Sometimes this may mean being on a hilltop overlooking the site. At other times you may have to settle for just seeing the SWAT team suiting up, because the street is closed and access is denied. The main thing, as in tape coverage, is to see action. If you cannot show the actual story, show the next best thing. Most of the time, the live shot will be a subject in front of the camera. You should be able to zoom past the subject into anything happening in the background as the reporter talks about it. Be prepared to ride both the iris (try never to use auto-iris) and the focus. The lighting will probably be of little concern as long as the subject is visible. If the lighting is particularly bad, it may be necessary to place the subject in better lighting with a worse background and simply pan to the action.

The use of the tripod is generally determined by proximity to the action. If you are in the middle of things, it is probably best to hand-hold the camera. If you are at a distance, then you should use sticks. Hand-holding the camera can add to the drama of a live shot. The reporter can be talking to eyewitnesses or authorities; the freedom to move around can make the background interesting regardless of where the guest stands. Keep in mind that handheld shots look best at wider focal lengths. The biggest problem with moving is the cables. If you outdistance the cable, it can pull the camera off your shoulder. Make sure you know how much cable is available and if anyone is likely to be standing on it at any time. A good trick is to coil about 3 feet of cable at the camera end and tuck it in your back pocket or through your belt. Then if the cable gets stuck during a move, it will pull out of that safety coil and not yank on the back of the camera. The reporter should do the same with the mic cable. Doing spot news live is the ultimate in news coverage. Every bit of talent, experience, and training comes to bear in this situation.

Scheduled Events

Most live shots for news are done at events planned well in advance. Parades, city council meetings, and demonstrations are typical live situations. In fact, many organizers purposely schedule their events to coincide with the news time to get live coverage. In situations like these, there is usually sufficient time to set up in a more relaxed manner, or even site-survey the location well in advance for the best location. With more setup time it is possible to get just the shot you want. You may have to run extra cable or use a 13-GHz short hop back to the van, but you have the time to do it.

For these types of live situations, the basic rules for doing a simple stand-up apply. Find a location where there will be some action in the background, but not action that would interfere with what you are doing. The shot should convey the event easily and quickly to the viewer. Some identifiable aspect of the event should be present in the background.

Two aspects of these types of live shots need special consideration: graphics and guests. Most TV stations tend to add a lot of written information on the screen during a live shot. Not only is the bottom third of the picture taken up with the location, reporter's name, and station call letters or slogans, but the upper corners of the picture may be filled with words reminding the viewer that the picture is live. The photographer needs to be aware of where this information appears and when it is in the picture. You may spend much time lining up a background only to have it covered by a graphic. This can be particularly troublesome when the reporter has a guest. In a two-shot their heads tend to be at the two upper corners of the picture; if the "live" graphic is also there, it will cover one of the subjects' faces. Your shots must be designed around the graphics as well as the scene.

The best technique for taping guests during a live shot is to have them on camera only when they are introduced or talking. One way to set up such a shot is to block it before you go live by having the guest and reporter stand side by side at a comfortable distance. The reporter should already be in the best place for the background. The guest should then take one large step to the side away from the reporter and one step back away from the camera. The guest should maintain this position throughout the live shot. This allows the photographer to start the shot on a single shot of the reporter without being zoomed in too closely. As the reporter introduces the guest, the camera can widen out to reveal the guest; the reporter then turns on the foot closest to the guest and faces him or her. This puts the two in a more traditional position for an interview, so that the camera can zoom in to the guest as a single shot without the reporter and not have a one-eye or profile view of the guest. As the interview is wrapping up, the camera can zoom back out to a two-shot and the reporter can pivot back to face the camera. The camera can now zoom in to the reporter; the guest is free to leave.

Live for the Sake of Live

Many times in local news, photographers and reporters are asked to do live shots from places where nothing is going on. It may be an empty field, a house where a shooting happened the night before, or just a street corner. Many stations feel it is necessary to use the live technology just to show the viewer that they have it. Even though it serves no journalistic purpose, it can be seen as a good excuse to train for the more important times and to experiment with different styles and techniques. You should always be looking for ways to make live shots look like they are live. For live-for-the-sake-of-live situations this may not be easy. Try to include some action indicative of the time of day, such as a setting sun, rush-hour traffic, or maybe totally empty streets if it is for the late news.

The weather and sports segments are other examples of this type of live TV. With these two segments, it is possible to be more creative and possibly practice hand-holding the camera during live shots. The sports segment may come from a pregame warm-up where the sports anchor walks around among the players asking how their spirits are. The weather segment may be from a cultural fair where the weatherperson walks to a few booths to sample food before giving the weather. It may not be news, but it is a chance to hone some skills that can come in handy at another time.

ELECTRONIC FIELD PRODUCTION

More and more non-news productions are being done live. From the early days of teleconferencing to the expanding use of TV on the Internet, live television is becoming a common way to communicate. Stodgy studio teleconferences are giving way to individual managers doing their segments live from the

plant floor or inside a research lab. Viewers from all over the country could ask questions of the manager and key workers as they work. Live TV for corporate, business, and educational use has just begun. In the coming decade there is bound to be more of it. Already, video arraignments are taking place in courthouses so that prisoners do not have to leave jail to go downtown, and classes are being sent live to remote classrooms so that two campuses can be served by one teacher. These are just two examples of two-way interactive live TV. The possibilities are endless.

WHAT CAN GO WRONG?

At almost every step of the process of portable video production, problems can occur and cause delays resulting in missed shots, time wasted, and money lost. When something goes wrong on a live shot from the field, a newscast can become chaotic.

Know the System

Live TV has the most pressure of any form of this business. It is also the time when the most things usually go wrong: The station does not have your picture or audio; the talent cannot hear the cues; or the signal is full of breakup. The easiest way to deal with any of these problems is to know how the system works. If you work with a live truck (microwave or satellite), you must know the elements that make up the system and the order that they come in; you should be able to trace the signal from the camera to the antenna through every tiny part of the truck. If the receiver gets the color bars from the truck but not the picture from the camera, then you know the problem is not with the transmitter. You should have a checklist for the entire system within the van. The color bar generator/switcher, waveform monitor, tone generator/audio mixer, transmitter, power amp, and TV monitor are all clues to where any problem may be. If color bars are okay at the other end, and your waveform says that the video is correct, then any problem may be at the other end and not with you. The last resort is to bypass everything in the truck and put the video and audio directly into the transmitter. (Transmitters usually require line-level audio.) By eliminating possibilities, you can narrow any problem down to the piece of equipment or section of the truck.

Power in the Truck

All live trucks have a gas-powered generator to supply electricity to the video/audio racks and the transmitter. Larger generators can also provide enough power for lights as well; many are as strong as 20 amps for outside use (called **tech power**). A backup system, and sometimes the main system of power in small vans, is an inverter that runs off the truck's engine. This small device converts the DC power from the engine's alternator and turns it into AC power for use in the rack. Most large vans actually run all equipment off a battery system that is continually charged by the generator. In case of generator failure, this battery system can allow you to keep transmitting for a short period of time if the power load is kept to a minimum. Make sure you understand the power system in the truck and know what to do if any one element fails.

Lighting

If the live shot is indoors, the lighting will be similar to that used for most stand-ups. Time, of course, will be a factor in how fancy you will be able to get and how many lights you can set up. One consideration in doing live shots is matching the studio style of lighting. While in some cases you might do a stand-up in available light to make it fit with the rest of the story, a live shot should match more to the studio than to the story it may be introducing. That means a high-key flat style with little shadow or modeling detail. You must also take into account any guests that may be interviewed and the light level of the background. It would look silly to have the reporter brightly lit and the background almost black by comparison, although that is often the case when only one light is used. (See Figure 9.13.) Try always to set the light up on a stand and not on top of the camera, unless the camera must be panned beyond the range of the stand light.

Outdoor live shots may look easy when being set up, but the sun can move to the wrong place in the sky, such as directly behind the talent or below the horizon. You must always be conscious of what time of day the live shot will go, unless it is spot news. It may be daylight when you are setting up for the high-tide story, but at 5:30 P.M. when the live shot hap-

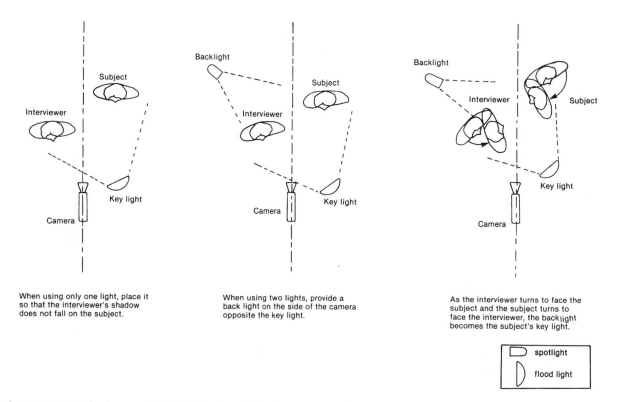

When using only one light, place it so that the interviewer's shadow does not fall on the subject.

When using two lights, provide a back light on the side of the camera opposite the key light.

As the interviewer turns to face the subject and the subject turns to face the interviewer, the backlight becomes the subject's key light.

spotlight

flood light

Figure 9.13 Light placement for a live interview with shadows.

pens, it may be pitch dark because it is no longer Daylight Savings Time. If you have not set up some powerful background lights to show the surf, the live shot location could come off looking like the parking lot at the station. Live shots should always have backgrounds, and at night this can be very difficult. You cannot light up the great outdoors. A good 1000-watt focusing spotlight can be used to punch up a detail in the background just enough to be visible over the talent's shoulder. Most of the time you would want to light the talent at a level where the camera's lens would be wide open to get the most exposure from the background. This would give the biggest advantage for getting something in the background to show up at night. Keep in mind the power limits of your generator if you do not have a reliable source of electricity. It is possible to blow an overloaded circuit anywhere. If you use battery lights, make sure they are not going to go dead in the middle of your shot.

Cables

The minimum cable to do a live shot is one video and one audio line. Many photographers keep a 100-foot bundle of twin-lead, or **Siamese** (an audio and video line in one cable), to use whenever they're in a very big hurry. They can simply throw it out on the ground, hook up the camera and mic, and be ready to go. More complex shots would make use of the multi-line cable that contains two video lines and four audio lines. This heavy cable, usually stored on a power reel, makes use of the full capabilities in the van. One video line is for the camera signal to the truck, another for an off-air TV signal from the truck's antenna to be used for the talent's monitor. One audio line is for the talent's mic to the truck, two lines are for IFB to the talent and camera operator being fed from the van, and one spare audio line can be used for a separate guest mic. A good live van should be able to send any audio down the cable from inside the van, including the two-way radio. Always make sure you have a backup cable in case any one of the primary cables fails. It is better to go live from next to the truck than not to go live at all because of a broken cable.

Batteries

Everything needed to go live should be able to be powered by battery. The rack and transmitter should function off the tech battery in the van for at least an hour without recharge in case the generator fails. The camera will most likely be powered by battery unless the shot is required for a very long time and AC is available. It can be very embarrassing if your battery fails while you are on the air. Always change to a fresh, fully charged battery several minutes before the

Figure 9.14 Even in a simple setup like this one, a live truck operator must know how all of the equipment works.

live shot. The off-air TV monitor should also be battery powered, and a battery-powered light should be available in case the power fails for any AC lights you may be using.

Live TV is the perfect case for knowing the condition and performance level of each of your batteries. A misjudgment here could cost the station dramatic coverage of a big story. Always have a backup battery handy. Some companies make a battery belt that uses two camera batteries in series, allowing one to be taken off the belt and replaced with a fresh one while not disrupting power to the camera. This type of battery system would be a good investment for any live van.

Crowds

Nothing can ruin a live shot faster than the talent being swallowed up by an overly anxious crowd of onlookers. Not only is this bad TV, but it can be dangerous as well. A live shot from an area of large crowds of young people can quickly get out of control. It is not unusual for such a group to turn violent, assaulting the reporter and crew. The type of people and the size of the crowd must be taken into consideration when setting up the shot. A nice quiet plaza at 3:00 P.M. might seem like a good place to do a simple live shot, except that at 5:00 P.M. the plaza is jammed with workers heading home. You may want that look, but sometimes you do not; it can get dangerous without some form of crowd control.

Many stations like to assign St. Patrick's Day live shots from inside bars. The most dangerous crowds are the crowds that are drunk. Do not let the station's desire for flashy live graphics push you into a situation that can cost you a camera or an injury. If the crowd cannot be controlled to your liking, then find a situation that will protect you. At times this may mean doing the live shot from the roof of the van or from behind a homemade barricade. Look at the traffic patterns of the area you are setting up in. Don't try to do a live shot from the busiest hallway in the building. Leave room for people to walk around you and stand and watch from behind you, the photographer, and not behind the reporter. Nothing looks worse than some idiot making faces behind the talent who is talking about what a horrible tragedy has taken place. Sometimes it may be necessary to tape off an area with duct tape to keep people out (some people will walk right between you and the reporter as if you're not there). If the situation is really bad, like a spring break story, if may even be necessary to have the police there to protect you.

Permission

Another nightmare that is quite common is to set up for a live shot and then find out the owner of the property is demanding you get out. This can happen at any time you are not on public property if you have not secured permission beforehand. In spot news, the situation is usually too chaotic for anyone to care, but if the shot does not come until after things have settled down, you may be in for a fight with an upset property owner. Police can do the same thing to you. You may set up in an area open to the press only to find that same area closed just before you are to go live. Pleading with them to give you just a few more minutes sometimes works, but you should not rely on this technique to come through. Be prepared to move and have an alternative site picked out.

Timing

We cannot emphasize enough the fact that you have no control over when your shot will be taken live. Whether it is the satellite time that has been booked or the producer's sense of flow within the show, it is someone else who will say, "You're hot." If you were hoping for a certain background, it may disappear just as the director comes to you. Unless you have total control of the picture's contents, you must live with the fact that things change. The only way to cover yourself is to be flexible. Never totally rely on any one thing to be there. It can be as simple as a fire truck pulling in behind the reporter and blocking the view of the fire, or as annoying as all of the people leaving the room 30 seconds before you go live. The only safe approach to live TV is to assume everything will go wrong because it usually does. If you consider all the factors mentioned, plan for the contingencies, and always stay two steps ahead of yourself, you should be able to surmount any obstacle to doing live TV.

10 Electronic Field Production Style

EFP style encompasses many different types and applications of portable video. An easy definition of EFP is simply professional portable video *not* for broadcast journalism or ENG. While this definition tells us what it is not, it does not give us a sense of what EFP is, or of what style is necessary to produce good-quality EFP work. A better approach to understanding EFP style is to look at the various applications of portable video, the conditions under which productions are made, and the audience for whom the video work is intended.

Unlike ENG, where the audience is the general broadcast viewer, EFP often has a very specific audience. ENG concerns an event that is about to or has already occurred; EFP has a very specific purpose, such as a commercial or public service announcement, the promotion of a new product line, or training about a new procedure.

In EFP, the key is planning. Careful preproduction and scripting help ensure that the final product is purposeful, effective, and affordable. In a corporate setting, the choice of EFP depends on whether it is the best way to get a message across; that is, whether it is cheaper or better than other methods such as face-to-face communication. There is a sequence of planning in any EFP project that closely follows the sequence of events in writing a script. When a decision is made to embark on a video project, the first questions that must be asked are "What do we hope to achieve by this project?" and "What are the objectives?"

In corporate work, the objective most often is to inform the audience of something, such as a new or old product, a new benefit to employees, a reiteration of an existing policy, or an introduction of a new corporate executive.

Another very common objective is to help create an attitude or stimulate motivation. A motivational tape may be created to inspire salespeople to promote and sell a new line of cosmetics or a new attachment to farm tractors. The project may include sales techniques, product information, or a demonstration of how the product is used. The goal for this type of project is to inform, create, or change an attitude and evoke a certain type of behavior. Corporate video is aimed at a *specific audience* to achieve a *specific purpose*. Rarely is it produced just for entertainment purposes.

Performance video, music video, nature and documentary video, and video art are generally produced for entertainment purposes. These styles are often carefully preproduced and scripted, but do not always have very specific objectives beyond entertainment; the audience targeted is often more general. Outlets for exhibition are also more general; this type of video may be shown on broadcast, satellite, or cable TV, in classrooms, theaters, festivals, or contests. In addition, the video may be part of a multimedia presentation or even be part of an Internet site. The audience often selects itself. The showing of the video is publicized in broadcast TV listings in the newspaper, in a flyer about a festival, or even in a class syllabus. The audience decides if it wants to view it.

This chapter covers seven common categories of EFP style: (1) corporate and professional videos, (2) public service announcements and commercials,

(3) performance videos, (4) sports videos, (5) music videos, (6) nature and documentary videos, and (7) video art. In addition, video for multimedia and video for use on the Internet will also be discussed.

CORPORATE AND PROFESSIONAL VIDEOS

The term *corporate video* has become a popular catch-all term for a number of types of EFP video. This category can include almost all professional nonbroadcast users of portable video whose purposes are not entertainment. Some users of this EFP style are not necessarily members of corporations; in fact, many are not. Educational institutions, governmental agencies, labor unions, professional associations, clubs, and civic organizations are common users of this type of video production.

Numerous types of video fit into the category of corporate video; the most common are news, information, and public relations videos. Especially popular in large and/or decentralized organizations where face-to-face contact among members is difficult or unusual, these videos are used as a means of disseminating information efficiently and maintaining cohesiveness among members. Another consideration here is the availability of information in-house to corporations whose employees' computers are tied together with a local-area network (LAN). These corporations are making web-type pages available in-house with information that is to be seen by employees only. These web pages now have the capability to show video as well as audio and other graphic material. This is similar to the Internet, except that these pages are not available to people outside the organization. The term for this in-house multimedia use of video is **intranet**.

Corporate News Show

Corporate video often takes the form of a company news show. The show consists of several common elements: messages from or profiles of top management; company-wide news such as recent achievements in sales, profits, safety, or growth; branch or regional news; and employee news. Although this communication is called news, it almost never includes hard news (for example, auto wrecks, burglary, or fires) and is never investigative in an adver-

sarial way. This type of video is pure internal public relations. It is a way of making a large organization seem more personal and familiar. (See Figure 10.1.)

The host or reporter on an internal company news show conducts on-location interviews, reads news copy over video, or gives lead-ins to packages of stories about the company and its employees. The shooting style is more like a magazine show (with features) than a news show. There is no sense of urgency, and the videographer can usually control what is happening in front of the camera.

Most of the rules mentioned for shooting general news and reporter stand-ups in previous chapters apply to this EFP style. The goal is to make the organization seem friendly and personal. Your style should reflect this goal. You may use wide shots to quickly establish your location, but close-up shots help convey a friendly mood.

Instruction, Training, and Demonstration

This general category includes instructional video production in classrooms designed to be viewed by persons other than those physically present in the classroom. This can mean a taped lecture for absent students, or a taped production of an entire course for students viewing the videotape rather than attending live lectures. It also may mean **distance learning,** where TV is used for live, real-time interaction between two classrooms separated by distance. In corporate and other professional settings, training tapes have become so common that they are an expected part of employee orientation and training. Using video for training purposes is the single most common use of portable video in the corporate world. If properly produced, a good training video can save many hours of boring repetition by an instructor. It can also provide location shots and event shots that could not otherwise be viewed by the audience.

While instructional video for distant learning may not have a verbatim script, it most often has a very carefully prepared outline for the instructor to follow, with graphic material specially prepared in a form conducive to good video. For example, graphic material should conform to analog TV's 4:3 aspect ratio or the 16:9 digital TV aspect ratio.

Instructional corporate video is used to convey very specific information to the intended audience. Its

Figure 10.1 Three shots from a corporate-style news show created by the Florida Department of Law Enforcement. It shows employees working together toward common goals and gives information about the activities of the department.

goal is to have the audience learn something specific, such as a procedure, a task, or a safety rule. (See Figure 10.2.) This requires a very accurate and organized script and storyboard. Two shooting rules are standard:

1. Each shot must be clear, accurate, and supported by explanatory audio when appropriate.
2. Close-up shots are critical for demonstrating procedures and showing small equipment or controls on larger equipment.

Extreme close-ups may be necessary. When shooting XCUs, make sure they are rehearsed. Because XCUs require high magnification, slight movement by either the camera or the subject may give your shot an amateurish look. Also, shots at high magnification often have a shallow depth of field. Small movement of the object can cause a loss of focus. During a rehearsal of a shot, mark off the area that defines your sharp focus area, keep the camera still and the object in the focus area. Hand-holding of small objects for XCU shots is not recommended.

Teleconferencing

A significant growth area for corporate video or non-broadcast video is teleconferencing. Although teleconferencing refers more to a method of distribution than a style of shooting, it became an enormous part of corporate and nonbroadcast TV in the 1990s. There are numerous reasons for this, but the most important are that teleconferencing can save much money by eliminating travel costs and that the technology needed is available at a reasonable cost. Executives of a given national organization in Boston and San Francisco can meet face to face through two-way TV, utilizing a satellite-distributed teleconference. A small university campus can reach out to employees of an engineering firm off campus with a graduate course in engineering through microwave distribution and audio call-in. Another university can distribute courses to its branch campus by using a two-way microwave TV system. (See Figure 10.3.) Students at both locations can ask the professor questions and get immediate answers.

The style of this type of video is a hybrid of studio and portable video. Most teleconferences occur in a room or location specially adapted for the purpose or in some type of TV studio. Teleconferences can be

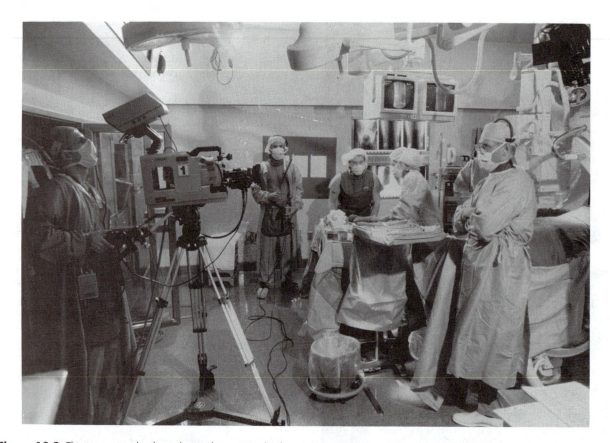

Figure 10.2 This instructional video is being shot in a medical operating room. The surgeon who will be performing the surgery gives an introduction about the procedure about to be performed. Courtesy Arizona Heart Institute.

shot in various formats that can include elements of a news show, demonstration, motivational video, panel discussion, and lecture.

Sales, Promotion, and Motivation

Public relations videos are shot with the intention of delivering information, but the desired effects are also behavioral and attitudinal. Corporations shoot these videos because they want their salespeople to know about the products and services that they must sell and also want to instill in them the positive attitude and energy necessary to get the sales job done. Sales, promotion, and motivational videos are characterized by high energy and dynamism. Enthusiasm is the key word.

As with the demonstration video, these videos require tight scripting to allow for the control necessary to keep the tempo of the video upbeat. Camera shots are dynamic, showing much movement. Sound tracks are crisp and lively; the music is upbeat. Lighting is usually bright, with strong direction and modeling

(not flat). Often, strong backlighting is used to separate the subject or the product from the background. Colors are often bright.

If editing is noticeable at all, it usually consists of quick cuts rather than slow dissolves to enhance the dynamic energy. Special effects are often employed to enhance the feeling that the product, service, or concept has special merit. These effects can be as simple as a star effect from a star filter on a camera lens, or a computer-generated special effect or animation costing thousands of dollars.

COMMERCIALS AND PUBLIC SERVICE ANNOUNCEMENTS

Commercials and public service announcements (PSAs) for broadcast and cable TV probably include every conceivable style of shooting. Styles vary by market size—usually in relation to the budget, which is directly related to market size and type of product

Figure 10.3 An instructional TV system connects a university with its branch campus and satellite locations that are located far away from the main campus. (A) A professor appears to viewers with a medium shot. (B) Students are in studio/classroom and see the professor and a large monitor that displays information from the pad cam or video that is shown from the control room. (C) Operators in the control room have cameras views that show the professor, students in the originating classroom, and the distant classrooms. (D) The faculty member has a view of a monitor that shows all of the classrooms that are connected for the class. The students at the remote locations can be seen and can ask questions in real time.

or issue to be discussed. Most videographers who shoot these short-format projects do so on a local level (for example, a local car dealership or the local United Way campaign).

Commercials

In broadcasting, all TV stations except those with educational or public television affiliations rely on commercials to pay for their operating costs. All non-premium cable programming services such as ESPN, CNN, or MTV also rely on paid commercials to keep them profitable. This presents an enormous opportunity for aspiring videographers to practice their skills. On the local level, tens of thousands of commercials are produced for airing.

Formats

Just about every style of video has probably been tried in a commercial. There are, however, a number of standard formats that have been used over the past 50 years that encompass most of the TV commercials produced.

Announcement   In the days before computer graphics and affordable yet powerful character generators, this commercial was of two general types: an announcer doing a stand-up with the product or in front of the store, and a series of still photos, shot on slides and fed through a telecine. New technology has made this type of commercial more sophisticated by allowing the addition of more complicated and sophisticated manipulation of video images.

Demonstration The introduction of a new product often requires that the use of the product be shown to the audience. Close-up work is common when the product is small or a very close look is needed by the audience. A new safety feature on the dashboard of a new model car or a new stamp issued by the post office requires close-up shots. If the shot looks best at a very short object-to-camera distance, the shot may need to be done with the lens in the macro mode. This type of shot also requires special lighting. As the camera lens gets very close to the object, the object size grows, but the lens and camera often block some or all of the light needed for proper exposure. Light aimed at 45-degree angles, similar to those on a copy stand, will illuminate the object without causing harsh shadows.

Testimonial This type of commercial is often done in a local grocery store, car dealership, or restaurant. Customers (nonperformers) are interviewed at the location and are asked questions that are intended to yield complimentary responses. Often several of these favorable sound bites are edited together to create the main body of the commercial.

Celebrity Spokesperson Famous people are often paid to go to a new store, attend an event like the county fair, or promote a product or service. The face and voice of the person help the commercial get the desired audience attention. Obviously, medium and close-up shots of the celebrity are needed to make sure that the audience recognizes the person. High-quality audio in the field is needed for this type of performer, because the audience knows the sound of the famous person's voice.

Dialogue This commercial is often shot on location in familiar settings like an ordinary kitchen. Two people might be discussing the pros and cons of an upcoming referendum. An establishing shot of the location is held long enough to show where the discussion is taking place. The technique often includes several over-the-shoulder shots that show the person speaking from over the shoulder of the other person. A child in a conversation with her mother would show shots from the perspective of the listener; a low angle shot when the mother speaks, a high angle down on the child when the child speaks.

Dramatization Often similar to a dialogue, this commercial is often told as a brief story. This is often shown in natural settings and therefore shot on loca-

tion. This could take the familiar before-and-after form—before using the product and after using the product. Humor or exaggeration is common with this format.

Institutional This format is often semi-documentary in form. It may show what a major oil company is doing to clean up the environment while producing a better grade of gasoline. This format is most often used by large corporations to promote good will toward the corporation.

Shooting Styles

Stand-up Presentation This format is an attempt at interpersonal communication by an announcer; actually, it is usually a simple and direct sales talk. The performer is shot straight on, with direct eye contact with the audience. This can be shot anywhere and is often done in an auto sales lot or grocery store. (See Figure 10.4.)

Hidden-Camera Testimonials This format is the typical "yes, this coffee does taste great" spot where real people are the stars of the commercial. The camera may not be visible to the real people, thus yielding a more natural response.

Music Orientation Often a musical piece is composed to sell a product and becomes almost more important than any other selling points. The visuals serve to accentuate the music. Producers of these shots hope that the music becomes closely linked to the product. This is especially helpful if the video spots are used in combination with radio spots.

Visual Orientation Commercials are sometimes produced with very little, if any, emphasis placed on the audio. In this case, the audio merely supplements the video; the message is almost completely visual. National spots for autos often show the auto on the road and keep the factual information minimal.

Comparative Demonstration This style often requires quite a bit of pre- and postproduction. In a very short time frame, the producer tries to show how a product is used or compares two products' performance and cost. A typical example would be the grease-cutting ability of two dishwashing liquids. Props such as glass kitchen sinks are needed to show how the product works. Another popular version has a split screen with shots of the two products, for example, Ford versus Chevy trucks. The screens show

Figure 10.4 These stills are from typical stand-up presentation commercials. Note the direct eye contact with the camera that enhances interpersonal communication. Courtesy John Wade.

superimposed facts about price, horsepower, load capacity, or other simple, numerically oriented comparisons over the shots of the trucks. The shots of the products are usually identical, but subtle lighting or other differences might be used to enhance the sponsor's product.

Animation   Animation is used to create a visual not possible in reality, or to draw attention to the product. Toy and cereal manufacturers have long believed that animation attracts and holds children's attention better than many real announcers. Obviously, this is a time-consuming and expensive approach rarely used locally. The advances in personal computers and software designed for computer graphics and animation may change this in the near future.

In addition to the above general categories, numerous combinations of formats and exotic variations of these are used. A celebrity spokesperson may by joined by an animated spokesperson for a theme park. A slice-of-life commercial may include a family trying two different products for comparison. A stand-up presenter may introduce a strongly visually oriented spot.

All the above approaches can be and often are accomplished in the field. Before high-quality, competitively priced ENG/EFP cameras were generally available, on-location local commercials for TV were usually shot on 16mm movie film or 35mm slide film. Low-budget commercials were shot on slides. Some slides (usually two to eight) from the shoot were loaded into the slide chain (telecine) at the studio and a sound track was added. Many commercials and PSAs are still done in this way, although the slides are often replaced with static video shots of the business doing the advertising.

It is easy to do better than that. Avoid static shots. Without overusing the zoom, add some dynamics to your shots with camera movement. If you have an on-camera announcer or subject, add interest to the shot by placing the subject in an unusual spot; for example, in a car lifted high above the ground with a crane, start on a close-up shot, then zoom out to reveal the exact location. If you add music, try to make some of your edits coincide with the beat of the music to draw your viewers into the message.

When doing a commercial or PSA, keep your time frame in mind. You will probably have only 30 seconds to convey your idea and the needed information. This calls for careful scripting and storyboarding. Commercials and PSAs offer excellent ways of sharpening your creative skills, both with the camera and in scriptwriting. Do not settle for the ordinary; use these short-format projects as a challenge to your ability to interest audiences and tell complete stories in a short time frame.

Public Service Announcements

Public service announcements (PSAs) are short (usually 30- to 60-second) announcements created and broadcast or cablecast for the benefit of the viewing audience. The sponsor is often a local nonprofit agency, such as the library, humane society, or police department. Many PSA campaigns are produced for nationwide broadcast by national groups, such as the Advertising Council, American Dental Association, American Cancer Society, religious organizations, and the U.S. government. The national campaigns often discuss themes of national concern, such as drug abuse, literacy, environmental safety, and health issues. Usually well financed and shot on film, these campaigns are distributed on videotape to broadcast and cable outlets throughout the country.

On a local level, state agencies and nonprofit institutions often attempt to create and produce a campaign with donated help and small budgets. This need often provides students and beginning professionals an opportunity to produce creative work aired (sometimes repeatedly) on local or regional stations or cable systems.

Budgets

Budgets for PSAs and commercials are usually quite small, limiting your alternatives for creativity and experimentation to those you do not have to buy. Forget about renting the helicopter for your aerial shot, but offer to trade-out with the local emergency health helicopter service—offer to shoot a public service spot or commercial for them in exchange for a free ride. If this does not work, try to get your bird's-eye view from the roof of the tallest adjacent building. Sometimes a wide-angle shot from above gives the desired aerial shot effect. Conveying the notion of acres of gleaming new and used autos may be easier from 100 feet than from a helicopter at 300 feet.

Instead of flashy digital effects, low budget retail commercials may force you to inject excitement and action with unusual camera angles and some dynamic editing. The point here is that network style and quality commercials require network-sized budgets. Ninety percent of video commercials are *low budget*; this is most likely what you will have to face, especially if you are a beginner. There is hope, however, for the aspiring producer. Computer programs that can manipulate video for special effects and editing are becoming more common and more affordable. These programs allow the low-budget producer to perform three-dimensional effects like rotation or image-to-image changes like morphing (for example, a smooth transition from one shape to another, such as an old, boxy-looking car becoming a sleek race car). The nonlinear editors allow an editor to make several versions of a commercial or PSA in less time than it takes a linear editor to complete one version.

PERFORMANCE VIDEOS

Two major types of performance video utilize EFP. The first is performance video for entertainment purposes done on location by one or more EFP cameras for later presentation to an audience. The other major type of performance video is shot for historical purposes; an event is captured on video and archived for future reference.

Entertainment

Many types of performances simply cannot be brought to the TV studio and still retain the mood or energy intended by the performers, directors, or choreographers. Part of the reason for this is that the TV studio is rarely large enough to permit an audience. Many performers accustomed to having an audience present strongly prefer having the audience there for feedback and energy. Also, TV studios can rarely duplicate the space or specific lighting, floor, or sound characteristics of a theatrical stage or auditorium. Because of these limitations, many performers have been captured on videotape in EFP style. If a good postproduction facility is available, a simple multiple-camera EFP shoot can yield a high-quality performance video suitable for broadcasting or showing to an in-house audience.

Switchable Camera Field Shoot. Two methods are used in practice for shooting on-location performance videos: (1) the switchable camera field shoot and (2) the isolated camera field shoot. The switchable camera field shoot uses multiple cameras with a field switcher that selects one camera to be the "taking" or on-line camera. (See Figure 10.5.) This system mimics the TV studio where a director makes real-time switching decisions to select which camera will supply the program video for any given shot. This system is convenient if the director is very familiar with the script of the performance and the look that the performance should have as a finished video product.

This configuration of equipment commonly has three cameras tied to one switcher and a videotape recorder connected to the program or outgoing line from the switcher. Because only one recording is made, the director decides on the spot which camera will be on line. If the wrong decision is made, or if the technical director pushes the wrong button, the videotape usually contains the bad decision or error with virtually no way of fixing it.

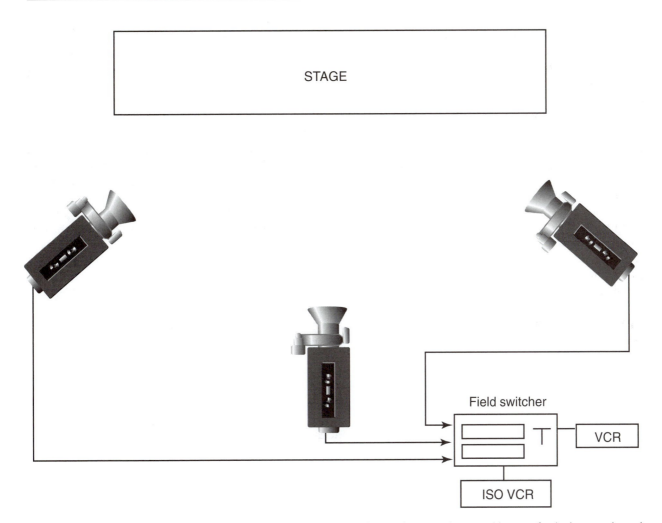

Figure 10.5 Three-camera remote shoot for a performance video. Switching is done in real time, yielding one finished tape at the end of the performance. An isolated VCR may also be used for close-up shots taken by one of the cameras.

Two ways exist to avoid the problem of having to live with your mistakes on a live-to-tape multiple-camera switched recording. The easiest is to have one wild camera not hooked to the switcher that shoots cutaway shots during the show, such as audience reactions, extreme wide shots, extreme tight shots, or any shot that could be considered nonsynchronous. Later these can be inserted to cover any mistakes made by the director, technical director (TD), or subject on the master recording with a minimum of editing time and without a jump cut or loss of continuity.

The second way is to have one of the switched cameras on an isolated line to its own VCR. Most switchers are capable of feeding an isolated (ISO) line from any of the cameras coming into the switcher. If the switcher cannot do this, then a separate deck can

be hooked up to one of the cameras. This can be a small price to pay and a minor hassle to ensure that the finished product meets the highest standards and does not look amateurish. The ISO camera is generally either the least used camera, the most stable camera of the group, or the one that gives a good wide shot. Very few big-time experienced directors would work without a safety net (that is, an ISO camera) unless the production is going to be aired live.

Whenever two or more cameras are brought together in the manner described above, they must be timed to avoid a glitch when the picture is cut from one of them to another. This method of timing is called **gen-lock**; there are two methods of doing this. Most professional multiple-camera setups make use of a special camera cable connection on the back of the camera called a triax adapter that allows most camera functions to be done at a remote location wherever the cables come together—generally near the switcher. A video control person can **shade** the cameras (control the iris and manipulate the color so that each camera looks as good as the other) as well as time them to each other. In lower budget productions, only a **coax** cable that attaches to the BNC connector on the side or back of the camera is used. Each camera must be matched manually before the shooting starts. To time them, a second coax cable must be run to each camera. This cable is attached to the genlock port on the camera and comes from the switcher, which is feeding a reference signal to each of the cameras that allows the cameras to synchronize their video scan rates. Without this timing function, nothing in a multiple-camera setup will work properly.

Isolated Camera Field Shoot. The alternative method for a multiple-camera shoot uses the same number of cameras, usually three, but they are not tied to a switcher. Instead, each has its own independent videotape recorder. The director's job using this method is more one of guidance, rather than final decision making, until the postproduction stage. This is because the director does not have a camera monitor for each camera. The director suggests certain shots to each camera operator, such as "Camera 1, look for Mr. X to enter from stage left, and make sure you get a CU of his face as he sees Ms. Y." If camera 1 misses the shot, the other two cameras may get it.

This method relies very strongly on postproduction. After the shoot, there are three complete versions of the performance, one from each camera. One version is commonly a master shot from the center camera; the other two versions are from the side cameras situated somewhat closer to the stage. (See Figure 10.6.)

Any time two cameras are being used to shoot one scene or event that will be edited on a high-

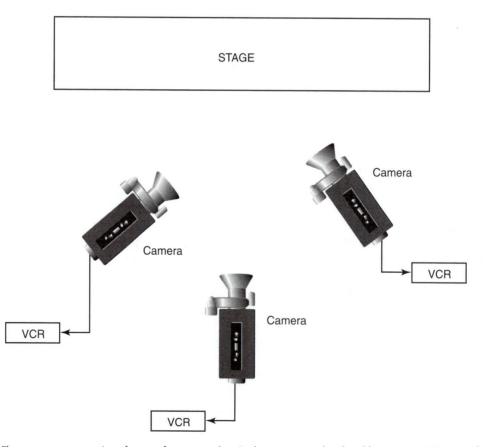

Figure 10.6 Three-camera remote shoot for a performance video. Each camera is isolated and has its own VCR. Tapes from each camera will be mixed in postproduction to yield a finished product.

quality edit system, the cameras must be gen-locked. On a two-camera interview, even without a switcher (each camera has its own deck), a gen-lock cable should be run between the cameras. One simple coax cable from the video out of one camera to the gen-lock port of the other will lock the two cameras together. Any number of cameras can be hooked together in series this way. This allows an edit machine to synchronize the two tapes in the edit process. Without it, even with common time code, the two tapes could be several frames off over the course of a 30-minute interview. (See Figure 10.7.)

The postproduction process consists of combining the three versions to get one high-quality version. The job is much easier if the three tapes have time-code information to provide a permanent address for each frame of the video. This makes synchronization much easier. In editing systems with three machines (two sources and a recorder to allow A/B roll editing where two sources of video permit transitions like dissolves and wipes rather than just cuts only), two versions (usually the center shot and one side shot) are synchronized on some action near the very beginning of the tape. Both tapes are then started. A switcher selects one of the two to feed the record machine at all times. The result is a mix of the center shot and one side shot.

This first tape is referred to as a two-**camera submaster**. The camera submaster is then used as a source tape with the third-camera tape. These two tapes are synchronized and fed to the record machine. The editor switches between the two sources to yield a final tape. This tape should be a final mixture of the three camera views.

The major advantage of this method is that you can try many different combinations before you decide on the final version. One major disadvantage is that many extra hours (and possibly dollars) are spent in postproduction. Another disadvantage is that parts of the final version of the tape may be

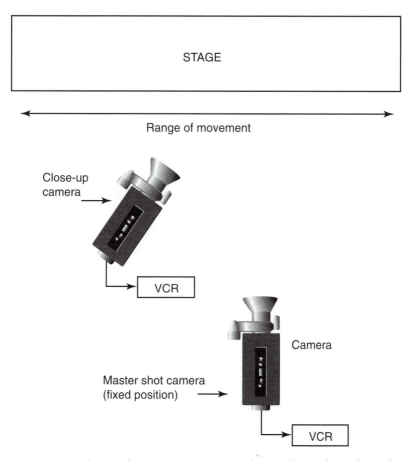

STAGE

Range of movement

Close-up camera

VCR

Camera

Master shot camera (fixed position)

VCR

Figure 10.7 Two-camera remote shoot for a performance video. Tapes can be mixed, or each may be used unedited.

third-generation video, technically of lower quality than first or second generation. This problem is avoided when digital videotape is used.

The easiest way to synchronize the tapes of a multiple-camera shoot is by using time code (providing the cameras are gen-locked). The method of doing this is called a **jam sync**. Any deck present, or a separate time-code generator, can be used as the master. A coax cable from the master's time-code OUT port can be run to the time code IN port of any deck. Just like gen-sync, this process can be done in series so that a separate cable does not have to run from the master to every single machine, but each machine needs to be connected to another. The time-code master machine can be set to internal time code, and all slaved machines need to be set to external time code on their control switches. Whatever the time code is set at on the master, each slave machine will record. If another deck is used as the master and the time code is in the record run position, it must be recording before it will send time code to the slave machines. This setup can make it easy to put a multiple-camera show together in the edit room.

Historical Archive

One of the most sensible and efficient uses of video is the historical archive. Unique events, such as celebrations, special performances, and groundbreaking ceremonies, are good reasons to use the inexpensive historical document that can be provided by good-quality videotape shot on location. The archive video is not the same as a performance-quality or entertainment video intended for later broadcast. It is a low-budget record of an occurrence worth keeping for future reference.

Choreographers and Directors. For the dance choreographer, archive video provides a representation of a creation as interpreted by the choreographer at a certain point in time and by the dancers available at that time. Video captures the movement and the staging for the choreographer to use during a later interpretation or reconstruction. (See Figure 10.8.)

In the same way, the theater director can obtain a record of a particular performance by the cast at a particular time, using the archive video. It creates a point of reference that a written script, review, or summary could never provide. The director can obtain a 1/2-inch videocassette copy and show it just about anywhere on a home video deck.

Figure 10.8 An archive video was shot for the choreographer of this dance to provide a record of how the space on stage was utilized and how the dancers performed.

Event Dictates Style. The style of the archive video is dictated by the event being recorded and the desires of the choreographer, director, or interested group that will use the tape. Choreographers and directors often want to have the entire stage visible to show not just the performers, but also the relationship between the performers and the space in which they are performing. This requires that the videographer avoid the temptation of zooming in on the action and framing it tightly. For both choreographers and directors, the expression of the performer on stage is not the only important aspect of the performance.

In dance, body positioning and articulation of the extremities should be included in all shots. Since dancers often move quickly, they can dance entirely out of the frame if the shot is too tight. Even cutting off the toes or hands in a shot of a dancer can lose what the choreographer needs to see. Directors often want to see entrances of characters while others are on stage. This also calls for a wide shot.

These types of requirements translate into a simple, static one-camera style. Use your tripod and set the camera on a wide master shot of the stage. Make sure that your shot is not so wide that it allows any stage lights to shine directly into your lens. If you are able to use two cameras, use the first camera for a master shot and the second for following action and close-ups of the main performers. You may want to edit these together into your final tape or simply provide two tapes.

This type of video may seem boring to you, or it may seem like unimaginative shooting. But keep in mind that the archive is *not* a commercial program to be viewed on broadcast TV; rather it is a tool used by professionals and scholars to preserve an historically significant event or creative endeavor.

SPORTS VIDEO

One of the reasons that sports are so popular is that they represent one of the few real live dramas available on television. Keep this in mind when you are planning to shoot any kind of sports coverage. As with any kind of video, make sure that you realize that sports coverage requires a story to be told. Because sports contests can be dramatic, remember the elements of known characters (well-known sports names), conflict (a history of hard fought battles between two teams), and suspense (the best games are those where the outcome is uncertain). These elements pull the audience into your video story; in this case, it is a game story. This requires some background work, such as a recounting of the events of the last meeting between the two teams or two competitors. One of the best examples of this kind of dramatic buildup can be seen on a pregame show for the National Football League. Often you will see highlights from a previous game (footage usually supplied by NFL Films), interviews with the coaches, the players, or even highly partisan fans. This pregame information helps orient the viewer to the drama of the game.

The two main types of sports EFP work are competition and features. Sports features are generally shot for use in pregame or highlight shows. EFP coverage of actual sports competition has two main purposes:

1. Live coverage of the event for broadcast or cablecast
2. Coverage for replay at a later time, usually in a highlights show.

Live coverage of a sports event is a complex, expensive undertaking that requires numerous cameras; a truck or van with camera control, videotape, switching, and other technical equipment; miles of camera cable; and a group of hardworking professionals. (See Figures 10.9 and 10.10.) Each sport has a particular sequence of shots compiled from the various cameras to give the viewer a comprehensive and complete view of the event as it occurs.

Features usually consist of four elements:

1. Interview with an athlete or participant (for example, the coach or auto racing pit crew member)
2. Shots of this person preparing for the sport or event (for example, lacing running shoes, changing a racing tire, taping a baseball bat)
3. Shots of an athletic performance, competition, or game
4. Shots of some type of previous success or future challenge.

These are all easy to shoot with one portable camera and can be easily edited together with a simple two-machine editing system.

Competition Coverage

The basic camera setup for a football game consists of six or more cameras. These cameras and the associated equipment are often brought to a big sports shoot in a large specially-designed production trailer. (See Figure 10.11.) Cameras 1, 2, and 3 are located in the stands about one-half to two-thirds of the way up to the top of the stadium. These cameras are used to orient the viewer as to the field location and direction. (See Figure 10.12.)

One of these three cameras will be used for the line of scrimmage, depending on the location of the ball. The camera closest to the line of scrimmage will

Figure 10.9 Cameras used for professional location video work are usually more like studio cameras. The large, heavy lens and the need for steady telephoto shots require a heavy support system. The camera operator can receive directions via an intercom system.

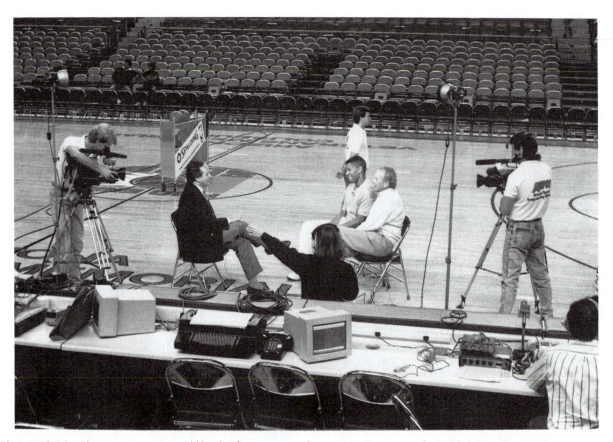

Figure 10.10 This sports interview could be shot for a pregame show segment or as part of a highlight program. Two cameras are used to let the director in the remote production van choose a shot of the interviewer or the interviewees.

be used to show the offensive team's huddle and one wide shot of their lineup at the line of scrimmage. Frame this shot so that about two-thirds to three-quarters of the screen is filled with the offensive team. (See Figure 10.13.) This allows screen space for the quarterback to move into when he drops back to pass or hand off.

Just before the center snaps the ball to the quarterback, the taking camera zooms in tighter on the quarterback. This camera will zoom in and follow the ball from the time the ball is snapped until the play is over. After the play has stopped and the players start to get back on their feet, the director will usually switch to the trucktop mounted camera, which should have a close-up shot of the ball carrier and the tackler or key defensive person involved in the play. If the play was a good offensive play, the shot will follow the offensive ball carrier. On a good defensive play, the camera will follow the defensive player as he returns to his huddle.

At this point, the director can choose one of several alternatives:

1. A videotape replay, sometimes with slow motion from the on-air camera or any one of the ISO cameras
2. A graphic superimposed over the real action as the players return to the huddle
3. A special graphic or videotape of the key player—his statistics or picture, or a short piece of videotape recorded before the game showing the player responding to a question
4. A wide shot from the end-zone camera or one of the other cameras (usually over a wide crowd shot), often used to frame statistics or a promotional graphic that is superimposed over the shot
5. A shot from the sideline camera, either of the coach, key players waiting to come into the game, an injured player, or some other color shot of cheerleaders, fans, mascots or the typical "Hi Mom" or "We're Number 1" shot of a player on the sidelines
6. As the end of the half or the game approaches, a shot of the clock or scoreboard.

Figure 10.11 This vehicle is custom designed and equipped for remote video work. It houses all necessary cameras, decks, switches, cables, and so forth, and provides the control room and hardware needed to shoot a remote event such as football.

If normal play is continuing, the sequence begins again with a wide shot from camera 1, 2, or 3.

Feature Coverage

Highlight shows are common to most professional and major college football teams. These shows consist of past matchups between the teams, a chronology of game footage with replays of key plays, coach interviews, player interviews, and previews of upcoming opponents. You may not have the equipment, personnel, or budget for live coverage of a football game, but one or two EFP cameras with competent camera operators can do a decent job of covering the game for a highlights show.

If only one camera is available for a football game, it should be the one placed at the 50-yard line, one-half to two-thirds of the way up to the top part of the stadium, or even on top of the press box if there is one. Many fields provide a designated space for video cameras. This camera will have a good view of the line of scrimmage for a high percentage of the plays. If the ball is followed closely, a viewer should be able to follow the entire game from the video of that one camera. The trick is to always stay with the ball.

Keep the framing loose until you are sure where the ball is and the play has already developed. Then you can zoom in as the running back crosses the line of scrimmage or the wide receiver pulls in the long pass. Obviously, a camera with a high zoom ratio or range extender is best. The biggest mistake you can make is to zoom in to follow a running back who has been faked a hand-off and does not have the ball.

A second camera would be best placed on a truck mount, but that requires additional personnel, a truck, and lots of expensive cable. A platform about 10 feet above the field at the 50-yard line is a possible second choice. Most likely, the only alternative for a second camera is a handheld one on the sidelines. This camera can provide very dramatic close-ups of the action but can also be blocked by players, referees, or even be run over by the play itself. This camera is most effective when it can shoot from the end

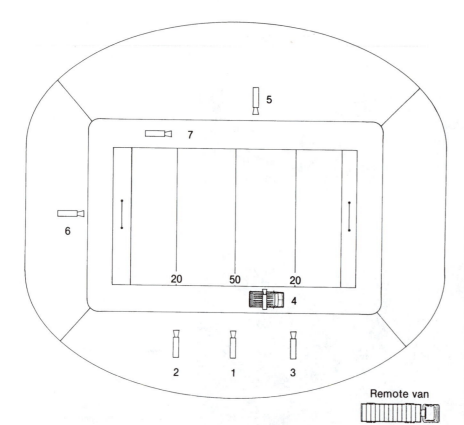

Figure 10.12 Multiple-camera remote professional sports shoot. Cameras 1, 2, and 3 are in the seating areas on the platform, one-half to two-thirds of the way up to the top of the stadium. Camera 4 is mounted on top of the truck. Camera 5 is in the seating area on the platform used for reverse angle shots. Camera 6 is in the seating area behind either goalpost. Camera 7 is the roaming portable camera. Sometimes additional cameras are attached to the goalposts to get shots of attempted field goals.

Figure 10.13 Line-of-scrimmage shot at beginning of football play. Note how the framing gives the quarterback room to move into for hand-offs or passing.

zone and get close-ups of scoring plays. For midfield coverage, the camera is best placed about 10 yards in front of the line of scrimmage. This is, however, far from ideal, since the field is often crowned with a center higher than the sidelines, yielding a low camera angle.

Other sports have slightly different requirements and camera placements (for example, golf and tennis, which are shot from the end of the green or court), but a few simple rules usually apply:

1. Get above and in the middle of the action (for example, midcourt in basketball or hockey).
2. Follow the ball (or puck or race car).
3. Frame loosely to avoid losing the object you are following.

MUSIC VIDEOS

The popularity of music videos is a recent phenomenon. Since the introduction of MTV (Music Television), the viewing world is now highly aware of the mixture of songs with visuals. This FM radio-to-TV product has stimulated enormous interest in music video style, as evidenced by the industry opinion that a band must have a music video in order to have a hit record. This has caused great demand for this type of material and is a boost to the employment potential of all aspiring EFP professionals.

The notion of setting visuals to music has been around for a long time. A viewing of Walt Disney's 1940 classic *Fantasia* will convince you of that fact. The idea of having the performers act to their own music has also been around for some time. For example, *A Hard Day's Night* is a mid-1960s Beatles' film in which the Beatles have good-natured fun and sometimes lip-sync to their songs.

Most music videos are shot on film, then either transferred to video for editing, or edited and then transferred to video for broadcast. Film, as mentioned in an earlier chapter, has a much better contrast ratio than video, and is better in very low light or very bright conditions. Many of the fancy digital effects in these videos are done on a video digital-effects generator during the editing process.

Variety of Settings

Despite the drawbacks of video cameras for the big-money music videos, the style of music video is perfect for the EFP videographer. Almost all of these videos have shots done on location outside of the studio. (Just imagine how dull they would be if all music videos only showed the musicians on a stage.) The fun in music videos comes from the unusual locations, camera angles, costumes, and sophisticated transitions between the major elements. Music videos generally are composed of a combination of two elements: (1) the musicians in the studio or on stage performing a song and (2) the musicians on location (somehow suggested by the song), either with instruments or in some dramatic vignette.

The variety of locations both for the performance and the vignette is virtually infinite, since almost anything is acceptable for a few minutes as an accompaniment to a song. Sometimes animation is used to create new locations and effects. Other times a mundane location such as a supermarket or basement apartment can provide you with the look or mood that you want for your music video. The biggest factor in changing an average setting into something unusual is creative lighting.

Style and Technique

Because the person and personality of the performers are the main interests of the music video, plan on shooting many more tight shots than long shots. You may use a brief long shot to give the viewer a sense of who is performing and where they are, but close-ups will probably be more interesting to the audience. You should also plan on low camera angles to accentuate the presence of the performers. You can shoot a music video in the style of the performance video. Using one camera on a master shot, or using three cameras, record a straight performance version of the song. If this is not a real performance and the performers are lip-syncing, make sure you have the audio to which they are performing recorded on videotape. During subsequent takes in various locations, make sure that you play that same version of the song while they lip-sync to it. This allows you to go back to the master version and synchronize your two audio tracks, then insert your video from your location shots. If you have a CD of the song, use a CD boom box at each location.

If you are well organized in keeping track of your various versions, putting together a finished composite music video even from six versions at six different locations can be relatively easy. Just make sure that your reference audio is on every tape. If numerous locations are not possible or desirable, use the multiple-take style. When using this style, record multiple takes of the song (or portions of the song) while the performers vary their performance, or while the focal length of the camera varies with each take. This style can yield a very respectable music video from an afternoon's shooting.

Music videos are an excellent opportunity for the beginning videographer to experiment with camera technique. Videographers and news photographers who usually have professional style restrictions placed on them can use music videos to loosen up and experiment with the camera. This even helps professionals become more familiar with the versatility and capability of their equipment.

NATURE AND DOCUMENTARY VIDEOS

Nature and documentary videos are perfectly suited for the portable video camera, just as they have been suited for the portable film camera for almost a century. This style requires a camera to be where the main characters (or animals or plants) are, or where the main events are occurring. The camera views the events as they actually occur, and the characters as they appear, not as they are staged in front of the camera. This is not to say that no editing is done to restructure events. By the use of editing, nature programs have created many encounters between wild animals that never took place. Even documentaries will sometimes use editing to create events that occurred but were missed by the camera.

The point is that the videographer is meant to be a passive participant, not an active one. This is not necessarily intentional in nature programs, but wild animals rarely take cues from directors. Documentaries are meant to present a reality that will enlighten its viewers, not a reality as created by the videographer or director. This style requires an unobtrusive camera to avoid influencing the events that occur in front of the camera. Therefore, retakes of these events are almost impossible, the addition of a large amount of artificial light may be nearly impossible, and getting every shot that you plan is certainly impossible.

Although the market for this type of video program is growing rapidly, the beginner should be aware of the fact that this type of work takes many long hours of shooting and editing. Because of this, the budget for this EFP style is necessarily large—at least in comparison to most commercials, performance videos, and many applications of corporate video.

VIDEO ART

This EFP style is still a well-kept secret. The main reason for this is probably that the number of outlets for this style is quite small. Video art is not the type of on-location video to choose if you need to earn a living doing one style of video work.

Video art serves an important role in a democratic society. It allows diverse views to be expressed, even if they are not the dominant ones in the culture. This diversity of viewpoints has a positive effect on a free society by stimulating people to think.

It is impossible to describe video art as a particular style. It is completely free form. It may resemble broadcast TV in length and form, while differing greatly in content. It can be a short piece that violates every known rule about pleasing an audience. Video art is the expression of the artist who looks at the same things that we do, yet sees something different. It is this difference in vision that makes video art an untapped source of creativity—video art has the capacity to show us a world at which we all look but do not see.

The process of creating video art is different from other EFP work in several respects. First of all, it is usually not done at a client's request, but because the video artist has the desire to express a topic or concept in a unique form. This means the time frame for creating the work is usually longer. It will generally be created in phases, with arts funding often sought for production and postproduction. Because the work is not being done for a client, the video artist has complete creative control.

Video art can combine EFP production, studio shoots, and complex postproduction techniques. It often entails use of advanced special effects equipment that allows the artist to manipulate the electronic signal. This can include digital processing of each pixel of information, varying the frequency of the signal, colorizing and polarizing, using multiple layers of wipes and dissolves, auditory processing, and using feedback as a visual effect. Artists gain access to signal-processing equipment through media arts organizations located in diverse areas of the country, including nonmetropolitan areas. In postproduction, the editing rhythm is often a different tempo than conventional TV, either faster, slower, or variable. The video artist has unlimited possibilities. The only constraint is to make choices that stretch and enhance the existing conventions and allow the viewer to experience the world in an imaginative way.

Broadcasters show various types of entertainment, nature and documentary programs, commercials, and sports. Corporations use and show training tapes, sales tapes, and demonstration tapes. But where do the video artists show their work? In competitions, festivals, and on a few scattered programs on cable or public TV. Innovative approaches in video art find their way into the mainstream by influencing approaches used in TV advertising. Many commercials are really a form of applied video art. Other mainstream areas that use video art approaches are the promotional IDs used for stations and the opening graphics and title sequences for all programs. Visual artists comfortable with electronic graphics equipment can apply their skill in these areas, as well as in helping create the overall design for these segments.

EFP equipment is affordable enough so that many college, art school, and university students can gain access to it. But without seeing it themselves, students are often slow in wanting to try this EFP style. The instant gratification of seeing your work on a monitor immediately after it is shot should lure many people to the video art EFP style. Unfortunately, however, with the exception of the very largest cities in this country, video art is virtually unknown.

Perhaps film still attracts so many artistic persons because of its long history and acceptance as an art form. TV, on the other hand, is often regarded as a medium of mediocrity, as evidenced by the constant stream of prime-time fare that is usually tasteless, slick, insulting, or all three. But broadcast TV is merely one method of delivering video; the networks are just some of the many programmers out to attract an audience. Other delivery systems for video exist and some of them do seek out video art. The Internet and World Wide Web offer tremendous potential for video artists. By creating a home page with video presentation capability, a video artist can have a site that can display the artist's video work to millions with very little cost to either the artist or the viewing audience.

There are more than 30 million camcorders in homes in the United States. This can only lead to what some call a democratization of portable video. Video can become a form of artistic expression for the masses, not just for the privileged minority with access to professional video equipment and broadcast air time. As portable video becomes more common and available in years to come, more creative individuals will attempt to use EFP equipment, computer equipment, and the Internet for art's sake. Perhaps then the Eisensteins, Griffiths, Chaplins, and Fellinis of video art will begin to surface.

MULTIMEDIA

Since the acceptance of video as a means of conveying information became popular in corporations and other nonbroadcast entities, videotape has been the dominant means of delivering the video to the viewer. During the 1980s, both video disc and CD-ROM emerged as a means to show video to the intended audience, but both required playback equipment that was not as common as videocassette machines. More recently, computers designed for home and office use are commonly equipped with internal CD-ROM and DVD players, sound cards, and stereo speakers to make these computers excellent playback machines for material produced on CD-ROM and DVD. This has further fueled the enormous growth in the use of video for playback in a storage medium other than videotape.

Multimedia has also grown because of the content of the material. By definition, it is a combination of media: not just video and audio, but all possible media that can be digitized and encoded onto a medium like CD-ROM or DVD. These storage formats are very popular because they have high storage capacity and are capable of high-quality images and sound. Because they are digital, they have the random access ability to find information anywhere on the disc in a very short period of time. Perhaps most importantly, multimedia allows **interactivity**, so the viewer can easily select information for viewing and input information that prompts the viewing selection. This interactivity can be simple, as in a kiosk in a hotel lobby that lists restaurants in the area surrounding the hotel. The viewer touches a TV screen to make choices like the type of food preferred from a list of types. The next video that might appear on the screen might be a list of restaurants of that type (e.g., Italian or vegetarian). The viewer can then select from that list and be shown a picture of the restaurant and a sample menu. This type of interactivity is called **reactive** interactivity, where the viewer reacts to questions or choices on the screen.

Another type of interactivity involves the viewer at a higher level. This could be something like game playing, where the viewer is giving feedback to the system regularly. Other videos at this level involve the viewer in complex tasks, such as storytelling, composing, or game-playing. This type of interactivity is known as **proactive** interactivity.

An even more complex level of interactivity is also gaining popularity. This level is differentiated from others because it requires quite a bit of input from the viewer, and this input results in constant change from the game or program being viewed. An example of this type of interactivity is a virtual reality program. This interactivity is called **mutual** interactivity.

Multimedia is distributed in a number of formats that include CD-ROMs and DVDs for personal computers, game cartridges, and laser discs. Enhanced CD-ROMs can play music on an audio system. They also have multimedia material for playback on multimedia computers. The DVD (digital versatile disk) format for CD-ROMs offers storage and playback of an entire movie with high resolution and excellent sound on one disk. In fact, DVDs can now be found that are two sided. One side contains an entire movie shown in standard television aspect ratio (4:3) and the other side will show a letterbox version of the movie (16:9). In addition, the DVD might contain sequences in which the director or actors offer ancillary information, such as commentary, about the film. Although CD-ROM recorders are common in computer systems, DVD recorders just became available in 2001. These "burners" are not nearly as common as tape recorders, and videotape will continue to be used for some time to come.

INTERNET

Another new outlet for video and audio production has emerged in the last few years. It is an outlet that allows individuals to access information from places all across the world. It has the capability to provide excellent quality audio and video information. Almost all of this information is free to those who seek it, if you have the appropriate computer equipment. This new outlet is the Internet. Broadly defined, the Internet is a collection of local networks gathered into a global network.

The Internet allows electronic mail, which is a method of sending text information to other individuals that can access the Internet. The speed of sending the message is faster than any kind of regular mail, even Federal Express, but the same as voice mail. One of the best advantages is that e-mail allows for text that can be a word or two, or chapters from a planned book, or results of a recent experiment. Since the information is sent as text, the receivers can capture the text with their computers, insert it into their word processor, and edit or just store for future reference. They can also delete the message without ever wasting paper.

Users of the Internet can download or upload programs, documents, pictures or even video. Essentially, anything that can be digitized and stored can be sent via the Internet. The Internet is a storehouse of information that is almost beyond belief in its diversity and depth. Research on almost any topic that can be described in a few words is easy, quick, and voluminous. Creating your own location on the Internet is relatively easy; searching for other sites is even easier. If you have an interest in the movies of Clark Gable or Brad Pitt, you can go to a search engine featured by one of the popular Internet browsers, type in the name Clark Gable or Brad Pitt, and the search engine will list many sites mentioning the name you entered. These sites can be visited through a clever system of links that allows you to travel from site to site by just clicking on your mouse. Your method might involve traveling first to a listing of movies that

won Academy Awards and their stars. One of the stars named would be the one you entered for your search. You could scroll down the list and find other stars from that movie. You could click on another movie and that movie site might have a link to a site that has contents of the script for that movie. Clicking on that link will take you to the script site, which would list the name of the scriptwriter and have it as a link to other scripts. It is this method of easy travel that makes the Internet so fascinating.

World Wide Web

A recent development that is part of the Internet is the World Wide Web or WWW. The web is a client/server system that allows for high-quality graphics, sound, and even moving images. From a location on the web you can often go to other locations by clicking on a link or "button." Getting around on the web requires that you use a web-browsing program like Netscape Navigator or Microsoft Internet Explorer. Several companies now sell a web interface box that can be used with your regular TV set to allow web browsing. This simplifies the entire process of getting on the web and also begins to utilize the family TV set (or home theater system).

This change in accessibility could revolutionize television delivery as we know it. Web sites that now have still images or small amounts of low-quality video clips might quickly evolve into sites that offer high-quality sound and full-motion high-quality video. Viewers who would ordinarily tune to a broadcast channel to get their favorite program might soon visit a web site to download or view their favorite program. Right now, the web has sites that are "radio stations" offering stereo sound that is streamed to simulate a typical broadcast radio station. Some stations and sites offer a menu of programs from which a listener can choose. This is much easier to accomplish than real-time full-motion video because audio requires far less storage space to digitize. Because of the technical limitations presented by narrow bandwidth, the videographer should be aware of some recommended techniques that will help maximize the impact of video shot for the web.

Preparing and Shooting Video for the Web

Video can be put on the Web and stored for two different types of transfer. The first type of storage is a video file that is downloadable. This file remains on a server's hard drive until a client requests the file. After a request, the server will send a complete copy of the file to the client. Once the copy of the file is completely received by the client, the client can then play the file for viewing. The second type of file transfer is called streaming. Files that are streamed are sent to the client in a continuous stream of data that can be played just after it is received. At the end of the streaming however, there is no file stored on the client's computer. Streaming, like broadcasting before it, does not leave a copy of the program behind for later viewing. Video for streaming requires software that can accomplish several tasks.

Software programs are available on the market and as shareware that can prepare video for streaming. These programs can be "stand-alone" programs designed to do the tasks required by streaming. Some video editing programs will have features that allow the edited video to be converted into a streaming file format. These programs generally have a few features in common. All of the programs must be able to take the video information and change the file format from the acquisition format to the streaming format. These programs should also be able to help the videographer adapt the video to the smaller size screen and lower resolution that will be shown on the web.

The process of converting video into a file format capable of streaming on the web begins with connecting a camcorder, player, or other video source to the computer that will be performing the encoding procedure. Raw video footage in the MiniDV or Digital 8 format can be loaded into a computer using a FireWire cable from the camcorder into the computer. The new video file is then placed into a Batch Window. At this point settings are chosen that will select the desired file format for the converted video information. Three choices have been generally available to video streamers: QuickTime, Windows Media Player, or Real Video. Obviously, the viewers of streaming can only view the project if they have a player program that is capable of reading files in the selected streaming format. Video producers who want to increase their business in production for the web should be able to use all formats and encoding software.

The next consideration is the screen or frame size. While a standard size like 640 pixels × 480 pixels is comfortable for viewers, it is simply too big for easy streaming. This screen size would require an enormous amount of information that is too large for streaming to be practical. A smaller screen size will require a smaller amount of information, but will yield a smoother picture. This is an important factor

because another variable in video playing quality is frame rate. Normally, standard NTSC video is shown at a rate of 30 frames per second. Most video projects on the web must slow the frame rate down enough to allow the size of the file to be manageable. Until bandwidth problems lessen, the rate for much of the video on the web is 5 to 15 frames per second. The rule of thumb for frame rates is simply the wider the bandwidth, the more frames per second allowable. Video is often prepared in several versions by connection rate: broadband, 56 kbps, and 28 kbps. Typically 15 frames per second works for broadband, 7.5 to 10 frames per second for 56 kbps, and as low as 5 frames per second for 28 kbps. These rates will yield video that is viewable, but a bit choppy. Generally speaking, the higher the data rate possible for streaming, the higher the frame rate. If your viewers have broadband connections, a higher frame rate is possible. If your viewers have slow dial-up connections (as slow as 28.8 kbps), the lowest frame per second rate may be the only choice.

Movement Because of the small screen size and slower frame rate, some adjustments must be made in the shooting of the project. To keep file size manageable, the videographer should avoid shots that have much camera movement. To the computer encoding the video information, movement requires more information for storage than still images. More information to be encoded results in larger file sizes. Avoid unnecessary camera movement because on-screen movement will be in the action you are recording. Don't add to the movement unless it is unavoidable.

Backgrounds Simple backgrounds should be used instead of cluttered, complicated ones. Too much meaningless detail in the background wastes bandwidth. Save bandwidth for the use of telling the story. Since your screen size is small, the viewer isn't always able to see it anyway. Make sure that you light everything that you want viewers to see. The encoding process often enhances the "grain" found in darkly lit parts of your picture. The smaller screen size demands that close-up shots be used frequently. Viewers need to be able to identify the subject and place it in the proper context. Therefore, wide shots should be used sparingly. Shots that have a canted or unusual angle should be used with great restraint.

Special Effects Although adding special effects like dramatic wipes or strobe effects are easy to accomplish with any digital editor, using special effects may be detrimental to your project. Because special effects require more information and thus more bandwidth, they can slow down the stream. Another consideration is the reality that special effects are much less discernable on the small screen than a large screen. It is best not to take up valuable bandwidth with effects that are all but lost on the viewers. An appropriate axiom here would be "Keep it simple!"

A final consideration for preparing video for the web is to make a decision about the audio that will be used for the project. Each file format used for video streaming treats the audio in slightly different ways. It is prudent to read the manual for the software program and make sure that the audio will be prepared in the appropriate way.

Once all of these variables are considered and choices are made, the video file is then ready to be sent to the processor to be converted from the video format to a streaming format. Some programs allow simultaneous viewing of the file while it is being converted. A split screen is shown with the original video on one side and the converted video on the other side.

Once the file is fully converted it can be sent to the web host, the computer that will store the video project information. The web host is then capable of making the video stream available on request to other computers or clients regardless of their location.

Besides the conversion process itself, some software will provide some publishing aids: shortcuts to uploading the converted file to the desired host web site and detailed instructions that are easy for novices to follow.

The host site will sometimes have information at the site to facilitate the transfer process. Often sites will give specific instruction on how to send a file using FTP (File Transfer Protocol) and how to make the video file available to the audience. Also the software should have precise instructions that will allow the videographer to prepare the file for being served from a host or server or embedded in a web page away from the host.

The above-mentioned suggestions will continue to be appropriate at least until a significant portion of the viewing public obtains broadband Internet connections. When this occurs, full-motion, full-frame video will become easier. This translates into shooting video for the web in a style that is similar to shooting video for typical exhibition on a broadcast station or any large monitor. In other words, as the technology improves, the restrictions on the videographer who shoots for the web will diminish.

The interest in Internet use among corporations increased dramatically after the web was introduced. Because web sites are capable of high-quality graphics and sound, corporations began to see these sites as promotional opportunities. Products are routinely promoted on the web in a variety of ways. Corporations are now creating **home pages** for institutional-type promotion. This presents an exciting opportunity for video producers in the future. Because web home pages are not expensive to create or maintain, most corporations are interested in having them. Soon, full-motion video will be readily available at the home page for any viewer or **web surfer** to visit. Where the home page once had a picture of the corporate headquarters or the main product of the company, soon we will be seeing videos of the president of the company or a chief spokesperson who might welcome you to the site and encourage you to check out the company's latest products or services by clicking on a button or linking to another page or site. These sites might contain information like a video brochure, or any of the standard, videotape-delivered corporate video products that have been in use for 20 years.

11 Budgeting and Pricing

Whether you are in broadcasting, in-house corporate video, or independent production, one of the first and most basic principles of video is that it is a business. Your work can be aesthetically superb, but if you do not know how much it cost to produce, or if you cannot price it to make a profit, you may soon be out of a job or out of business.

Budgets are statements of business goals in financial terms. One of the goals of a video project is to complete it for a designated amount of money, based on the best estimate of costs by the people making the budget. Budgets help keep video producers on target—they provide a disciplined approach to communication problem solving. They also help measure performance. In the business world, a video that truly gets the job done for $1000 is better than a video that does it for $2000.

Most managers see the use of video as an added cost, while most videographers and producers see it as a good investment. This difference of perspective is common throughout the industry. The best argument for using video is that it tells the necessary story and generates the desired effect more convincingly than other methods. In broadcast news operations, video can deliver the news stories from the field faster and cheaper than film. In the corporate world, video can deliver a message about a new benefit, procedure, or product more quickly and effectively than other methods. For example, a corporation that has a new health benefit option that cuts health costs to employees may want the president of the corporation to deliver the message to encourage employees to choose the new option and to enhance an image of a caring and concerned chief executive. The options available for delivery of the message include (1) a brochure with a picture and a message from the president, (2) a visit from the president to all branches of the corporation to personally deliver the message, or (3) a video of the president's message delivered to all branches of the corporation.

A simple cost analysis may reveal that the brochure is the least expensive of the options. But a good video manager may easily make the case that brochures are often read once, if at all, and then thrown away by most employees. A face-to-face video from the president may be viewed several times, especially when the specific details of the new health plan are explained. The video can be used for other public relations purposes, and the costs are relatively low. The president only has to do a good job delivering the message once and it doesn't even have to be in one take. Editing can help make the president's message perfect, and then the entire corporation sees an excellent delivery of the message every time the tape is shown. Obviously, the expenses incurred by the travel of the president and any assistants would probably exceed the cost of the video. Also, this would take the president away from other important tasks.

The size of the budget may not necessarily be the best indicator of the quality of the resulting video project. Creativity and skill can often substitute for dollars in a budget. This is especially true in corporate video where entertainment value is secondary to effectiveness.

Constructing an elegant set would enhance the aesthetics of a scene but may not help the audience remember the purpose of the video. The same is true of elaborate computer graphics and digital effects. These may be both beautiful and exciting but may not contribute directly to the effectiveness of the video project. This logic may apply to many aspects of the production. Big-name talent may be recognizable, but are they credible to the particular audience? A supermodel like Cindy Crawford may look great in your video, but is she credible when demonstrating and discussing a new high-powered multimedia computer? How about Madonna—would she be better? A local public school teacher with knowledge and confidence about using computers may be more convincing, and certainly less expensive, for getting the audience to focus on the goals of the video.

Big budgets can give you more flexibility because you have the option of high-priced talent, fancy post-production work, or a large crew. But solving a problem with video is similar to other problem-solving situations: Throwing money at the problem may help, but it is expensive and does not guarantee anything. For example, large-area lighting that requires numerous lights and people to set them may not be much better than a lighting strategy that relies on close-up lighting with a standard portable light kit. For any video production, creativity and skill can often compensate for a low budget.

ENG VERSUS EFP

Large differences between ENG and EFP emerge in the pricing and costs of portable video. Generally speaking, strict adherence to a budget is necessary in EFP work but only marginally important in ENG work. A big-budget EFP project usually results in a high-quality video piece, while the quality of ENG stories may have no direct relationship to the amount of money spent shooting them. EFP work usually begins when a budget is approved, but ENG work begins whenever an event worth covering is imminent, or an issue worth showing and discussing surfaces.

ELECTRONIC NEWS GATHERING

A majority of ENG work is shot and edited by news department employees in broadcast TV stations. The footage is owned by the station and is almost always shown during the station's own newscasts. Usually, these stories are not marketed to any other users.

A story or event coverage is sometimes sold to another broadcaster or news programmer (another TV station or the Cable News Network, for example). The sale may occur on a per-piece basis or may be part of a contractual agreement for numerous stories on one or more topics over a period of time. Video may also be traded for other services or video.

Prices for this type of ENG product may fluctuate wildly. The key determinants of price are the importance (news value) of the piece (which may depend on the importance of the event), the length of time it will be available, and how many other ENG photographers obtained similar footage. The price range may begin as low as $25 for a short piece of moderate interest, and increase to thousands of dollars for dramatic footage in high demand.

Many ENG stories sold by TV stations are sold to that station's network, or, if the station has no network affiliation, to a news service or state or regional cooperative. These stories are sometimes made available to other members of the group or network via some type of closed-circuit, satellite-distribution system or feed.

Cable News Network (CNN) has become the leader in acquiring and distributing video news from every corner of the world. Because of all of CNN's arrangements with various TV stations and foreign networks, they are a 24-hour per day trading service for news pictures.

Freelance ENG photographers, sometimes called "stringers," shoot news stories and cover events for a variety of buyers. These professionals, like their counterparts in EFP who do freelance work or have independent production companies, are often found in larger markets or locations that tend to generate many news stories, such as state capitals.

Because most ENG stories are not shot to be sold, most pieces are not budgeted as in EFP work. Local news budgets are not broken down by story. A news director for a TV station looks at ENG costs by a time unit (such as a typical broadcast week or month) that includes the salaries of the photographer, editor, and reporter, knowing that maintenance and overhead expenses are met by other departments. Most often the only factor that varies in the budget is the cost of overtime payments. News departments do create emergency funds in case of big, expensive stories to keep the station on a relatively stable and predictable budget.

ELECTRONIC FIELD PRODUCTION

Whether you are the manager of an in-house video production unit in a corporation or a manager/owner of a small independent production house, knowing the worth of your video product is the key to staying in business. Knowing the worth of your product helps you to charge your clients reasonable prices while allowing you to make a fair profit. The profit allows you to reinvest in your future through the purchase of new production or business equipment, or to provide special benefits such as bonuses to employees for high-quality work.

Costs in EFP production are somewhat different from those in studio TV. In EFP work, the setting does not come to you; you must go to the setting. This often generates large expenses for transportation of equipment and personnel. Because of the extensive handling that portable equipment receives, all equipment requires more frequent maintenance.

Tape costs in EFP are higher than in studio production. Film-style shooting of EFP requires many takes of each scene, resulting in a minimum of two to three times more tape than studio work. In addition, most tapes shot in the field, whether for ENG or EFP, are edited before being shown. Far less editing occurs in studio work, but studio costs are generally higher because of overhead expenses, such as rent or mortgage payments and regular utilities expenses.

IN-HOUSE VERSUS INDEPENDENT PRODUCTION UNITS

When video services are needed, an individual can do the work or a professional can be hired. When a corporate entity has repeated need for video services, it may decide to start its own video production unit or contract with an outside production business, often referred to as an independent production house.

In-House Production Unit

The purpose of establishing an in-house corporate video production center is to provide the corporation with a much-needed service for less money and more control than contracting outside the firm. Almost always the size of this unit grows or shrinks in a way that corresponds to the corporate need for the service

and the health of the business environment. The corporate video production unit receives money in two general ways: (1) by charging the in-house customers for services rendered (sometimes referred to as a chargeback) or (2) by a direct flat-rate budget based on projected expenses.

The first method simulates an independent production unit in the marketplace. In-house clients go to the video manager and agree on services to be rendered by the video unit and the cost of those services. The payment is made through some type of interdepartmental transfer. Often when this type of system exists, the video manager competes with other media or even with outside production units.

This keeps the pricing structure of the in-house unit very realistic. A good production team can do well in this system by keeping busy and providing excellent services at good prices. This system forces the video unit to earn its salary; in other words, the only financial support it receives is obtained directly through the amount of work it does.

A second method for financing an in-house video production unit is through some type of annual or flat budget. The production unit is automatically funded on a year-to-year basis without actually charging the in-house client on a per-piece basis. Variations on these two basic funding systems are common. Video units may receive some type of annual budget and may charge certain in-house clients for some kinds of services. In-house units that usually work on a chargeback basis may perform some services or provide services to in-house clients without charge.

Regardless of what type of financial system the company utilizes, it is essential to know the costs of providing necessary services to your clients. Because managers of corporate video units that receive annual funding are expected to provide the production service on the given budget, the manager should know how much work can be done with a given finite budget in order to avoid operating at a deficit. Unrealistic prices by a video unit on a chargeback system either result in a noticeable deficit or a surplus that might anger the in-house clients.

Independent Production Unit

Independent production units generally have more freedom in their pricing. The only limitations are the goals set by the owners and managers and the need to make enough money to stay in business. Often the marketplace exerts a great deal of influence on the price. The general rule is that the price is what the market will bear. This is directly related to competition. Numerous competitors lead to lower prices.

This is not to say that quality and reliability are not pricing factors. High-quality work and a high degree of reliability are certainly worth a higher price, but competition limits your pricing range and flexibility. Too much competition often leads to underpricing and cutting corners to get the job done. Too little competition might prevent your prices from having credibility. Without any competition, your client has no point of reference on prices. Keep in mind that few clients actually understand and appreciate all the time, equipment, and labor required to produce a professional-quality EFP video project.

CREATING AN ACCURATE BUDGET

The secret to creating an accurate budget is understanding all the possible sources of costs for the production. Most production units have some type of guide or budget sheet that lists possible costs for productions based on those done in the past by that unit. As new sources of cost are incurred, these new sources are added to the list.

These costs can be broken down into categories to help the organization of the process. Various strategies and systems exist. For many, especially smaller operations and most in-house corporate video units, the categorization follows a more generic approach that would be typical of any business that sells a product. The categories typically found in this system include materials cost, services cost, labor cost, and overhead cost.

A tradition handed down from the movie industry regarding budgets consists of two very general categories: creative and executive talent and production; postproduction and related expenses. This system uses the terms "above the line" and "below the line."

Line Costs

Budgets for large-scale productions in both the film and broadcast industries have traditionally delineated costs in a specific way. The first classification consists of costs encountered in securing the story rights and script, the producer and producer's immediate staff, the talent, the director, and the costs for travel and fringes (fringe benefits) of these people. These costs are referred to as above-the-line costs.

All other costs directly incurred by the production are categorized together (though listed separately) and referred to as below-the-line costs. These are for materials, services, labor, and so forth—costs not included in the above-the-line category. The below-the-line costs are sometimes categorized by the stage in the production process (for example, preproduction or postproduction) in which they are incurred.

The above-the-line costs and below-the-line costs are combined with the indirect or overhead costs to give a grand total. Although this budgeting procedure works for major studios, it is not as functional for smaller operations that have not had as much budget and budget-tracking experience.

Materials

Some materials for video projects, such as lamps, set or scenery construction, and materials used for graphics preparation (slides or graphic cards) are expected to provide only one usage. For every project that requires a script, a certain amount of paper and office forms are used. Other materials may have some leftovers or reusables, but it is not safe to expect this to occur. Include the full cost of these materials in your budget.

Typical materials costs include the following:

Videotape

Audiotape

Computer disks or other storage material

Film stock (slides, still, movie)

Set construction (lumber, paint, nails)

Graphics materials (markers, paper, paint, photocopies)

Tools (purchased for a specific project)

Props (furniture, equipment for a specific project)

Miscellaneous (gaffers tape, special adapters).

The videotape and audiotape used in the project may or may not have later use. Some of it will not be recycled: For example, the edited master will remain in use only for the project for which it was purchased for a long time, or at least until the client is thoroughly satisfied with the finished program. However, some of the raw footage shot on location may come in very handy for future productions that require a specific shot or cutaway from that location or type of location. It is sometimes amazing how creative and resourceful video people can be if reusing video or audiotape can save a return trip to a location. If you keep these things in mind, you can be more accurate when assessing your materials cost for videotape.

Services

This cost category includes the services purchased specifically for the project that are not provided by in-house personnel or equipment. When you must rent a vehicle, do a special effect at another facility, or cater meals at a location, categorize these as services costs. A slightly different type of cost that falls under this general category is the cost incurred when you must use copyrighted materials and pay a fee for that privilege.

Typical services costs include the following:

Rental of equipment/vehicles

Rental of locations

Rental of facilities (for example, postproduction)

License fees (music, stock photo/slides, or video)

Catering for meals

Outside contracts (security, construction)

Production of graphics materials or special effects

Photo processing

Duplication (videotape or audiotape).

Labor

The general definition of labor costs is the total cost of all hours (or days) spent by all employees involved in a project. Assigning exact costs for this category is most accurately done after the project is completed. However, you must try to predict exactly how many hours or days a key crew member like a director will or can spend on a given project. The price for the project is often needed well ahead of the project's completion—usually before the project is even begun.

Typical labor costs include the following:

Executive producer

Producer

Director

Writer(s)

Researcher(s)

Assistants

Camera operators

Videotape recorder operators

Engineer(s)

Lighting director

Art director

Grip(s)

Production assistants

Editor

Office staff.

Labor costs call for accurate predicting if your production is to be successful. To budget for the cost of a director on a project, we must try to get an accurate picture of how much effort will be required. Predictions are most accurate when two types of information are available: (1) the number of hours spent by your director on a similar project and (2) the number of hours generally spent by other directors on similar projects or amount of work. Very simply, once you have predicted the amount of time, multiply this figure by the director's unit rate. The unit rate is determined for any convenient length of time (for example, hour, day, or week) by dividing the director's total pay for a known period by the appropriate number of units.

For example, your director earns $3000 per month. What are the unit rates for each (1) day or (2) hour worked by the director? The following equation will give the daily unit rate (we assume here that each month has 20 workdays):

Daily unit rate = total monthly salary divided by the number of workdays per month

= $3000 per month @ 20 workdays per month

= $150

To find the hourly unit rate use this equation:

Hourly unit rate = daily unit rate divided by the number of work hours per day

= $150 per day divided by 8 work hours per day

= $ 18.75 per hour

NOTE: On larger productions, or when freelance help is hired, the number of work hours is usually 10 hours, but longer days are not uncommon.

The hourly rate should be multiplied by the projected number of hours that will be spent by the director on this particular project. This procedure needs to be repeated for all persons involved in the production. (See Figure 11.1.)

For most union or personal service contracts there is a base-pay unit, usually set at one full day. Along with this rate for union and nonunion people are overtime and other compensations agreed to by employee and employer. In some cases, flat rates can be negotiated.

Once the labor costs for all production personnel are added, you then have a general idea of what the actual costs will be. This first sum is merely the dollar amount that will be going directly to the employees. What must be added to this direct payment is the amount that your company pays for employee benefits, such as life insurance, hospitalization, retirement, or bonuses.

These fringe benefits can add anywhere from 30% to more than 100% of the cost of the work to your direct labor costs. These added costs are almost always associated with full-time employees. Failure to include these costs will cause you to underestimate your overall costs, which may result in underpricing your product and lead to some red ink. When using contract or freelance help, fringe benefits are not involved.

Overhead Expenses

Overhead expenses are those expenses generally associated with being in business. Typical overhead expenses include the following:

Salaries (nonproduction)

Benefits

Office/studio space rental

Utilities (heat, light, water, telephone)

Internet service

Dues (professional organizations)

Subscriptions (magazines)

Reference/library materials (books, sound library, graphics clip art)

Equipment depreciation (office/production equipment)

Maintenance (janitorial, grounds keeping)

Miscellaneous (donations).

Certain kinds of labor costs may also be associated with overhead. Salaries of others not directly involved in the project (a secretary, for example) can be included in labor costs if the employee spends an easily definable amount of time on the particular project being priced. Often this is not the case, and the project is merely assigned a portion of this type of office salary in the overhead cost. Equipment depreciation costs may also be included in a general category of overhead expenses. Without going into great detail or accounting theory, depreciation can be thought of as the value that your equipment loses as a result of use and aging. For example, if a Betacam camcorder costs $60,000 and is expected to last 5 years, the cost of owning and using the camcorder can be calculated as $60,000 divided by five or $12,000 per year.

There are numerous ways to deal with these costs, but for use in pricing your product, follow a simple procedure in which you ascertain a unit rate of overhead costs in the same way you obtain a unit rate for labor costs. Total the previous year's overhead costs and then divide that total by the number of working or operating days:

$$\frac{\text{Total Previous Year's Overhead Costs}}{\text{Number of Operating Days}}$$

The result is a daily overhead cost. This daily cost, or fraction thereof, should be added to other costs.

Keep in mind that this cost may fluctuate from year to year. If you are aware of definite fluctuations in overhead that would change the overhead unit rate in your current year, you should adjust the figures accordingly. Salary raises or bonuses for office or executive employees, increases in utility use or rates, or changes in tax rates can influence current overhead expenses.

If you think that changes like those mentioned above have occurred, you can adjust the unit rate by

```
                           BUDGET


Production Requirement          Rate          Budget

A.   Production Operating Expenses
  1. Off-Line Editing (Rough Cut)           $ 10,000
  2. On-Line Edit                           $  6,000
  3. Equipment Rental                       $ 14,000
  4. Video Tape Stock                       $    800

Production Operating Expenses Sub-Total     $ 30,800


B.   Professional Services
  1. Computer Animation & Graphics          $  3,000
  2. Archive Research & Purchase            $  1,000
  3. Music Composition & Audio Production   $  3,000

Professional Services Sub-Total             $  7,000


C.   Personnel
  1. Producer/Director
       Pre-Production (5 days)    $   100    $    500
       Shoot (10 days)           $   250    $  2,500
       Post-Production (10 days) $   250    $  2,500
  2. Audio/Engineer (10 days)    $   200    $  2,000
  3. Dir. of Photography (10 days) $ 250    $  2,500

Personnel Sub-Total                         $ 10,000


D. Travel/Scouting/Meetings
  1. Hotel                                  $  2,400
  2. Ground Transportation                  $    500
  3. Meals                                  $    450
  4. Telephone/Fax                          $    500

Travel/Scouting/Meetings Sub-Total          $  3,850


E. Talent & Rights
  1. Writer                                 $  1,000
  2. On Camera/ Voice talent               $  1,000

Talent & Rights Sub-Total                   $  2,000


TOTAL BUDGET                                $ 53,650
```

Figure 11.1 This budget for an in-house industrial video project shows per day and project costs for personnel in Section C. Courtesy of VAS Communications.

first adjusting last year's total overhead expenses by the amount of the expected changes. Another method is to arrive at your overhead cost more often than once per year. A quarterly assessment of overhead costs will sometimes help to keep your unit rate closer to reality.

When the four general cost categories (materials, services, labor, and overhead) are added together, you have a total cost for the project. This is also the price at which you or your company can break even with no financial loss or gain. But if your price is set to break even, chances are that your department or company will lose money. As unforeseen expenses always crop up, it is good business policy to add something to your total cost to provide for a rainy day.

If you include another factor—profit—in your pricing formula, you will help guarantee that you will be able to meet any cost overruns and perhaps save some money to buy more or better equipment in the future.

BUDGET TRACKING

The best way to give accurate prices for your video work is to have accurate information regarding what the actual costs are. You can do this by keeping accurate records of expenditures for the projects your company produces. This record keeping or book-keeping process is called budget tracking.

This procedure allows you to compare the projected budget for a video service with the actual cost. By making this comparison, you not only can assess your ability to cover your incurred costs and attain your desired profit amount, you also gain valuable data for pricing future projects. If you track your budgets after you make them, you can easily evaluate your ability to predict costs. This procedure is a relatively easy one to establish.

First, whenever you give a budget estimate for a project, make sure that it includes a dollar amount for all possible items within each of the cost categories (see Table 11.1). Set up this budget breakdown so that each cost item has a line with at least two columns: one for the budgeted or predicted cost, and a second for the actual cost.

A third column might also be included for cost overruns—when actual costs are more than the estimated costs. Or the third column may be used for budget surpluses—when the actual costs are less than the predicted costs. This third column is derived by subtracting the actual cost from the predicted cost. The sum of the positive and negative numbers in the third column will give you a report on your pricing accuracy: A positive number shows that you have safely assessed your costs and have some money left over to contribute to profit (as in the example above); a negative number means that you have underestimated costs and you may have to use money initially earmarked for profit to pay for the costs of producing the project.

Computer Assistance

Just as computers and computer programs have become essential for business managers to organize, track, project, and plan in their areas of responsibility, these new technologies are helping EFP producers with the planning and business aspects of portable video production. (See Figure 11.2.) Computer programs created by video professionals allow producers and their staffs to generate budget figures in standardized categories in very short periods of time, whereas the tedious paper-and-pencil mode formerly took days. This type of program also allows the individual producer to create special tailor-made budget categories.

Table 11.1. Budget Tracking

Cost Category	Budgeted	Actual	Difference
Materials			
Videotape	$450	$275	$175
Set	$150	$175	($25)
Paint and lumber	$85	$80	$5
Total Materials	$685	$530	$155
Services			
Van rental	$150	$150	$0
Special effects	$250	$350	($100)
Costume rental	$75	$75	$0
Total Services	$475	$575	($100)
Total			$55

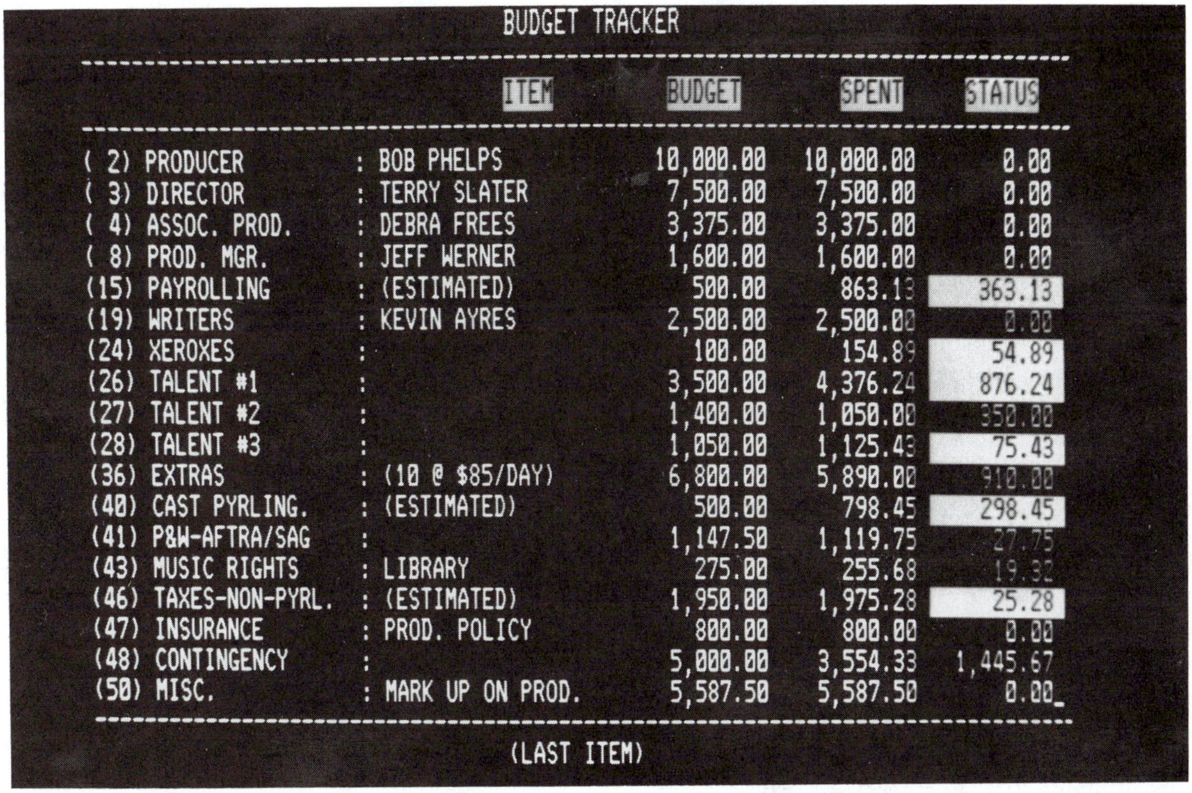

```
                        BUDGET TRACKER
--------------------------------------------------------------
                         ITEM      BUDGET     SPENT     STATUS
--------------------------------------------------------------
( 2) PRODUCER        : BOB PHELPS    10,000.00  10,000.00     0.00
( 3) DIRECTOR        : TERRY SLATER   7,500.00   7,500.00     0.00
( 4) ASSOC. PROD.    : DEBRA FREES    3,375.00   3,375.00     0.00
( 8) PROD. MGR.      : JEFF WERNER    1,600.00   1,600.00     0.00
(15) PAYROLLING      : (ESTIMATED)      500.00     863.13   363.13
(19) WRITERS         : KEVIN AYRES    2,500.00   2,500.00     0.00
(24) XEROXES         :                 100.00     154.89    54.89
(26) TALENT #1       :               3,500.00   4,376.24   876.24
(27) TALENT #2       :               1,400.00   1,050.00   350.00
(28) TALENT #3       :               1,050.00   1,125.43    75.43
(36) EXTRAS          : (10 @ $85/DAY) 6,800.00   5,890.00   910.00
(40) CAST PYRLING.   : (ESTIMATED)      500.00     798.45   298.45
(41) P&W-AFTRA/SAG   :               1,147.50   1,119.75    27.75
(43) MUSIC RIGHTS    : LIBRARY          275.00     255.68    19.32
(46) TAXES-NON-PYRL. : (ESTIMATED)    1,950.00   1,975.28    25.28
(47) INSURANCE       : PROD. POLICY     800.00     800.00     0.00
(48) CONTINGENCY     :               5,000.00   3,554.33 1,445.67
(50) MISC.           : MARK UP ON PROD. 5,587.50 5,587.50     0.00
--------------------------------------------------------------
                        (LAST ITEM)
```

Figure 11.2 Sample computer program for video producers.

This type of software can also perform budget tracking. After a final budget for a project is entered, expenses are entered as they are incurred, either at some regular interval or at the end of the production. This type of program allows you to quickly recall the amount budgeted for a particular category of expense, the number of expense entries in that category, and the remaining balance. The program also allows you to update the budget when hourly or unit rates change.

EFP PRICING FORMULA

Every production situation brings a unique problem to the person who must accurately assess costs and set prices. This section presents a general formula for the identification and categorization of costs associated with EFP video projects.

A combination of five factors makes up the components necessary to set the price for an EFP video project. The first four factors are materials, services, labor, and overhead costs. These can be combined into one major category of cost:

$$
\begin{array}{r}
\text{Materials Cost} \\
\text{Services Cost} \\
\text{Labor Cost} \\
+\text{Overhead Cost} \\
\hline
\text{Total Cost}
\end{array}
$$

These four, when combined and added to the fifth factor, profit, yield the formula for price:

$$
\begin{array}{r}
\text{Total Cost} \\
+ \text{Profit} \\
\hline
\text{Price}
\end{array}
$$

or

$$
\begin{array}{r}
\text{Materials Cost} \\
\text{Services Cost} \\
\text{Labor Cost} \\
\text{Overhead Cost} \\
+\text{Profit} \\
\hline
\text{Price}
\end{array}
$$

The fifth factor, profit, is considered separately because the amount of profit is often under the control of the price setter. Profit is the amount of money you want to make over and above all of your costs for the project. Profit may be used for reinvestment in equipment, facilities, real estate, bonuses, or simply to build the company's cash reserves. A closer look at these factors gives a better understanding of the role each plays in price setting.

The profit factor in the pricing formula is often the most difficult to quantify. How much money do you want to make on a project? Enough to buy dinner? Enough to buy 10 cases of tape? Enough for a new video camera? Enough to pay off your mortgage? Obviously, the amount of profit is related to the total cost of the project. It would be great to make $800 profit on a project that involves only $200 of real cost, but this percentage of profit is rare in everyday business.

A good manager would not settle for a $50 profit on an $8000 job unless there were some unusual circumstances. A $50 profit for that much expense is too much work and too much risk for such a small profit. The base profit percentage in the production business is about 20%. In other words, you can usually add 20% of the total cost as the profit factor in your pricing formula (or multiply total costs by 1.2).

Some projects may justify a higher profit figure. Low-priced jobs usually have a minimum dollar amount included for profit. Some projects may be risky, require crucial deadlines, or present difficult or unpleasant conditions. If any of these conditions are present, a 25 to 50% profit margin may be quite reasonable.

You may feel you should do certain projects for reasons other than direct economic gain. These are the jobs that may enhance your credibility, give you desired publicity, give your creative desires a boost, or simply give you a shot at working for a highly desired clientele. Foregoing profit even in these cases may not be necessary, but it may assure you of getting the job because you are the lowest bidder.

In some instances, you may want to take on a video project at a loss, even if the client is not a highly desired one. For example, the price structure in a voluntary loss situation may look like this:

Materials cost	$100
Services cost	50
Labor cost	100
Overhead cost	50
Total cost	$300

The above figures are the costs for a small video project (for example, a public service announcement or commercial). If the client pays only $275, you are left with a negative profit of $25. For what reason would you undertake this project?

A quick look at the cost of being in business can shed some light. Some costs, such as labor and overhead, are incurred whether you have a project to do or not. Your overhead costs are fixed, and your labor costs might come from full-time employees who get paid whether they have a project to do or whether they are reading magazines in the office. If you do not have a project, you still have some costs:

Labor cost
$100

Overhead cost
+50

Total cost
$150

If you do not take on this project, you still have to pay $150 in costs. By taking on the project, you cover most of your costs and lose only $25 instead of $150. Besides, it is better to have your employees gaining experience in video production instead of in magazine reading.

This policy of accepting negative-profit jobs is risky. If client X finds out that client Y paid less for a similar job, the integrity of your rate structure may suffer and you may have to continually justify your prices to clients. Except for highly unusual circumstances, it is best to take on jobs at your normal profit rate.

ENTRY INTO THE VIDEO MARKETPLACE

The above discussion makes the assumption that you are already in business and have the equipment or procedures to obtain the equipment you need to produce portable video projects. Many new entrants in the field of portable video decide to be in business for themselves and try to acquire the equipment and related materials and people necessary for them to conduct business. This can be a daunting and dangerous endeavor. The cost of obtaining the equipment is quite high. A full traveling kit for high-quality professional EFP work, which includes a professional camcorder, light kits, wireless mics, audio accessories, cables, and cases, and a two-wheel hand truck to carry the cases, can easily cost $150,000. This does not include a vehicle to transport the equipment or personnel. This also doesn't include any studio facilities or editing facilities. A digital editor with playback and record video decks can cost $50,000 to $200,000 more. Obviously, this kind of capital outlay bars many new video professionals from casually entering the field of high-quality production.

Leasing

Some of this initial cost outlay can be reduced by leasing or renting some of the equipment. You may find that it is much more realistic to lease a camcorder for $400 or more per day than to purchase a new one for $60,000. Extended leases that are not on a day-to-day basis may reduce your per day cost. Like all leases, you don't really own the equipment, the leasing company does. At the end of the lease period you must return the equipment or buy it from the company. This can be problematic when unexpected business comes your way.

Using the Web for Video

The World Wide Web offers some relatively new opportunities for video producers to improve their business. The first opportunity allows a video producer to market services. A video producer can use a typical web site home page to display a resume, both in text and audio/video forms. The site can also be used to store drafts of work for clients. After posting on the web, clients can have easy access to projects that may be in a rough edit stage. By showing the client a draft copy, the producer can gain valuable insight into what the client expects in the finished product. This procedure saves the video producer time. By posting the video on the web, the producer need not travel to the client with a tape or have the client come to the producer. The client views the video when convenient and can give immediate feedback via e-mail.

Examples of scripts, storyboards, and actual projects can be seen or played when prospective clients go the web site. Obviously, the web site is a 24-hour-per-day marketing tool that can reach many people from all parts of the world.

Video Producers as Hosts. The use of the web for video production business is still in its infancy. People who shoot video professionally are just starting to explore the video applications on the web. At present, bandwidth problems prevent easy distribution of video on the web. Video professionals are cautiously approaching business on the web, due in part to video quality issues. One business that has emerged is the video professional using the company web site as a host for all work done for all clients. By providing this service, the clients need not be web "savvy" because the work is exhibited from the same source it is produced.

Being Realistic

It may be best for you to start your business in a smaller way and build up to a more professional or high-end level after you have more experience and a strong track record or reputation. Instead of a state-of-the-art camcorder, you may opt for a low-end professional or industrial digital camcorder. Instead of an extensive light kit, you may choose to start with a much smaller kit that is very flexible and can adapt to many lighting situations. An extra video recording deck may be nice, but when it is absolutely necessary, you can rent one. Top-of-the-line wireless microphones are the best for most situations involving sound bites from subjects, but you can also get less expensive wireless mics and supplement them with some good-quality cabled mics.

The point here is that you must avoid overextending yourself financially. Portable video may be your life's desire—your ambition is to shoot terrific video and produce video projects that are both aesthetically pleasing and entertaining to your audience. Unfortunately, if you decide to go into portable video as an independent businessperson, your work must produce enough money to pay the bills and your salary. This reality has resulted in many individual and small business failures. The rule of thumb is to make sure that your equipment is the best that your business can justify economically.

12 Copyrights and Legal Issues

One of the best aspects of producing portable video is that a large number of people may see your work. In fact, if you are in a city, many people may even see it while you are shooting. While this exposure is a blessing for video makers in added recognition, the high profile can also be a blessing through higher ratings, more sales, a larger corporate budget, and so on. But with the two rewards of exposure and money can come some very substantial legal problems. For those who plan to produce video programs or segments, a cursory knowledge of how to protect yourself from legal entanglements and your material from being stolen or misused is as necessary as any video techniques.

Most videographers encounter two major areas of the law: the right to privacy and the right of ownership (or copyright). The former is the most common problem in ENG and the latter in EFP. Either issue can certainly create more trouble than you would suspect. The safest thing to do before shooting anything, whether news or not, is to be sure not only of your rights but also of the rights of everyone or everything that appears in your video or had anything to do with it. This sounds complex, but the level of complexity is somewhat a function of the amount of money involved. A student project only seen by a class or school can do many things that a multimillion-dollar network TV show could never dream of doing without having every legal *i* dotted.

LIBEL, SLANDER, AND PRIVACY

A major concern of all broadcast journalists is **libel**. Most libel laws come from issues regarding the print media, but libel laws do apply to electronic media as well. Libel involves the **defamation** of character through the printed word, whereas **slander** is defamation with the spoken word. Defamation is the act of making a statement that negatively impacts a person's reputation. Using these definitions as a guideline, you would expect slander to apply to broadcast and video, since it involves speaking through narration or reporting. Because broadcasting is ubiquitous, defamation in broadcasting falls under the guidelines that apply to libel.

One of the basic rights of all Americans is the **right to privacy**. Many areas within our laws are interpreted by measuring them against this right. The greatest concern for video producers regarding privacy comes in two areas: using people's images and using their names. Any time a person writes about anyone else or picks up a camera and photographs anyone else, the right of that person's privacy has to be considered. A person's privacy can be limited for a number of reasons, and some people seem to have no privacy at all. Broadcast, cable, and industrial video producers need to be constantly aware of this right in order to avoid what can be major legal problems after a program or segment is shown.

NEWS PRODUCTIONS

Broadcast journalism has a great many freedoms under the law that other types of video production do not enjoy. How the end product is used is very crucial to the rights of the makers as well as the subjects. Because news is a public service and the right of a free press is guaranteed under the Constitution of the United States, there are very few ways to stop someone from covering an event or showing a particular picture or scene on a newscast. However, if the news staff does not understand the subtleties of interpreting the right to privacy, the results can range from loss of prestige to high-priced civil suits. Being wrong can be costly to you and to your employer.

The Public's Right to Know

The courts have made it very clear that the public's right to know is one of our most secure freedoms. The right to know generally applies to anything that could be considered interesting to the public, is in the public eye, or affects any portion of the populace. The public's right to know allows the news to show the victim of a car crash, the president on vacation, or the unsanitary conditions inside a poorly run meat-packing plant. This does not mean a news broadcast has the right to libel or slander someone or otherwise misrepresent the pictures shown or the words read. However, it is very difficult to prove claims of such wrongdoing against a news organization.

In the late 1980s, Las Vegas singer Wayne Newton sued NBC News for linking him to known organized crime figures, thereby damaging his public image. It was alleged that NBC's combination of words and pictures created a defamatory impression. Newton won a large judgment ($19 million) in a local court, but a higher court deemed the award to be too high. If the news organization had a legitimate reason for doing a story on a particular person (such as Mr. Newton) because he is in the public eye, that person's complaint would have to show that the information used was not only totally false but also that the news reporter knew it was false. Stories done about corporations can be equally costly. A story done on a Chicago TV station about the Brown and Williamson Tobacco Corp. was deemed defamatory by a jury, and the corporation was awarded more than $5 million dollars in damages. Subsequently, the award was reduced to about $3 million, but $50,000 was to be paid by the TV reporter who did the story.

A reporter's ability to protect the identity of sources can make it hard to prove how much a reporter really knows about what was written. This legal loophole applies to any news media and explains why supermarket tabloids get away with saying the most outrageous things. The small chance of proving malicious intent and falsity is usually not worth the time, trouble, added publicity, or money

needed to sue the paper. What separates tabloid journalism from the mainstream is ethics. Any news organization seeking the respect of the public should try to uphold not only the letter of the law but the spirit of the law as well.

Besides the public's right to know as a defense against libel, two other issues should be kept in mind. The best defense against a libel suit is that the information you have presented is the truth. If you are doing your job properly and not misrepresenting the facts, this should be easy when producing news. In 1996, ABC News learned the hard way that news coverage cannot be deceitful in any way. As part of their investigation into unsanitary conditions at a popular food market, an employee of ABC applied for and got a job at the market using a false resume. A jury found ABC's allegations of unsafe practices in the store to be true but gave an extremely large settlement to the store's management because of the deceptive way ABC uncovered the story. The end does not justify the means, and a jury can drive that point home in a big way. The second defense is to present the story as opinion, because there is no penalty for libelous opinion. However, when doing general news, opinion is not appropriate.

The public's right to know permits great freedom in a story but also requires great responsibility. Suppose that your videotape of a well-known politician showing affection to a member of the same sex implies that he is gay. You may have the right to show it, but if he has not made public his sexual preference, is it ethical to show it? Would his being gay mean anything about his ability to be a good public servant? The public may find it interesting, but it may also cost him his office. There is an ongoing debate as to how far the media can go in this type of reporting. It may be legal, but you must always weigh the benefits of what you do against the harm it may cause. Often it rests on you, and you alone, to decide.

Public Property

A common misconception on the part of the public upon seeing a TV camera is what the right of privacy means. For example, a storeowner may see a news photographer taking pictures and order the photographer to stop. If the photographer does not, the storeowner may call the police, even though there are no legal grounds for doing so as long as the photographer is on public property. If the photographer is not harassing the owner or creating a public disturbance, any action against the photographer by the owner could end with the owner going to court, not the photographer. As long as a photographer is on public property, practically the only reasons that can prevent videotaping are public safety or risk to national security.

Although most people think they have the right to reject any coverage of themselves or their property, they often have no legal basis for that belief. The factors that determine the right of privacy in video are the location of the camera and the context in which the pictures are used. Generally, if a photographer is on public property, or even on private property with the permission of the owner or management, anything the camera can see is fair game, regardless of where it is in relationship to the photographer. Even when former President Reagan vacationed at his Santa Barbara ranch, the public saw fuzzy pictures of him riding horses. The news media had permission to be on adjoining property, and with special telephoto lenses, they could see and photograph Reagan.

Exercising the right to take pictures can be overdone. When pop singer Madonna was married, the press hired helicopters to survey and photograph her outdoor wedding. The resulting air show with its noise spoiled the wedding and became almost as big a story as the event. Unfortunately, celebrity status brings attention. Everyone would agree that the helicopters were an invasion of privacy, but any news show or newspaper would pay to have the pictures because the public really wanted to see that wedding. This does not make it ethical, but the public's right to know is a powerful force, and, in this case, it did make it legal.

Context

Being in the news media does not, however, give you the right to misrepresent what you see or imply criminal wrongdoing without reasonable proof. The context in which the scene is used must reflect the reality of the situation at the time of taping. While most problems of misrepresentation or accusation come during editing or because of narration used over the pictures, the photographer should still be aware of any potential problems.

Here is a typical situation in which you could find yourself when shooting news. Suppose the assignment is to shoot people smoking in a public restaurant for a story on a proposed change in smoking laws. The owner of the Dinner Bell Cafe has agreed to let you shoot there. With the owner's permission, you do not need the consent of each individual patron. However, it is considered polite and ethical to seek permission of any customer that your camera approaches or anyone who needs to be lit by your sungun or stand light. If you can make the same shot using your zoom lens and existing lighting, then you need not ask them. Let's suppose that you shoot the cafe when it is lit well enough for you to shoot with natural light, and you do most of it on a tripod from the sides of the room so that many of the diners do not even notice your presence. The video airs on the news and one of the shots depicts an easily recognizable couple who are having an affair and are discovered only after appearing on the news. The two sue the station for airing their pictures.

Is the station liable? No. The station cannot be held responsible. The couple may sue the restaurant, but they have no legal grounds for suing the broadcaster. If the story was about people having affairs and they showed this couple, it would be quite different. Even if it were true, it would be an unjustified invasion of privacy, unless the story was actually about that particular couple. This is the reason why videotapes of people apparently committing crimes show their faces covered by a video effect so that they are unrecognizable. These people have not yet been charged with any crimes. The safest way of dealing with questionable situations is to apply a good measure of caution. Do not say or imply anything bad about someone unless you are prepared to defend that accusation in court, or you know for certain on advice from an attorney that you are within your rights.

Public Figures

The really gray area of the privacy issue concerns people who can be considered public figures: politicians, movie stars, business leaders, and so on. The media hid outside presidential candidate Gary Hart's condo during his campaign for president in 1988. They could not have done that to just anyone. Hart put himself in the public spotlight and yielded most of his right to privacy to the public's right to know. There is still a large debate as to whether that media stakeout was ethical, but it was legal. The unfortunate part of this area of the law is that not all public figures attain this status by choice. Some are the innocent bystanders caught up in events not of their making. The victims of crimes and disasters, relatives of the famous, and even witnesses to events can suddenly find themselves the center of media attention—and powerless to do anything about it.

Trespassing

In the pursuit of an important story or shot, many news photographers have found themselves breaking other laws. The most common law broken is trespass. A property owner is powerless to stop a news crew from taping while the crew remains on public property, but this does not apply to private property, where not only can they be removed but also arrested. Trespassing charges are seldom filed against news crews for two main reasons. First, property owners usually do not want the added publicity or hassle; second, courts are generally sympathetic to the media if the story is in the public interest. The public's right to know is an area of the law with a wide latitude for abuse by the media. The news technique made famous by *Sixty Minutes*, where the photographer and reporter barge into a private place and thrust the camera into the face of the accused, is a prime example. The reporters fire accusations at the accused who screams for them to leave while covering his or her face. It produces very dramatic pictures and can make any subject look guilty. *Sixty Minutes* does this successfully because the producers are *very* sure of the person's guilt or inability to prove innocence. However, this *is* trespassing.

Most trespassing by news crews goes unnoticed until after the fact. It may be as simple as a photographer hopping a farmer's fence to get a better shot of a beautiful sunset, or as serious as sneaking into a building to show that foreign workers removing asbestos are not provided with protective clothing and masks. The former is done out of the innocence of the story; the latter, out of the public's right to know that people are being unfairly exploited and their lives put at risk. In both cases, the photographer may have ended up in jail. The charges may later be dropped or the fine, if any, inconsequential. Regardless of the reason for the trespass, you may experience at least some trouble.

In the majority of cases, the trespassing photographer would be ordered to leave and that would be the end of it. There will be cases, however, when just the opposite can happen. The photographer shooting the sunset could be held at gunpoint by an angry farmer tired of too many vandals. The farmer can make the photographer wait until the sheriff shows up. When you are an uninvited interloper, you increase the chances of being in the wrong place at the wrong time.

A law that makes it an acceptable risk for so many news crews to trespass is the one against robbery. If you are caught taking pictures on private property, the property owner can order you to leave, or even detain you until the police arrive, but cannot take your camera, videotape, or any other of your possessions, because this is your property. Taking it against your will or by threat is defined as robbery. It does not matter that you are on someone else's property; your things, including the images recorded on the tape, belong to you or to your employers who have you as their representative. Unfortunately, just as the law often allows you extra leeway in cases of trespass, it also tends to allow leeway to angry property owners who may destroy your tape or damage your equipment. You may be told that pursuing any charges against the property owner is inadvisable, because there is virtually nothing to gain from it. You can easily appear to be the bad guy breaking the law or harassing the property owner. You must weigh the worth of what you are trying to do against the risks you are taking. The laws do not bend in your direction only.

Hidden Cameras

A common technique for taking news pictures on private property, where the owner would not allow a crew access, is to use a hidden camera. With digital tape formats like Digital 8 and MiniDV that are at or near broadcast quality, videotape recorders can be hidden with ease in a handbag, briefcase, or even under clothing. With the use of fiber optic lenses, miniature color cameras can be placed almost anywhere. For this type of setup, a wide-angle lens is often no larger than a small button and can easily look just like one. Fiber optics allow the camera to be placed some distance from the lens in the same way that a microphone is run by cable to a recorder.

The use of a hidden camera is as old as photojournalism. News organizations as well as law enforcement agencies have set up sting operations using a camera concealed behind a false wall or shooting through a two-way mirror to capture subjects doing everything from selling phony health insurance to the elderly, to selling cocaine to well-known public figures, as in the famous John DeLorean (a former automobile manufacturing executive) case. While such uses often lead to grand jury investigations or even arrests, this does not mean that the accused will be found guilty. DeLorean was acquitted of the charges against him despite the videotape evidence. The jury thought he had been pressured into buying the cocaine by government agents. If it had been a news crew doing the taping and DeLorean suing them, it could have cost the news organization millions of dollars to be wrong. You must make sure the law is on your side before you engage in or make public your investigative activities.

The most common situation involves going onto private property to show illegal or questionable activity where the visible presence of a camera would cause the activity to stop. The photographer usually uses the disguise of an interested party to the activity, for example, a spectator at a pit bull dogfight or a buyer of child pornography. Making use of a wide-angle lens, the hidden camera can merely be pointed in the direction of the activity to show an overall view of what is happening. This use of photography can be quite dangerous. Before engaging in any risky form of photojournalism, you should consider what the worst possible outcome might be and how you can minimize your risks. In some cases, it could cost you your life.

Because this technique pushes the limits of the right to privacy, the laws concerning the use of a hidden camera can vary from state to state. Check with your state's attorney general's office before using a hidden camera on private property; check with your lawyer before airing any part of it. Not only the context in which the video is used, but also the way in which it was obtained can determine liability in any criminal or civil complaint. At least one state in the Midwest has made it illegal to use such a camera to videotape on farms in reaction to the use of hidden cameras by the news media and by animal rights' groups who were protesting the treatment of livestock. Disguised protest group members and TV journalists in that state were visiting "puppy mills" to expose the horrible conditions under which the dogs were bred and raised. The resulting public outcry did not lead the state to clamp down on the offending "mills" but rather on the journalists. Laws that restrict journalism will surely be tested in the courts, but it does point out the complexity of interpreting the right of privacy versus the public's right to know.

Names and Numbers

Another aspect of privacy involves information. Credit card numbers, tax returns, addresses, social security numbers, and bank account and telephone numbers cannot be made public by the news media. Showing an audience this type of information without good cause can be a serious violation of the right to privacy, even for people who fit the category of a public figure.

The U.S. Post Office has one hard and fast rule: You may not show the names and addresses of any letters or packages in a photo, because it is not public information any more than the parcel's contents; it is meant only for the sender and the addressee to know. This situation would also exist in a department store if you were shooting a story on consumer credit. You cannot show someone's credit card number on the screen. In both situations, there are ways to get all the shots needed, including extreme close-ups, without violating anyone's rights.

It may be part of a story to show the destination of mail. By carefully arranging the letters in a pile, you can have successive letters stacked so that only the city line of the address can be seen. Without the name and street, the city cannot be linked to any one individual. The same can be done with credit cards. By asking the customer to hold the card with a finger covering the name and part of the card's number, a viewer would have no way of getting the name and credit number to misuse.

Anytime you shoot names and numbers, you must pay special attention to the rights of the people associated with them. Sometimes the most innocent situation can lead to a nasty legal conflict. If you are in a real estate office doing a story on home buying and you shoot a close-up on some bid papers, you may inadvertently show the name of the bidder. If other business associates see the story and confrontation results in a deal falling through, you may be sued for invasion of privacy. Permission was never given to make the deal public and the bidder was not a public figure.

Regardless of the situation, you must always consider how much personal information you may be revealing about someone, especially if that person has nothing directly to do with your story. The safest thing to do is never to show anyone's name or any of their personal identification numbers unless you have their permission or that information is already public knowledge, such as the address of a criminal charged in a serious crime. Because someone's name and number are listed in the phone book does not give you the right to use this information, unless that particular person is the subject of public interest.

Police Orders

Many times a police officer will try to stop the videotaping of crime or accident scenes and will threaten a photographer with arrest. The photographer usually complies with this request to maintain good media/police relations but also attempts to find a way to circumvent the officer's orders. Usually the photographer will simply back away and use a telephoto lens to continue shooting. Nonetheless, the threat of arrest is real, although the officer knows charges are unlikely to be filed against the photographer; the police usually release the photographer after a short time. The official reason for detaining the photographer can simply be interfering with a peace officer. This offense can be hard to prosecute but gives the police legal grounds to lock a photographer in the back of a squad car. The reality is that most police know that keeping the photographer locked up until the event is over accomplishes what they want: no pictures. If you are threatened with arrest, believe the officer regardless of your opinion about your rights.

There will be times when the police and the media seem to be at cross-purposes and you must take extra care to make sure you are not pointlessly exercising your rights at the expense of good police work. One of the reasons police often do not want pictures at the scene of a crime is to prevent valuable evidence from becoming common knowledge. Only the criminal, the police investigators, and the prosecutor should know the details of the crime scene until the trial. This eliminates the innocent but disturbed individuals who confess to the offense, or false witnesses who come forward to throw off suspicion from someone else. If the police are sure that only the real criminal would know certain details about the crime scene, then the fakers can easily be spotted.

The greatest problems arise when the police do not make clear their reasons for denying pictures. The public's right to know can be on a collision course with the ability of the police to do their job. If the news organization has well-established good relations with local law enforcement, most problems will not arise. One part of the constitutional responsibility of a free press is to question authority. This aspect of journalism can put you at odds with the police. In the absence of a good working relationship, the news media can hamper an investigation by its aggressive coverage. Knowing where the line is between your rights and the duty of the police to protect the public can be almost impossible. You must decide in a split second whether the shot is worth the chance of getting arrested. Sometimes you have to lose a battle to win the war.

Part of your duty to serve the public's right to know is to be able to actually do just that. The police or any other agency or organization may try to stop your coverage for any number of reasons. It is your job as a journalist to decide if their reasons are valid (not showing a rape victim), are simply self-serving (no bad publicity), or are an attempt to cover up wrongdoing (the police using excessive force). If you are locked in a squad car, you will not be able to make any decisions or take any pictures for that matter. Your most important goal is to keep shooting video without getting arrested. You can be a very powerful person with your camera; with that power comes a great deal of pressure to direct what you do or do not do. Remember that without your camera, you are powerless. Many people will want to censor what you are shooting.

Avoiding Problems

Almost all TV stations have lawyers who scrutinize pictures or scripts that might lead to legal problems before the material is aired. Of course, there will always be times when a lawyer is not available for this purpose. A news organization may have to rely on the judgment of the producer or other news management. If you, as a news photographer, know that something you are taping could result in a potential legal problem, try to head off as much as you can in the field while still covering the story. If some people really do not want their pictures taken and they are not directly part of the story, don't shoot them. Avoid problems that serve no purpose in covering the story. If you know that the video you are shooting in our cafe example earlier is for a story on couples having affairs, then you should provide plenty of shots of couples where the audience would have no way of identifying them. Shoot only their clasped hands, shoot them out of focus, use a potted plant in the foreground to block the view of their faces, shoot them from behind, do not let the particular cafe be recognizable in the shots, and so on. This makes the job of the editor easier and adds another layer of safety to keep you and the station out of trouble.

On the other hand, you should not censor yourself so heavily that you cannot get the job done or get all the pictures you need. You will have to rely a certain amount on the other people involved with putting the material on the air. You may not always be the best person to make the decision on what to show or how to show it. Unless you know for a fact that you cannot show something, or were given explicit instructions on how to shoot it, do the shooting with several options in mind. Trust the editors and the news management to make the best use of the pictures. After all, the pictures are not public until they are aired. You can shoot anything but you cannot always air everything shot. If you at least avoid the obvious problems (like showing the faces of undercover police officers), other problems can be dealt with in postproduction by not using the shot or by applying special effects.

NON-NEWS PRODUCTIONS

Any video product that does not fall under the category of news does not enjoy the same latitude regarding privacy. Without the backing of the Fourth Amendment to the Constitution, violating someone's right to privacy can quickly lead to the courtroom. The way the courts interpret privacy laws is much stricter for non-news productions than for news. Even if the method of shooting and the presentation are the same as news, if the videographer is not shooting for a news organization there are no "free press" rights.

Profit and Publicity

Most non-news production is done not to serve the public but to serve the producer or subject of the video. Because one or both of these parties are benefiting from the video, they are not allowed to do so at the expense of someone else's rights. Non-news production normally brings to mind commercials or entertainment and informational programs, but it also includes areas like public service announcements, charity promotions, and business presentations. Although an organization may be nonprofit and its 30-second video spot shot free, the organization still benefits from the publicity. People see the spot and donate money to that charity. While a community service may be important and have the best community needs in mind, the organization is not allowed to invade the privacy of anyone. It is easy to see that showing the face of a down-and-out person on skid row in a commercial for a trade school without permission is violating a right to privacy for simple monetary gain. It may not be as easy to see that a skid-row charity using the same face in a public service

announcement without permission still violates this same right.

Content

Even with permission, you cannot use a person's image in any way you please. It is not acceptable to misrepresent what you are doing. If you ask permission to photograph someone and give either a direct answer or implication of how the pictures will be used and then use the pictures in a totally different manner (for example, one that shows the person in a negative way), you could still be in for a big lawsuit. Also, unlike news, the plaintiffs in cases like this tend to be more aggressive, because the producers were doing it for money and not for journalistic reasons. A news organization may be able to show that the misuse of the picture came about by error due to the rush to meet a deadline and the material was not double-checked. A production company does not have the problem of on-air deadlines only hours from shooting, because it has the time to make sure that everything is right and legal.

Intended Audience

The greater the number of people who see your product, the more you need to make sure that every little legal detail is properly handled. In the case of a student video, the rights of some subjects may be overlooked because only a very small number of people will ever see the video. A student is generally allowed to gather video in the same way as a news crew even without a press pass. Context can be overlooked because no one outside the class will see the video. It is similar to art students copying a great painting for a class project; any use of that copy outside the classroom would be illegal. If a student video is to be judged in a contest, the student had better start worrying about the rights of the people in the video.

Most corporate videos are not too concerned with the right of privacy in their video presentations if the intended audience is only the workers within the company. Just as in the student video example, the size of the audience is small enough that any infractions of the law will more than likely go unnoticed. The key word here is unnoticed. As a corporate video producer you may tape in public areas and never get permission to use people's pictures in your presentation, because they and anyone who knows them will probably never see the end product. Of course, there is a remote possibility that someone portrayed in a negative fashion will find out and sue.

The feeling that if your audience is small enough you need not worry at all about anyone else's rights can lead to real trouble. Most of the time this belief will work. The one time that it does not could cost the company or you a fortune. The key to this issue is that the image of a person who has not given permission for its use must be recognizable in a video. If the shot is wide enough or done from behind or lasts such a short time that the subject cannot be recognized, then a charge of invasion of privacy will be hard to justify. Unless you know for certain that no one you are shooting will complain or even find out how their pictures are used, you had better secure an okay from all parties involved in any recognizable on-screen appearance. (See Figure 12.1.)

COPYRIGHTS

A TV news photographer can shoot almost anything and air it. But an editor cannot take just any source of video and insert it into a news story. One TV station cannot simply tape another's newscast and use video from it as its own. Nor can segments of any other program or movie be used in its news stories unless it is used by permission of, or by purchase from, its owner.

Violations

One of the most common copyright violations is the use of movie clips in news stories. Without the permission of the owner or copyright holder of the movie (the studio or producer), you cannot use any part of a movie in your news story. If, however, the studio has sent you a video press kit made up of the trailer and several clips from that film, you can use the pictures in any news story where they would be appropriate. By sending you the press kit, the copyright holder has in a sense given you permission to use the film clip. The same rule applies to any other TV show or program.

Often TV stations in smaller markets will break the copyright rules because no one from the movie or TV industry will see the story. This is similar to making copies of your favorite movie and giving them to your friends. It seems innocent, but it is illegal. The FBI warning at the head of each tape applies to newspeople as well as to the public. If you want people to respect your right of ownership for what you produce, you must respect their rights. If you are caught using parts of movies or TV shows without permission, the owner can charge you a rental or licensing fee that may be as high as several thousand dollars a minute for what you used, plus residual payments to those who worked on the show.

Fair Use Rules

The news media can exercise an exception to copyright laws in certain cases. By invoking a standard called **fair use**, a new organization can use a wide variety of copyrighted material in a news story. The most common example of this is when a famous actor dies. His or her obituary can be filled with clips from all of their work without permission from the copyright holders. It comes back to the idea of the public's right to know. The law allows any material that is directly related to the telling and understanding of a story to be used in that telling. Especially at the network level such use is carefully scrutinized to make sure it is not abused. Fair use material is generally limited to one-time use only and it does have to adhere to a strict and direct relationship to the subject of the story. Showing a scene from the movie *Titanic* in a feature story about a local woman that has a Titanic diner plate collection would not qualify as fair use of the movie clip. But a story about a major scandal concerning the making of the movie (there are none as far as we know) could allow the news organization to use clips without permission.

In stories involving controversy it is often best not to make the video being fair used too prominent in the piece. In other words, the video shouldn't "wallpaper" the piece. A good method of distancing the material from your original portions of the story is to play the fair used material in a monitor and then shoot the set as well as the video so it is obvious that the video is being copied and not simply used as normal B roll.

While fair use can shield a news organization from copyright fines it cannot shield them from lawsuits trying to assess damages. The suits may fail in court but the cost of simply defending against them to that point can be more trouble and costly than paying off the copyright holder.

Piracy

In 1989, a United jumbo jet crashed at the Sioux City, Iowa, airport. Only one TV photographer was there to capture the horrible event on tape. Within hours,

MODEL RELEASE

I hereby assign rights to the videotape and sound recording made of me this date, _____, by, _____ and I hereby authorize the reproduction, sale, copyright, exhibition, broadcast and/or distribution of said videotape without limitation for the purpose of

_____

I certify that I am over 21 years old.

Signed _____

Dated _____

MODEL RELEASE

For and in consideration of my engagement as a model by _____, hereafter referred to as the videographer, on terms or fee hereinafter stated, I hereby give the videographer, his legal representatives and assigns, those for whom the videographer is acting, and those acting with his permission, or his employees, the right and permission to copyright and/or use, reuse and/or broadcast and republish videotape recordings of me, or in which I may be distorted in character, or form, in conjunction with my own or fictitious name, on reproductions thereof in color, or black and white made through any media by the videographer at his studio or elsewhere, for any purpose whatsoever, including the use of any printed matter in conjunction therewith.

I hereby waive any right to inspect or approve the finished videotape, sound track, or advertising copy or printed matter that may be used in conjunction therewith or to the eventual use that it might be applied.

I hereby release, discharge and agree to save harmless the videographer, his representatives, assigns, employees or any person or persons, corporation or corporations, acting under his permission or authority, or any person, persons, corporation or corporations, for whom he might be acting, including any firm publishing and/or distributing the finished product, in whole or in part, from and against any liability as a result of any distortion, blurring, or alteration, optical illusion, or use in composite form, either intentionally or otherwise, that may occur or be produced in the taking, processing or reproduction of the finished product, its publication, distribution, or broadcast of the same even should the same subject me to ridicule, scandal, reproach, scorn, or indignity.

I hereby certify that I am over twenty one years of age, and competent to contract in my own name in so far as the above is concerned.

I am compensated as follows

I have read the foregoing release, authorization and agreement, before affixing my signature below, and warrant that I fully understand the contents thereof.

DATED _____

_____ L.S.   _____ L.S.
WITNESS   NAME

_____   _____
ADDRESS   ADDRESS

I hereby certify that I am the parent and/or guardian of _____ an infant under the age of twenty one years, and in consideration of value received, the receipt of which is hereby acknowledged, I hereby consent that any videotapes which have been, or are about to be made by the videographer may be used by him for the purposes set forth in original release hereinabove, signed by the infant model, with the same force and effect as if executed by me.

_____ L.S.
PARENT OR GUARDIAN

_____
ADDRESS

Videographer 1 - Fill in terms of employment.
           2 - Strike out words that do not apply.

Figure 12.1 Two examples of model release forms. If a videographer or producer has a subject complete a release form, the chances of being sued for unauthorized use are greatly reduced. Forms like these are used extensively in non-news production. Note that the term model is the same as subject.

every TV news outlet in the world was running the tape. How did others get access to it? The news director of the Iowa station said they stole it.

The age of satellite transmission has not only made it easier to get images from one place to another, but it has also made it easier for more people to have access to these images. Unless a signal is scrambled, anyone with a satellite dish and the proper tuner can tap into any channel on the satellite. Because so many different organizations use the few satellites available for occasional use, scrambling has not been a practical method of protecting news material. Entertainment outlets, such as HBO or pay-per-view shows, control one particular channel on the satellite for extended periods of time or even own a particular channel. They can easily have their signals scrambled to protect against piracy.

News organizations have traditionally shown a low concern for piracy because the ease of accessibility and speed of delivery are always more important. News organizations in the past have generally respected each other's rights of ownership even when they share the same satellite channel. It is not unusual to see NBC, ABC, CBS, and CNN stories all being fed one after another on a single channel from the satellite. Sometimes only their mutual cooperation allows any network to get material from a distant location in a timely manner. Unfortunately, the expanding number of news organizations has made the competition to get exclusive pictures more important than ever. The expanding market for the pictures has also made the ability to keep them exclusive harder and harder.

A picture taken by an NBC affiliate can be sent via satellite to NBC network in New York, which can in turn send the picture to all NBC affiliates across the country on their regular news feed by satellite. One of the affiliates that receives the feed may have a contract to provide pictures to CNN News and uses the shot in a story sent to CNN. CNN puts the story on its feed to all its subscribers. One such station happens to be a CBS affiliate, who repackages the story and sends it to CBS network in New York. In the evening the shot appears on both NBC and CBS. If the special group-owned stations' news services contain affiliates of all three networks, the picture may end up on every news show in America. The lightning speed of satellite delivery makes each of these transfers possible and explains how one picture can make it to every TV channel in the country in a few short hours and not openly break any copyright laws (individual agreements notwithstanding).

The case of the Sioux City plane video is more complex. It was alleged that the video never made the more legal rounds and was simply stolen off the original feed to the Iowa station's network. If it was taken at that point by anyone else, it would be a case of copyright violation. However, once the pictures start to travel from one station or from one company (a broadcasting company can own stations with different affiliations) to another through network or smaller news service feeds, the copyright laws can be stretched to the limit. This will become even more confusing as full-motion, full-frame video becomes easily accessible to most homes via broadband connections to the World Wide Web. Because the web is digital, any news video put on a web site by a news service (such as CNN or MSNBC) can be easily downloaded by unscrupulous individuals, edited for their own purposes, and then resent or "webcasted."

Exclusivity

Because of the way business is generally done in TV news, it can be almost impossible to keep a particular picture exclusively in your organization if the picture is of great interest to the public. On the other hand, if proper legal precautions are taken and the pictures are tightly controlled, you may be able to maintain exclusivity. It can be easier to control pictures not produced by members of your station or company. Previous agreements can make pictures shot by staff members available to other members of the group or company automatically. An independent producer or freelance photographer may offer you exclusive pictures, and as part of the agreement to let you air them, the pictures come with tight restrictions on their use. The famous Zapruder film showing the assassination of President John F. Kennedy is not the property of the public or any news organization. It requires special permission from the owners to air it, and you must comply with many restrictions in its use. As in any legal contract, you are bound by the agreement you have signed and it can take precedence over other agreements. The agreement may say that only your station and not other parts of your network or group can air the video.

Bugs

One way producers keep track of their video and avoid any unauthorized use of it is by marking the video as theirs. In a manner similar to putting a brand on cows, video makers can "brand" their tape. In TV terms, it is called a **bug**: A small logo or abbreviation, much like the rancher's brand, is superimposed in one corner of the picture when the video is dubbed or transmitted. While it is widely used in news throughout the world, it is most common in sporting event highlights. Instead of recording hours and hours of sports, a local station may simply contract with an authorized highlight producer. Several times a day this company will feed by satellite condensed highlights of all the important sporting events of the day. All the video will have a bug in the corner of the screen to identify the origin of the pictures. If the bug should appear on another station or anywhere else that has no agreement with the producer, then legal action may be taken to stop this activity.

Courtesies

The easiest way to get other people's material is to simply ask for it. For pictures that are not controversial or have little competitive advantage, most stations or producers allow their use if the owner of the video gets an on-screen credit. This credit is somewhat like the bug only larger. Usually displayed across the bottom of the screen, it will say "Tape courtesy of (producer's name)," whether it be CBS News or Paramount Pictures or John Doe. You must obtain permission to use this method of protection.

The use of the "courtesy" is usually granted by verbal agreement and not written up or signed. If you or your company has a reputation for honesty in this type of agreement, then getting permission is usually quite easy. But when the video is very important, it is more difficult to get permission for use in this way.

There is a point where the escalation of fighting within the media to keep exclusive rights to something does slow down. A news organization that should happen to get video of a dramatic or history-making event when others did not may indeed share the pictures with or even without a credit because they feel the public, not just their viewers, must see it. A private party might not feel that sense of duty to inform the public and reserve the rights to the pictures, as in the case of the Zapruder film.

Pool

In some situations, only one camera is allowed to enter a restricted area or there is only enough room for one camera. In the course of daily news coverage and during large national stories, this situation arises time and time again. The solution is to form a pool. One camera goes, but its video is shared among all interested organizations. If you have ever seen the president of the United States outside the White House, you would have noticed a small band of press people who have a slightly closer position than the larger group of press. This small group is the White House Pool. These few TV cameras are from the broadcast networks and CNN, but the video from each of them is made available to anyone who wants it. Because every TV news photographer covering the president would want this front-row advantage, it would be a madhouse of pushing and shoving without the pool arrangement.

The most common use of pools in the TV news industry is in the courtroom. As in the example of the president above, it would be too disruptive to have many cameras in a courtroom. Usually one person or group in every market coordinates the pools to make sure the burden of having to do the extra work involved (wiring a courtroom for sound, providing a multiple outlet box, or making dubs) gets handled fairly. Often the pool photographer cannot be in position in the hallway to get the crucial just-out-of-court statements by the defendants. In these cases, it is common practice for a nonpool photographer to let the pool organization use their hallway interviews.

Some situations in the field may require the photographers present to form an impromptu pool on the spot without the time or ability to check with management before doing so. An example might be a group of photographers at the command post of firefighters battling a raging forest fire. The commander is going via helicopter to see if the fire lines are holding in a remote village cut off from the usable roads; one seat is offered for a photographer from the group. In this situation, the photographers present would decide among themselves who is the best to go. The video will be dubbed either at the site later or at the station. The group can enter into an agreement on the ownership of the tape independent of any outside input.

This ability gives the photographer in the field the power to negotiate access to restricted or dangerous areas. Setting up a pool so that the tape can be shared and no other cameras need to access the site makes dealing with the media just that much easier for the emergency services people. If the media can be satisfied with one photographer, then it becomes an easy solution to a growing problem: throngs of photographers all wanting pictures or, worse yet, trying to sneak their way into a very dangerous situation. Once a deal is made, all parties must abide by the agreement or the possibility of it working out again in the future will be jeopardized. The emergency agency cannot let anyone else into the area, so the pool photographer must make the video readily available to any news organization actively covering that event.

Certain restrictions apply if the organization allowing the pool is made fully aware of them and understands them. The pool may be restricted to only those present at the time of departure, or to those there by the time of arrival back from shooting. In this case, a news organization that showed up several hours late, or simply did not send anyone to the site, would not have a right to the tape. Usually any media outlet that was trying to cover the event, whether present at the time the pool was formed or not, gets a share of the tape.

Public Domain Materials

Many portable video producers have the need to obtain video or audio but cannot obtain it through their own shooting and have no musicians on staff to compose or perform it. There is an answer to this general and widespread problem. An abundance of film footage is available that can be used because its copyright has expired. Many films are sold on videocassette in discount or grocery stores for less than $10. Often these films no longer have copyright protection and a video producer may use this footage as desired. Buying these videocassettes from the grocery store may be convenient, but the quality derived from the VHS copy may not be acceptable. Companies exist that can, for a reasonable fee, supply a copy of the material you need in the format of your choice.

Music or soundtrack material is similarly obtained. Excerpts from some old radio shows are often available at a very reasonable price and a tape format is less of a problem. You should note that sound quality is always an important criterion for the decision to use this type of material. If you have a musician or vocalist available, you may choose to have a fresh version of a song produced for you. This may yield a high-quality soundtrack, but the producer must either obtain permission from the publisher or use music that is not copyright protected. Material in this category, both audio and video, is referred to as being "in the public domain," meaning that it is owned by the public in general, or includes traditional songs

that may never have been copyrighted. For example, your musicians could perform songs like "Turkey in the Straw" or "She'll Be Comin' Round the Mountain" without fear of copyright problems, but strangely enough, not "Happy Birthday." Classical music has this benefit as well, but not other artists' performance of classical works, because their performances are their property even if the music is not.

If you choose to use copyrighted music, you may find that the copyright holder has an organization that will provide assistance in obtaining clearance and collecting fees. For much of the popular music recorded in the last 30 years, this organization would be either BMI (Broadcast Music Inc.) or ASCAP (American Society of Composers, Authors, and Publishers).

COPYRIGHT GUIDELINES FOR THE WEB

The responsibility for following copyright law falls on the user of other people's material that has been obtained from the web. The following are some guidelines to use when getting material from the web:

- Works on the web are considered copyrighted as they are created, even if copyright is not claimed in the material.
- If you use other people's web content you can be sued even if there is no money involved. This is especially true if it damages the profitability of the original material. The recent Napster case illustrates the general concept here. Napster distributed copyrighted audio material via a system of peer-to-peer information sharing. Numerous musical groups and their publishers claimed that this activity limited the profitability of the original product. The legal system has judged that this is a violation of copyright law, and Napster was ordered to stop distributing copyrighted material unless they begin to pay copyright fees to the copyright holders.
- Material that was originally posted on an electronic mailing list is not in the public domain unless specifically stated by the originator of the material.
- Copyright holders do not have to defend themselves or their material, because it is protected unless permission is granted for the material's use.

- Copyright violation is a crime that can result in monetary fines, but some violations can be treated as felonies.
- Reposting or reusing material that was received in an advertisement or promotion has the same protection as other material unless permission is granted for its use.

PROTECTING YOUR WORK

A common violation of copyright laws occurs when copyrighted material is copied and used improperly. This law concerns all VCR owners. Broadcast material recorded off the air or from cable TV can be reused for some length of time for personal or educational use. After this period of time has elapsed, you must rerecord the program from its broadcast in order to have a legal copy to use.

After putting many hours and dollars into an original creation, it would be quite annoying to have your work stolen by unscrupulous video producers who decided that it was easier to use your video rather than produce their own. This is difficult to prevent; a copy of your video can easily be duplicated especially if it is in a digital format. But you may be able to be compensated for this theft. As mentioned earlier, copyright law provides legal protection against unauthorized use of your work. Intentional theft of your copyrighted work can be penalized with very stiff fines of up to $100,000. Criminal penalties (for example, a jail term) may be levied as well. Accidental use of copyrighted material carries penalties of $500 to $20,000 per incidence of such use.

Obtaining Protection

Protection of your creative work is guaranteed by law. This protection is easy to obtain through the U.S. Copyright Office in Washington, D.C. You can obtain all of the information and forms you need on the web. Go to the U.S. Copyright Office forms site at www.loc.gov/copyright/forms. The site lists the different types of material that can be copyrighted and provides links to forms that can be filled out and returned to the office. Form PA is used for motion pictures or other audiovisual works. (See Figure 12.2.) Each form comes with line-by-line instructions to help you fill out the form. For voice information about copyright registration you can call (202)707-3000, or you can call the copyright hotline at (202)707-9100 and ask that an application form be sent to you. Forms can also be obtained by fax. The application form, along with a small fee, registers your copyright. The office will send you a certificate as proof of the registration. If the work you wish to protect is to be exhibited to the public (for example, broadcast or shown to a large, public audience), or if your script is to be published, send two copies of the work along with your application. Unpublished work requires only one copy of the product.

Alerting Others of Protection

Perhaps the most effective way to discourage others from unauthorized use of your work is to indicate that you hold a copyright on the work. This is simple and straightforward. If you want to copyright a videotape, simply put the word "copyright" with your name and the year on the label. The Copyright Office recommends that you include this information in the video itself. The abbreviation "Copr." or the symbol "C" can also be used. For written work, the notice of copyright should appear on each page. The copyright notice protects you in the United States. To protect your work in other countries, add the words "All Rights Reserved."

Scope

What aspects of your creative project can be copyrighted? The complete project can certainly receive this protection. Some components of the project can also be protected. The entire script and the music and/or audio track are also subject to copyright protection. Any portion of these aspects of the work is protected as well. But it is important to note that the idea for the video project cannot be copyrighted. Others may use your basic idea and produce another project. In fact, they can obtain their own copyright protection for their work. In other words, your ideas can be stolen, but the specific way you have expressed them cannot, at least not legally. Another video producer can take your idea but must express it differently in the final project. If the methods are too similar, you may be able to sue the infringer for monetary damages.

INSURANCE

No matter how many precautions you take, something always goes wrong. Most of the time the problem is simple, such as a broken cable or a deck that

FORM PA
UNITED STATES COPYRIGHT OFFICE

REGISTRATION NUMBER

PA   PAU
EFFECTIVE DATE OF REGISTRATION

Month   Day   Year

DO NOT WRITE ABOVE THIS LINE. IF YOU NEED MORE SPACE, USE A SEPARATE CONTINUATION SHEET.

1
TITLE OF THIS WORK ▼

PREVIOUS OR ALTERNATIVE TITLES ▼

NATURE OF THIS WORK ▼ See instructions

2
a
NAME OF AUTHOR ▼

DATES OF BIRTH AND DEATH
Year Born ▼   Year Died ▼

Was this contribution to the work a "work made for hire"?
☐ Yes
☐ No

AUTHOR'S NATIONALITY OR DOMICILE
Name of Country
OR { Citizen of ▶_____
Domiciled in ▶_____

WAS THIS AUTHOR'S CONTRIBUTION TO THE WORK
Anonymous?   ☐ Yes ☐ No
Pseudonymous?   ☐ Yes ☐ No
If the answer to either of these questions is "Yes," see detailed instructions

NATURE OF AUTHORSHIP   Briefly describe nature of the material created by this author in which copyright is claimed. ▼

NOTE
Under the law, the "author" of a work made for hire" is generally the employer not the employee (see instructions). For any part of this work that was "made for hire" check "Yes" in the space provided, give the employer (or other person for whom the work was prepared) as "Author" of that part, and leave the space for dates of birth and death blank.

b
NAME OF AUTHOR ▼

DATES OF BIRTH AND DEATH
Year Born ▼   Year Died ▼

Was this contribution to the work a "work made for hire"?
☐ Yes
☐ No

AUTHOR'S NATIONALITY OR DOMICILE
Name of country
OR { Citizen of ▶_____
Domiciled in ▶_____

WAS THIS AUTHOR'S CONTRIBUTION TO THE WORK
Anonymous?   ☐ Yes ☐ No
Pseudonymous?   ☐ Yes ☐ No
If the answer to either of these questions is "Yes," see detailed instructions

NATURE OF AUTHORSHIP   Briefly describe nature of the material created by this author in which copyright is claimed. ▼

c
NAME OF AUTHOR ▼

DATES OF BIRTH AND DEATH
Year Born ▼   Year Died ▼

Was this contribution to the work a "work made for hire"?
☐ Yes
☐ No

AUTHOR'S NATIONALITY OR DOMICILE
Name of Country
OR { Citizen of ▶_____
Domiciled in ▶_____

WAS THIS AUTHOR'S CONTRIBUTION TO THE WORK
Anonymous?   ☐ Yes ☐ No
Pseudonymous?   ☐ Yes ☐ No
If the answer to either of these questions is "Yes," see detailed instructions

NATURE OF AUTHORSHIP   Briefly describe nature of the material created by this author in which copyright is claimed. ▼

3
a YEAR IN WHICH CREATION OF THIS WORK WAS COMPLETED This information must be given in all cases.
◀ Year

b DATE AND NATION OF FIRST PUBLICATION OF THIS PARTICULAR WORK
Complete this information ONLY if this work has been published.
Month ▶_____ Day ▶_____ Year ▶_____   ◀ Nation

4
COPYRIGHT CLAIMANT(S) Name and address must be given even if the claimant is the same as the author given in space 2.▼

See instructions before completing this space

TRANSFER If the claimant(s) named here in space 4 are different from the author(s) named in space 2, give a brief statement of how the claimant(s) obtained ownership of the copyright.▼

APPLICATION RECEIVED

ONE DEPOSIT RECEIVED

TWO DEPOSITS RECEIVED

REMITTANCE NUMBER AND DATE

DO NOT WRITE HERE
OFFICE USE ONLY

MORE ON BACK ▶
• Complete all applicable spaces (numbers 5-9) on the reverse side of this page
• See detailed instructions
• Sign the form at line 8

DO NOT WRITE HERE
Page 1 of_____pages

Figure 12.2   Form PA is used to obtain copyright protection.

EXAMINED BY

CHECKED BY

☐ CORRESPONDENCE
  Yes

FORM PA

FOR
COPYRIGHT
OFFICE
USE
ONLY

DO NOT WRITE ABOVE THIS LINE. IF YOU NEED MORE SPACE, USE A SEPARATE CONTINUATION SHEET.

PREVIOUS REGISTRATION Has registration for this work, or for an earlier version of this work, already been made in the Copyright Office?

☐ Yes ☐ No If your answer is "Yes," why is another registration being sought? (Check appropriate box) ▼

☐ This is the first published edition of a work previously registered in unpublished form.

☐ This is the first application submitted by this author as copyright claimant.

☐ This is a changed version of the work, as shown by space 6 on this application.

If your answer is "Yes," give: **Previous Registration Number** ▼   **Year of Registration** ▼

5

DERIVATIVE WORK OR COMPILATION Complete both space 6a & 6b for a derivative work; complete only 6b for a compilation.

a. **Preexisting Material** Identify any preexisting work or works that this work is based on or incorporates. ▼

b. **Material Added to This Work** Give a brief, general statement of the material that has been added to this work and in which copyright is claimed. ▼

6

See instructions
before completing
this space

DEPOSIT ACCOUNT If the registration fee is to be charged to a Deposit Account established in the Copyright Office, give name and number of Account.

Name ▼   **Account Number** ▼

7

CORRESPONDENCE Give name and address to which correspondence about this application should be sent. Name/Address/Apt/City/State/Zip ▼

Area Code & Telephone Number ▶

Be sure to
give your
daytime phone
◀ number

CERTIFICATION* I, the undersigned, hereby certify that I am the

Check only one ▼

☐ author

☐ other copyright claimant

☐ owner of exclusive right(s)

☐ authorized agent of_____
    Name of author or other copyright claimant, or owner of exclusive right(s) ▲

of the work identified in this application and that the statements made
by me in this application are correct to the best of my knowledge.

8

Typed or printed name and date ▼ If this application gives a date of publication in space 3, do not sign and submit it before that date.

_____ date ▶ _____

☞   **Handwritten signature (X)** ▼

**MAIL
CERTIFI-
CATE TO**

Name ▼

Number/Street/Apartment Number ▼

City/State/ZIP ▼

**Certificate
will be
mailed in
window
envelope**

YOU MUST:
• Complete all necessary spaces
• Sign your application in space 8

SEND ALL 3 ELEMENTS
IN THE SAME PACKAGE:
1. Application form
2. Non-refundable $10 filing fee
   in check or money order
   payable to *Register of Copyrights*
3. Deposit material

MAIL TO:
Register of Copyrights
Library of Congress
Washington, D.C. 20559

9

* 17 U.S.C. § 506(e) Any person who knowingly makes a false representation of a material fact in the application for copyright registration provided for by section 409, or in any written statement filed in connection with the application, shall be fined not more than $2,500.

June 1989—200,000   ☆ U.S. GOVERNMENT PRINTING OFFICE: 1989—241-428/80,026 will not thread the tape. The delays and breakdowns may cost the news photographer a shot or cost the production photographer much money. Sometimes people can be injured by a falling light or their business can suffer losses due to a water pipe you broke. You can violate someone's rights even without turning on a camera. In the case of physical injury, your troubles may skyrocket. As an employee, you may not have to worry about the ultimate outcome of such events because your employer is covered by insurance. If you are a freelancer or working as an independent contractor, however, then you should protect yourself with insurance.

Comprehensive Liability

Everyone doing business needs some type of protection in case of accidents. When you are in an automobile, you may, through no real fault of your own, cause someone to be injured or even killed. This is why you need car insurance. You also need insurance at work for the same reason. Working for a TV station or corporation, you usually can rely on them to have such insurance. A news photographer who causes an accident (such as setting up a light that eventually falls on someone) would be able to turn to the company for protection against a lawsuit. A freelance photographer hoping to sell a video would be responsible and held liable for the injuries.

Anyone making videos on their own for news, production, and other uses needs to consider what being held liable means if they are without insurance. Suppose you agree to shoot a public service announcement for a charity at a very wealthy person's mansion. A light falls, starting a fire that gets out of control and burns the house to the ground along with its priceless art collection. If the owner does not sue, then the insurance company will. Without insurance, you may lose everything you own and end up in personal bankruptcy court for a simple 1-hour shoot.

In recent years, the average coverage for an independent video maker was $1 million in liability insurance. This amount covers most common claims filed as a result of property or bodily injury or death. This sounds like a great deal of money, but if you look back at the burned-down mansion example, you can see that even this may not be enough. More than likely, it would be more than enough for any problems you would normally encounter. One million dollars' worth of coverage may cost several thousand

dollars a year in premiums, but if you want to stay in business, it is a necessary cost.

Comprehensive liability insurance is required if you want to do any taping on public property that requires a permit. Many rental companies require it before renting you any equipment. Even production companies asking you to work as an independent contractor want you to have liability coverage. Everyone who has anything to do with you, your equipment, or the location in which you are shooting will want some assurance that they will be protected in case anything should happen and you are found at full or partial fault. Not having liability insurance can cause prospective video clients to take their business elsewhere.

Equipment Loss or Damage

When you work for yourself, people routinely want to know if you have appropriate loss or damage coverage and the means to cover any damages you might cause to the equipment you are using. The bank may still own part of your gear, and the rental house does own the gear. If your $30,000 camera should fall from a tripod and topple over a second-story balcony, then you would want some means of replacing it without a second mortgage on your house. If you rented the camera from a rental company, the company would also want to know about your coverage.

If you are using equipment owned or rented by your employer, then you need not worry about who pays if something happens but only about preventing something from happening. People working for themselves more than likely would own their own equipment or rent or borrow it. A freelance photographer can invest anywhere from $10,000 to $200,000 for a set of broadcast-quality gear. Having insurance can mean the difference between losing everything, including your ability to make a living, and going right on to the next shoot.

Rental Floaters

A good insurance policy not only covers anything you own but also any equipment you need to rent. This additional rental coverage, known as a floater, covers you in case anything should happen to the rental gear while it is in your possession. Each floater is issued for a certain dollar maximum; it is priced according to how high the coverage is. If you are renting a VCR, then a $15,000 floater would probably be enough. The amount must be high enough to replace, at current cost, all the equipment rented at any one time. The floater also needs to be made out to the company or person from whom you are renting the equipment before you take the gear. You will need a floater for each company or person from whom you rent. Most insurance companies charge a fee for each company named, and a copy is sent to that company. A floater is usually good for 1 year, no matter how many or how few times you need it.

Rental houses can offer insurance on the spot to qualified renters who do not have a floater. The cost of this type of insurance is usually 10% of the rental fee. You can also get an uninsured renter's policy if you rent equipment you own to other people. This type of coverage would be added to your own equipment loss policy and would not only cover you in case the person damaged your gear but also in case of that person's inadequate coverage.

Restrictions

In almost every policy there are exceptions to what is covered and when it is covered. Some policies may not cover your equipment if it is stolen from inside a vehicle. Others may not cover injuries that happen from operating or riding in a boat or airplane. By reading the fine print, you can discover any number of things that a particular policy does not cover. You may find that the videotape in the machine is not covered but the recorder is.

Other Coverage

You can get insurance for just about anything concerning a video production that is non-news. As the cost of the production increases, a small expense for some protection in an uncertain world may not be a bad idea. The average coverage required for the video business is aimed at protecting the people around from getting hurt either physically or financially. Many exceptions to the coverage are things that can hurt you if you are the producer of the project. For a price, you can get things like cast insurance for your production. This covers any additional expenses incurred because the person appearing in your program or segment cannot finish the project due to sickness or injury.

You can insure the videotape for the cost of producing it so that if it is stolen everyone can still get

paid. You can even insure the camera against failure in case you miss the shot because a chip goes bad. Other coverage includes sets or props you may use, as well as the wardrobe of the people appearing on camera. If you are working with any union or guild contracts, they may require special coverage. While most of these extra types of coverage are out of the budget range for small video productions, anyone dealing with large amounts of money for an ever-increasingly complex production should consider them. This type of coverage usually is required when people have invested money in your project and want some guarantees of at least seeing the project finished in case something goes wrong. There are several special types of coverage that all video makers might consider as their budgets grow.

Errors and Omissions

A special type of coverage called **errors and omissions (E&O)** can protect you from an oversight in the use of copyrighted material. You may think you have received licensed permission but find out after the production airs that the person who gave you the rights did not own them. This coverage protects you from this and also covers plagiarism, unfair competition, libel, breach of contract, and invasion of privacy. Any complete production that you plan to sell or syndicate for public viewing often requires this type of insurance before anyone will buy it or show it.

Workers' Compensation

Should you be in charge of a production large enough that you are hiring people to work for you, many state and federal laws determine how much protection you must give employees. Workers' compensation insurance is required in most states for anyone having employees or independent contractors. This coverage provides medical, disability, or death benefits to any cast or crew member who becomes injured in the course of their employment. This coverage is needed in addition to normal liability insurance.

Completion Guaranty Bond

This coverage is used to guarantee that the video project you have agreed to do will get the funding necessary for completion. When independent producers finance a project with a bank, a company, or a group of investors, they will often ask for this type of policy to protect their investment from poor budget planning on your part or some other reason. The bondholder is saying that the program will be made so that it will at least have a chance to make money or otherwise satisfy those concerned.

Producers' Insurance Policies

Almost all the above-mentioned types of coverage can be combined into one blanket policy, referred to as **producers' insurance policies (PIPs).** PIPs come with different combinations of coverage to fit almost any type of production. You can often design your own package to fit the exact needs of your production. By working with an insurance company experienced in the film and video industries, you can tailor the coverage to suit your budget as well as your risk.

The cost of any insurance coverage is dependent on several factors. The higher the budget, the higher the insurance costs. The ceiling of the policy also determines the price: a $10,000 floater costs less than a $50,000 one. The amount of the deductible can change your premiums. Some deductibles are rather high, but the annual premium is significantly lower. Most small independent photographers and produc-

ers have year-round policies that cover all of the work they do in that year (within the limits of the policy). You can often determine the cost of insurance before you actually have to buy any special coverage for a particular production. The premiums are usually based on the cost of the project and run between 2 to 4% of the total budget. With extra coverage, a long shooting schedule, or any hazards, the cost can be as much as 10% of the project's budget. Often, for small productions, it ends up being 10% of the budget because the premiums cannot go below certain minimum amounts. In some cases, the insurance might be the major cost of the shoot if you are doing things on a shoestring.

The more you have to interact with the public or any public agencies, the more you are going to have to know about insurance. Even if you do not have the coverage, knowing what you are not covered for can be a great help. Having insurance takes some of the risk out of what you are doing. Many people, especially at the low end of the budget scale, go without any coverage. They have chosen to assume all the risk themselves. Most of the time they play the odds and win. You should always step back and ask yourself what would happen if something should go wrong. It may be a risk you are no longer ready to take.

13 New Trends and Technologies

The future of video production is digital. More so than ever before, the transition between analog video and digital video is proceeding at a rapid pace. Many of the analog formats are being phased out and replaced with digital formats. Broadcast stations, corporate, and educational video users are looking more at digital editors and avoiding high-end analog editors. Off-line editing is becoming possible with personal computers equipped with affordable software programs and video inputs and outputs. As improvements are made in the method of compressing digital video information, digital video storage techniques, and editing software, the entire process of editing is becoming easier and less expensive today than ever before—a trend that will surely continue in the future.

The industry is moving rapidly toward a **tapeless environment.** Rather than acquire video footage shot with video cameras or camcorders and recorded onto videotape, there is considerable pressure from video users to be able to shoot directly into a digital and nonlinear storage device like a high-capacity DVD drive or hard drive. This would decrease the time needed to input video into editing systems and allow quicker access to desired shots for viewing and logging.

One thing is clear for the future of digital TV: **The industry needs to cooperate and decide on a standardized method of digitalization, encoding, and decoding.** More so than any other issue, the lack of standardization presents many problems and causes a general hesitancy by users to adopt new technologies. Often, professional video users are prepared to upgrade their equipment, but don't because of the fear that they might be buying a system from a manufacturer that may soon be obsolete or inferior to a newer system brought to the market shortly after the purchase. This hesitancy has been common for corporate and educational users, but is more of a recent phenomenon for broadcast and high-end independent producers. Since the mid-1980s, Sony's Beta and Beta SP formats have been standard choices for most television station ENG operations and virtually all production houses throughout the country; therefore producers have become used to compatibility using Beta tapes almost exclusively. The challenge to manufacturers of digital video equipment will not only be to standardize, but also to find a method of easily digitizing existing video footage in libraries of production houses, networks, and local news operations across the country.

BUYING EQUIPMENT

Although it is not essential to keep up with each and every innovation or product change that surfaces from the myriad of companies that sell equipment to the video production industry, keeping track of trends is worth doing for several reasons:

1. New equipment may be available to enhance the performance of the equipment that you have.
2. You may be asked to make a purchase recommendation for a major piece of equipment and selecting a soon-to-be-obsolete format or technology (for example, buying an expensive analog format editing system) may make you look less than knowledgeable.

3. Generally, newer equipment is not only of a higher quality but often more economical to use, less expensive to maintain, and more durable than older equipment.

While it is true that a young ENG photographer may have little or no input into major buying decisions at a broadcast TV station, corporate video specialists may be responsible for a capital equipment budget and equipment selections soon after taking a job.

Keeping current with new trends and technologies in the video and related fields (for example, desktop video and computers that can be used to produce multimedia) will help you make better recommendations for future purchases and prepare you for needed technique changes when appropriate. Knowing that a good portable video projection system is now available at a reasonable price may convince you to shoot video instead of film for exhibition to several large audiences at a convention. Several years ago, before liquid-crystal display video projectors were marketed, film might have been the better choice.

DIGITAL TECHNOLOGY IN PORTABLE VIDEO

Digital recording, manipulation, and rerecording of audio and video signals are part of a revolution that has been occurring for some time. Digital recording is a highly accurate, totally reproducible method that allows amazing special effects and no signal loss from generation to generation.

Although the biggest changes have not yet arrived, digital applications are changing the way portable video work is produced. This is especially true for EFP, where postproduction can utilize digital effects to enhance a program to get more attention and appear more professional.

Digital audio is a reality as shown by compact discs, digital audiotape (DAT), and audio portions of videotape recording (for example, the DV format) that can be done with an inexpensive camcorder. Audio editing for video has changed considerably. Sound libraries that formerly consisted of numerous LP records (where some of the most used tracks wore out after numerous uses) now consist of a smaller number of compact discs that take up less space, are almost impervious to wear, and supply amazing sound. Audio editing has forgotten the cut-and-splice days of reel-to-reel recorders. Digital audio stations are commonplace in the professional studio, the educational facility, and even the home. Most home computers can be easily adapted with software (and an add-in card) to allow digitization of audio and drag-and-drop audio editing.

Digital video for ENG and EFP is now commonplace. The process of production is still a hybrid of analog and digital, linear and nonlinear processing because of all the Beta systems and library tapes still out there. In the upper levels of video production and network news, almost all the editing is done on digital formats even when the raw material was acquired on analog systems. Simply because of the sheer volume of Beta analog equipment in the field, it is still the most popular format to shoot with on location.

CAMERAS

The biggest changes in cameras for the foreseeable future concern conversion to digital encoding, overall quality, and size. The solid-state CCD image sensors in most professional cameras can provide more than 850 lines of resolution and the capability to shoot with just a fraction of a foot-candle. The camera can still outperform the rest of the TV system. Until the high-definition video question is resolved, there will be a limit to how good a camera needs to be. Any video camera purchased today will be a true digital camera.

Camera size and weight continue to decrease while quality increases. In fact, many industrial and consumer cameras are so small that they cannot be shot from the shoulder and must be held with two hands directly in front of the operator's face. While this allows small people to shoot for long periods of time without fatigue, getting a steady shot without a tripod is more difficult. Camera manufacturers have partially solved this problem by incorporating image stabilization circuitry into the camera to help get steadier shots. Professional cameras generally do not have this internal feature, but at least one lens manufacturer has marketed an image stabilization device that can be added to the front of the camera lens to provide a steadier shot.

Cameras the size of lipstick tubes have been marketed that have a fairly high degree of quality and are used by ENG operations and news feature programs that try to bring the "inside story" to the viewers with hidden camera shots. Because there is a point at which a camera can be too small and thus impossible to hold steady on the long shots so necessary in TV photography, the bulk of the camera/recorder unit may simply be filled with other bells and whistles to enhance the number of possible functions and refinements.

VIDEOTAPE

Video manufacturers have raced to bring digital tape formats to the market. Numerous formats have been developed during the last 10 years that feature superior-quality recording, excellent tolerance of postproduction manipulation (like video layering), and multiple-generation dubbing without quality deterioration. These formats include D-1, D-2, D-3, and D-5 and make full use of the already existing digital effects machines and digital audio sources to give postproduction an incredible range of possibilities. Other digital formats exist (like Digital-S, DVCPRO, DVCAM, and Digital 8), but it is important to realize that digital encoding onto linear videotape is not the desired product for the future. What seems logical is a nontape digital storage medium, one that could be nonlinear and allow for very quick input into an editing system.

Two developments from the late 1990s are worth noting here. The first is a hybrid system from Sony (Betacam SX) that is a digital-to-linear videotape camcorder that can be paired with a hybrid video recorder. The video recorder allows transfer of the digital tape information to a hard-drive type storage system. The advantage of this system over analog-to-digital transfer is that it can transfer information at four times the normal speed. In addition, the system solves the problem of dealing with all of the Betacam tape that is currently in tape libraries across the country. The video recorder can play back analog Betacam SP tape or store it on its hard drive. This recorder can be used with a laptop-type edit controller to yield a digital nonlinear editing system for on-line editing. The system also allows simultaneous digitizing by shooting with the Betacam SX camcorder with a direct link to the laptop editor, which has the capacity to store about 40 minutes of digital audio/video material. The advantage of the system is that it can accept analog tapes; the disadvantage is that it still employs linear tape that requires downloading for editing.

The second development was a system developed jointly by the makers of Avid editors and Ikegami cameras. It is an all-digital system that features an Ikegami camcorder with a removable hard drive that stores digital video and audio. When the hard drive is removed it is placed in an Avid digital nonlinear editing system. Conceptually, this system is a response to the need for all-digital video recording and editing. The system requires several expensive hard drives for shooting because they are removable and must be placed into the edit system for transfer. In addition, it is not compatible with other systems.

Both of these systems are steps in the right direction—toward the all-digital future. Both have advantages and disadvantages, but neither is a complete solution to the all-digital question. A new entry into the marketplace appeared in 2001. It was a video camera with a storage medium other than videotape. Hitachi entered the digital camcorder market with a camera that records full-motion, high-quality video on a DVD-RAM disk. In addition to high-quality recording, this camera has editing capabilities built into it. This camera might signal the beginning of the end for videotape as the only choice for field video recording.

EDITORS

Editing technology for the everyday user has not changed much, except that the machines involved have generally become better and more reliable. The most common editing bay still features two VCRs, two monitors, and an edit controller. More and more editing systems have become open ended to allow the video input from a large variety of machines with different formats. It is not uncommon to see a Beta editing system with two source machines, one Beta SP format, the other perhaps a DV. This allows video to be acquired in one format and edited to another without having to dub or bump the first-generation video to a second generation for it to be used on the editing system.

More production facilities are upgrading their editing bays from cuts-only systems to digital systems that allow more sophisticated transitions. The technology to do this has been around for some time, but the demand for more sophisticated transitions between shots and edits of multiple-camera field shoots has grown considerably.

Most edit systems sold today are nonlinear. The quality has risen to match that required by program producers and program outlets such as the networks and cable channels. Most of what you see on TV today has been edited on a nonlinear system. (See Figure 13.1.)

The other change to look for in editing is the size of the equipment. As in so many home units, the

Figure 13.1 This editor is using a computer-based nonlinear editor that can edit more quickly than a linear editor. This system can also manipulate video images, provide transitions, and perform special effects. Courtesy of Scitex Digital Video.

player side of the edit setup may simply be the camcorder. The record side may not be much larger either. Because of all of the built-in digital functions, you can do a version of A/B roll-editing with two machines that together can fit inside a small suitcase. For news this means being able to edit anywhere, including the hallway floor at the courthouse, or the backseat of the van as the reporter drives to the next location.

EXHIBITION MONITORS

TV monitors have ostensibly changed little in recent years. They are still large and heavy and also utilize a glass vacuum tube for a direct view of the video picture. Projection sets, both front- and rear-projection types, are basically unchanged in concept but much

improved in performance. There are some very useful and accurate portable video projectors that through the use of liquid-crystal display technology can project a good-quality picture in variable size from 10 to 100 inches in diameter onto any screen with very little distortion and good resolution.

Direct-view monitors have become much more accurate in recent years, especially as measured by the horizontal lines of resolution. Monitors are now designed for home use that can reproduce well over 400 lines of resolution. These monitors have been developed because consumers can now record in several videotape formats (S-VHS, DV) that can play back a signal with that much resolution. To do this, these monitors have added new signal inputs that allow for the separation of the luminance and chrominance portions of the video signal.

Laptop computer monitors have high-quality LCD flat screens. If professional video recording could use DVDs as a field recording medium (an innovation that has appeared), laptops equipped with DVD players will become digital field editing machines.

DIGITAL TV

In 1996 the U.S. Congress mandated that broadcasters give up the current spectrum of frequencies used for analog television and switch to a new spectrum using digital broadcast signals. Every station was to have a working digital broadcast tower by May 2002 and have vacated their original channels by January 1, 2006 (although a loophole allows some broadcasters to maintain their analog signals until 2025). As of 2000, nearly 1500 stations still had not converted to Digital TV (DTV) transmissions despite the fact that DTV is on the air in more than 100 cities in America. Industry analysts concede that the deadline cannot be met.

Add to that the growing debate over the digital standard chosen by the FCC. The United States is the only country in the world to have chosen the ATSC standard 8-VSB. The Advanced Television Systems Committee (ATSC), established in 1982, decided the broadcast signal should be the **eight** discrete amplitude level **vestigial side-band** broadcast technology. That technology was rejected by the Digital Video Broadcasting Group (DVB) representing Europe and by the Japanese government. The Europeans went with a system called DVB-T based on a transmission scheme called COFDM or coded orthogonal frequency-division multiplexing. This system spreads the signal over a large number of carriers to reduce the chance of a common signal interference called multipath or reflection. The Japanese adopted a similar system called ISDB or integrated services digital broadcasting that also uses the OFDM technology. Both the European and the Japanese systems are up and running with few if any problems after the first year in operation. The 8-VSB transmissions in the United States are so problematic that only a tiny handful of U.S. consumers are able to receive the signals despite the hundreds of stations already on the air. As of early 2001, the only way to receive a digital signal in the United States was by use of an outdoor antenna pointed directly at the transmission tower with no objects in the path between them. This doesn't seem like too big of a problem when you consider that more than 60% of the American public receives their TV signals over cable systems. But the reality is that most if not all cable systems did not carry digital TV channels as of October 2000.

This Catch-22 for the broadcast industry has put the United States years behind the rest of the world in the development of digital TV. Consumers simply will not put out thousands of dollars for new digital or high-definition TV sets when they can't receive any programming in digital. In 2000 the average cost of a DTV set was more than $4000. Analog sets cost as little as $200. That in turn has an effect on the producers of program material. Why go to the added expense if no one can see the better quality? Is it the field of dreams theory: Build it and they will come? Or is it a matter of Congress and the FCC stepping in and mandating yet another change? Or will the marketplace simply sort this all out on its own?

HIGH-DEFINITION TV

High-definition television (HDTV) gets its name from the fact that it can offer about three to four times as much visual information per frame as the standard definition NTSC television (SDTV) in use today. SDTV has about 300,000 picture elements and HDTV has about 2 million picture elements. This large amount of visual information gives a picture that is very high in resolution and puts the picture quality in a class occupied currently by 35mm motion picture film. High-definition TV also has a different aspect ratio. While current technology allows for a 4:3 width-to-height ratio, HDTV will have an aspect ratio of 16:9, closer to the aspect ratio of films shown in a movie theater.

Much has been said about this new system for TV recording and transmission for many years, going back to at least 1985. Unfortunately, this change is still years away from everyday use for several reasons. Calling the transition to digital TV in the United States a disaster would be an understatement. As discussed above, massive technical problems, financial difficulties with individual stations, and consumer indifference have combined to slow the progress of DTV to a near standstill as of 2000.

Very few programs on a DTV signal are high definition. While most networks had some programming in HDTV in the fall 2000 TV schedule, the vast majority of programs are simply upconverted SDTV. The future of HDTV is still up in the air for the broadcast networks and local stations alike. While the rules are subject to interpretation, there doesn't seem to be a mandate for local stations to run HDTV programming under their new DTV license. The rules only state that programming has to be at least as good as NTSC. Since HDTV uses a 19-Mbps transfer rate and a SDTV signal would only use 3 to 4 Mbps, that leaves a large chunk of space open for other uses in the assigned bandwidth. Local stations across the country are toying with the idea of broadcasting data, interactive enhanced programming, or simply other channels of video programming in that remaining 15 Mbps. If that happens, the consumer will not be able to receive HDTV through a local station.

As broadcast stations and networks wrangle over the myriad of problems facing them, computer makers have been quietly working to integrate HDTV into their hardware by turning PCs into HDTV receivers. At a fraction of the cost of a new HDTV television, a simple card can be installed in the computer and the consumer is DTV ready on a platform already used in a digital world. The reception problem of the DTV signal is still there, but the investment is relatively minor and the technology is ready to go. But how many people are willing sit at their desks to watch TV instead of their living rooms?

The bottom line is that there is no real outlet for an HDTV product at this time in broadcast TV. In the late 1990s it seemed as though HD was just around the corner and manufacturers rushed to design equipment and tape formats to be ready. By 2000 most have slowed their HDTV consumer units to a crawl and found little interest in camera and field recorder sales. While many productions and news sources use digital formats, very few use HD formats. A good HD camcorder by the leading manufacturers—Sony and Panasonic—costs nearly $60,000 with a good lens. With very few edit facilities available around the country to handle an HD product, it takes a major programming commitment and large budget to shoot anything on HD compared to a similar product done in SDTV or DTV. On a national scale, only a few cable and nature segments seen on outlets like National Geographic Explorer and some Discovery shows are HDTV, but an ever-increasing number of commercials and low-budget movies are being done on HD. In fact, HDTV's greatest advances are in projects where film, particularly 16mm film, would have been the normal choice just a few years ago. Today those programs are increasingly shot on HD video even if they are to be released on film for theatrical showings. A tiny number of local stations use HDTV.

To put the entire HDTV debate in real terms, the Consumer Electronics Association (CEA) figures show that approximately 60,000 set-top demodulator/decoders and integrated DTV receiver/players (necessary to view DTV programs) have been sold to retailers by late 2000. Even if all of those products have been sold to consumers, it still shows that compared to the 300 million SDTV sets in the United States, no one is watching digital broadcast TV in this country despite the fact that more than 100 stations are broadcasting it. On the other hand, approximately 400,000 DTV displays (CEA's term for digital TV sets) were shipped from the manufacturers in 2000. The assumption is that those sets are being sold to consumers for watching DVDs and the very few satellite channels that are beaming HDTV pay movies to home dishes—what's known as home theater. With almost no local cable companies carrying digital signals and off-air reception via an antenna almost impossible for the vast majority of the public, how will broadcast DTV—let alone HDTV—establish itself? Any guess as to the future made today will almost certainly be wrong by tomorrow.

STREAMING VIDEO

With the faster computer connections now available to the consumer through DSL phone lines and cable modems through the cable TV services, home computers are now capable of both watching live video

pictures and downloading video programs with relative ease. Without special hardware or software, anyone with one of these fast connections can log onto msnbc.com, go to the Nightly News with Tom Brokaw section, and download any story from that evening's newscast to play on their computer. The story may be paused, rewound, and played multiple times. Where once a viewer may have missed a line or fact in a TV news story and never been able to recover it, they can now replay the story as often as they like to understand just what was said. The quality may be bad compared with the broadcast signal, but the story is now on demand and not limited to just those who were home at 6:30 P.M.

This advancement means that an entire new outlet is ready and waiting for a video product. Whether it's the replay of a national or local newscast or a newscast that originates on the Internet itself, the video product is becoming more and more like the newspapers and magazines: ubiquitous. The Forrester Research Company estimates that by 2004 around 36.4 million households will have broadband Internet service. That's not quite a video mass medium but it is still nearly one-third of all households.

The infrastructure of the Internet makes delivering a video product shaky at best. Poor picture quality, especially with live video streaming, network delays, lost data packets, and its still relatively narrow bandwidth make the end product less than picture perfect. But the basic information is there—you can still see and hear the presentation. On the plus side, a site operator can make the video just one component of an overall package. By adding links, additional information, and other interactive devices, the viewer gains as much information as he or she wishes. As technology advances, these services can improve not only in quality but in content.

A CAUTIONARY NOTE

We find it worth mentioning at this point that not all of these new technologies are as benign as they might seem. As digital effects become more and more sophisticated with the addition of faster and more powerful computers, reality and technology are being blended into a seamless picture. While this is great fun for commercial and entertainment video makers, it can lead to real moral and ethical problems for the news and documentary photographers. If you can make it happen in the computer, why not? A subtle manipulation in a picture can be made to look so real that it could fool anyone. People can be placed in a scene that they never attended with the look of total reality. If just one case of this type of manipulation occurs in the future, it may cost the entire news industry its credibility with the public just as its attempt to use recreations in newscasts did in 1990. The practice was halted almost immediately, but the damage it caused was real and lasting.

A FINAL NOTE

As mentioned above, the future of video is digital. Soon we will have digital cameras and a digital storage medium that is not tape. Video images will be edited on digital editors. Video programs and projects will be broadcast or "webcast" digitally. The number of outlets for video projects and programs will increase, not decrease. Broadcast television stations are in the middle of the changeover from analog broadcasting to digital broadcasting. Where television stations could transmit one program at a time, stations may soon have the ability to transmit several simultaneously. Just as the introduction of cable created more jobs for videographers on channels like CNN, ESPN, and MTV, the digital revolution will create more jobs for videographers who can shoot video for regular broadcast-type programs for the Internet. Principles of composition, framing, proper exposure, and the ability to tell a story with video images will not change. Learning how to shoot high-quality video is a skill that will not become obsolete, regardless of the changes in how these images are shown to audiences.

Glossary

Italicized terms within the definitions may be found elsewhere in the Glossary.

above the line   The personnel costs and expenses involved with securing a script and the rights, a producer and the staff, the talent (performers) and the director.

ampere   A measure of the amount or volume of electrical current.

ampere hours   A way of rating a battery according to how much electrical current it can generate over a period of time.

angle   The location of a camera relative to the camera's subject.

ASA   A rating of the ability of photographic film to record light as determined by the American National Standards Institute. The higher the rating, the less light is needed to record an image.

aspect ratio   The relationship of the width of a TV screen to its height; for standard NTSC television it is 4:3. Digital television has the capability to have a 16:9 ratio.

assemble   A type of edit that transfers all information from the source machine to the editing recorder; it is similar to a *dub*.

audio-limiter switch   This control prevents the recorded audio signal from becoming distorted because of too much signal strength.

auto-iris   A feature on video cameras that allows the exposure to be automatically set by the camera.

available light   The natural light in a scene; the light that exists before additional light sources are added.

background light   A light illuminating the background of a scene or shot. It is usually the fourth light in a lighting kit.

backlight   A directional light used in three-point lighting. It is placed in line with the camera but positioned behind and above the subject and aimed at the back of the subject's head and shoulders.

balanced audio input   An input into an electronic device that accepts signals with two conductors of equal voltage. It is used in professional work to ensure a better signal.

bandwidth   The measure of the capacity of a data line. Also, the difference between the upper and lower frequency limits of an audio or video component.

barndoor   A rectangular piece of dark metal attached to a light to modify the direction of the beam, often used around a light in a set of four.

bass/roll-off/switch   A microphone switch that prevents the microphone from reproducing low-frequency sounds below a certain set level.

batt check   A control that when depressed or engaged gives an indication of the amount of remaining power of the battery in use.

behavioral effects   The changes in the things people say and do as a result of viewing a video program. See *cognitive effects* and *emotional effects*.

Betacam   A professional 1/2-inch component video format from the Sony Corporation that was most popular with professional ENG operations in the 1980s.

Betacam SP   The improved Betacam format which replaced Standard Betacam; SP stands for "superior performance."

bite   A piece of video with a person speaking and their audio is heard clearly. Also called a sound bite.

black bursting   Recording a tape with a pure black signal (a control track, but no viewable picture), usually used for insert editing.

blocking   The talent and camera movements specified by the director for each scene.

BNC connector   A connector with a twist lock or positive grip feature used with single conductor video cable.

boom A pole (often extension type) mounted on some type of tripod base used as a microphone mount that can bring the mic close to the subject without being in the picture. See *fishpole*.

bottomers A flag used below a light source to shade the lower portion of the scene.

bounced light A diffuse, indirect light that reflects onto a desired subject. See *reflector*.

brick battery A powerful rectangular battery usually used to supply DC current to a video camera.

broad light A rectangular-shaped video light that casts bright light over a large area.

budget tracking A record-keeping process in which one records actual expenditures from a production and compares them with the projected expenses.

bug A small logo or abbreviation that identifies the source of the video being shown, usually located in one corner of the picture.

burn-in The image retention by a pickup tube caused by shooting a very bright object or by aiming the camera at a static scene for a long period of time.

butted Two scenes edited together without the benefit of an electronic transition such as a *dissolve;* sometimes called a straight cut.

camcorder A one-piece, combination video camera and recorder.

camera control unit (CCU) An electronic device used to properly set up and maintain the quality of a video camera's image.

cannon connector A high-quality multi-pin connector with a positive lock feature used for audio input and output. See also *XLR connector*.

capacitor An electrical device used in condenser microphones that stores an electrical charge.

cardioid A microphone pickup pattern that resembles a heart shape. A mic with this pattern is also known as unidirectional and is most sensitive to sounds in front of it.

centrifugal force The force that tends to pull a thing outward when it is rotating rapidly around a center; this force may affect the operation of some videocassette recorders if they are physically moving while recording.

chargeback The amount paid by one unit of a corporation to an in-house production unit for services rendered on a piece-by-piece basis.

charge coupled device (CCD) An imaging device made of solid-state microelectronics that changes light into an electrical signal. It is used in place of a vacuum *pickup tube*.

chrominance The combination of the red, green, and blue information in video.

cinéma vérité A portable shooting style developed in France in the 1950s that popularized handheld camera work.

clearance The permission granted by a copyright holder to allow use of copyrighted material.

clogged heads A condition that occurs when minute pieces of dirt or magnetic particles from the videotape attach themselves to the video head of a VCR and cause poor-quality recording or playback.

close-up lenses Lenses designed to allow focusing on an object located a very short distance from the front of the lens.

close-up shot A shot in which the subject is framed tightly; for example, when a person is framed from the neck up. Also called a tight shot.

coax Wire that carries audio and/or video signals; the wire has one central conductor and a braided shield for grounding that surrounds it.

codec An abbreviation for compression/decompression of information. A software program that can convert the data from a video project to a much smaller file.

cognitive effects The changes in knowledge as a result of viewing a videotape for training purposes. See *behavioral effects* and *emotional effects*.

color *Chrominance*—the control on a TV set that varies the amount or intensity of the chroma information.

color enhancement filters A piece of glass or a gel that functions to brighten (or increase the saturation of) the colors of the subject being shot.

color gels Cellophane material placed in front of lights to alter the color of light that reaches a subject or object to be shot.

color temperature A measure in degrees of Kelvin of the tint or wavelengths of a light; helpful in color balancing between shots. A light with high color temperature is blue; a light with a lower color temperature is red.

color temperature blue (CTB) A color-correction gel that, when placed in front of a light, raises the color temperature of that light toward the blue (daylight) end of the scale.

color temperature orange (CTO) A color-correction gel that lowers the color temperature of a light source toward the red (tungsten) end of the scale.

comet tailing The smearing of light that occurs when a bright image source is moved across a darkened background.

compensator group Two lenses in a typical zoom (compound) lens.

component recording A recent development in videotape recording in which the color information is recorded separately from the brightness and synchronization information.

compression The reduction of size or value of a signal.

condenser The transducing element in a microphone that generates electrical signals as a result of changes in capacitance between the diaphragm and the backplate.

contrast ratio The relationship between the brightest portion and the darkest portion of a picture (for example, 20:1).

convertible or systems mic A microphone that can be modified in shape, pickup pattern, or sensitivity to accommodate various audio situations.

cookie A metal sheet with a pattern cut-out that is used to project light patterns on floors, cycloramas, and so on. Also called a cucalorus.

corporate video Video for nonbroadcast purposes used mainly by private enterprise, government, nonprofit organizations, and associations.

crab dolly A movable camera mount that can be steered and is designed to allow the camera operator to sit on the device to operate the camera.

cut A signal or command to stop cameras and tape during a production. See *take*.

cutaway Shot related to, but slightly away from, the action being recorded; often used to cover unsatisfactory parts of a scene or interview.

cutter A narrow *flag*.

daylight blue A full CTB gel that when placed in front of a standard video light, gives off light similar to sunlight or daylight in color.

depth of field The area in front of the camera where all objects appear in focus.

dew Moisture that may form or condense inside a camcorder or VCR due to environmental conditions; when dew is sensed inside of a VCR, a sensor may light, warning the user that the VCR or camcorder will not work.

diaphragm A moving part of a microphone. See *element*.

diffuser A piece of material (glass, fiberglass, cloth) that reduces the intensity or amount of light from a source and makes it less harsh; it may also be placed in front of a camera lens.

Digital 8 A digital video format available to consumers. It utilizes 8 MM wide videotape.

digital effects Special effects for transitions, such as picture compression, tumble or page peel, accomplished by the digital encoding of the video picture to be manipulated.

digital video recording A method of recording a video signal that changes the signal into bits of data stored as numbers (0 and 1).

diopter A single lens designed to magnify an image.

director The person who translates a written script into a video program.

dissolve A transition in video where one video source is faded out while another is simultaneously faded in. See *fade*.

distant learning Instructional TV that utilizes two-way communication over a distance, often accomplished by microwave or satellite transmission.

doorway dolly A small platform on wheels used to carry a camera on a tripod and small enough to fit through an average doorway.

double fog filter Lowers the contrast of the overall scene but only looks like fog over the very brightest areas.

draw The shadow on a subject created by directional light.

DTV Digital television.

dual redundancy Two small (tie-clip) microphones placed on a single clip to provide a backup mic if one fails while recording.

dub A copy ("dupe" or duplicate), or the process of copying a video- or audiotape. See *assemble*.

dynamic A description of a shot or edit that shows movement, power, strength, or energy.

edit To put together, rearrange, or eliminate segments of video or audio information on tape.

EFP Electronic Field Production—portable video for non-news applications.

element A basic moving part of a microphone that generates the basic electrical signal.

emotional effects A desirable effect of a video project where the audience experiences feelings as a result of viewing the video.

ENG Electronic News Gathering—portable electronic journalism.

extender A device used on a zoom lens that can double the focal length of the lens.

external time code Time code sent to a VCR that is generated outside the VCR.

eye light A small light used in dramatic shots to illuminate the subject's upper facial area.

fade Gradual change from a video source to a black screen, or vice versa. See *dissolve*.

faders Sliding rheostats used to adjust the volume in audio, the intensity in lights, *or* the mixing of two video signals.

fast lens A lens that is capable of gathering a *large* amount of light; a lens capable of an f-stop of 1.4 would be a fast lens in comparison to one that was only capable of an f-stop of 4.0.

fat side The side of the face most visible to the camera. Also called the long side. See *short side*.

feeders Microwave-equipped trucks used in *ENG* to relay video and live pictures back to the station.

field One-half of a complete TV picture, that is, 262.5 scanning lines. See *frame*.

fill light Light used to soften the shadows caused by the *key* or main directional light.

film style A type of portable production that utilizes a single camera and often uses many takes of a scene for later editing.

filter Cellophane, glass, spun glass, or similar material used in lenses, cameras, or in front of lights that somehow modulates or changes the light passing through it.

fishpole A handheld extension pole used to get a microphone close to a subject. See *boom*.

flag A solid or opaque light modulator used to direct light or create shadows.

flat An upright square or rectangular frame covered with cloth or other material that can be painted for a scenic effect.

flat lighting A type of lighting that does not yield shadows, often created with nondirectional lighting or soft light from the camera position.

flat rate A nonvariable payment made on a regular basis; for example, a regular payment made to an in-house media production unit for services rendered.

floater An insurance policy that provides coverage for rented production equipment.

flooded When an adjustable or focusable spotlight is in the least focused position; when a scene is lit with a large quantity of nondirectional light.

floodlight A video light that produces a diffuse, wide beam of light.

focal length The distance from the optical center of a lens to the point at which the light rays converge on the face of the image sensor. Determines field of view.

focal plane The point where the light rays that pass through a lens converge and are in focus; when in proper focus, this point falls on the image sensor.

focusing group The front three lens elements in a compound zoom lens which determine the position of the focal plane.

footcandle A measure of the amount of light used in countries that have not adopted the metric system. The amount of light given by one candle one foot away from it.

frame One complete picture in video, equal to two *fields*, that is, 525 scanning lines. *See field*.

fringe benefits Items used to pay employees other than salary or wage dollars; for example, health insurance.

f-stop A designation of the size of the *iris* opening in a video lens.

gaffer grip A device used to hold equipment in place.

gaffer tape A wide, strong tape used to hold various pieces of equipment or wire in place.

gel A cellophane-type material placed in front of a video light that changes the color of the light.

gel frames A frame used to hold gel in place in front of a video light.

gen-lock A timing signal that allows the synchronization of two or more video sources.

graphic card An art card, especially prepared for use in a video production, that conforms to the aspect ratio and other restrictions of TV.

grip A person who helps carry and place equipment.

gyro A stabilizing device on the lens to reduce the shakiness of telephoto shots or pictures taken from aircraft or other unstable locations.

hard news A news story that is serious, timely, and deals with important issues in society; for example, crime or politics.

HDTV High Definition Television.

head light Slang term for a camera-mounted light.

head room The amount of space from the top of the subject's head in a shot to the top of the frame. In audio, the term means the ability of a recorder to accept a degree of over-modulated signal without distortion.

hertz (Hz) A unit of measurement for frequency equal to one cycle per second.

Hi8 A videotape format that uses 8mm metal particle tape and features high-resolution and high-quality audio reproduction.

high-definition/high-density TV A recently developed TV format that yields a higher-resolution picture due to an increased number of scanning lines per frame.

high-intensity discharge A type of mercury or sodium vapor arc discharge lamp that uses a low amount of electricity but generates a large amount of light.

high-key lighting Lighting that is bright with a few shadows used when an upbeat mood is desired.

hot A video picture with too much light; any signal whose level is too high.

house sound   Sound that is available from the audio board of the "house" (the theater, concert hall, etc.).

house sync   A synchronization signal created by a sync generator for the purpose of having all equipment in a production facility use the same timing.

hyperfocal distance   A measurement from the lens to the closest point that an object will be in focus when the lens focus ring is set at infinity.

impedance   The opposition or restriction to the flow of current, usually measured in ohms.

incandescent   Lamps that give off light when they glow from electrical current passing through a filament located inside a vacuum.

insert   A type of *edit* in which video, audio, or both are put into an existing video piece.

internal optical system   In almost all video cameras available now, a prism block that separates the white light into red, green, and blue light before the light strikes the image sensors.

internal time code   An electrical signal generated by a VCR that labels each frame of videotape it records.

Internet   A worldwide computer network where information can be stored and retrieved by users.

intranet   An in-house computer network used by corporations where information can be stored and used by in-house users.

inverse square law   The rule that the amount of light that falls on an object decreases by the square of the inverse of the distance from the light to the object. If the distance from the light to the subject is doubled, the amount of light falling on the object is one-fourth the original amount of light.

iris   The adjustable diaphragm inside a lens that varies the amount of light that enters the camera—the aperture.

jam sync   Synchronization signals sent into camcorders and VCRs from one central source.

jump cut   An uncomfortable edit juxtaposing two shots that do not go together smoothly; for example, a medium shot to a medium shot of the same subject with little difference between them.

keyframe   An image used as a reference for a video clip

key light   A directional video light used to focus attention and give proper shadow and contrast to a subject. The main source of illumination.

lag   The after-image seen trailing a moving object on screens.

lamp   A bulb for a video light.

lead-in   A news anchor's introduction to a story.

LED (light emitting diode)   A small light (usually red, yellow, or green) used as an indicator light.

lens flare   When a strong light shines directly into a lens, an optical distortion can be seen, often appearing as a series of pentagons. This problem can be avoided by changing the camera angle or deflecting the direct light.

lighting grid   In a TV studio, a cross-hatch system of bars mounted below the ceiling that allows the mounting of video lights.

lighting panel   The electronic device in a TV control room or studio that allows connection for, and control of, the lighting system.

line   (1) One of 525 scanning lines in a video picture; (2) in audio work, a level of signal that has been amplified and is higher in level than a signal from a microphone; (3) in a TV control room, the signal path that leads out from the switcher to the transmitter or videotape recorder—the on-air signal.

line level   A signal level in audio that is amplified and therefore stronger than a microphone-level signal.

line of interest   Sometimes called the stage line or the 180-degree line, it is a line drawn through a scene to maintain continuity of screen direction when editing together shots taken from different angles to the subject by keeping the camera always on the same side of that line. Two people talking to each other create a line of interest drawn from one person to the other that extends to infinity in both directions.

lip-sync   The accurate or synchronized combination of sound and picture, especially matching words with a talking person.

live   In *ENG* work, a shot from the field that is transmitted back to the TV station and broadcast as it is being photographed.

live on tape   A method of recording a program on videotape where the program is performed as if it were done live, all in one take, with no editing.

low-key lighting   Lighting that creates strong, well-defined shadows used to create a serious or even somber mood.

luminance   The brightness information in a TV signal and picture.

MII   A professional $1/2$-inch component videotape format from Panasonic used in portable video, especially *ENG*.

macrofocus   A focusing ring at the rear of the lens element that allows the focal plane to be brought very close to the front element.

macro ring/macro lever The device on the barrel of the lens that engages the macrofocusing capability of the lens.

male A type of plug with prongs or pins designed to fit into a corresponding socket.

matched action A technique in which one camera is used to shoot the same action from different angles and the raw footage is edited to give the appearance of multiple cameras shooting the action at one time.

matte box A rectangular bellows-shaped hood that fits over the front of the lens to aid in shading the lens and as a holder for large filters that do not attach to the lens.

media player A program that plays back audio or video from the Internet.

medium shot A relative description of a video shot, usually framing a subject from waist up.

mic level 150 ohms, the standard impedance level of a professional microphone.

microphone A device for translating sound energy into electrical energy for amplification or recording purposes.

miniboom A small crane-like arm used for camera mounting.

MiniDV A digital video format that is available to consumers through a number of different manufacturers. The cassette size is considerably smaller than VHS or 8MM cassettes.

mix The combination of two or more signals.

mix select switches Levers on a VCR that control which channels of audio are to be monitored.

modeling effect The effect of showing depth and texture by creating shadows with directional light.

modular camera A portable video camera that allows for a variety of on-board videocassette recorders to be attached, or for others to be connected by cable.

modules A rectangular light made up of rows of individual *PAR* lights.

moire The rainbow distortion seen on videotaped subjects with a very small, repeated geometric pattern, such as a tie with very thin, evenly spaced stripes.

moving-coil A type of microphone transducer that has a coil suspended in a magnetic field. A *diaphragm* reacts to sound pressure and displaces the coil in the field to create an electrical current, often referred to as a dynamic microphone.

multi-pin cable connector A cable plug designed to connect a single cable containing many smaller individual wires that must always stay insulated from one another.

needle drop fee A cost incurred when using a copyrighted musical piece for production purposes.

neutral density gel (ND) A gray gelatin filter in varying densities that cuts down the amount of light without affecting any other characteristics of the light source.

nickel-cadmium cell A rechargeable battery unit made from nickel and cadmium; often referred to as a "nicad."

non-segmented videotape A type of videotape recording format in which information for one entire frame is recorded by one head without being broken into two parts, allowing for easier special effects, such as slow motion or still frame.

NTSC (National Television Standards Committee) The U.S. government group formed in 1953 to set standards for TV's video signal.

off-axis A sound source coming from some place other than where the mic is pointed.

omnidirectional A microphone that receives sound equally well regardless of the direction the mic is pointed from the source.

on-axis Sound coming from directly in front of the microphone.

overhead expenses Costs incurred as a result of being in business, such as rent and utilities, but not directly related to a video production.

PAL (Phase Alteration by Line) The video signal standard set by Germany, England, and Holland in 1966.

parabolic An inward curved reflector that focuses the light or sound it receives to a single point in front of it.

Parabolic Aluminized Reflector (PAR) A sealed-beam light with the bulb built into a reflector at its focal point, such as the headlights of a car.

party colors A slang term for colored gels that change a light source to a single color of light, such as deep red, forest green, and so on.

photons Units of energy that make up light waves.

pickup tube An imaging device of vacuum tube construction used in video cameras to change light into an electronic signal.

pinned A position on an adjustable video light that yields its narrowest beam; the maximum reading that a needle-type meter can show.

pixels The extremely small light-sensitive surfaces that make up the image-recording area of a charged couple device (CCD); the more pixels, the sharper the image will be.

plumb-bubble bullseye A circular container with a single bubble in a liquid; when the bubble is in a ring painted on top of the container, the device (tripod, camera, and so on) is level to the horizontal plane.

plumbicon tube A vacuum tube designed to produce a video picture using a lead oxide coating on its light-sensitive surface.

polar pattern A diagram of a microphone's sensitivity or pickup capability.

polarizing filter A glass filter over the lens that reduces glare and reflections by preventing certain angles of reflected light from passing through it.

portable Refers to production equipment that can be easily transported to an on-location shoot; implies that it can be run on direct current or battery power.

Porta-pack The first portable video system developed by Sony that used a reel-to-reel VCR and a black-and-white camera.

post-production The last stage in the process of creating a video project; the stage in which editing is accomplished.

pre-production The first or planning stage in the process of creating a video project.

presence boost An audio filter that emphasizes frequencies in the upper midrange, around 5 kHz, to enhance voices.

press pass A photo identification card issued by law enforcement agencies to bona fide members of the news media.

primary additive colors Red, green, and blue. A TV camera reduces a picture to varying amounts of these three colors to make up the chroma segment of a video signal.

prime lens A fixed focal length lens.

prime lens group The series of lenses at the rear of any type of lens that focuses the image onto the recording surface.

prism block A device in a video camera that consists of several prisms that split the incoming light into its red, green, and blue components and guides the light to the appropriate chip.

processing amplifier A device to boost a video signal with control over the strength and black level of that signal (similar to brightness and contrast controls).

producer The person in charge of a production.

production The middle stage in the process of creating a video project when images and/or sound are recorded.

prop An abbreviation for property used on the set of a video shoot or scene.

public domain Film, video, or sound recordings on which no one holds the creative rights and no royalties can be collected.

pull-ups Subtractions or changes done to an edited piece of video causing a change in the total length of the piece.

quality light By professional consensus, light from a very large source that produces soft-edged shadows.

quality of light A measure of both the color temperature and the harshness or softness of the light source.

random access The ability to retrieve information from any point in a system without having to search through or scan information in a linear fashion. Also known as nonlinear.

real-time switching The changing of video sources done *live* or when a program is recorded live on tape.

record and playback controls The buttons to put the VCR in either the record or playback mode.

reflector Hard or soft surface covered with a highly reflective material to redirect light to fall on a desired area.

registration The alignment of the three color *image sensors* in a video camera to give one full color image.

Rembrandt lighting The style of lighting made famous by the Dutch painter and characterized by the use of alternating areas of light and shadow in his scenes. Creator of the *modeling effect*.

remote An on-location shoot that relays a signal to another location, such as a broadcast station.

resolution A measure of sharpness or clarity in a video picture.

retrozoom A multi-element glass lens that attaches on a zoom lens to decrease the focal length throughout the zoom range; a wide angle attachment.

RF interference Noise in a video signal caused by unwanted broadcast signals (often from AM radio signals).

rim light Similar to *backlight* only striking the subject from a lower angle. Also called edge light.

roaming Having the automatic iris constantly changing due to a portion of the scene fluctuating in brightness.

"rocker"-style switch A long switch operated with a finger at each end and the axis of the switch in between. As the switch is rocked downward in the front, the servo runs forward; as the switch is rocked down at its rear, the servo reverses direction.

routing system A system that allows the video and/or audio signal to be channeled or directed to multiple locations by cable.

rule of "three to one" or rule of thirds When lining up a shot, it is aesthetically more pleasing to have the major elements in the frame fall on lines created by dividing the screen in thirds both horizontally and vertically.

saticon   A type of *pickup tube* used in industrial-quality and some professional-quality video cameras.

saturation   The amount of overall color in a picture.

scoop   A type of artificial light that provides generally diffuse light for fill purposes.

scrim   A piece of metal screen material placed over a light to reduce its output. See *diffuser* and *filter*.

SDTV   Standard definition television (NTSC).

SECAM (Sequential Couleur a Memoire)   The 1962 TV signal standard developed and used in France.

segmented video   A videotape format in which two (or more) video head passes are necessary to record a *frame* of video.

servo   A small electric motor used to turn a set of gears.

shade   (1) To prevent light from falling on a certain area. (2) To remotely set the iris and black levels of a camera.

shaky camera   Having too much movement of the camera while recording.

shoot   The actual production work of a video project.

short side   The part of the face least seen from the camera position. Generally the side of the face lit by the *key light*. See *fat side*.

shower curtain   A slang term for a heavy plastic fire proof diffusion material used over a light source.

siders   Flags that are used to the side of a light source.

signal-to-noise ratio   A ratio that compares picture strength to noise strength. The higher the ratio, the better the picture.

single-element wide-angle lens   A glass lens that fits on a zoom lens to reduce the focal length to one specific wide angle focal length; thus, the zoom elements cannot be used with it in place.

skew knob   On older-style VCRs, this control would manually adjust the tension of the videotape across the playback heads.

sliding element   A group of lenses within a complete lens that is able to move closer to or further from the other lens groups.

slow lens   A lens whose iris does not open very wide and thus does not let very much light pass through it.

smearing   An undesirable aspect of a video picture with too much gain; smearing appears as colors trailing or flaring off of objects in the *frame*.

snap zoom   A very fast-changing zoom, accomplished by manually rotating the zoom control with a quick wrist motion.

soft frost   A type of diffusion gel used over a light source to soften the harshness of the light.

soft light   A large diffuse light source that creates soft-edged shadows. A light fixture designed to create soft-edged shadows, sometimes called a soft box.

softnet filter   A very fine net material within a glass filter used over the lens to soften the look of a scene.

soft news   News stories that are more entertaining in nature and not as serious or timely as *hard news*.

special effects filters   Glass filters on the lens that manipulate the image's color, focus, or position.

speed   A photographic term for describing how sensitive a lens or chip is to light.

split-field effect   A filter on the lens that changes the plane of focus for only one-half the picture.

spotlight   A directional, often adjustable, type of artificial light source for video.

stand-up   A shot in which a reporter or other on-camera host talks directly to the viewer.

star filter   A glass filter in front of the lens with a screen material in it that makes highlights such as light bulbs appear pointed like stars.

sticks   Slang term for a tripod.

stopped down   To have the iris at a very small opening or even completely closed.

storyboard   A two-dimensional pictorial representation of a script that represents the visual theme and important shots.

streaming   Playing sound and/or video in real time as it downloads over the Internet, rather than storing it in a file for later playing.

studio arcs   Large carbon arc lights used in movie production.

studio pedestal mount   A professional, heavy-duty mounting system with wheels for studio cameras; it can only be used on very smooth surfaces.

subtractive primary colors   Magenta, cyan, and yellow used in paint mixing and color photo printing to obtain all the other colors but not used in video recording.

sungun   A small battery-powered light, usually camera-mounted.

switcher   A device to combine or switch video signals and special effects from a variety of sources into one video output.

sync generator   An electronic device used in a video studio that gives timing pulses to the cameras, VCRs, and all other pieces of equipment that need to be time coordinated.

take   An individual shot or scene, usually one of several; an instantaneous change from one video source to another. See *cut*.

talent   The persons who are performing in front of the camera.

talking head   A shot of a person speaking, usually a static head and shoulder or head-only shot; generally slang for an interview shot.

teasers   Large black flats used to prevent light from falling on certain areas.

telecine   A device that transfers film or slides to video, consisting of a film projector, slide projector, video camera, and multiplexer; a device to direct projection into a video camera lens. Also called "film chain" or "film island."

teleconverter   A multi-element glass filter that fits onto a zoom lens to increase its focal length while still being able to zoom.

tilt   Angling the camera either up or down.

time base corrector (TBC)   An electronic device that corrects for speed and mechanical errors in a videotape machine, giving the videotape a broadcast standard horizontal sync.

toppers   *Flags* used above a light source.

tracing paper   Slang for a heavy paper-like diffusion material used in front of a light source.

tracking   The speed and angle at which the videotape passes the video heads, often adjustable during playback to maximize picture quality.

tracking knob   A manual adjustment when playing back a videotape to align the video heads of a VCR with the video tracks laid down on the tape.

transition shot   A shot used to bridge two video segments that otherwise might not smoothly connect.

treatment   A preliminary synopsis or storyline that describes plot, characters, setting, and so on, for a forthcoming script.

tungsten-halogen lamp   The standard light source for film and video production using a tungsten filament inside a sealed glass globe that gives off light at 3200 degrees Kelvin.

two-X range   The range of focal lengths created on a zoom lens after the 2X extender is used.

U-Matic format   The first color video cassette format developed by Sony for use in the field and often referred to as 3/4-inch because of the tape's width.

U-Matic SP format   An improved version of the original U-Matic format using metal particle tape for better sharpness and color; SP means superior performance.

umbrella   A device shaped like a regular rain umbrella that is mounted on a portable video light. The reflective underside of this umbrella reflects a diffuse light on a subject.

unit rate   The amount of cost incurred in a particular time frame; for example, the cost per day of owning a portable camera.

UV   Ultraviolet.

vanishing point   A point on the horizon or outside the frame where parallel lines when viewed at an angle in a shot seem to converge.

variator group   The lens grouping within a zoom lens that changes image size by moving toward or away from the main lens groups.

vertical interval time code   The series of numbers stored in the vertical interval of a video signal that mark each frame of that video so those frames can be cataloged for later reference.

video digital effects   A sophisticated video manipulation that allows the video picture to be compressed, flipped, tumbled, and so on.

video level control   A device that can adjust the amplification of a video signal either up or down.

video processors   Electronic circuits that control the amount and quality of all the components of a video signal.

video switcher   An electronic device that allows an individual to select among many video inputs.

viewfinder   A small black-and-white TV monitor with an eyepiece used by the camera operator to see what the camera sees.

vignetting   Dark areas in the corners of a picture caused by lens problems or the lens not being properly lined up with the camera's internal optics system.

voice coil   A small wire coil used in a microphone to transduce sound into electric energy so that it can be recorded.

VU meter   A device to measure volume units of audio on a tape machine or sound mixer/amplifier.

wide angle lens   A lens with a large field of view and focal lengths starting around 5.5mm for video lenses.

wide shot   A camera shot with a short focal length, therefore a wide field of view, that includes a large amount of the area in front of the camera. Also called a long shot.

World Wide Web   The portion of the Internet that allows use of graphics, audio, and video information.

wrong-field edits   When the edit machine mistakenly cuts from a position or negative field of one shot to the like field of the next shot, thereby breaking the required pattern of alternating fields.

XCU   An extreme close-up video shot.

XLR connector   The standard three-contact plugs used in all professional sound work, originally the part number of this type of audio connector by the Cannon Company and sometimes still called cannon connectors.

zebra bars The diagonal white lines superimposed over parts of the picture that have a certain level of video signal and can only be seen in the viewfinder. Many cameras have the zebra bars set at 70 units of video, which aids the operator in determining proper exposure.

zip light A type of soft light fixture in metal housing.

zoom control The device that operates the zoom servo to determine the direction and speed of the zoom.

zoom lens A lens capable of changing focal lengths without affecting the plane of focus, thus allowing continuous change in image size from widest to narrowest field of view with no other adjustments needed.

zoom ratio This ratio compares the longest focal length to the shortest, such as 120mm to 10mm, or 140mm to 10mm; often expressed in ratio form, for example, 12:1 or 14:1. Also called the zoom range.

Bibliography

BOOKS

Aesthetics

Arijon, Daniel. *Grammar of the Film Language*. Boston, MA: Focal Press, 1976.

Douglass, John S. and Harnden, Glenn P. *The Art of Technique: An Aesthetic Approach to Film and Video Production*. Needham Heights, MA: Allyn & Bacon, 1996.

Lester, Paul M. *Visual Communication: Images with Messages*. Belmont, CA: Wadsworth Publishing Co., 1995.

Ward, Peter. *Picture Composition*. Boston, MA: Focal Press, 1996.

Zettl, Herbert. *Sight, Sound, Motion: Applied Media Aesthetics*. 3rd ed. Belmont, CA: Wadsworth Publishing Co., 1999.

Audio

Alten, Stanley R. *Audio in Media*, 5th ed. Belmont CA: Wadsworth Publishing Co., 1998.

Bartlett, Bruce. *Introduction to Professional Recording Techniques*. Indianapolis, IN: Howard Sams & Co., 1987.

Clifford, Martin. *Microphones*, 2nd ed. Blue Ridge Summit: PA, Tab Books, 1982.

Huber, Miles. *Microphone Manual: Design and Application*. Indianapolis, IN: Howard Sams & Co., 1988.

Budgeting/Business

Marsh, Ken. *Independent Video*. San Francisco, CA: Straight Arrow Books, 1974.

Van Deusen, Richard E. *Practical AV/Video Budgeting*. Boston, MA: Focal Press, 1984.

Wiese, Michael. *Film & Video Budgets*. Studio City, CA: M. Wiese Productions, 1995.

Corporate Video

Hausman, Carl. *Institutional Video*. Belmont, CA: Wadsworth Publishing Co., 1991.

Gayeski, Diane. *Corporate and Instructional Video*, 2nd ed. Englewood Cliffs, NJ: Prentice Hall, 1991.

Dizazzo, Ray. *Corporate Media Production*. Boston, MA: Focal Press, 2000.

Directing

Blumenthal, Howard J. *Television Producing and Directing*. New York, NY: Barnes and Noble Books, 1987.

Cury, Ivan. *Directing and Producing for Television: A Format Approach*. Boston, MA: Focal Press, 1998.

Hickman, Harold R. *Television Direction*. Santa Rosa, CA: Cole Publishing Co., 1991.

Kennedy, Thomas. *Directing Video*. Boston, MA: Focal Press, 1989.

Editing

Anderson, Gary. *Video Editing and Post Production: A Professional Guide*, 4th ed. Boston, MA: Focal Press, 1999.

Browne, Steven E. *Nonlinear Editing Basics: Electronic Film and Video Editing*. Boston, MA: Focal Press, 1998.

Ohanian, Thomas, A. *Digital Nonlinear Editing*. Boston, MA: Focal Press, 1993.

Reisz, Karel and Millar, Gavin. *The Technique of Film Editing*. Boston, MA: Focal Press, 1986.

Rubin, Michael. *Nonlinear 4*. Gainesville, FL: Triad Publications, 2000.

Schneider, Arthur. *Electronic Post-Production and Videotape Editing*. Boston, MA: Focal Press, 1989.

Legal

Blue, Martha. *Making It Legal*. Flagstaff, AZ: Northland Publishing Co., 1988.

Miller, Philip. *Media Law for Producers*. Boston, MA: Focal Press, 1990.

Lighting

Carlson, Verne and Carlson, Sylvia. *Professional Lighting Handbook*. Boston, MA: Focal Press, 1985.

Hunter, Fil and Fuqua, Paul. *Light: Science and Magic*, 2nd ed. Boston, MA: Focal Press, 1997.

LeTourneau, Tom. *Lighting Techniques for Video Production*. Boston, MA: Focal Press, 1987.

Lyver, Des. *Basics of Video Lighting*. 2nd ed. Boston, MA: Focal Press, 2000.

Millerson, Gerald. *The Technique of Lighting for Television and Motion Pictures*, 3rd ed. Boston, MA: Focal Press, 2001.

Ritsko, Alan J. *Lighting for Location Motion Pictures*. New York, NY: Van Nostrand Reinhold Co., Inc., 1979.

News

Hausman, Carl. *Crafting the News for Electronic Media*. Belmont, CA: Wadsworth Publishing Co., 1992.

Cremer, Charles F., Kierstead, Phillip O., Yoakam, Richard D. *ENG: Television News and the New Technology*, 3rd ed. New York: McGraw-Hill, 1996.

Production

Compesi, Ronald. *Video Field Production and Editing*, 5th ed. Boston, MA: Allyn and Bacon, 20000.

Gross, Lynne, and Ward, Larry. *Electronic Moviemaking*. 4th ed. Belmont, CA: Wadsworth, 2000.

Mathias, Harry and Patterson, Richard. *Electronic Cinematography*. Belmont, CA: Wadsworth Publishing Co., 1985.

Schroeppel, Tom. *The Bare Bones Camera Course for Film and Video*, 2nd ed. Miami, FL: Tom Schroeppel, 1982.

_____. *Video Goals: Getting Results with Pictures and Sound*. Miami, FL: Tom Schroeppel, 1987.

Shook, Frederick. *Television Field Production and Reporting*, 3rd. Ed. New York: Longman Publishers, 2000.

Smith, David. *Video Communications*. Belmont CA: Wadsworth Publishing Co., 1991.

Utz, Peter. *Today's Video*. Englewood Cliffs, NJ: Prentice Hall, Inc., 1987.

Zettl, Herbert. *Television Production Handbook*, 7th ed. Belmont CA: Wadsworth Publishing Co., 2000.

Technology

Beaulieu, Mark and Okon, Chris. *Demystifying Multimedia*. San Francisco, CA: Vivid Publishing, 1993.

Grant, August and Seele, Peter, eds., *Broadcast Technology Update*. Boston, MA: Focal Press, 1997.

Writing

Garvey, Daniel and Rivers, William. *Broadcast Writing Handbook*, New York, NY: Longman, Inc., 1982.

Meeske, Milan. *Copywriting for the Electronic Media*, 3rd ed. Belmont, CA: Wadsworth Publishing Co., 1998.

PERIODICALS

Digital Video. CMP Media, 600 Harrison St., San Francisco, CA 94107

Videography. P.S.N. Publications, 2 Park Ave., Suite 1820, New York, NY 10016

Videomaker. Videomaker, Inc., 290 Airpark Blvd., Chico, CA 95926

Index